A-Z OXFORDSHIRE

D1685857

CONTENTS

REFERENCE

Motorway	**M40**
Primary Route	**A34**
A Road	**A4095**
Under Construction	
Proposed	
B Road	**B4030**
Dual Carriageway	
One-way Street	
Traffic flow on A Roads is also indicated by a heavy line on the driver's left.	
Restricted Access	
Pedestrianized Road	
Track / Footpath	
Residential Walkway	
Railway	Station / Heritage Station / Level Crossing / Tunnel
Built-up Area	BARNS RD
Local Authority Boundary	
Posttown Boundary	
Postcode Boundary (within Posttown)	
Map Continuation	88 / Large Scale City Centre 5 / Road Map Pages 144

Airport	✈
Car Park (Selected)	P
Church or Chapel	†
City Wall (Large Scale Only)	
Cycleway (Selected)	
Fire Station	■
Hospital	H
House Numbers (A & B Roads only)	20 40
Information Centre	i
National Grid Reference	²05
Park & Ride	Pear Tree P+
Police Station	▲
Post Office	★
Toilet: without facilities for the Disabled / with facilities for the Disabled	▽ / ▽
Viewpoint	☀
Educational Establishment	
Hospital or Hospice	
Industrial Building	
Leisure or Recreational Facility	
Oxford University College / Hall	
Place of Interest	
Public Building	
Shopping Centre or Market	
Other Selected Buildings	

SCALE

Map Pages 6-139	Map Pages 4-5
1:16,896 3¾ inches (9.52 cm) to 1 mile 5.9 cm to 1 km	1:8,448 7½ inches (19.05 cm) to 1 mile 11.8 cm to 1 km
0 ¼ ½ Mile	0 ⅛ ¼ Mile
0 250 500 Metres	0 100 200 300 400 Metres

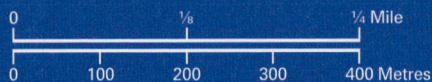

Copyright of Geographers' A-Z Map Company Limited

Fairfield Road, Borough Green, Sevenoaks, Kent TN15 8PP
Telephone: 01732 781000 (Enquiries & Trade Sales)
        01732 783422 (Retail Sales)
www.a-zmaps.co.uk

Ordnance Survey® This product includes mapping data licensed from Ordnance Survey® with the permission of the Controller of Her Majesty's Stationery Office.

© Crown Copyright 2006. All rights reserved. Licence number 100017302

Edition 1 2007

KEY TO MAP PAGES

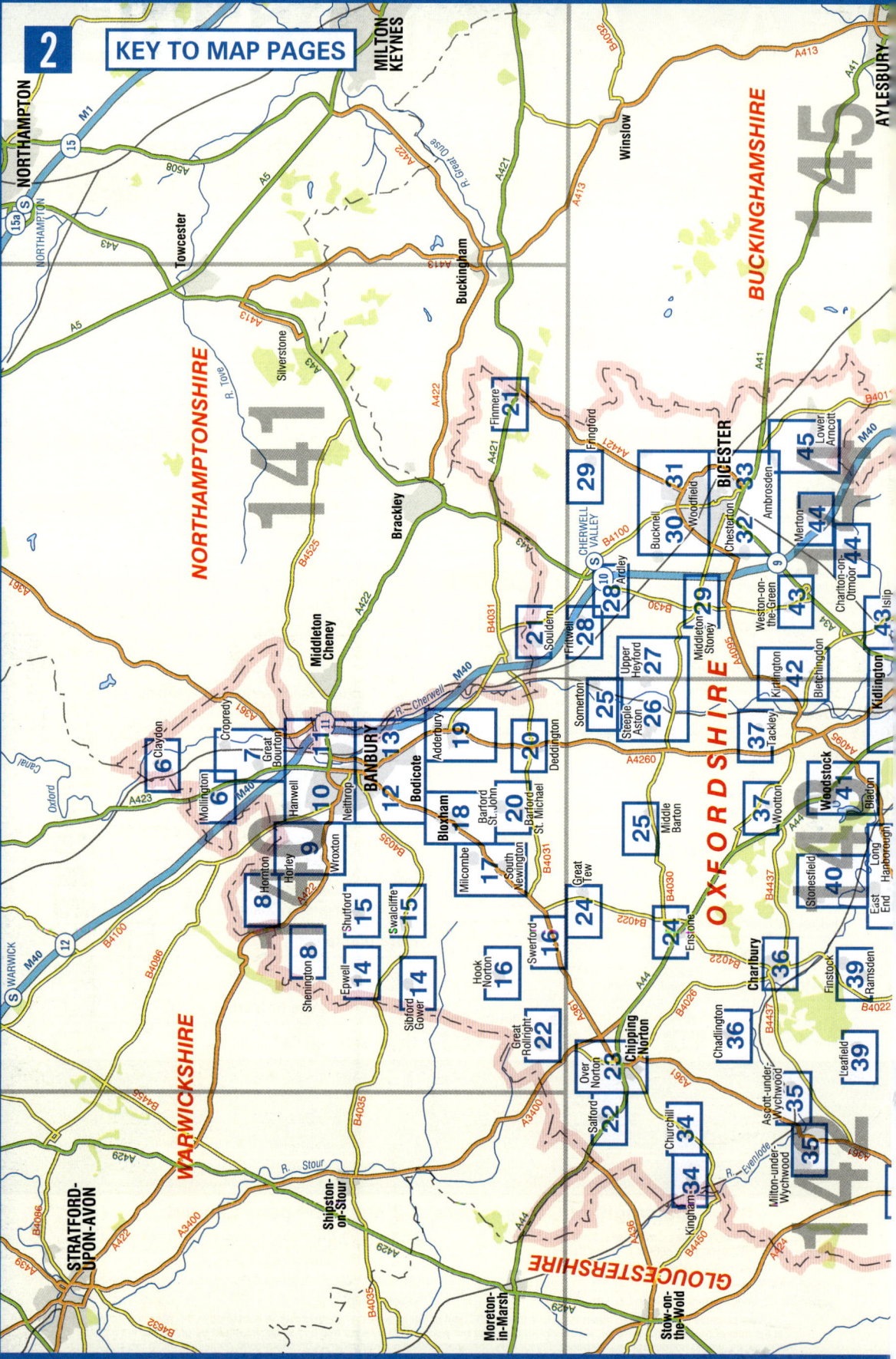

MILTON KEYNES

NORTHAMPTON

AYLESBURY

BUCKINGHAMSHIRE

NORTHAMPTONSHIRE

WARWICKSHIRE

OXFORDSHIRE

GLOUCESTERSHIRE

141

145

Towcester

Silverstone

Buckingham

Winslow

Brackley

Middleton Cheney

BANBURY

Bicester

Finmere

Fringford

Woodfield

Bucknell

Chesterton

Ardley

Ambrosden

Merton

Weston-on-the-Green

Charlton-on-Otmoor

Lower Arncott

Islip

Kidlington

Middleton Stoney

Souldern

Fritwell

Kirtlington

Bletchington

Somerton

Upper Heyford

Steeple Aston

Middle Barton

Tackley

Wootton

Stonesfield

Woodstock

Bladon

Long Hanborough

East End

Charlbury

Finstock

Ramsden

Leafield

Ascott-under-Wychwood

Milton-under-Wychwood

Chadlington

Churchill

Kingham

Stow-on-the-Wold

Moreton-in-Marsh

Shipston-on-Stour

STRATFORD-UPON-AVON

WARWICK

Claydon

Mollington

Cropredy

Great Bourton

Hanwell

Nethrop

Bodicote

Adderbury

Bloxham

Deddington

Barford St. John

Barford St. Michael

Milcombe

South Newington

Great Tew

Wroxton

Horley

Horton

Shenington

Epwell

Shutford

Swalcliffe

Sibford Gower

Hook Norton

Swerford

Enstone

Great Rollright

Over Norton

Chipping Norton

Salford

CHERWELL VALLEY

6 7 8 9 10 11 12 13 14 15 16 17 18 19 20 21 22 23 24 25 26 27 28 29 30 31 32 33 34 35 36 37 39 40 41 42 43 44 45

LARGE SCALE
4 5
OXFORD CITY CENTRE

Princes Risborough

Chinnor

Towersey

Thame

Sydenham

Tetsworth

Kingston Blount

Lewknor

Watlington

Chalgrove

Great Haseley

Little Milton

Stadhampton

Drayton St. Leonard

Benson

Ewelme

Warborough

Shillingford

Dorchester on Thames

Berinsfield

Shepherd's Green

Sonning Common

Nettlebed

Stoke Row

Woodcote

Ipsden

Crowmarsh Gifford

Wallingford

Brightwell-cum-Sotwell

Cholsey

Moulsford

Goring

Aston Tirrold

South Moreton

Blewbury

West Hagbourne

Harwell

Chilton

Steventon

Ardington

East Hendred

Henley-on-Thames

Lower Shiplake

Binfield Heath

Tokers Green

Mapledurham

Pangbourne

READING

CHIEVELEY

MEMBURY

Lower Shiplake

Cane End

Horton-cum-Studley

Stanton St. John

Holton

Wheatley

Cuddesdon

Gatsington

Marsh Baldon

Clifton Hampden

Long Wittenham

Appleford

Sutton Courtenay

Milton

Drayton

Caldecott

Shippon

Wootton

Boars Hill

Witham

OXFORD

Marston

Headington

Iffley

Littlemore

Kennington

Bayworth

ABINGDON

DIDCOT

Elsfield

Barton

Cassington

Yarnton

Gosford

Wolvercote

Eynsham

Farmoor

Cumnor

Appleton

Stanton Harcourt

Brighthampton

Southmoor

Marcham

Lyford

West Hanney

Denchworth

Stanford in the Vale

East Challow

Wantage

Letcombe Regis

Sparsholt

Uffington

Fernham

Little Coxwell

Faringdon

Longcot

Watchfield

Shrivenham

Bourton

Idstone

Ashbury

Highworth

SWINDON

Lechlade on Thames

Burford

Minster Lovell

Hailey

WITNEY

Coggs

Curbridge

Ducklington

Brize Norton

Carterton

Alvescot

Clanfield

Bampton

Aston

Langford

Freeland

OT MOOR

CHILTERN HILLS

BERKSHIRE

WILTSHIRE

VALE OF WHITE HORSE

SCALE
Miles
Kilometres
Oxfordshire County Boundary

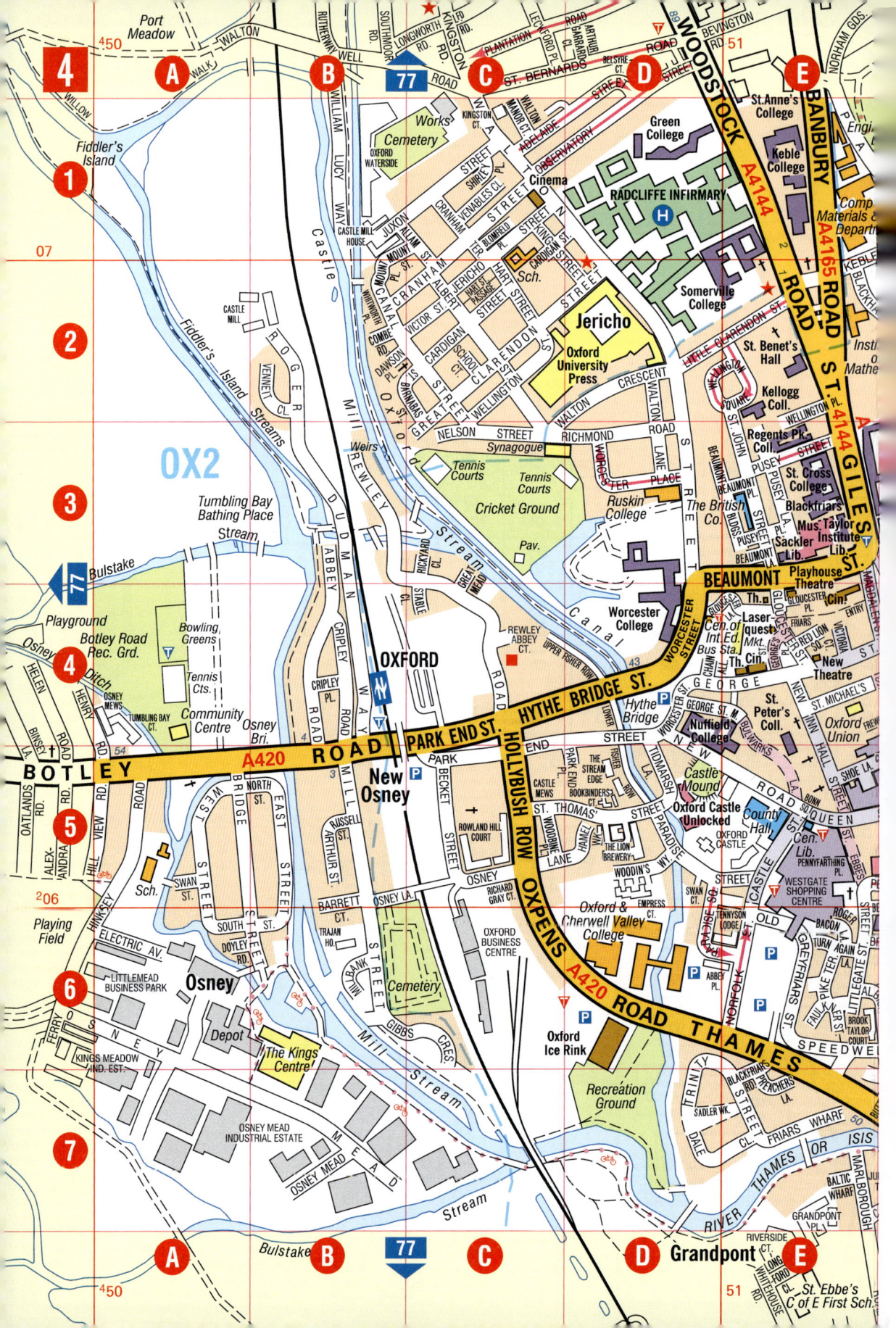

OX2

Grid references (top): 4 A B 77 C D E

Grid references (left): 1 07 2 3 77 4 5 206 6 7

Grid references (bottom): A B 77 C D E

Port Meadow
450
Fiddler's Island
WALTON
WALTON WALK
William Street
Lucy Way
Juxon St.
Mount Pl.
Walton Well
RUTHERWAY
SOUTHMOOR RD.
LONGWORTH RD.
KINGSTON RD.
PLANTATION RD.
LEOFRED CL.
ARTHUR GARRARD CL.
ROAD
BEVINGTON RD.
WOODSTOCK
NORHAM GDNS.
51

Works
Cemetery
Kingston Ct.
ADELAIDE
St. Bernards
ST. BERNARDS
Manor Ct.
Observatory
BELSYRE CT.
STIRLEY
STREET
St. Anne's College
Keble College
Green College
Comp. Materials & Department
BANBURY ROAD
A4144
A4165

OXFORD WATERSIDE
Cinema
Castle Mill House
SHIRLEY PL.
SHIRLEY
CRANHAM
JERICHO
BLOMFIELD PL.
KING STREET
RADCLIFFE INFIRMARY
H
Somerville College
WOODSTOCK ROAD
A4144
Institute of Mathematics

Castle Mill
ROGER ST.
VENNET
Fiddler's Island Streams
COMBE RD.
CARDIGAN
DANSON PL.
VICTOR ST.
ALBERT ST.
CLARENDON ST.
GREAT CLARENDON STREET
JERICHO STREET
CRANHAM STREET
HART STREET
HART STREET PASSAGE
KINGSTON CT.
Sch.
Oxford University Press
Jericho
CRESCENT
WALTON STREET
CRESCENT
St. Benet's Hall
Kellogg Coll.
Regents Pk. Coll.
WELLINGTON SQUARE
St. Cross College
Blackfriars
Mus.
Taylor Institute Lib.
ST. GILES
LITTLE CLARENDON ST.
WELLINGTON ST.
PUSEY ST.
PUSEY LA.
PUSEY ST.
A4144

Tumbling Bay Bathing Place
Stream
77
Bulstake
Playground
Botley Road Rec. Grd.
Bowling Greens
Tennis Cts.
Osney Ditch
Osney Helen Henry
Osney Mews
Tumbling Bay Ct.
Community Centre
Osney Bri.
DUDMAN
ABBEY ROAD
CRIPLEY PL.
CRIPLEY ROAD
RICHYARD CL.
STABLE CL.
BREAM MEAD
Weirs
Tennis Courts
Tennis Courts
Cricket Ground
Pav.
Ruskin College
The British Co.
Stream
Canal
BEAUMONT
Worcester College
REWLEY ABBEY CT.
Rewley Abbey Ct.
Cen. of Int. Ed.
Laser quest
Bus Sta.
Mkt.
Th.
Th. Cin.
Playhouse Theatre
GLOUCESTER
GLOUCESTER ST.
RED LION SQ.
VICTORIA CT.
Cin!
New Theatre
GEORGE STREET
FRIARS
MAGDALEN ST.

OXFORD
PARK END ST.
HYTHE BRIDGE ST.
Hythe Bridge
P
Nuffield College
GEORGE ST. M.
St. Peter's Coll.
New ROAD
NEW INN HALL STREET
Oxford Union
St. Michael's
Oxford Frewin

BOTLEY
OATLANDS RD.
BINSEY RD.
HINKSEY RD.
ALEXANDRA RD.
BINSEY LA.
A420 ROAD
NEW OSNEY
NORTH ST.
EAST STREET
WEST STREET
BRIDGE ST.
SWAN ST.
ARTHUR ST.
RUSSELL ST.
BARRETT CT.
OSNEY LA.
RICHARD GRAY CT.
ROWLAND HILL COURT
BECKET ST.
PARK END
LOWER FISHER ROW
WOODBIN ST.
ST. THOMAS'
The Stream Edge Bookbinders Ct.
The Lion Brewery
HAMEL
PARADISE STREET
WOODIN'S WY.
Castle Mews
Castle Mound
Oxford Castle Unlocked
Oxford Castle
County Hall
BONN SQUARE
Cen. Lib.
Pennyfarthing Pl.
WESTGATE SHOPPING CENTRE
QUEEN STREET
CASTLE ST.
ROGER BACON LA.
TURN AGAIN LA.
SHOE LA.
PEMBROKE ST.
BULWARKS LA.

Playing Field
ELECTRIC AV.
Littlemead Business Park
Osney
Depot
The Kings Centre
Kings Meadow Ind. Est.
FERRY
HILL VIEW
SWAN ST.
DOYLEY RD.
SOUTH ST.
BANK STREET
MILL STREET
TRAJAN HO.
GIBBS CRES.
Cemetery
Oxford Business Centre
OSNEY MEAD
MILL STREAM
Oxford & Cherwell Valley College
EMPRESS CT.
SWAN CT.
TENNYSON LODGE
ABBEY PL.
OLD
GREYFRIARS ST.
FAULKNER ST.
PIKE TER.
LITTLEGATE ST.
BROOK ST.
BACON
TAYLOR COURT
SPEEDWELL
TRINITY ST.
A420 ROAD THAMES
OXPENS ROAD

Oxford Ice Rink
P
Recreation Ground
BLACKFRIARS RD.
PREACHERS LA.
SADLER WK.
DALE CL.
FRIARS WHARF
BALTIC WHARF
MARLBOROUGH RD.
GRANDPORT PL.
RIVERSIDE
THAMES OR ISIS
Grandport
LONGFORD CL.
WHITEHOUSE CL.
St. Ebbe's C of E First Sch.

Osney Mead Industrial Estate
MEAD
Stream
450
206
51

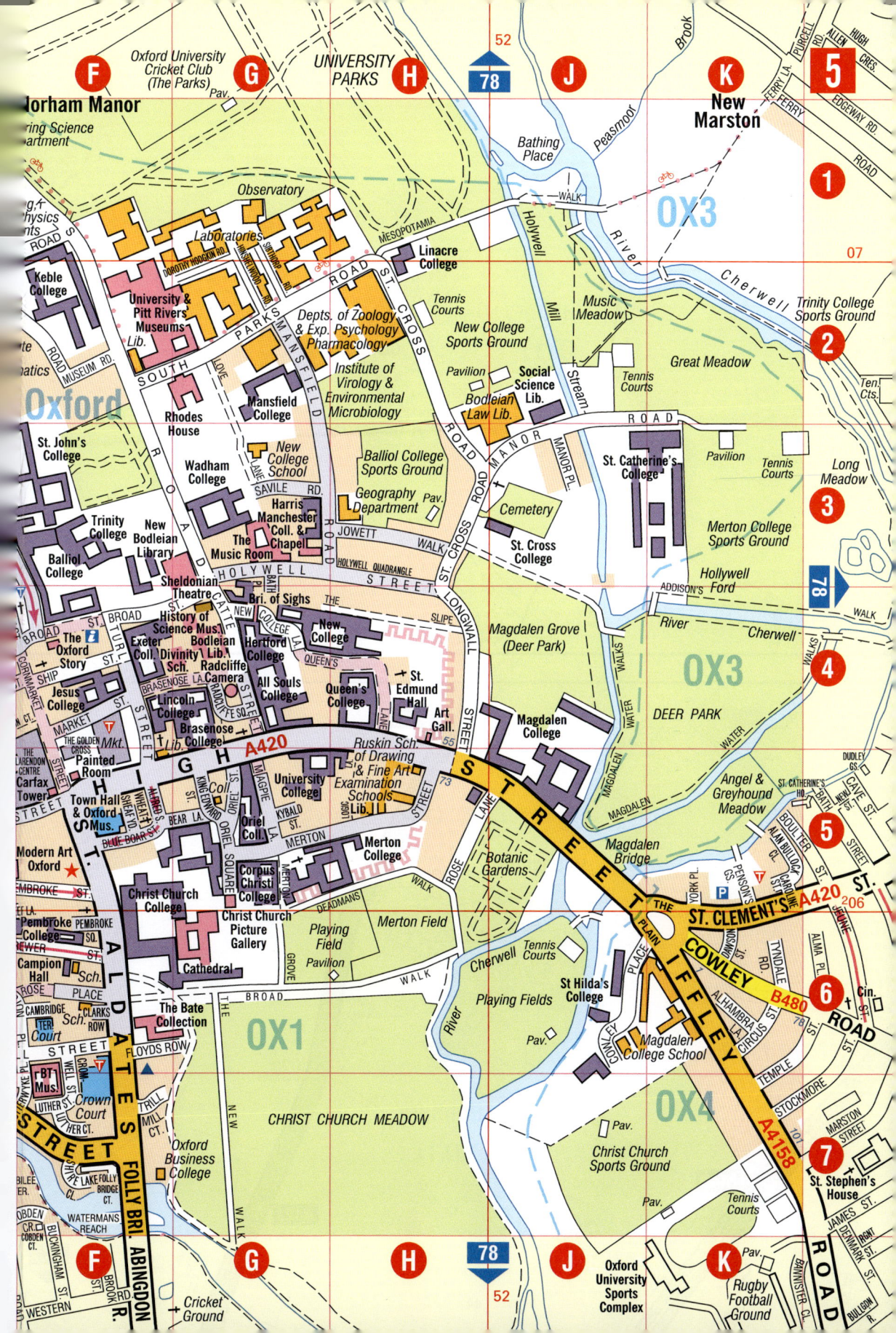

F Oxford University G Cricket Club (The Parks) UNIVERSITY PARKS H 52 78 J K 5

Norham Manor

New Marston

...ring Science ...partment

Observatory

OX3

1

07

Laboratories

DOROTHY HODGKIN RD.

Linacre College

Cherwell

Trinity College Sports Ground

Keble College

University & Pitt Rivers Museums

Lib.

Depts. of Zoology & Exp. Psychology Pharmacology

Tennis Courts

New College Sports Ground

Music Meadow

Great Meadow

2

Ten. Cts.

Oxford

ST. CROSS

Mansfield College

Institute of Virology & Environmental Microbiology

Pavilion

Social Science Lib.

Bodleian Law Lib.

Tennis Courts

Pavilion

Tennis Courts

Long Meadow

3

St. John's College

Rhodes House

Wadham College

Balliol College Sports Ground

Geography Department

Pav.

Cemetery

St. Catherine's College

Merton College Sports Ground

Trinity College

New Bodleian Library

Harris Manchester Coll. & Chapel

SAVILE RD.

JOWETT WALK

St. Cross College

Hollywell Ford

78

Balliol College

The Music Room

HOLYWELL

Sheldonian Theatre

Bri. of Sighs

STREET

LONGWALL

Addison's

River Cherwell

4

History of Science Mus.

Exeter Coll.

Bodleian Divinity Lib. Sch.

New College

Hertford College

THE SLIPE

Magdalen Grove (Deer Park)

OX3

DEER PARK

The Oxford Story

Radcliffe Camera

All Souls College

Queen's College

St. Edmund Hall

Art Gall.

Magdalen College

Jesus College

Lincoln College

Brasenose College

Lib.

55

A420

HIGH

University College

Ruskin Sch. of Drawing & Fine Art Examination Schools Lib.

73

STREET

Magdalen Bridge

Angel & Greyhound Meadow

ST. CATHERINE'S HO.

DUDLEY GS.

5

Carfax Tower

Painted Room

Town Hall & Oxford Mus.

Oriel Coll.

Kybald St.

MERTON

Merton College

Botanic Gardens

THE PLAIN

PENSON'S GS.

YORK PL.

ALAN BULLOCK CL.

CAROLINE ST.

ST. CLEMENT'S

A420

206

Modern Art Oxford

Christ Church College

Corpus Christi College

DEADMANS

WALK

Merton Field

Cherwell

Tennis Courts

COWLEY

B480

6

ROAD

Pembroke College

Christ Church Picture Gallery

Playing Field

Pavilion

Playing Fields

St Hilda's College

IFFLEY

ALHAMBRA LA.

CIRCUS

Campion Hall

Cathedral

THE BROAD

WALK

Pav.

Magdalen College School

TEMPLE

STOCKMORE

MARSTON STREET

The Bate Collection

FLOYDS ROW

OX1

River

OX4

A4158

7

BT Mus.

Crown Court

TRILL MILL CT.

Oxford Business College

CHRIST CHURCH MEADOW

Christ Church Sports Ground

Pav.

St. Stephen's House

ABINGDON

WATERMANS REACH

NEW

WALK

Tennis Courts

BANNISTER CL.

ROAD

F G H 78 52 J Oxford University Sports Complex K Pav. Rugby Football Ground

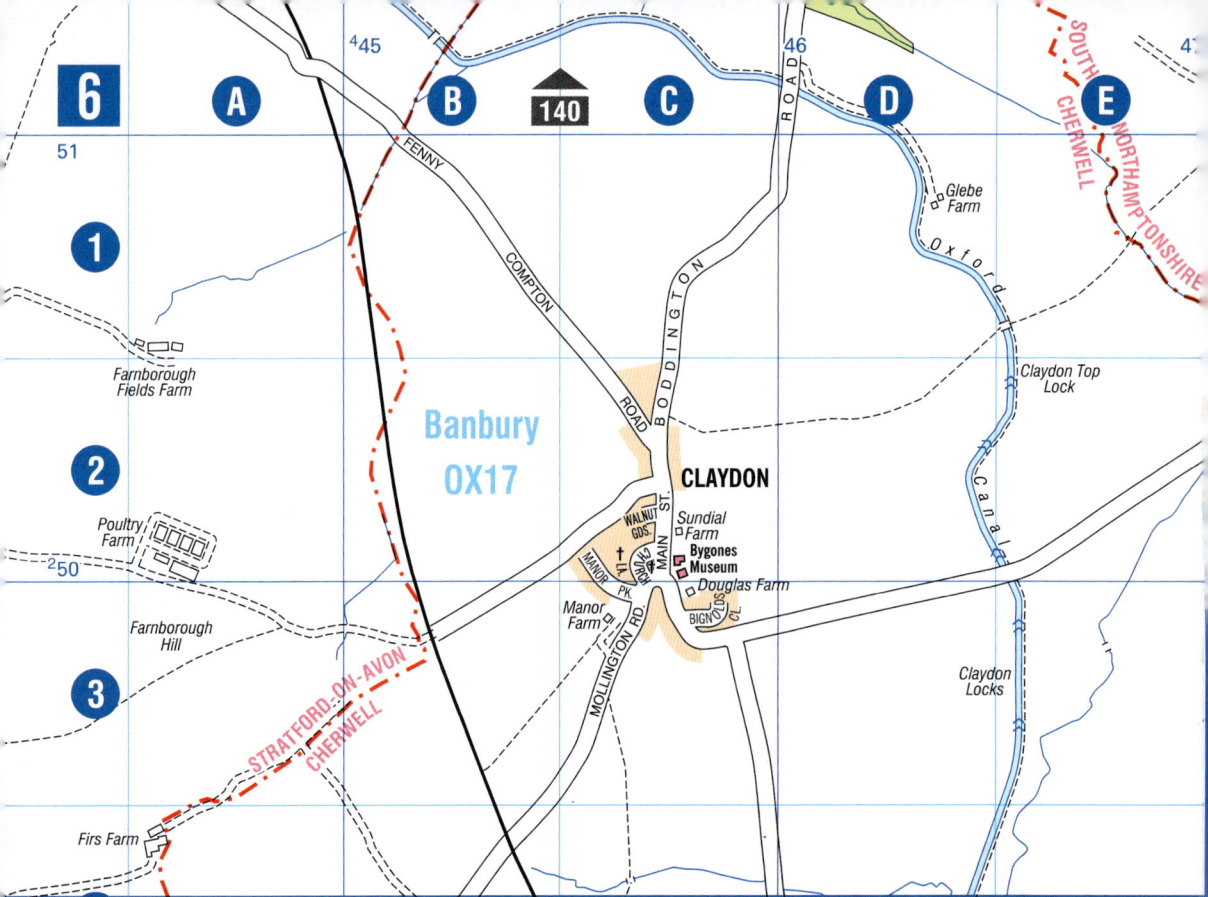

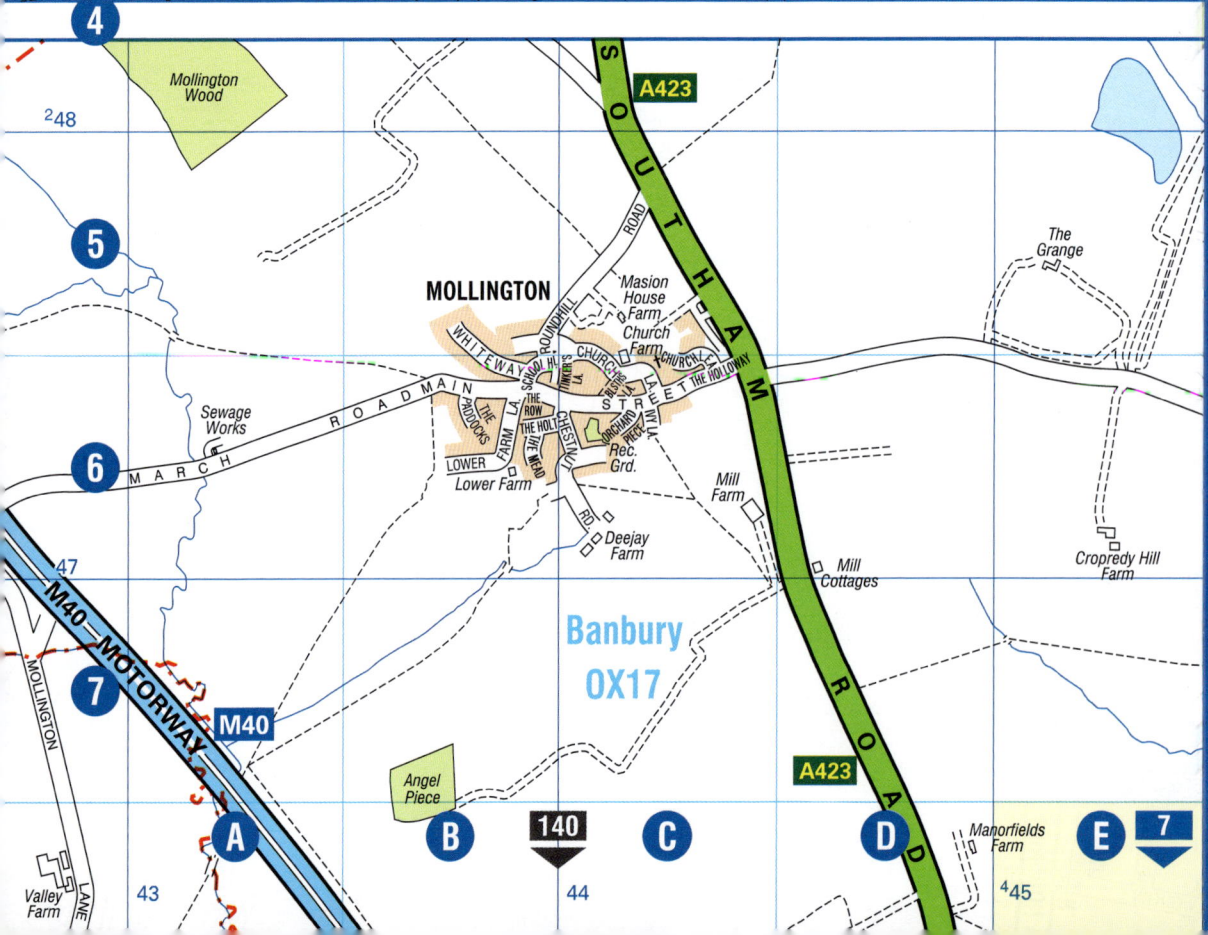

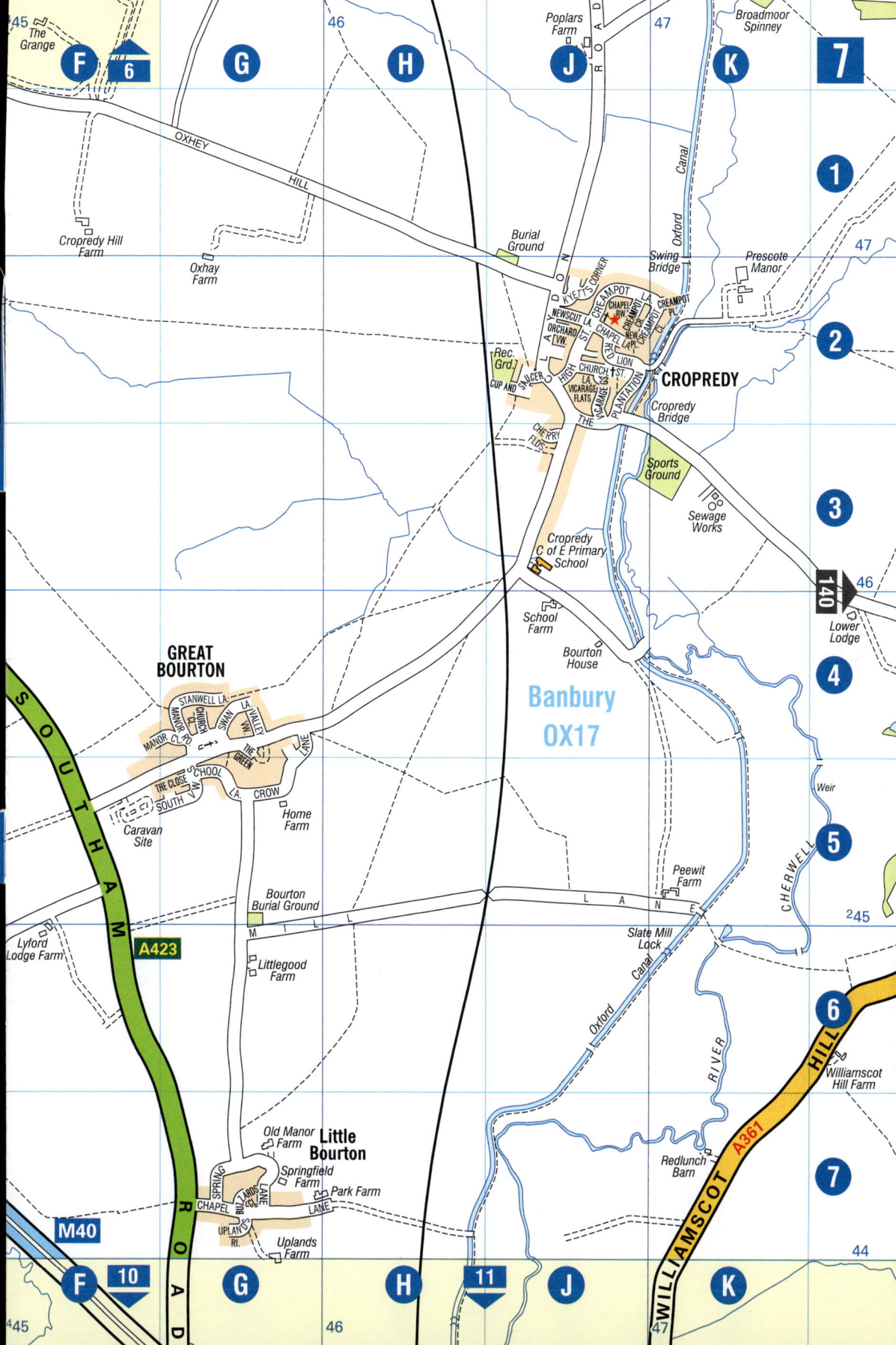

F 6 G H J 7 K

1

The Grange
Cropredy Hill Farm
OXHEY HILL
Oxhay Farm

Poplars Farm
ROAD
Broadmoor Spinney

Burial Ground
KYETT'S CORNER
CREAMPOT LA.
CREAMPOT CL.
CHAPEL
NEWSCOT LA.
ORCHARD VW.
NEW CREAMPOT CL.
Swing Bridge
Oxford Canal
Prescote Manor

2

LONDON
Rec. Grd.
CUP AND SAUCER
HIGH ST.
CHURCH
LA.
VICARAGE FLATS
THE VICARAGE
CHERRY FLDS.
PLANTATION
LION ST.
RED LION
CROPREDY
Cropredy Bridge

3

Sports Ground
Sewage Works
Cropredy C of E Primary School
School Farm
Bourton House

140 46
Lower Lodge

4

GREAT BOURTON
STANWELL LA.
MANOR RD.
MANOR CL.
CHURCH
SWAN LA.
THE GREEN
VALLEY LA.
SCHOOL LA.
THE CLOSE
SOUTH
CROW LANE
Home Farm
Bourton Burial Ground

Banbury OX17

Peewit Farm
CHERWELL
Weir
245

5

SOUTHAM
A423
Lyford Lodge Farm
MILL LANE
Littlegood Farm
Slate Mill Lock
Oxford Canal
RIVER
WILLIAMSCOT HILL
A361
Williamscot Hill Farm

6

Old Manor Farm
Little Bourton
Springfield Farm
Park Farm
SPRING LANE
BILLARDS LANE
CHAPEL LANE
UPLANDS RI.
Uplands Farm
Redlunch Barn

7

M40
ROAD
445
46
47
44

F 10 G H 11 J K

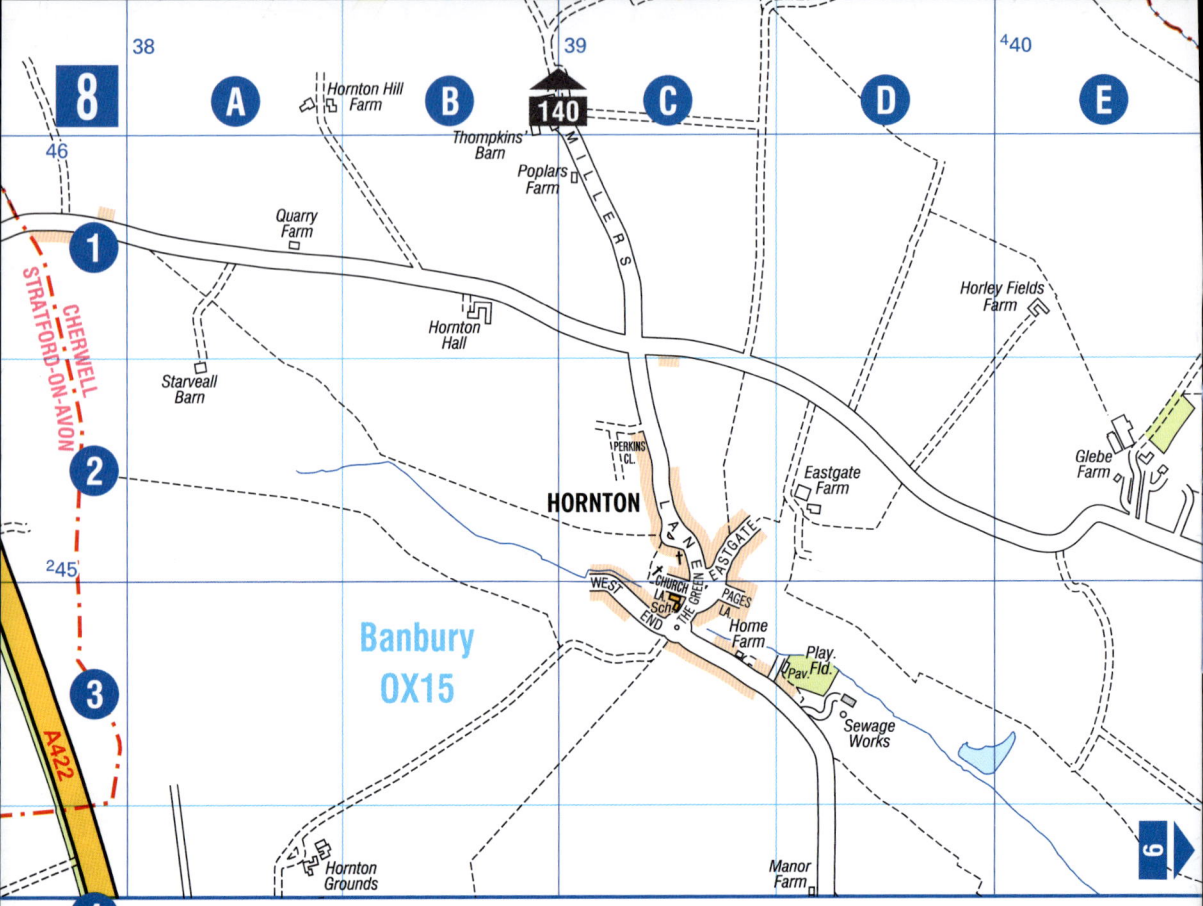
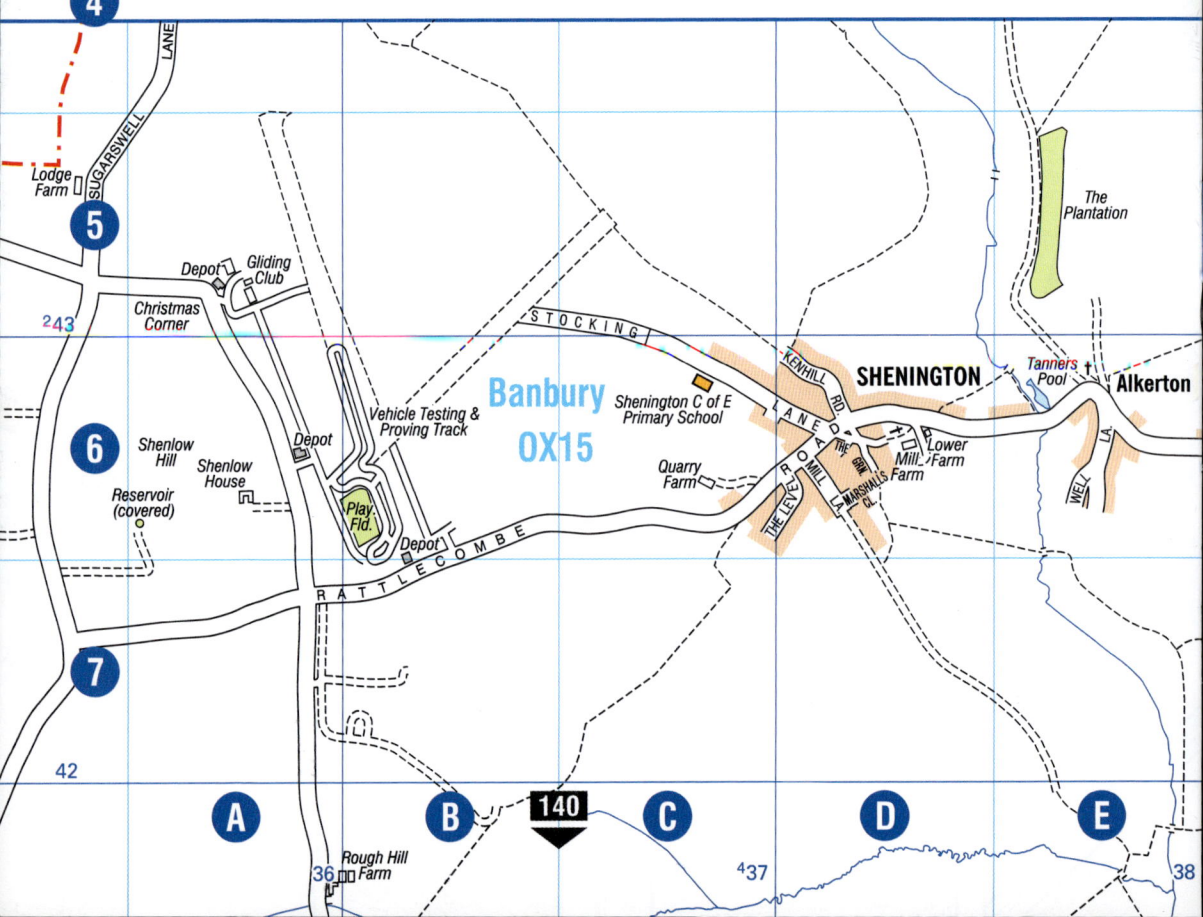

F G H 140 J K 9

8

OX17

STRATFORD-ON-AVON
CHERWELL

WARWICK

B4100

1

Manor
Farm

New
Farm

140

41 42 43

44

Lower Field
Barn

DUMP

LANE

Bramshill Park
Farm

HORLEY

Pav.
Cricket
Field

LITTLE

MANOR ORCHARD

LANE
CL.

LA.

GULLIVER'S CL.

Manor
Farm

Banbury

Rec.
Grd.

ROAD

2

Horley
Mill

Sewage
Works

3

Sor

43

Brook

Nature
Reserves

OX15

Drayton
Lodge

4

Playing
Field
Works

Pav.

FRIARS
HILL

Cemetery

Lord's
Spinney

10

Club
House

Drayton Leisure
Golf Driving Range

5

42

WROXTON

HORLEY PATH RD.

Sports
Grd.
Pav.

SILVER LANE

STRATFORD

ROAD

A422

STRATFORD

A422

QUEEN'S CL.

METCALFE CL.

Drayton

6

STRATFORD

A422

ROAD

THE FIRST

LEYS CL.

WOODWAY CL.

MAIN

STREET

LAMPITTS GN.

MILLS LA.

CHURCH

DARK LA.

Hall

STREET

Wroxton Gardens
Cottage

MILL LANE

ARDEN

ROAD

Run

Wroxton C of E
Primary School

Laurels
Farm

Wroxton
College

Abbey
Wood

Fish Pond

Obelisk

7

F G H 140 J Keeper's K
Covert

41

French's
Buildings

42 43

41

43   44   B   140   C   D   E   445

A   B   C   D   E

1

Recreation Ground

Hanwell
Sewage Works

HANWELL CT.

STREET

SPRINGFIELD

PARK

Sunview Farm

MAIN   CHURCH
Hanwell Castle

SACK-VILLE CT.

GULLICOTE LA.

Park Farm

Banbury Crematorium   Cemetery

2

OX17

243

Hardwick Gorse

3

Drayton Lodge

Hanwell Fields

MEADOW   DRIVE   GRANDISON RD.

ELWES RD.

Laboratory

DUKES   HURST   ASH   CHAMOMILE PL.
WINTER   MEADOWSWEET WY.
SAGE CL.   GARDENS

Playing Field

SIR HENRY   RE CL.

BOOTH RD.   GRIFFITH RD.

Hanwell Fields Community Sch.

Club House

Drayton Leisure Golf Driving Range

USHER DR.   USHER DR.   CHESTER CL.   HEREFORD
PITMASTON CL.   FRENSHAM WY.
WINSON DR.   LAXTON   GUERNSEY CL.   CONIFER
ELLISON   RD.   SIME   BARLOW   KERBY   STARINA   PRIMROSE   RISE   SYRINGA
FIRTREE RD.   ROTHER RISE   JASMINE WK.   CAM.   ELMS
MAGNOLIAS

4

HARDWICK   RISE   CHEVIOT   CHICHESTER   ALFRISTON GR.   SALVIA CL.   FUCHSIA   PEN WK.
SUSSEX   BANESBERIE CL.   HIGH   LAVENDER   Depot
ROMNEY   LUNDBOURNE   HEATH   HIGHLANDS
RED POLL CL.   ANGUS CL.   Sch.   Community Centre

42   QUEEN'S   OX15   ALVIS   DAIMLER   BEAUMONT   INDUSTRIAL ESTATE
GR.   METCALFE CL.   Running Track   TALBOT   BYFORD   AVENUE   Sub.   LOCKHEED CL.   BANBURY CROSS RETAIL PARK

5   Drayton   LUDLOW DR.   HUMBER RD.   LANCASTER   WOLSELEY   RUSCOTE   ARCADE
STRATFORD   A422   ROAD   MORRIS   DR.   Hill View Primary School   RUSCOTE   A422   AV.   A361   Factory

Drayton School   Games Court Play Fld   Ruscote   RUSCOTE   AV.   NURSERY

6   William Morris Prim. Sch.   THE   AVENUE   RUSCOTE   AVE.   NEITHROP   Depot   Cemetery   SOUTHAM
BRAMBER   APPLEBY   CROMWELL   LINK   ROAD   WARWICK   PARKLANDS   NURSERY
PENRHYN   HASTINGS RD.   WARWICK   B4100

Neithrop   WITHYCOMBE   MALLORY   ORCHARD   COPE   ROAD
CHESTER WY.   FAIRWAY   MILLER   Funtasia
7   HIGHCLERE   PRESCOTT   Orchard Flds Prim. Sch.   KENNEDY HO.   Club   King's   People's Park   HORSE FAIR
St. Joseph's Cath. Prim. Sch.   PENROSE   Lib.   Leisure Cen.   NORTH BAR
BRADLEY ARCADE   Pav.   WEST BAR

41   Withycombe Farm   ARUNDEL PL.   12   WOODGREEN   Frank Wise School   College

A   B   44   C   D   445   E

43   KENILWORTH WY.   HILL   ROAD   ROAD

F CHERWELL ST. G H 11 J K

ROAD 48 CHETWODE

Castle Quay Arts Cen
Shopping Centre
Market Pl
Bowl Bridge
CHURCH St.
George
Sorting Off.
Mosque
Banbury

M40

BANBURY

Industrial Estate

Depot
Works
Gas Holder
Works
The Tramway Ind. Est.
Spital Farm Depot
Spital Farm Sewage Works

Superstore
Greenhill
Banbury United FC (The Spencer Stadium)

1

240

2

Blackpits Farm

HORTON HOSPITAL
FIENNES CENTRE
HOSP.
Calthorpe
HIGHTOWN

Oxford Canal

RIVER

CHERWELL

SOUTH NORTHAMPTONSHIRE

3

140 39

4

A4260

Recreation Ground
Superstore
Prim. Sch.
The Hanithorns Prim. Sch.
Comm. Cen.
CHATSWORTH

M40 MOTORWAY

OX17

Pav.
Cricket Ground
Recreation Ground Hall
Tapper's Farm
School
Council Offices

5

38

M40

BODICOTE
Town Furlong Farm
Bodicote Park Rugby Ground

Bushy Furze Barn

6

Cotefield Farm
Cotefield House

A4260 BANBURY ROAD

Manor Farm

7

The Brook
Mill
OX15

37

F G H 19 J K

Reservoir
Mill
The Paddock
Twyford
Green Hill Farm
Homestead Farm

Bloxham Grove Farm
46
Windmill
47
48

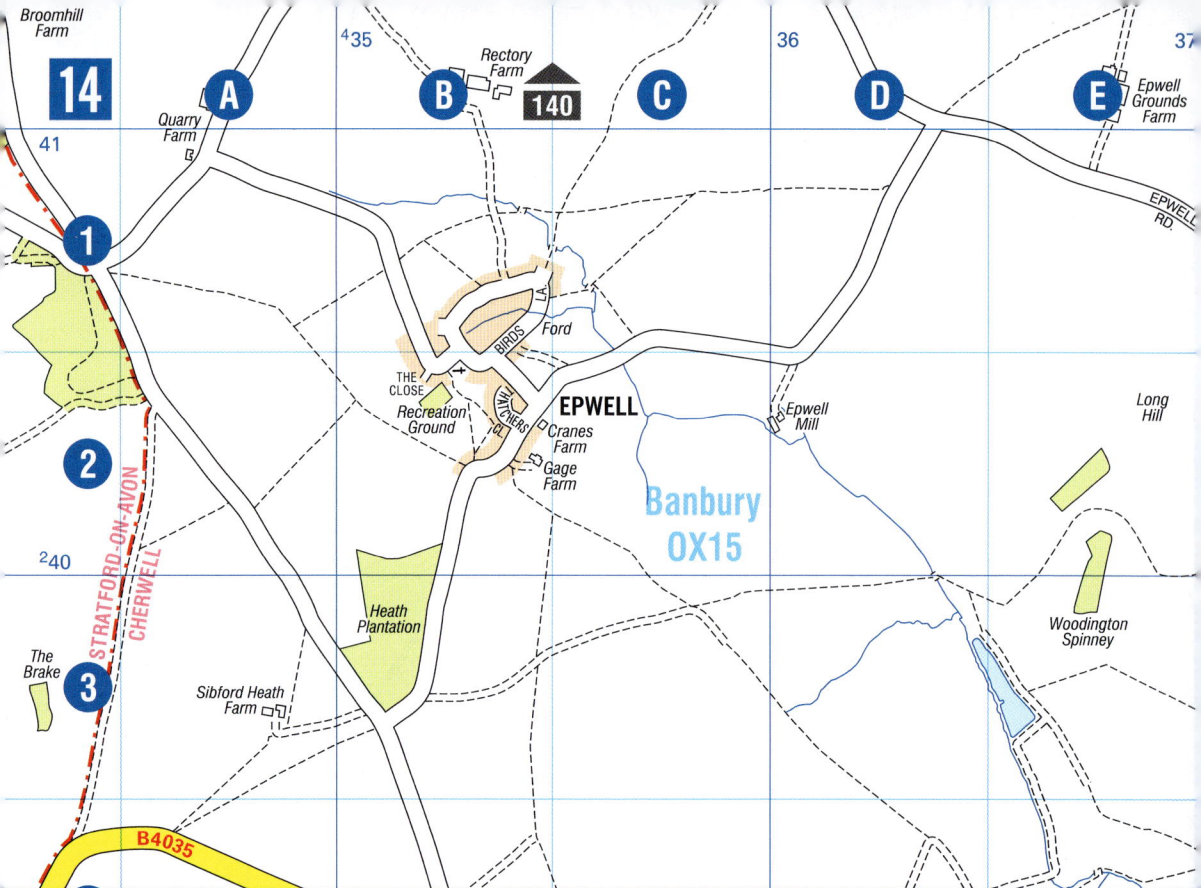

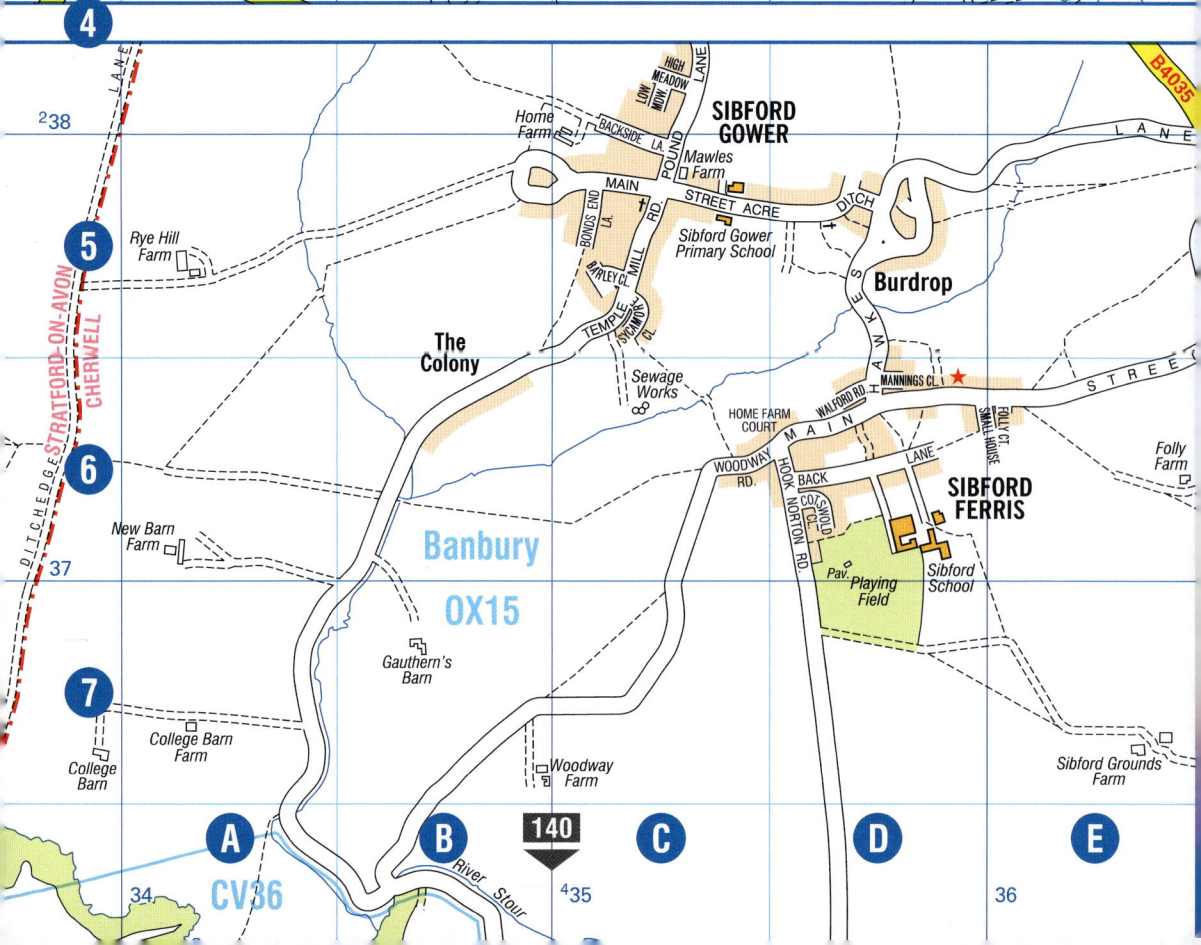

14

41

Broomhill Farm

Quarry Farm

⁴35

Rectory Farm

▲ 140

36

37

Epwell Grounds Farm

EPWELL RD.

BIRDS LA.

Ford

THE CLOSE

Recreation Ground

THATCHERS CL.

EPWELL

Cranes Farm

Gage Farm

Epwell Mill

Long Hill

Banbury OX15

Woodington Spinney

²40

Heath Plantation

The Brake

Sibford Heath Farm

STRATFORD-ON-AVON

CHERWELL

B4035

²38

LANE

HIGH MEADOW LANE

LOW MOW

BACKSIDE LA.

POUND LANE

SIBFORD GOWER

Home Farm

Mawles Farm

B4035

LANE

Rye Hill Farm

BONUS END LA.

MAIN

STREET

MILL RD.

ACRE

DITCH

Burdrop

BARLEY CL.

Sibford Gower Primary School

STRATFORD-ON-AVON

CHERWELL

DITCHEDGE LANE

TEMPLE MILL

SYCAMORE CL.

The Colony

Sewage Works

HAWKES

MANNINGS CL. ★

STREET

37

New Barn Farm

HOME FARM COURT

WALFORD RD.

MAIN

FOLLY CT.

SMALL HOUSE

Folly Farm

WOODWAY RD.

HOOK

BACK

LANE

SIBFORD FERRIS

Banbury

NORTON RD.

COTSWOLD CL.

OX15

Gauthern's Barn

Pav. Playing Field

Sibford School

College Barn Farm

Woodway Farm

Sibford Grounds Farm

College Barn

34

CV36

¹35

▼ 140

36

River Stour

38   39   40   41

1
Padsdon
Bottom

Sewage
Works

Balscote
Mill

Tythe
Farm
2

SHUTFORD

THE DAIRYGROUND ST

Middle Hill
Farm

E P W E L L

COOK'S
MALT HOUSE
MILL LA.
LWR END PLOT
THE
SMALL HOUSE
IVY
Depot
Works
WEST   HIGH ST.
CHURCH LA.   BANBURY LA.
THE
RICK YARD
Manor
House

R O A D

R O A D

Cemetery

S I B F O R D

THE
PLAIN RD.
BANBURY RD.

Five
Ways

S H U T F O R D

²40

Five Ways
Cottage

Shutford
Bridge

3

Weir

**Banbury
OX15**

Barton
Hill

Round
Hill

Jester's
Hill

R O A D

Heathnell
Spinney

Langley
Hill

4

S W A L C L I F F E   L E A

Swalcliffe
Lea

S H U T F O R D

L E A

5

SWALCLIFFE LA.
GREEN LA.

SWALCLIFFE

THE THINGS
Swalcliffe
Barn Mus.

BRICK
ROW

THE SQUARE
BAKER LA.

LANE

PARK

B4035

SWALCLIFFE RD.   M A I N

Preedys
Farm
College
Farm

18
OLD GLEBE
1

Home
Farm

BAKERS LA.

²38

6

Home
Farm

Swalcliffe
Park Sch

Hill
Farm

TADMARTON

Austins
Farm

Brick
Farm

**Banbury
OX15**

BROMFIELD

RISE

R O A D

R O A D

DRIFT

B4035

7

Ushercoombe
Copse

Ushercombe

Works
High Meadow
Farm   37

ACRE

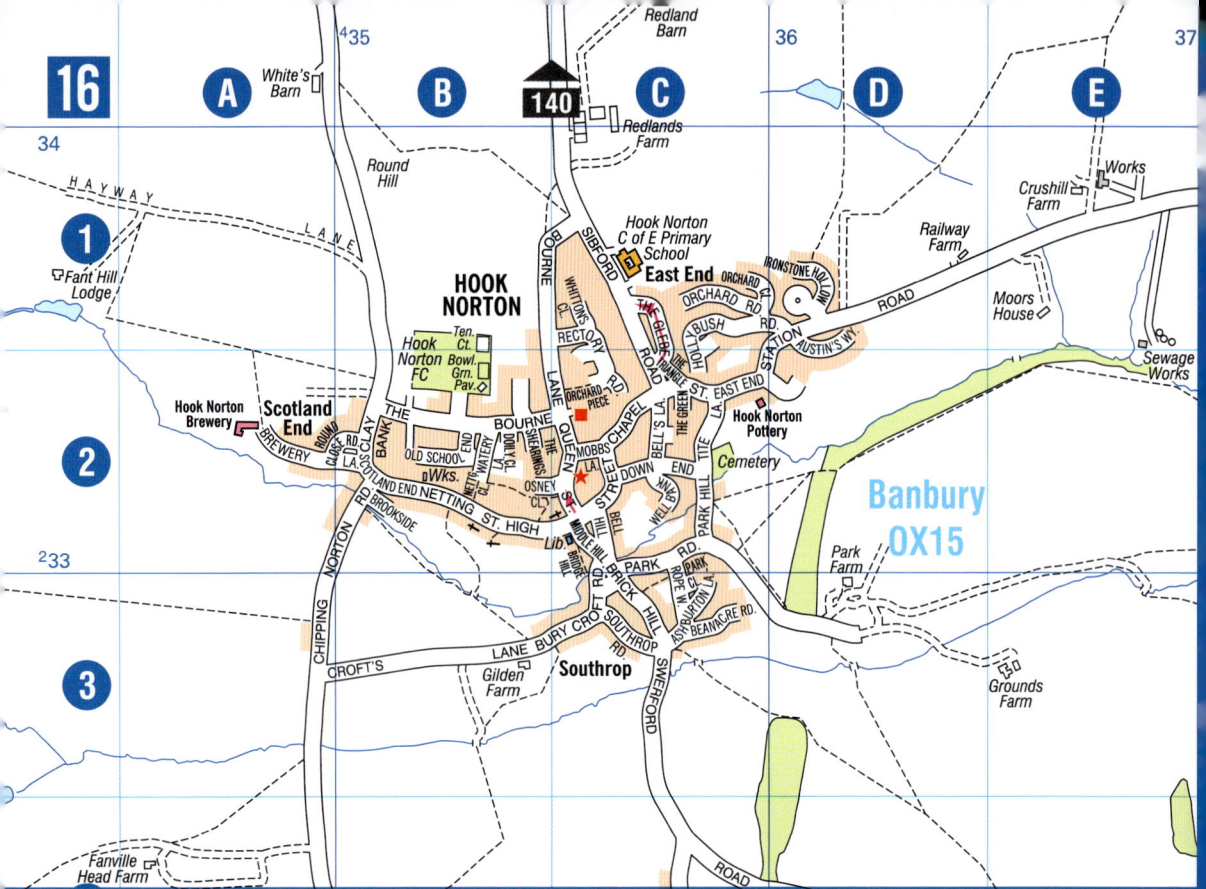

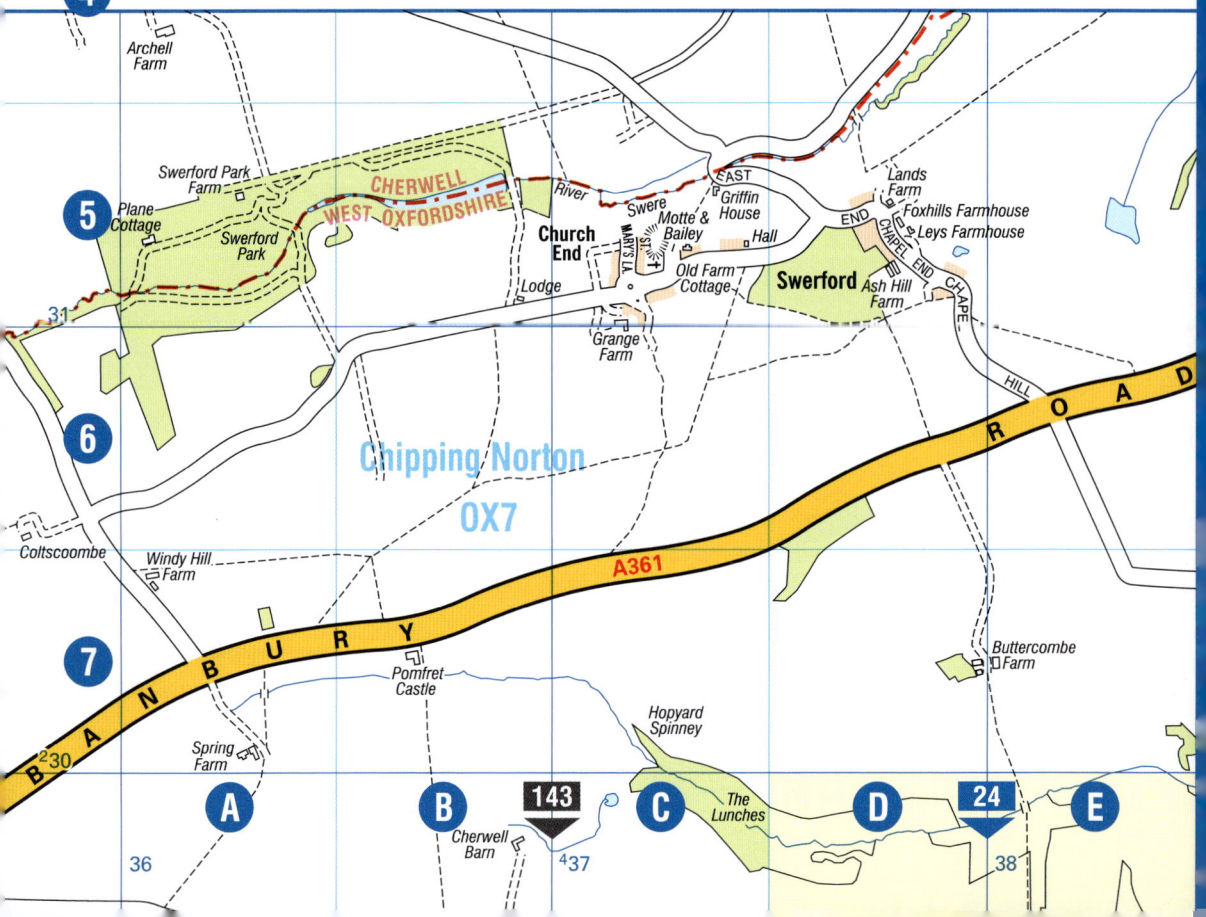

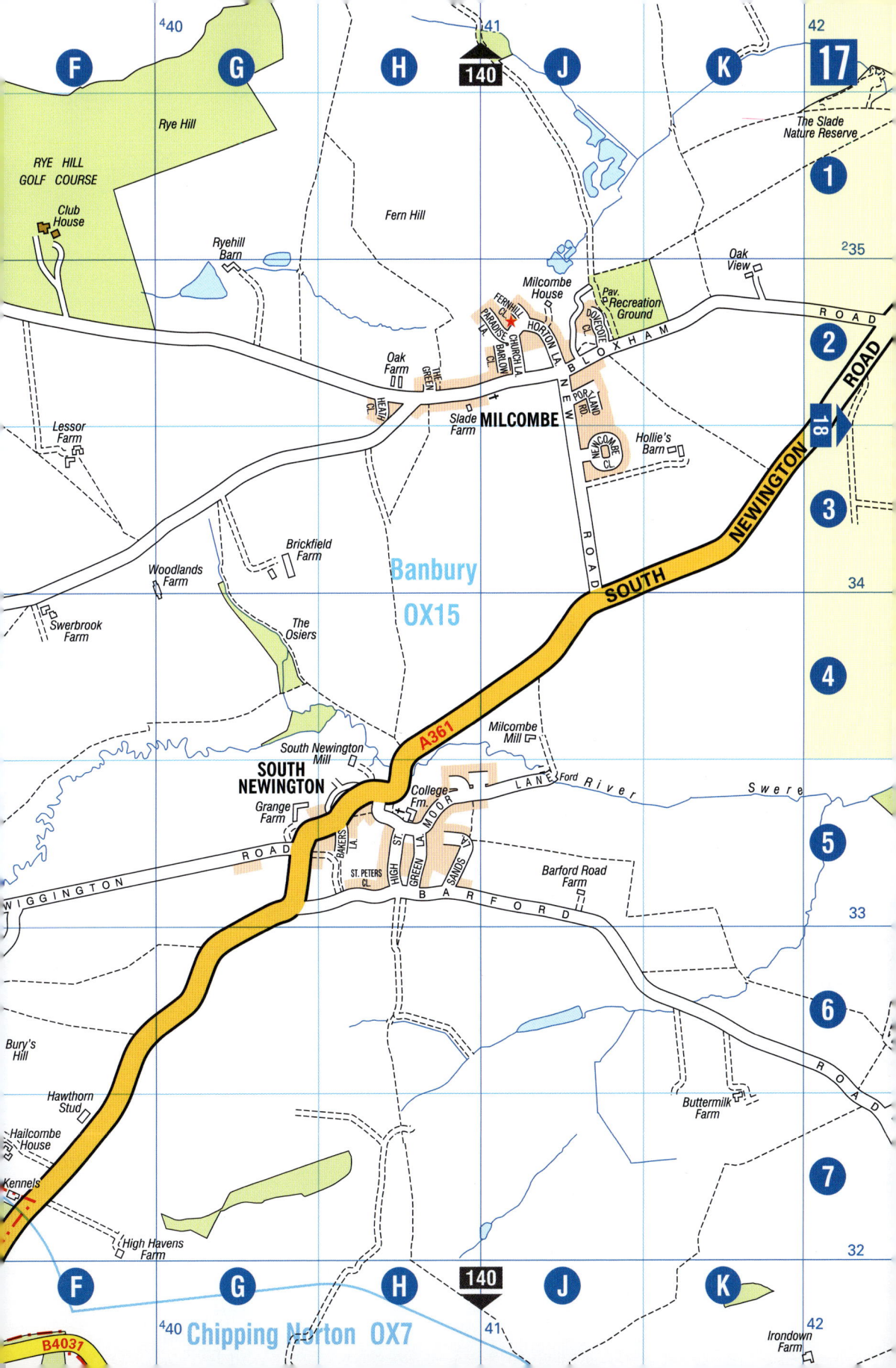

440 41 42

The Slade
Nature Reserve

1

Rye Hill

RYE HILL
GOLF COURSE

Fern Hill

²35

Club
House

Ryehill
Barn

Milcombe
House

Oak
View

Pav. Recreation
Ground

R O A D

2

Oak
Farm

FERNHILL
CL.
PARADISE
BARLOW LA.
CHURCH LA.
HORTON LA.

PORTLAND RD.
DOVECOTE CL.

ROAD

18

Slade
Farm

HEATH CL.
THE GREEN

MILCOMBE

NEW

Hollie's
Barn

NEWINGTON

3

Lessor
Farm

MILCOMBE CL.
BLOXHAM

ROAD

SOUTH

34

Brickfield
Farm

Banbury

OX15

Woodlands
Farm

Swerbrook
Farm

The
Osiers

4

A361

Milcombe
Mill

South Newington
Mill

Ford River

Swere

**SOUTH
NEWINGTON**

College
Fm.

LANE

5

Grange
Farm

ROAD

BAKERS LA.
HIGH ST.
ST. PETERS CL.
GREEN LA.
MOOR
SANDS

Barford Road
Farm

33

W I G G I N G T O N

B A R F O R D

6

Bury's
Hill

ROAD

Hawthorn
Stud

Buttermilk
Farm

Hailcombe
House

7

Kennels

High Havens
Farm

32

440 41 42

Chipping Norton OX7

B4031

Irondown
Farm

140

140

18

42 · A · B · 43 · C · 12 · D · 44 · E

37 Nayland Farm

Ell's Farm

Chaddle Barn Farm

BLOXHAM GROVE ROAD

Old Barn Farm

1

140

Firs Hill Farm

Hobb Hill

Firs Hill

Woollen Hale

Reservoir (covered)

Hillside Farm Golf Driving Range

LANE

ST. BANBURY ROAD A361

Swim. Pool

Games Court

The Warriner School

Playing Field

CHIPPERFIELD RD.

Warriner Farm

2

TADMARTON

36

Park Farm

Bloxham C of E Prim. Sch.

Playing Field

Playing Fields

THE POUND

LANE

WORKHOUSE

GAUNTLETS CL.

COLEGRAVE RD.

SALMON

LAWRENCE LEYS

SCHOFIELDS WY.

GREENS GTH.

STRAWBERRY TER.

STRAWBERRY HILL

Play. Field

Pav.

Sch.

WATER LA.

Recreation Ground

The Dewey Sports Centre

BRICKLE

BARLEY CL.

The Bowl. Grn.

Yew Tree Farm

3

COURTINGTON

Play. Fld.

LITTLE BRIDGE RD.

STONE HILL

HUMBER

ROSE BANK

OLD BRIDGE RD.

RIDGEWAY

ST. HOGG END

Chapel CL.

STEEPLE CL.

BLOXHAM

Sewage Works

THE AVENUE

WINTERS ROAD

PAINT.

HORNTON HOLLOW

QUARRY CL.

FLINT PL.

CLIBFORD

WALSINGHAM CL.

GREENHILLS

PARK

MALTINGS

LITTLE GREEN

KINGS RD.

GOOSE WK.

UNICORN ST.

TANNE

MERRIVALE'S LA.

BRAYDON CT.

Bloxham Village Museum

Coates's Spinney

4

The Slade Nature Reserve

BROOKSIDE

HYDE GRO.

CHERRYS CL.

COLESBOURNE

ORCHARD GRO.

CUMBERFORD HILL

QUEENS RD.

ALBERT RD.

QUIN

CHURCH ROAD A361

WESTBOURNE GR.

HAMILTON ROAD

Caravan Site

Brickhouse Farm

Recreation Ground

Pav.

NEWINGTON ROAD

BARFO

GASCOIGNE WY.

MANNING CL.

MAPLE CL.

Banbury OX15

Brooklands House

5

35

Oak View

BLOXHAM ROAD

Brompton Farm

Happy Valley Farm

6

17

SOUTH

Wooden Hill Farm

Mast

Wireless Station

ROAD

BLOXHAM RD.

7

34

Rifle Range

River Swere

42 · A · B · 43 · C · 20 · D · 44 · E

Barford St. John

F G H 13 J K 19

46 447 48 37

ROAD ROAD

Twyford Wharf

Oxford Canal

1

The Paddock

Reservoir

TWYFORD

Homestead Farm

M40 MOTORWAY

Mill

OX15

Green Hill Farm

Water Tower

Bowling Green

Greenhill House

BANBURY ROAD A4260

TWYFORD CL LESTER GS TWYFORD AV. TWYFORD GRO. GARRET RD. RAWLINS CL. MARY CL.

ROCHESTER

WALTON RD.

Kemps Farm

M40

2

SUMMERS CL.

Twyford

THE CRESCENT KEMPS RD.

AVENUE WAY

THE RISE CAWLEY RD.

DEENE CL.

36

School

East End

ADDERBURY

Tennis Courts

Weir Club

Sorbrook Manor

Library

AYNHO ROAD

ADDERBURY CT. CALDECOTT MITCHELL CROFT LA.

THE GREEN

KEYTE CL. LONG GEORGE WAY WALL CL.

East Adderbury

Sydenham House Farm

Home Farm

B4100

3

Croft Farm

CHAPEL LA.

MEADOW

HIGH STREET

SIR GEORGES RD.

PARSONS ST.

CHURCH LA.

LAMBOURNE CL.

HOME FM. CT.

EAST END LA.

KATHARINE HOUSE HOSPICE

140

West Adderbury

MANOR RD.

CROSS HILL

DOG CL.

NEW RD. WATER LA.

LANE

Lib.

ROAD

ADDERBURY PARK

ROUND CL.

HILL RD. CLOSE RD.

MILL

The Old Mill

Duchess Bridge

OX17

Home Farm

BANBURY BUSINESS PARK

BALLIOL HO.

TRINITY WY.

PEMBROKE HO.

SOMERVILLE

4

235

Burial Ground

Recreation Ground Club

TANNER'S LA. THE LEYS

HORN

ST. MARY'S RD.

Nursery

NORRIS CL.

MILTON ROAD

BERRY HILL ROAD

OXFORD ROAD A4260

Station Yard INDUSTRIAL ESTATE

Weir

Caravan Park

Bo-Peep Farm

Sor

5

BANBURY GOLF COURSE

Warehouse

Park Farm

Weir

Club House

6

Banbury

Wyatt's Barn

Quarry Farm

Brook

34

Bellow's Covert

7

St. Mary's Farm

Adderbury Grounds Farm

Swere

Paper Mill Cottages

F G H 140 J K

OX15

46 447 48

Bloxham Bridge

Adderbury Bridge

River

LITTLE LA.

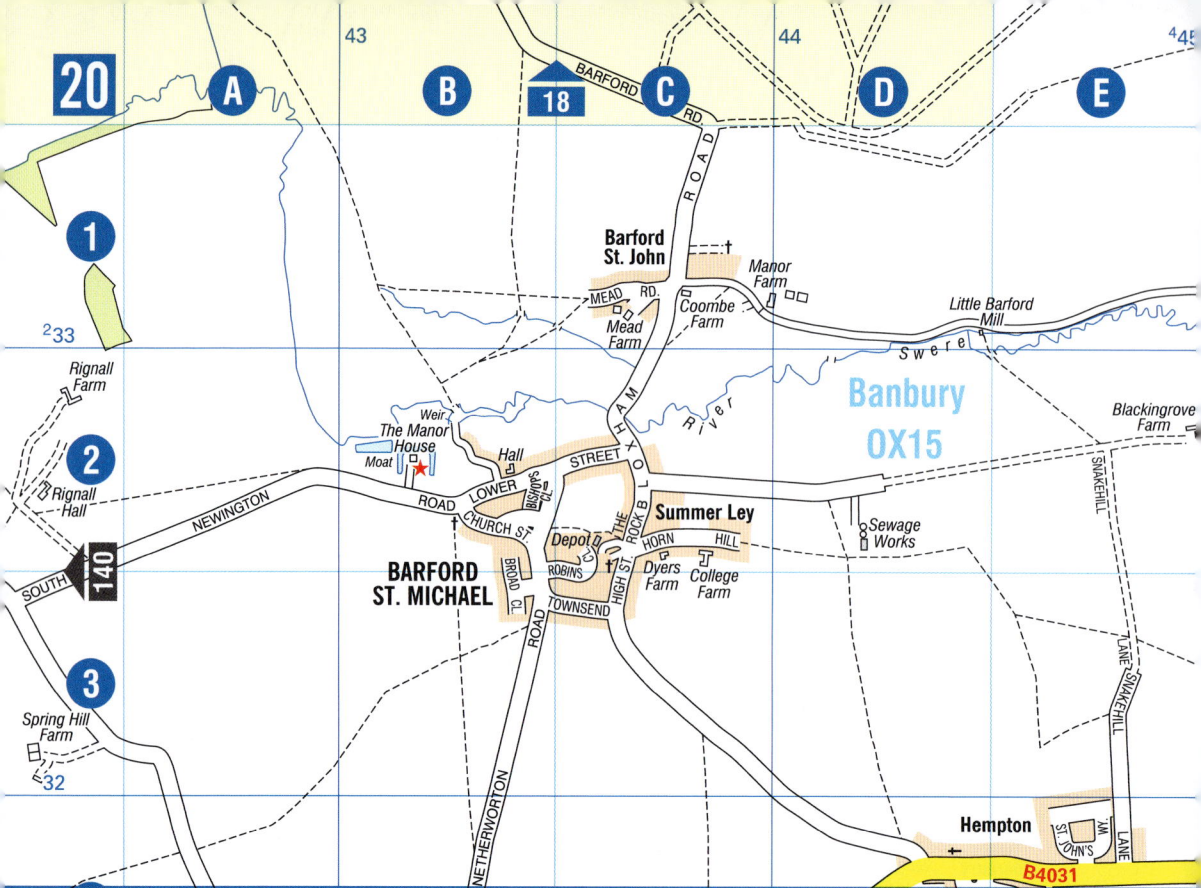
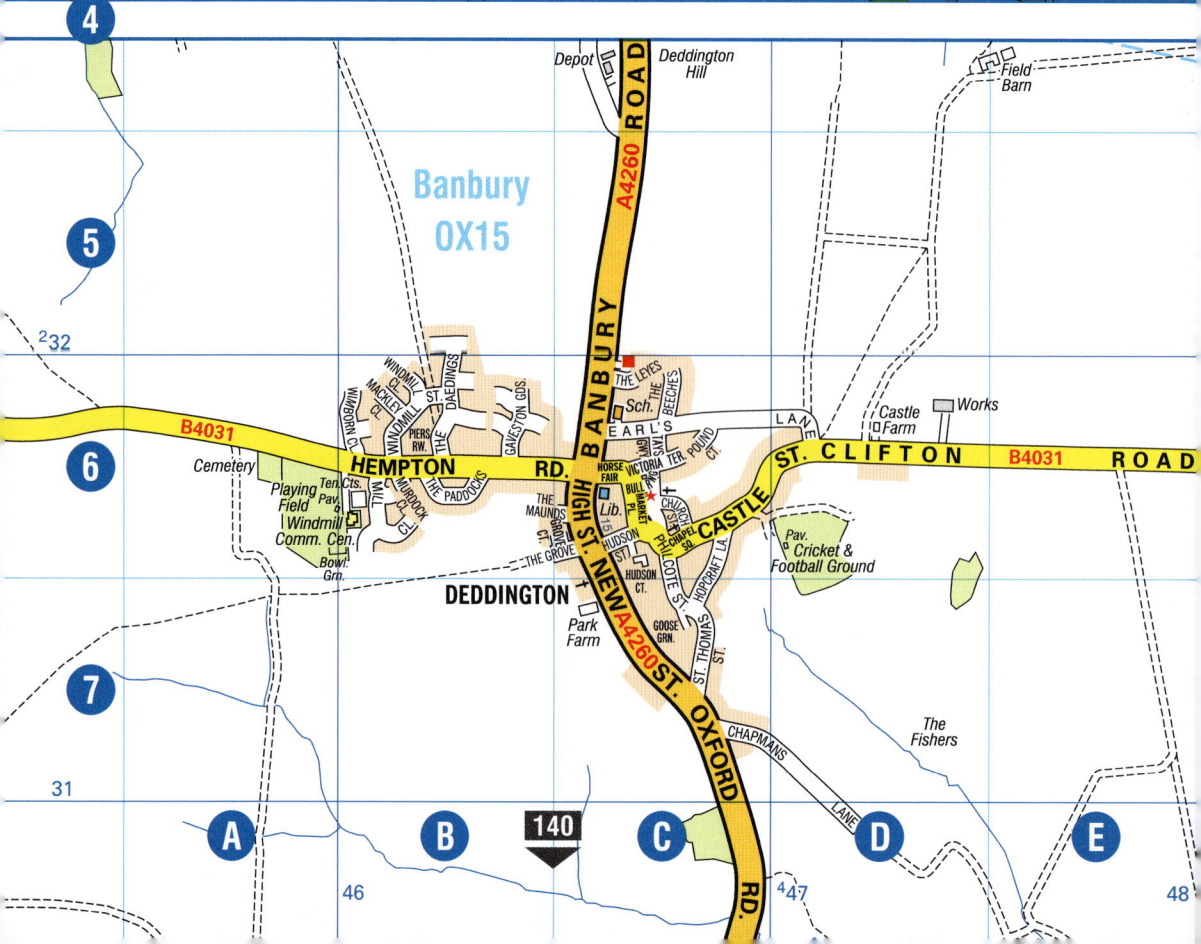

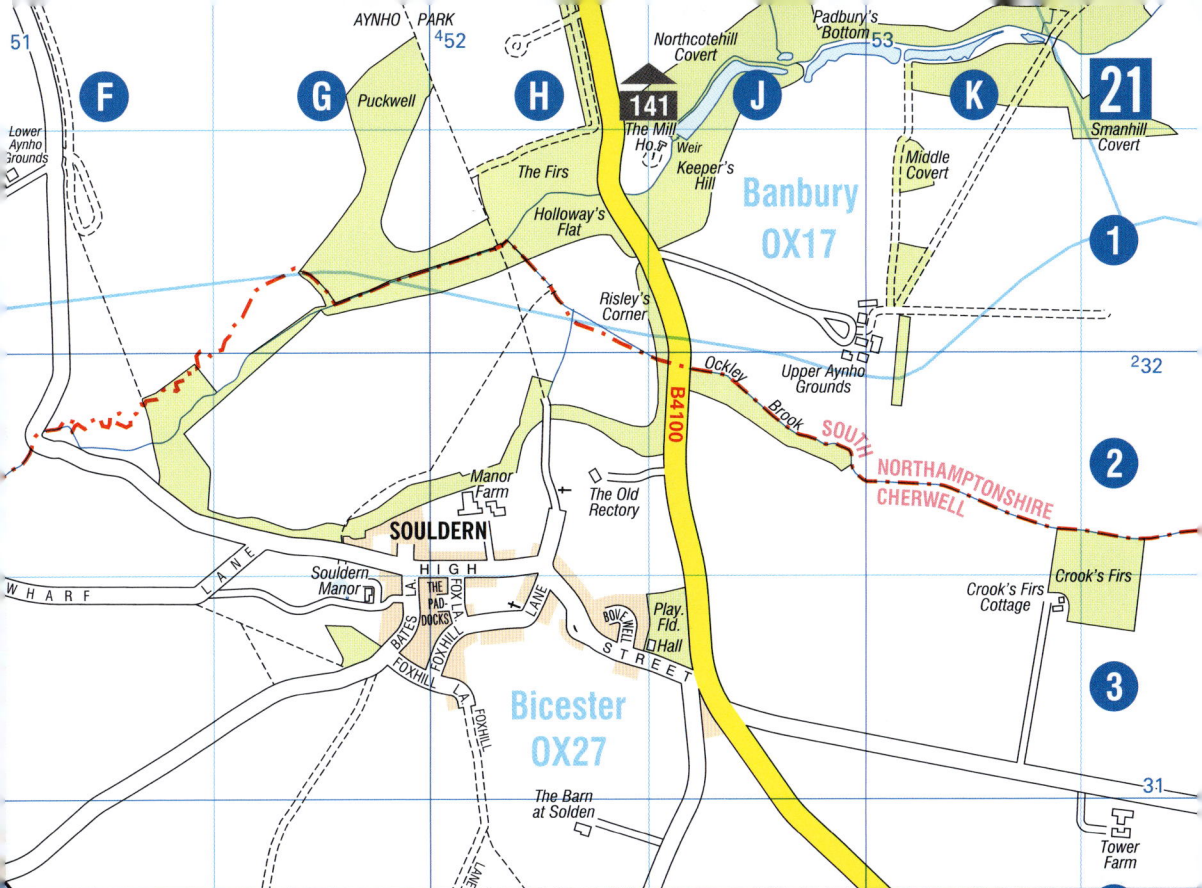

F Lower Aynho Grounds — AYNHO PARK — 51 — 52

G Puckwell

H The Firs — Holloway's Flat

J Northcotehill Covert — 141 — The Mill Ho. — Weir — Keeper's Hill — Padbury's Bottom — 53

K Middle Covert — Smanhill Covert

1 Banbury OX17

Risley's Corner

Ockley Brook — Upper Aynho Grounds

2 SOUTH NORTHAMPTONSHIRE CHERWELL

Manor Farm — The Old Rectory — SOULDERN

HIGH — Souldern Manor — BATES LA. — THE PADDOCKS — FOXHILL LA. — LANE — Bowell Well — Play. Fld. — Hall — STREET

Crook's Firs — Crook's Firs Cottage

3 Bicester OX27 — FOXHILL LA. — FOXHILL LANE

The Barn at Solden — 31

Tower Farm

WHARF LANE

B4100

4

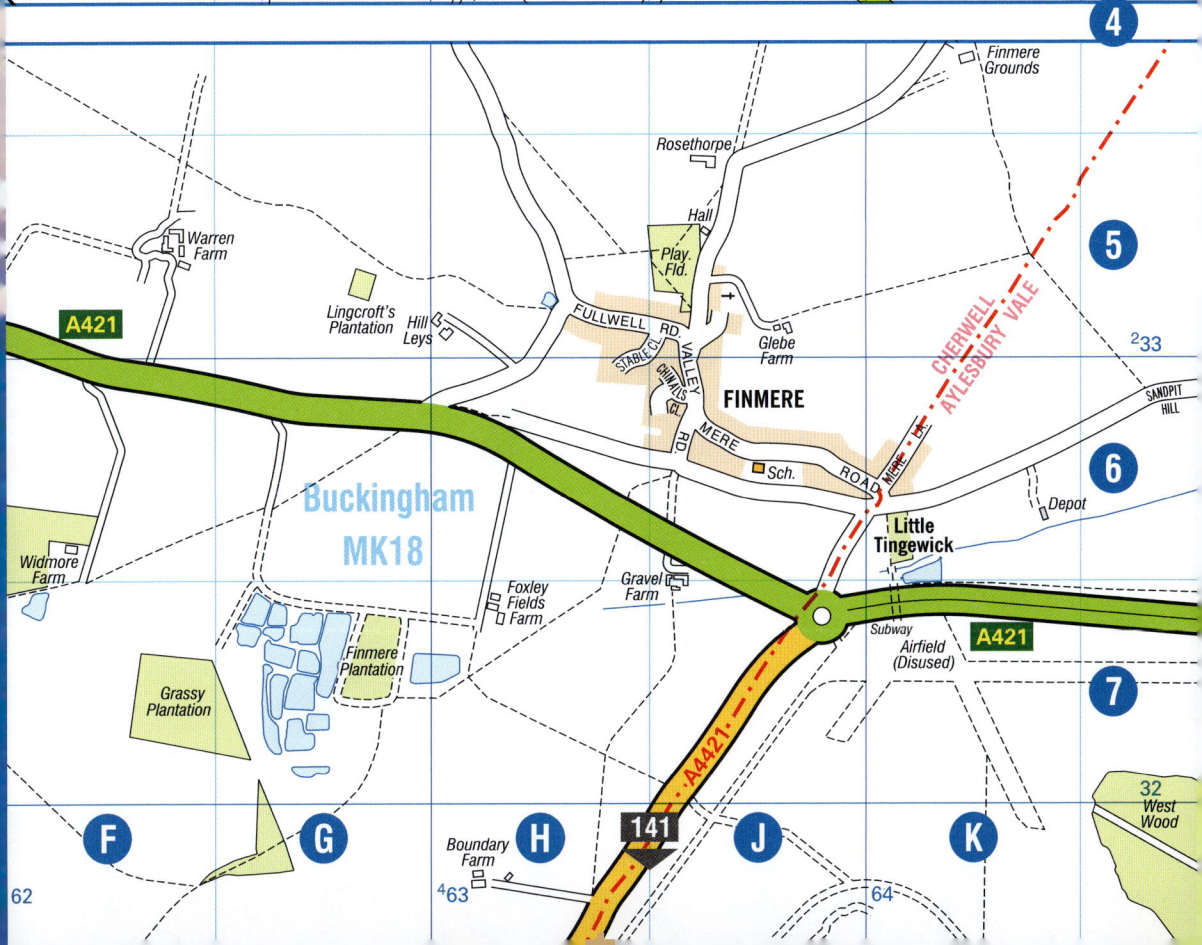

Finmere Grounds

Rosethorpe

Warren Farm — Hall — Play. Fld.

A421 — Lingcroft's Plantation — Hill Leys — FULLWELL — STABLE CL. — VALLEY RD. — CHINALIS RD. — Glebe Farm — FINMERE — MERE ROAD — Sch.

CHERWELL AYLESBURY VALE — SANDPIT HILL — 33

5

6 Depot

Little Tingewick

Buckingham MK18

Widmore Farm — Foxley Fields Farm — Gravel Farm — Subway — Airfield (Disused) — **A421**

Finmere Plantation

Grassy Plantation

A4421

7 32 West Wood

F — **G** — **H** Boundary Farm — 141 — **J** — **K** — 62 — 63 — 64

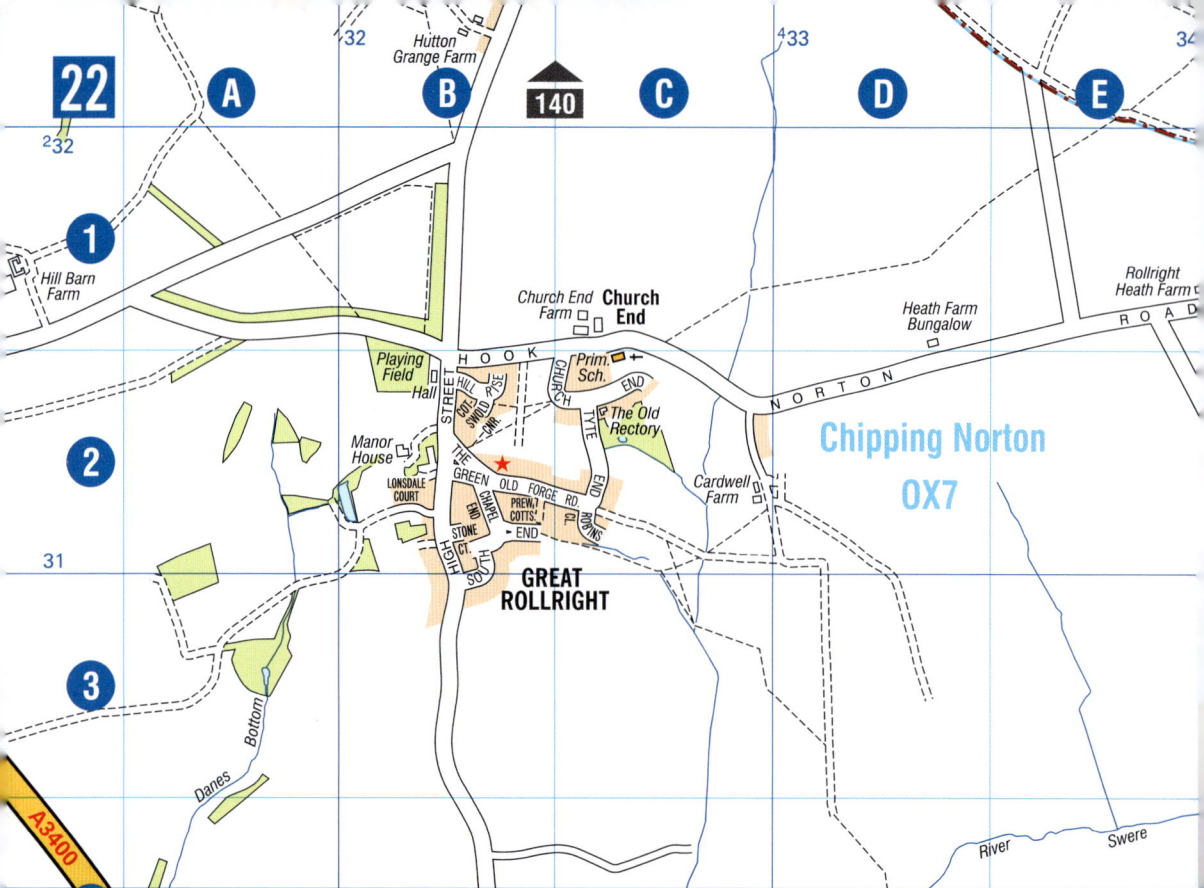
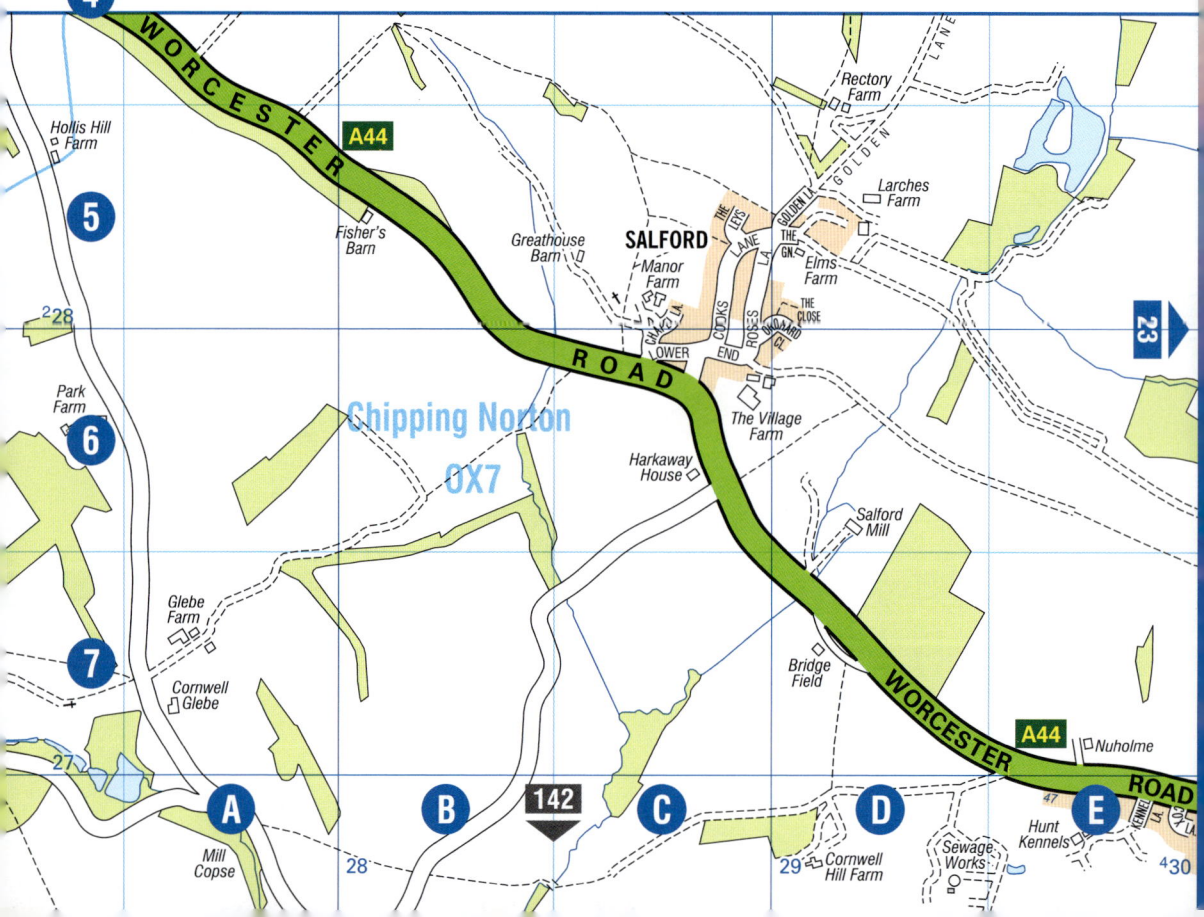

22

140

23

142

A   B   C   D   E

1
2
3
4
5
6
7

Hill Barn Farm

Hutton Grange Farm

Church End Farm   **Church End**

Heath Farm Bungalow

Rollright Heath Farm

NORTON   ROAD

Playing Field

Hall

Manor House

LONSDALE COURT

THE GREEN

HIGH ST.

CHAPEL END

STONE CT.

SOUTH END

HOOK STREET

THE HILL

COTS. SWOLD CNR.

CHURCH TYTE

OLD FORGE RD.

PREW. COTTS.

END

END

ROBINS CL.

Prim. Sch.

The Old Rectory

Cardwell Farm

GREAT ROLLRIGHT

Chipping Norton OX7

31

Danes Bottom

River   Swere

A3400

WORCESTER

A44

Hollis Hill Farm

Fisher's Barn

Greathouse Barn

SALFORD

Manor Farm

Rectory Farm

GOLDEN LA

Larches Farm

THE LEYS

LANE

CHAPEL LA

COOKS LA

ROSES

TOWER

END

LA

THE GN.

Elms Farm

THE CLOSE

ORCHARD CL.

Chipping Norton OX7

The Village Farm

Harkaway House

Salford Mill

ROAD

228

Park Farm

5

6

Glebe Farm

Cornwell Glebe

7

27

WORCESTER

A44

Bridge Field

Nuholme

Hunt Kennels

KENNEL LA

Sewage Works

Cornwell Hill Farm

ROAD

Mill Copse

28   29   30

A   B   C   D   E

32   33

Choicehill Farm
Caroline Colyear Cottages
F G H 143 J K 23

Little Meadows
1
29
B4026
A3400
Sandfields Farm
2
OVER NORTON PARK
The Orangery
Over Norton House
Witts Farm
Over Norton
PENFIELD
Home Farm
BLUE ROW
CLEEVES CL.
QUARHILL CL.
Play. Fld.
THE GREEN
Slad Lodge
Piggery
Reservoir (covered)
3
RADBONE HILL
MAIN ST.
Cleeves House
Hit or Miss Farm
28
Chipping Norton
OX7
Nursery
A361
Chipping Norton Cricket Club
4
The Cleeves
B4026 NORTON ROAD
PARK AV.
CLEEVES AV.
WILCOX RD.
INSALL RD.
MAR. RD.
CHALFORD RD.
COLBOROUGH RD.
Cromwell Park
ROCKHILL FARM CL.
The Mount
Castle (site of)
Pool Meadow
ELMSFIELD FARM INDUSTRIAL ESTATE
John Cory House
CHURCH LA.
The Theatre
CHURCH ST.
SPRING ST.
HORSE FAIR
HOSP.
LONDON ROAD
BANBURY
NORTON PK.
AKRN.
Sch.
A44 Factory
ROCK HILL
PORTLAND PL.
DICKENSON CT.
SHEPARD CL.
COOPER CL.
BRASSEY CL.
5
Cemetery
WORCESTER ROAD INDUSTRIAL ESTATE
PRIMSDOWN INDUSTRIAL ESTATE
A44
Rec. Grd.
ROAD NEW ST.
HIGH ST.
MARKET ST.
GOSTE
MARKET PL.
WITHERS CT.
ROWELL
WARDS
FOXFELD
Tank Farm
27
CHIPPING NORTON
WORCESTER
STATION YARD INDUSTRIAL ESTATE
CRAFTS MILL TER.
STATION RD.
LEWIS RD.
WEBB
THE
DUNSTAN
WITHERS WY.
MILLVN.
ALBION
FOX
CLOVERS CL.
HITCHMAN DR.
ROAD
Chipping Norton Lido
Chipping Norton School
6
Chipping Norton Common
Bliss Mill
CROSLEYS AV.
CROSLEYS RD.
SPRING
THE GREEN
BURFORD ROAD
VERNON HO.
Glyme Farm
7
Ponds
Westend Farm
LORDS PIECE
TILSLEY RD.
HAILEY CRES.
HAILEY RD.
CORNISH RD.
CORNISH CL.
WALTERBUSH RD.
ALEX. FER.
MITRA FER.
RAMSKE FER.
BLENHEIM TER.
MARSHALL
HILL CL.
COTSWOLD CRESCENT
Rec. Grd.
Rec. Grd.
St Mary's C of E Prim. Sch.
A361
Westfield Farm
B4450
Club
Football Grd.
CHURCHILL
CHARLBURY B4026
Play. Fld.
Oldner House
26
F G H 143 J K
Play. Fld.
Greystones (Council Offices)
Greystones Leisure Centre
ROAD
30 31 32

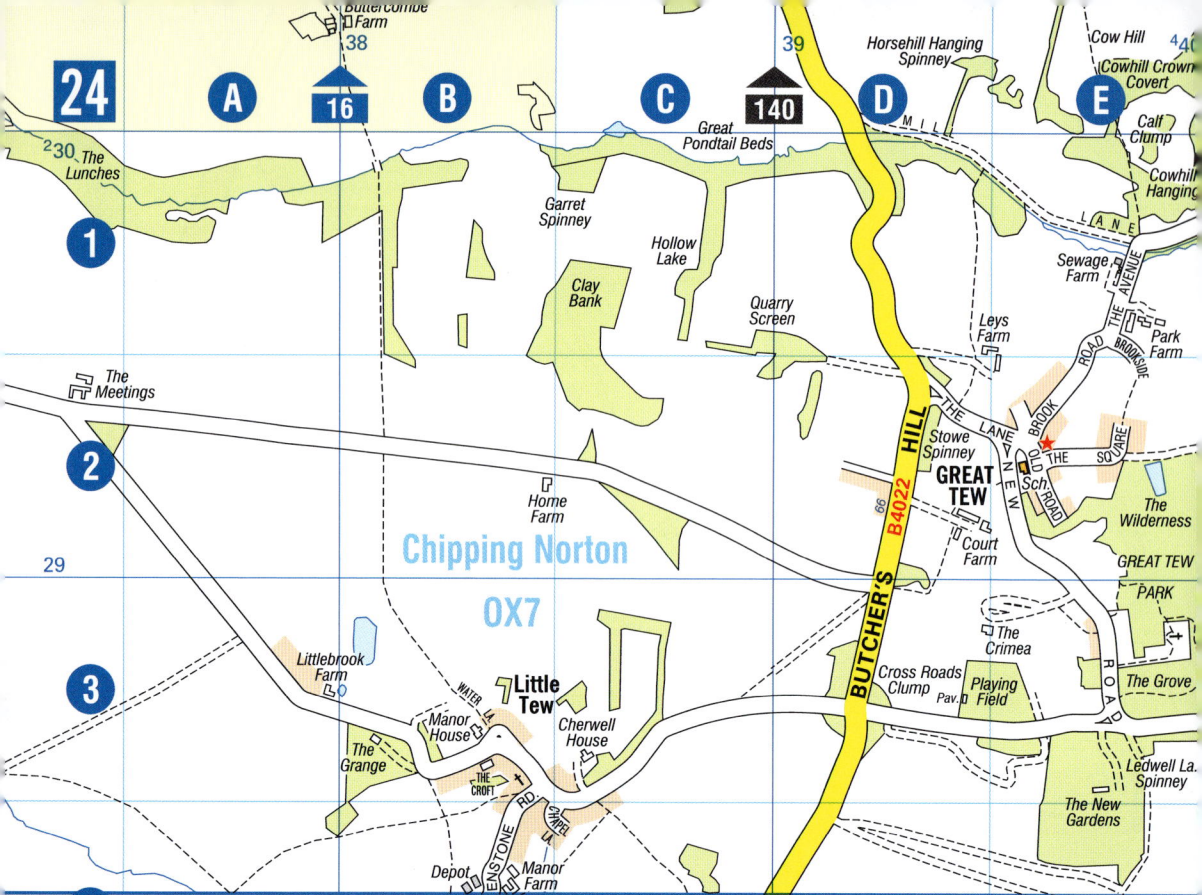

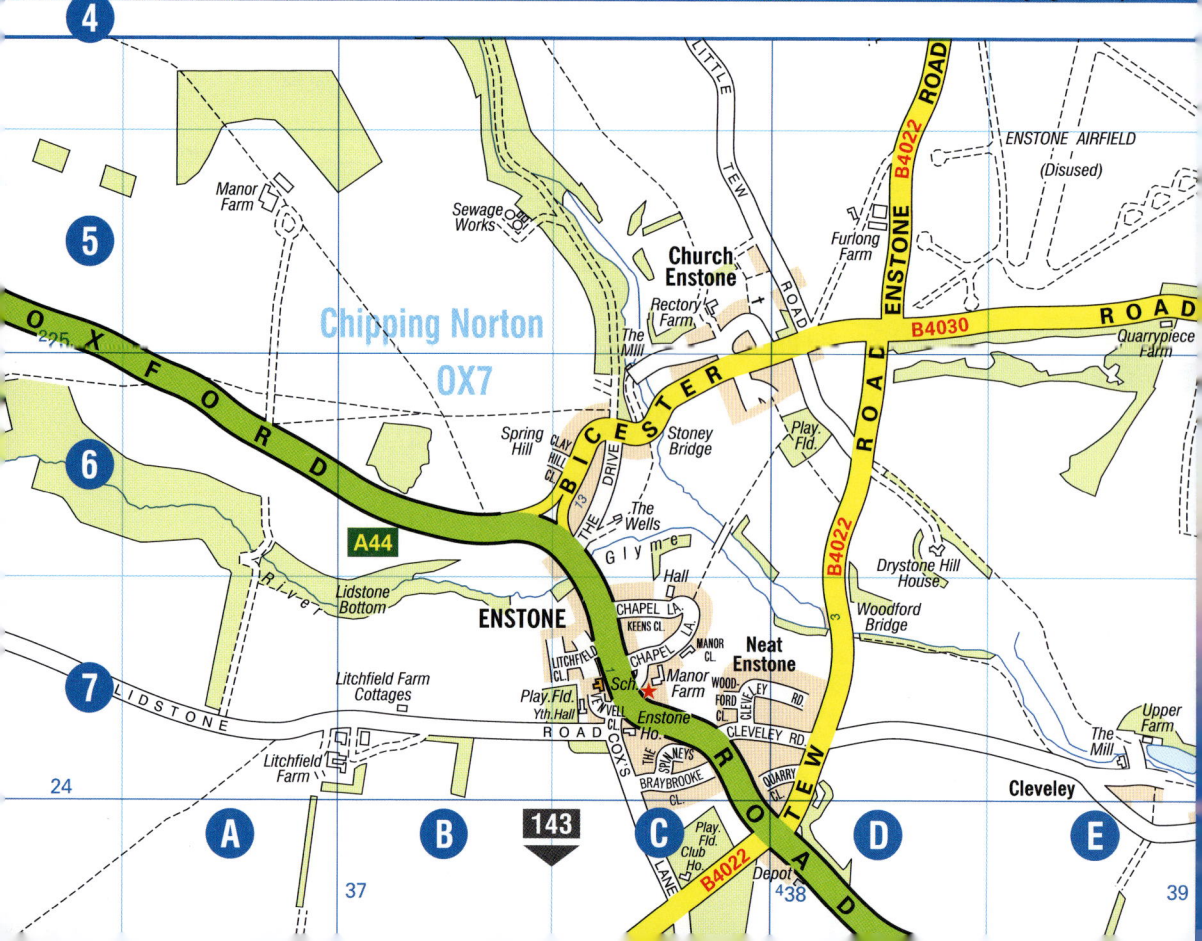

Buttercombe Farm 38

A **16** B C **140** D Horsehill Hanging Spinney Cow Hill Cowhill Crown Covert Calf Clump E 40

30 The Lunches

Great Pondtail Beds

Cowhill Hanging

THE LANE

Sewage Farm

THE AVENUE

Park Farm

BROOKSIDE

ROAD

1

Garret Spinney

Hollow Lake

Clay Bank

Quarry Screen

Leys Farm

THE SQUARE

2

The Meetings

BUTCHER'S HILL

B4022

66

Stowe Spinney

THE LANE

Sch

THE OLD ROAD

GREAT TEW

BROOK ROAD

The Wilderness

29

Home Farm

Chipping Norton

OX7

Court Farm

GREAT TEW PARK

3

Littlebrook Farm

WATER LA.

Manor House

Little Tew

Cherwell House

Cross Roads Clump Pav. Playing Field

The Crimea

The Grove

The Grange

THE CROFT

ENSTONE RD.

CHAPEL RD.

Ledwell La. Spinney

The New Gardens

Depot

Manor Farm

4

Manor Farm

Sewage Works

LITTLE TEW

B4022 ROAD

ENSTONE AIRFIELD

(Disused)

5

Chipping Norton

OX7

Church Enstone

Rectory Farm

The Mill

Furlong Farm

ROAD

ENSTONE ROAD

B4030

ROAD

Quarrypiece Farm

25

OXFORD

Spring Hill

CLAY HILL CL.

THE DRIVE

Stoney Bridge

Play. Fld.

ROAD

6

BICESTER

The Wells

Drystone Hill House

A44

River

Lidstone Bottom

G l y m e

Hall

Woodford Bridge

7

LIDSTONE

Litchfield Farm Cottages

ENSTONE

CHAPEL LA.

KEENS CL.

CHAPEL

LITCHFIELD CL.

MANOR CL.

Neat Enstone

WOOD FORD CL.

CLEVELEY RD.

TEW ROAD

Upper Farm

The Mill

Litchfield Farm

VELL

Sch

Play. Fld. Yth. Hall

Enstone Ho.

COOK'S

SPINNEYS

BRAYBROOKE CL.

ROAD

Manor Farm

CLEVELEY RD.

QUARRY CL.

Cleveley

24

A B **143** C Play. Fld. Club Ho. B4022 Depot D 38 E 39

37

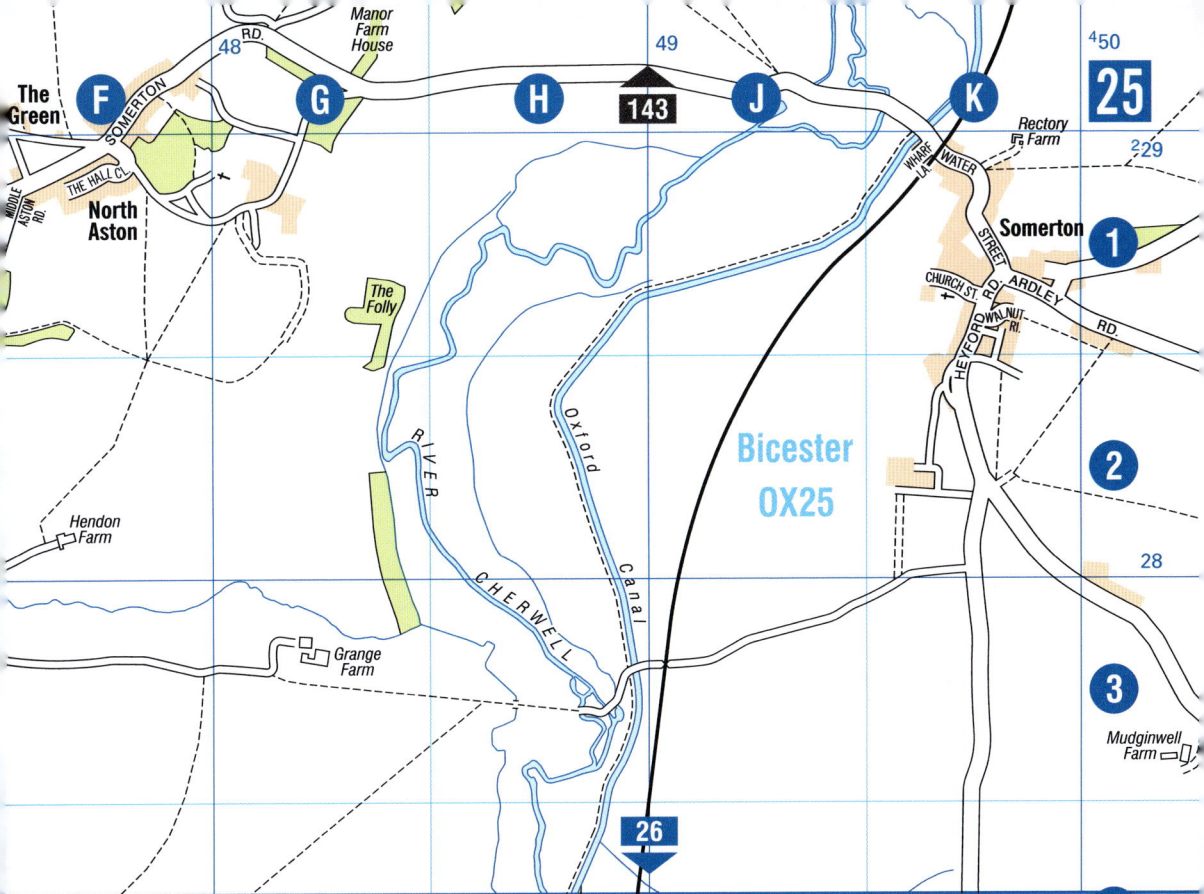

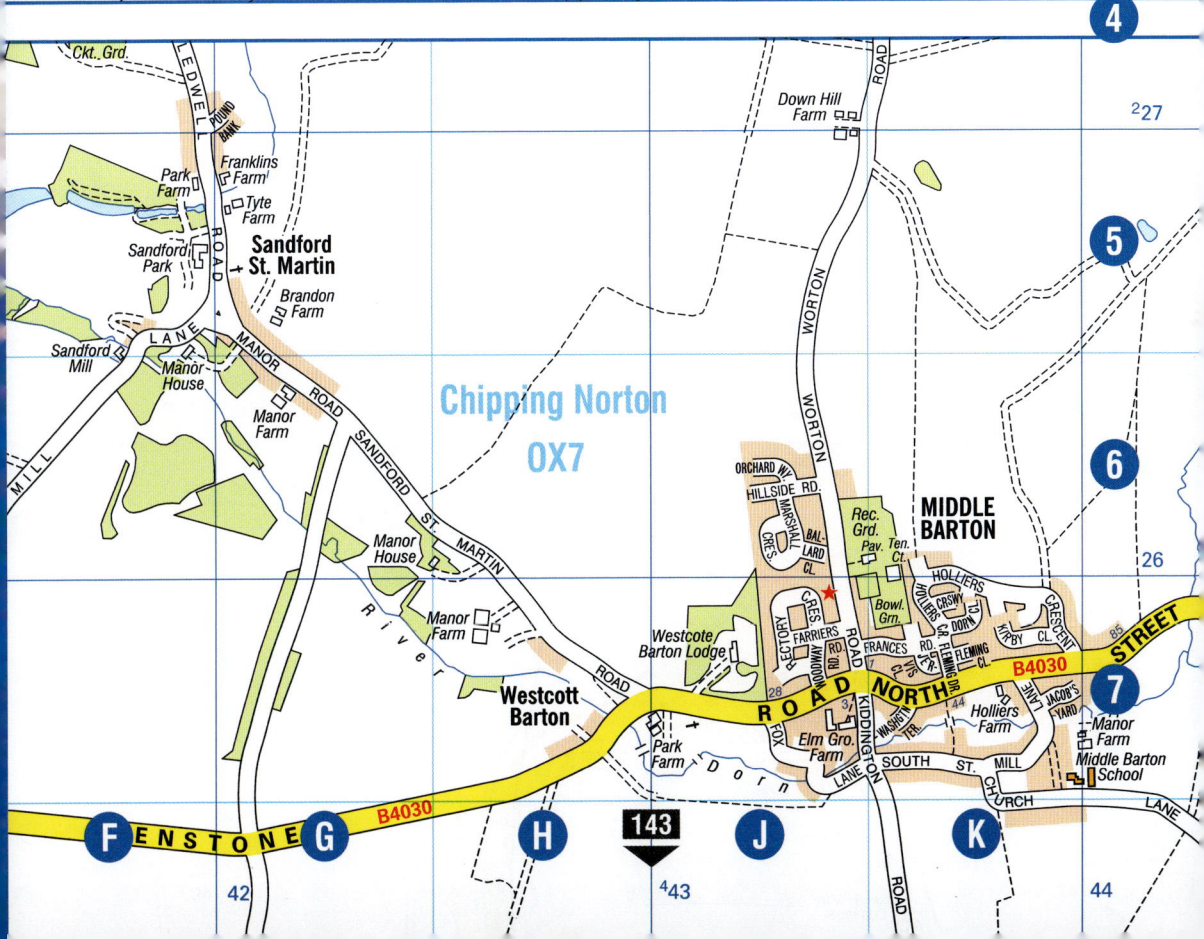

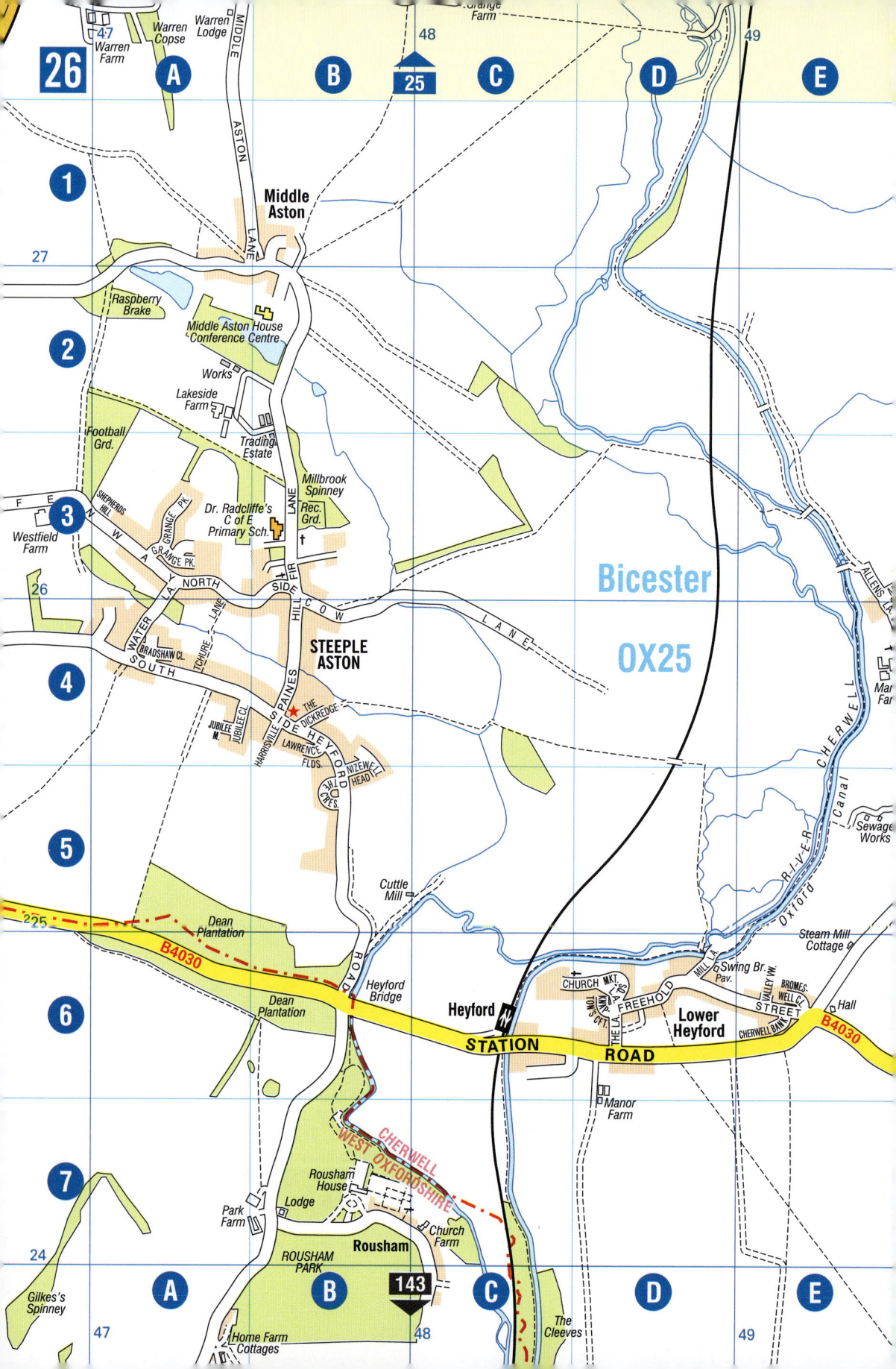

A   B   25   C   D   E

1

27

Warren Farm
47
Warren Copse
Warren Lodge
MIDDLE ASTON LANE
Middle Aston

2

Raspberry Brake
Middle Aston House Conference Centre
Works
Lakeside Farm
Trading Estate

3

F E
Westfield Farm
26
SHEPHERDS HILL
NEW WAY LANE
GRANGE PK.
GRANGE PK.
NORTH
Dr. Radcliffe's C of E Primary Sch.
Millbrook Spinney Rec. Grd.
SIDE
FIR HILL
LANE
COW

4

WATER LA.
BRADSHAW CL.
TCHURE LANE
SOUTH
STEEPLE ASTON
LANE
Bicester
OX25

JUBILEE M.
JUBILEE CL.
HARRISVILLE
SPAINES
DE
THE DICKREDGE
LAWRENCE FLDS.
HEYFORD
SH. CL.
NIZEWELL HEAD
ALLENS LA.
Mar Far
RIVER CHERWELL

5

Cuttle Mill
Sewage Works
Oxford Canal

225
B4030
Dean Plantation
ROAD
Heyford Bridge
Steam Mill Cottage
MILL LA.
Swing Br.
Pav.

6

Dean Plantation
Heyford
STATION
ROAD
CHURCH
MKT.
TONS CL.
THE LA.
FREEHOLD
Lower Heyford
WHITELEY W.
CHERWELL BANK
BROMES-WELL CL.
Hall
B4030

7

Park Farm
Lodge
Rousham House
CHERWELL
WEST OXFORDSHIRE
Manor Farm

24
Gilkes's Spinney
47
ROUSHAM PARK
Rousham
Church Farm
143
48
The Cleeves
Home Farm Cottages
49

A   B   C   D   E

1

Mudginwell
Farm

2

UPPER HEYFORD AIRFIELD
(DISUSED)

3

Letchmere
Farm

26

SOMERTON

LANE
STREET

UPPER
HEYFORD

Cemy.

ORCHARD LA.
ORCHARD PL.
SCHOOL LA.
HIGH

ROAD
CAMP
WAY

HOMESTEAD
EGLIN ST.
ALTUS ST.
SCHILLING ST.
CR.
CR.
HOMESTEAD

ROAD   C A M P

P

DRIVE
GORDON
ROAD
ROPER
WHIT...
CHESHIRE RD.
EADY
DACEY
PORTAL DR.
GIBSON DR.
BADER
TAIT DR.
RDD PL.
HARRIS
NETTLETON DR.
PORTAL DR.
DR.
PORTAL
DR.
ROAD

DOW ST.
RD.
RHEE
P

SODEN RD.
LARSEN RD.
RENCHARD CIRCLE

ROAD
CHILGROVE DR.

4

Caravan
Park

Heyford
Leys Farm

The
Heath

Sewage
Works

5

²25

Cheesman's
Barn

The
Gorse

6

Timberyard
'Clump'

Lime
Hollow

ROAD

DITCH HILL

B4030

LOWER   HEYFORD

PORT
WAY

Hill View
Farm

New
Nursery

7

Park
Farm

Caulcott

SOUTH STREET

Daisy Head
Farm

Caulcott
Farm

24

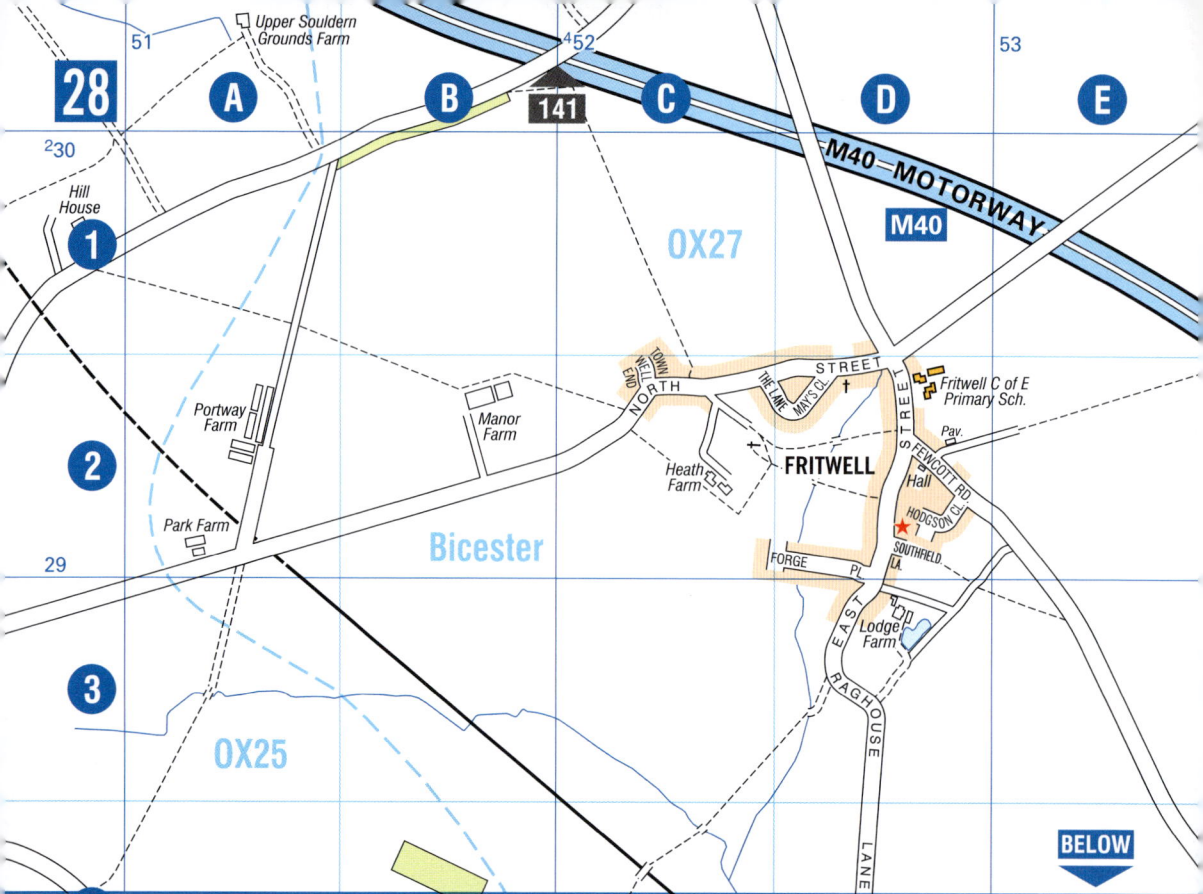

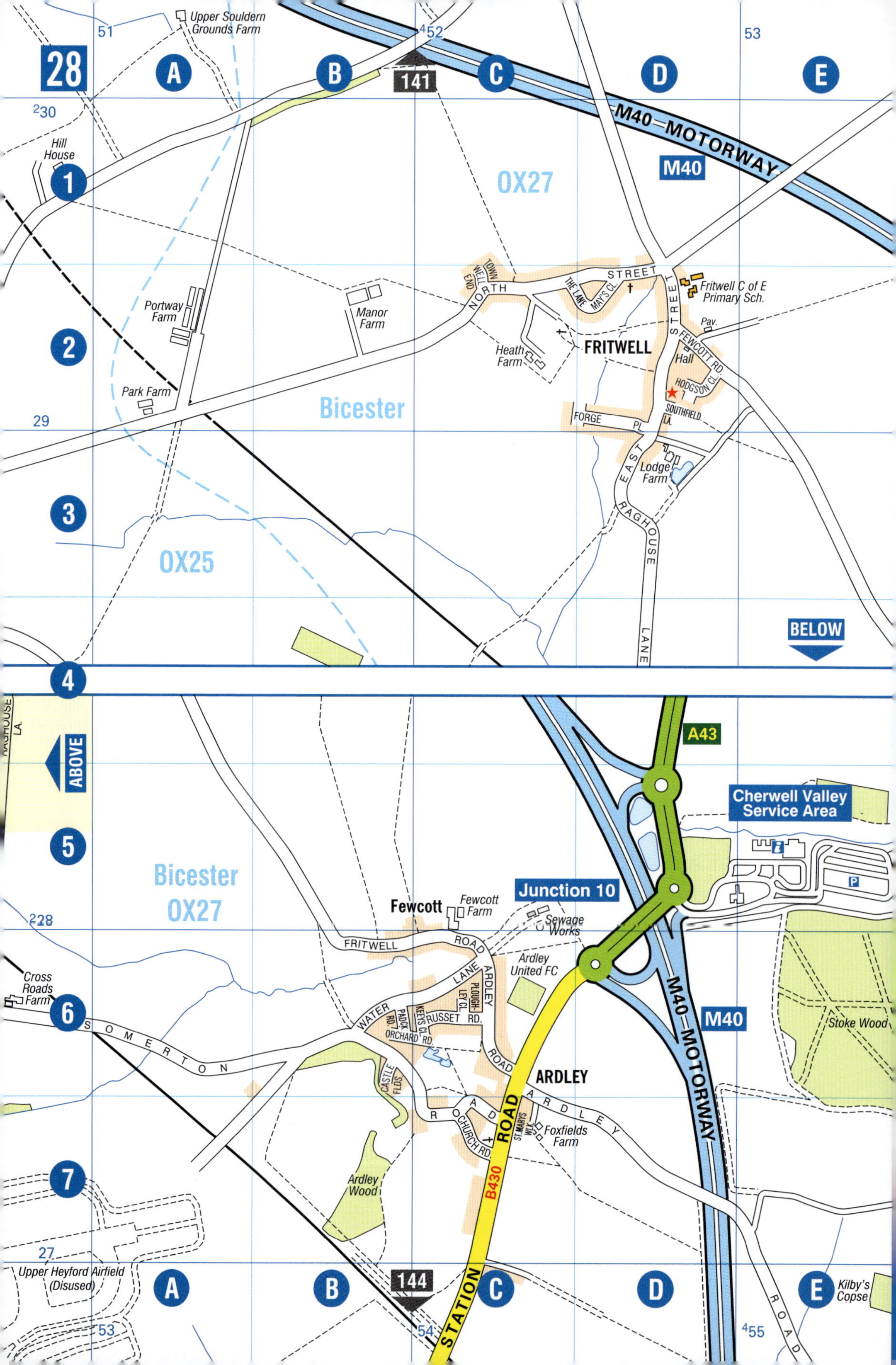

28

Top map (sections 1–4)

A **B** **C** **D** **E**

51   452   53

²30

141

M40 — MOTORWAY

M40

OX27

Upper Souldern Grounds Farm

Hill House

Portway Farm

Manor Farm

Park Farm

Bicester

Heath Farm

29

OX25

TOWN WELL END

NORTH

THE LANE

MAY'S CL.

STREET

STREET

FEWCOTT RD.

Fritwell C of E Primary Sch.

Pav.

HODGSON CL.

Hall

FRITWELL

FORGE PL.

SOUTHFIELD LA.

EAST

RAGHOUSE LANE

Lodge Farm

BELOW

Bottom map (sections 4–7)

RAGHOUSE LA.

ABOVE

A43

Cherwell Valley Service Area

Junction 10

M40

M40

Bicester OX27

Fewcott

Fewcott Farm

Sewage Works

Ardley United FC

Cross Roads Farm

SOMERTON

FRITWELL ROAD

ARDLEY LANE

PLOUGH CL.

WATER RD.

PADDA RD.

KEYS CL.

RUSSET RD.

LEY CL.

ORCHARD RD.

ROAD

ARDLEY

Stoke Wood

CASTLE FLDS.

CHURCH RD.

ST MARYS WAY

ADD RD.

ARDLEY

ROAD

ARDLEY

ST MARYS WAY

Foxfields Farm

ARDLEY

B430

ROAD

STATION

Ardley Wood

²28

Upper Heyford Airfield (Disused)

27

144

Kilby's Copse

A **B** **C** **D** **E**

53   454   455

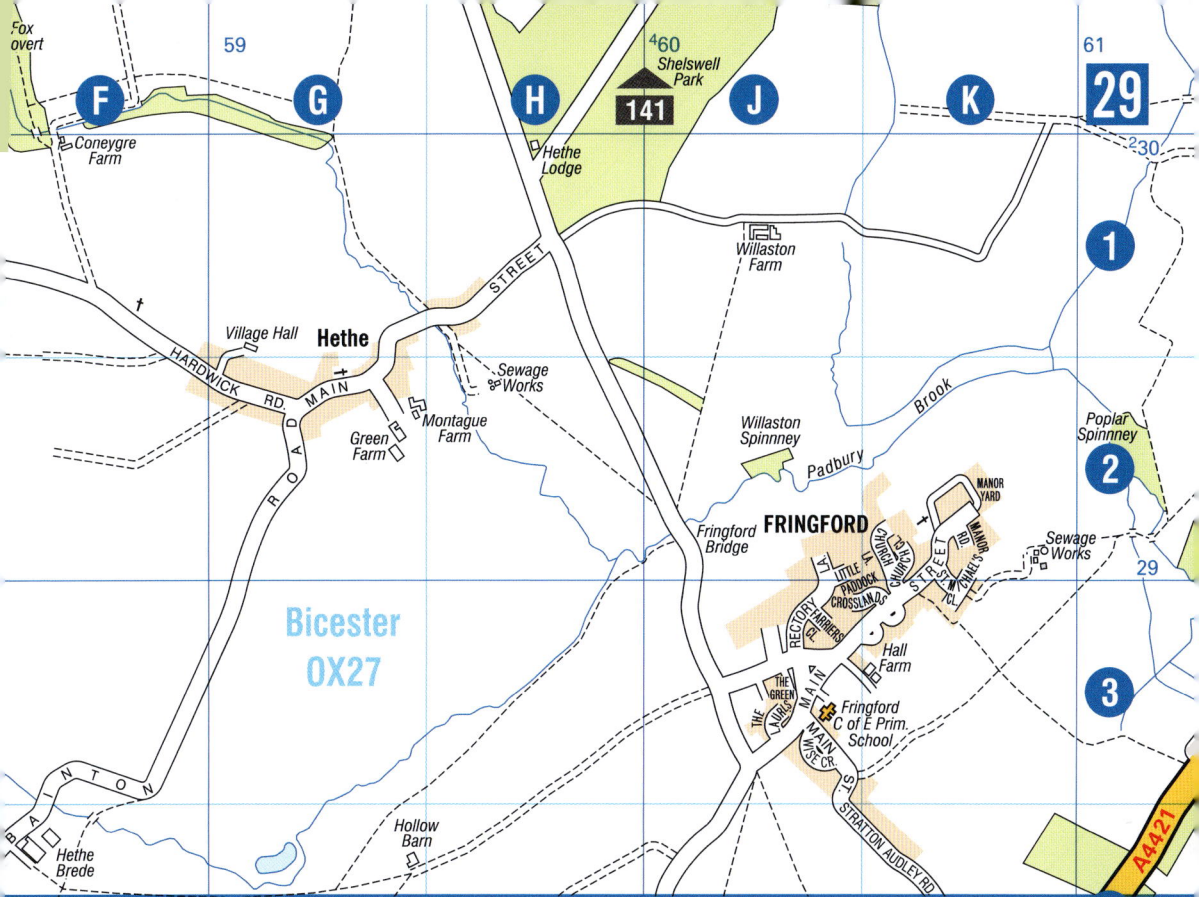

Fox overt

Coneygre Farm

Hethe Lodge

141
Shelswell Park

Willaston Farm

1

Village Hall

Hethe

HARDWICK RD.

ROAD MAIN

STREET

Brook

Poplar Spinnney

2

Green Farm

Sewage Works

Montague Farm

Willaston Spinnney

Padbury

Willaston Spinnney

Fringford Bridge

FRINGFORD

MANOR YARD

Sewage Works

29

Bicester OX27

LITTLE CROSSLANE

PADDOCK CROSSLN 2

CHURCH ST.

CHURCH LA.

MANOR

STREET

MICHAELS CL.

BAINTON

RECTORY LA.

HARRIERS CT.

MAIN

THE LAURELS

THE GREEN

Hall Farm

3

Fringford C of E Prim. School

Hethe Brede

Hollow Barn

WISE CR.

MAIN ST.

STRATTON AUDLEY RD.

A4421

4

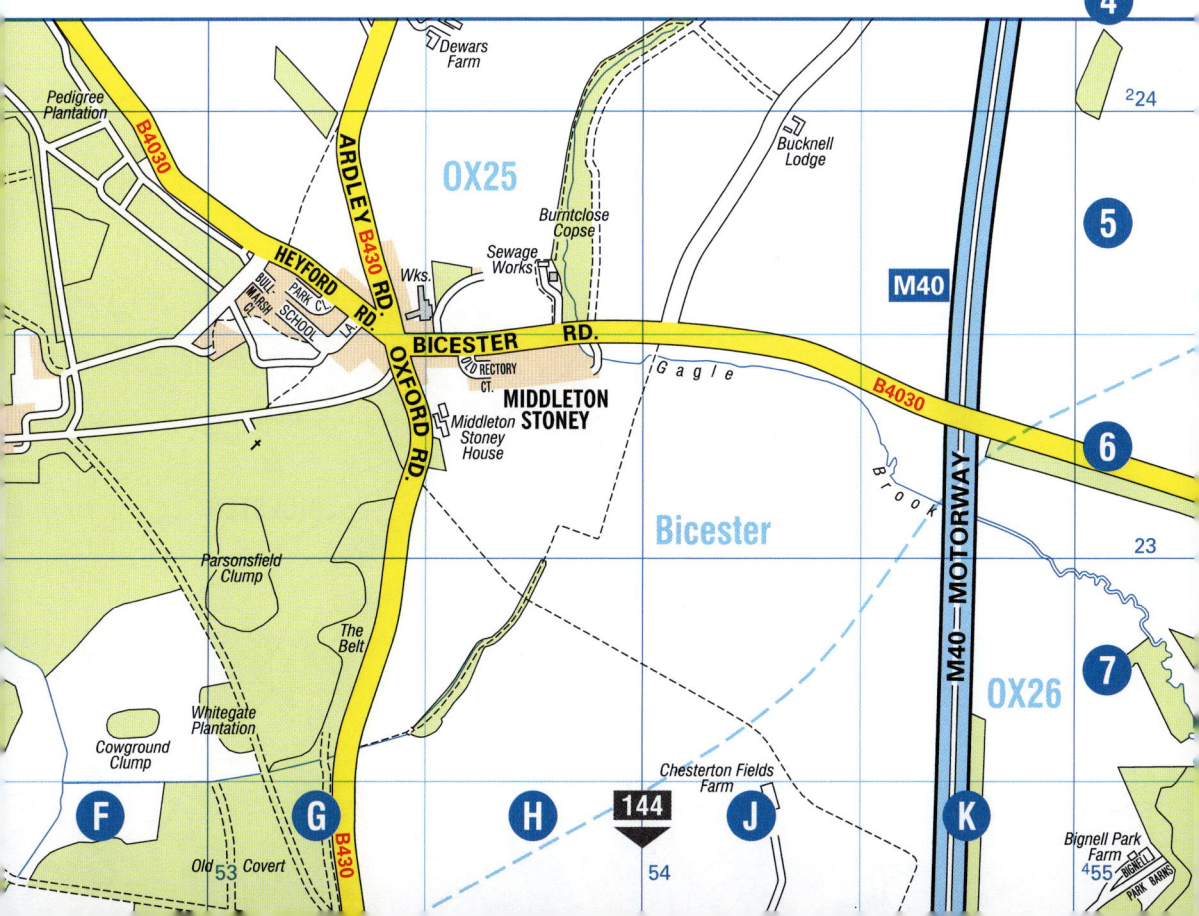

Dewars Farm

Pedigree Plantation

B4030

ARDLEY

B4030 RD.

OX25

Bucknell Lodge

224

Burntclose Copse

5

HEYFORD

RD.

Wks.

Sewage Works

M40

BULL MARSH CL.

PARK CL

SCHOOL

LA.

BICESTER RD.

B4030

6

OXFORD RD.

RECTORY CT.

MIDDLETON STONEY

Gagle

Middleton Stoney House

Brook

23

Parsonsfield Clump

Bicester

M40 — MOTORWAY

The Belt

7

Whitegate Plantation

OX26

Cowground Clump

Chesterton Fields Farm

Bignell Park Farm
455
BIGNELL PARK BARNS

B430

Old 53 Covert

54

A B 144 C D E

56 57 58

Bainton Manor

Watergate Farm

Twelve Acre Copse

Great Copse

Nettle Copse

B4100

Bainton Copse

1

26

ARDLEY ROAD

Manor Farm

Bucknell ROAD

2

SCHOOL PADDOCK

MIDDLETON ROAD BAINTON RD

ROSE CL NEW ROW CL

Lower Farm

Bucknell Manor

BICESTER

3

225

Caversfield House

South Lodge Riding Stables

Home Farm

B4100

4

Crowmarsh Farm

Hawkwell Farm

Bicester

5

OX25

Aldershot Farm

Lords Farm

A4095

BANBURY

24

Woodfield

BICESTER

Bure Park Prim. Sch.

6

Himley Farm

Gowell Farm

Police Depot

AVONBURY BUSINESS PARK

LANE

B4100

Playing Field

OX26

7

23

A4095

HOWES

School

TAMAR CRES.

SHAKESPEARE DRIVE

GEORGE AVENUE

ROWAN RD.

Highfield

Brookside Prim. Sch.

BUCKINGHAM ROAD

B4030

56 57 58

Bignell

MIDDL

Comm. Cen.

Sports

Bicester Comm. College

St. Mary's

Sports Centre

Brookside Ct.

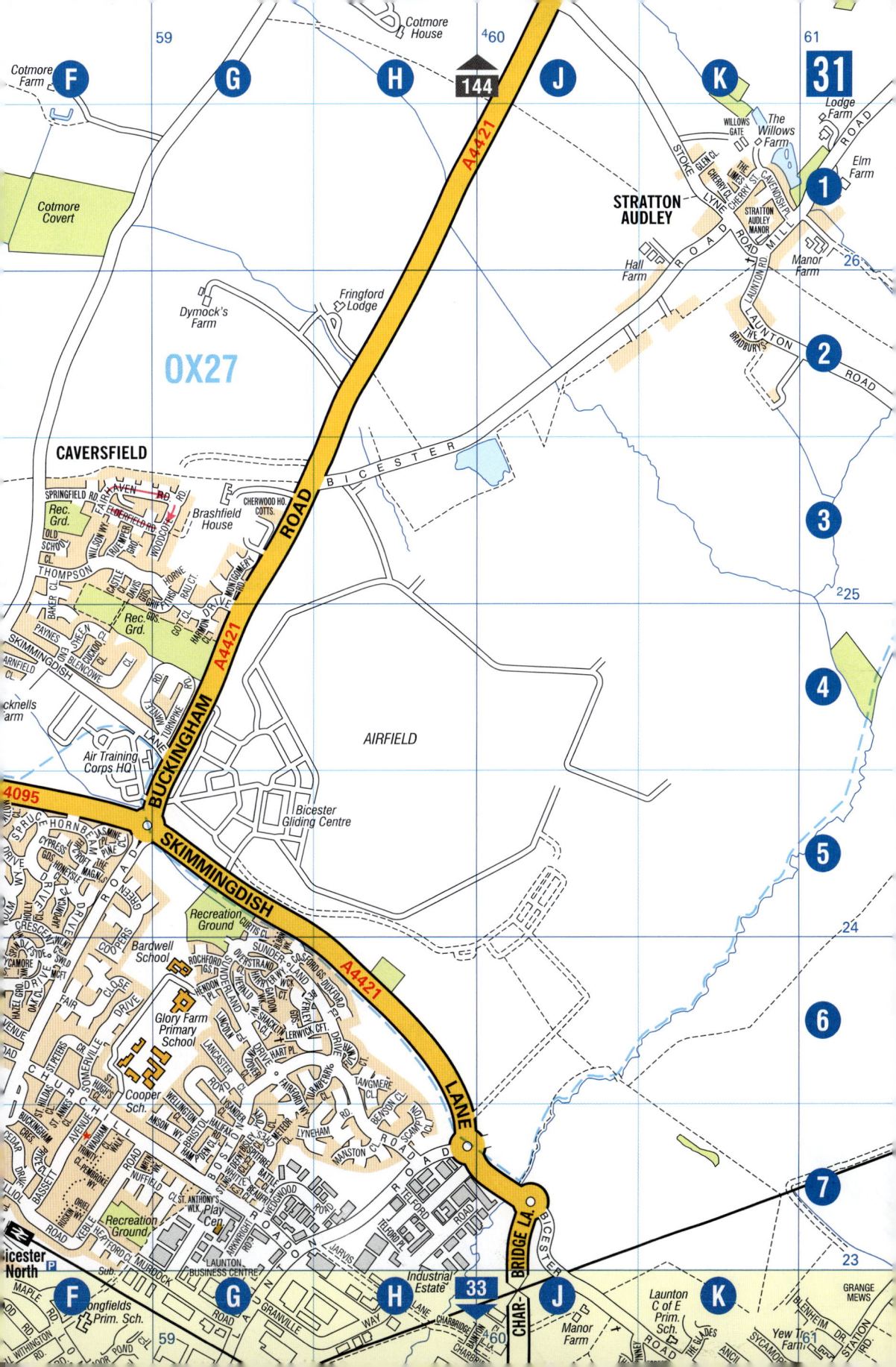

F
G
H
144
J
K

59
460
61

Cotmore House
Cotmore Farm
Lodge Farm
Willows Gate
The Willows Farm
Elm Farm

Cotmore Covert

STRATTON AUDLEY

STOKE LYNE ROAD
GLEN CL
CHERRY CL
THE LIMES
CHERRY CT
CAVENDISH PL
CAVENDISH RD
MILL ROAD

Stratton Audley Manor

1
26

Hall Farm
Manor Farm

OX27

Dymock's Farm
Fringford Lodge

LAUNTON RD
THE BRADBURY'S
LAUNTON ROAD

2

3
225

CAVERSFIELD

SPRINGFIELD RD
RAVEN RD
FARM WY
ENDERFIELD RD
Rec. Grd.
OLD SCHS CL
WILSON WY
BUTTMEAD
PRY
WOODCOCK
CHERWOOD HO. COTTS.
Brashfield House

BICESTER ROAD

THOMPSON
BAKER CL
CASTLE
DANS
GRIFY
HORNE
RAU CT
MONTGOMERY
HANNON DRIVE
Rec. Grds.

PAYNES
GREEN
CUCKOO
BLENCOWE CL
RD
FENWAY
TURNPIKE LANE
Rec. Grd.

SKIMMINGDISH CL
ARNFIELD CL.

cknells arm

BUCKINGHAM ROAD
A4421

Air Training Corps HQ

AIRFIELD

4

4095

SPRUCE
HORNBEAM
JASMINE
CYPRESS
CROFT
PINE CL
HONEYSLE
MAGNO
HOLLY
GREEN ROAD

Bicester Gliding Centre

SKIMMINGDISH LANE
A4421

5

Recreation Ground
CURTIS CL
Bardwell School

Glory Farm Primary School

24

ROCHFORD GS
OVERSTRAND
SUNDER
OXFORD GS
DUXFORD
HENDON PL
HERALD
W. SHACKL CL
LERWICK CFT.
HART PL

Cooper Sch.

6

WELLINGTON
ANSON WY
BRISTOL
HALIFAX
LINCOLN
LANCASTER
TURNBERRY RD
TANGMERE CL
BENSON CL
SCARP RD

ST. ANTHONY'S WLK
Play Cen.

LYNEHAM RD
MASTON RD
MITOR RD
LANE ROAD

7

Recreation Ground
KEBLE
HERTFORD CL
MURDOCK
Launton Business Centre

TELFORD
TELFORD PL

BRIDGE LA.
BICESTER LANE

23

icester North

Industrial Estate

GRANGE MEWS

F
G
H
33
J
K

ongfields Prim. Sch.
GRANVILLE ROAD
WAY
CHARBRIDGE
A4421
CHAR-
Manor Farm
Launton C of E Prim. Sch.
BLENHEIM DR
STATION
Yew Tr Farm
SYCAMORE
59
460
61

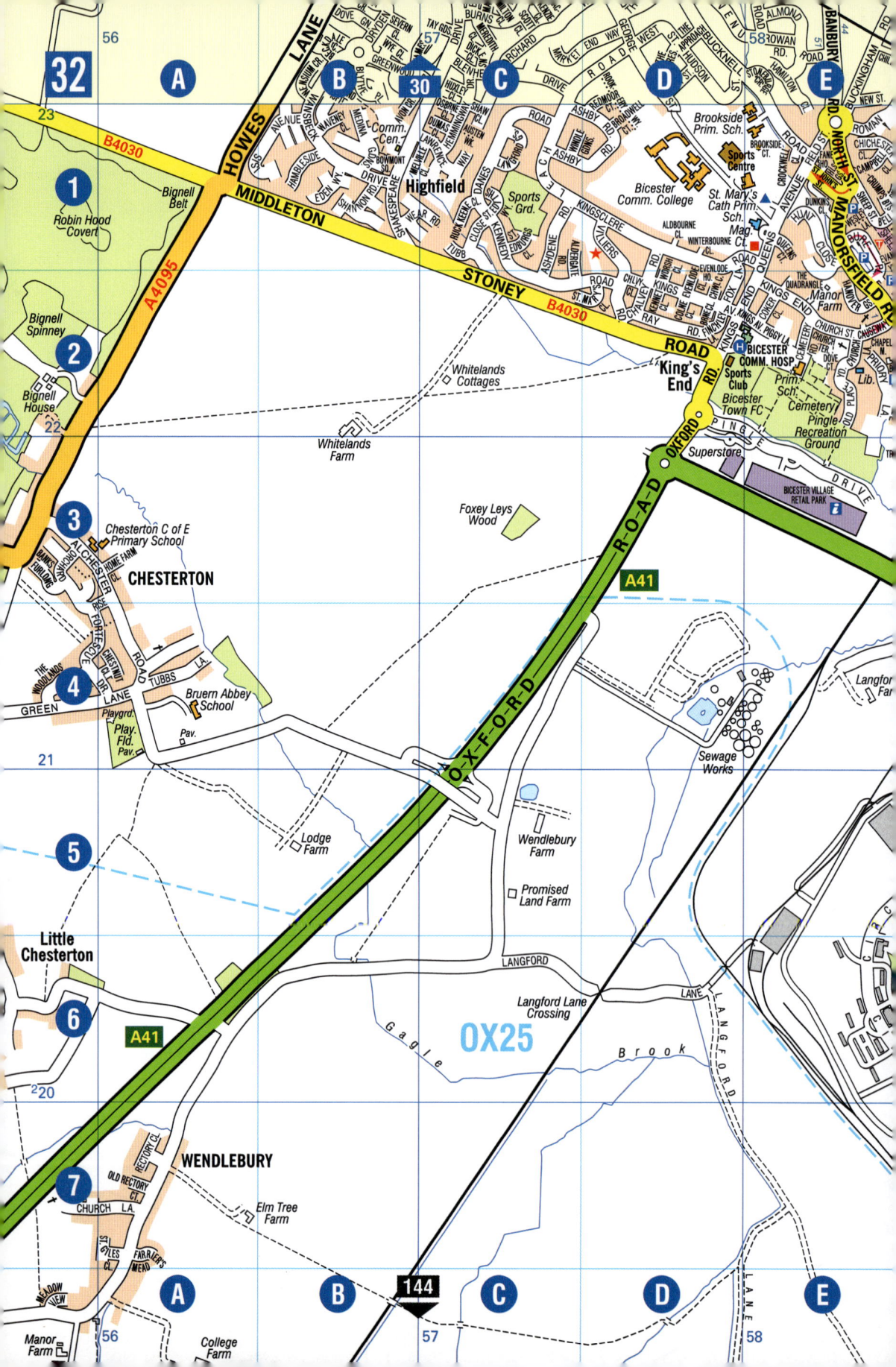

56 | A | B | C | D | E

23

B4030

1

Robin Hood Covert

Bignell Belt

HOWES LANE

MIDDLETON

A4095

DOVE CL · DRYDEN CL · SEVERN · TAY GDS · DRIVE · BURNS · GREENWOOD · BLYTH · BLUM CL · WAVENEY · MEDINA · HAMBLESIDE · WANSBECK · WYE CL · BLENHEIM · SHAW CL · RICHARD · GEORGE · WEST · ST. JOHN · APPROACH · BUCKNELL RD. · HAMILTON · HUDSON ST. · ROWAN RD.

30

Highfield

Comm. Cen.

BOWMONT

DUMAS · LAWRENCE WAY · PENNINGTON WK. · AUSTEN WK.

SHAKESPEARE · NEVILLE · MELVILLE · MERE RD. · EDEN WY. · DANES · BUCK KEENE CL · KINNY LANE · ASHBY · ASHBY · DINGLE LANE · BROWNELL · ASHBY RD.

Sports Grd.

58

BANBURY RD.

NEW ST. · ROMAN · CHICHESTER · CAMPBELL

Brookside Prim. Sch.

CROCKWELL · LANE · Sports Centre · St. Mary's Cath Prim. Sch.

Bicester Comm. College

KINGSCLERE

ALDBOURNE CL · WINTERBOURNE CL · EVENLODE

NORTH ST.

MANORSFIELD RD.

DUNKINS · CLOSE · SHEEP ST. · CROMWELL CL

THE QUADRANGLE · Manor Farm

2

Bignell Spinney

Bignell House

22

STONEY

B4030

ROAD

King's End

Whitelands Cottages

Whitelands Farm

ROAD

CHLVEY · KENNET · FINCHEY · COLNE · KINGS · RAY RD. · ST. MK. · KINGS · KINGS AV. · PIGGY LA. · CHURCH ST. · DOVE · CHAPEL

Bicester COMM. HOSP.

Sports Club · Bicester Town FC

Cemetery · Pingle Recreation Ground

Prim. Sch. · Lib.

PINGLE DRIVE

Superstore

Bicester Village Retail Park

3

Chesterton C of E Primary School

ALCHESTER · HOME FARM · DUNKINS FURLONG · ARCHWAY RD.

CHESTERTON

Foxey Leys Wood

OXFORD

ROAD

A41

4

GREEN · THE WOODLANDS · FORTESCUE DRIVE · CHESTNUT CL · LANE · CHESTNUT · TUBBS · ROAD · TUBBS LA.

Bruern Abbey School

Playgrd. · Play Fld. · Pav. · Pav.

21

Lodge Farm

Wendlebury Farm

Promised Land Farm

Sewage Works

Langford Far

5

Little Chesterton

Gagle

Brook

OX25

Langford Lane Crossing

LANGFORD LANE

LANE

6

A41

20

7

WENDLEBURY

OLD RECTORY CT. · RECTORY CL. · CHURCH LA.

Elm Tree Farm

ST. GILES CL. · FARRIERS MEAD · MEADOW VIEW

Manor Farm

College Farm

56 | A | B | **144** | C | D | E | 57 | 58

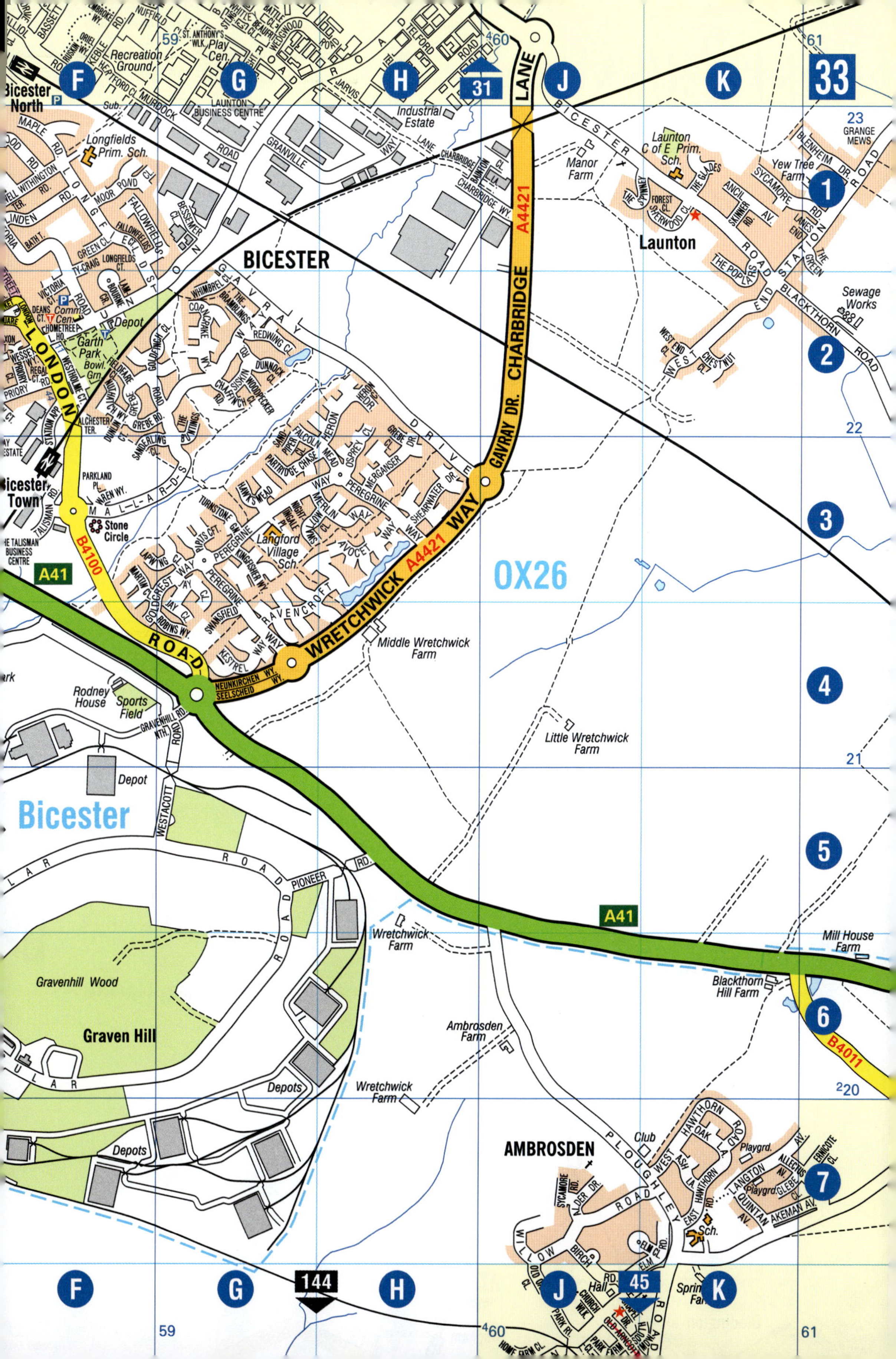

BICESTER

Bicester North

Longfields Prim. Sch.

St. Anthony's Wlk. Play Cen.

Recreation Ground

Launton Business Centre

Industrial Estate

Manor Farm

Launton C of E Prim. Sch.

Launton

Yew Tree Farm

Grange Mews

Sewage Works

Garth Park Bowl. Gm.

Depot

Bicester Town

The Talisman Business Centre

Stone Circle

Langford Village Sch.

Middle Wretchwick Farm

OX26

Little Wretchwick Farm

Rodney House

Sports Field

Depot

Bicester

Gravenhill Wood

Graven Hill

Wretchwick Farm

Wretchwick Farm

Depots

Depots

A41

Mill House Farm

Blackthorn Hill Farm

Ambrosden Farm

Club

AMBROSDEN

Spring Farm

A B 142 C D ROAD E

25

Kingham Hill House 27 Sports Fld.

Boulter's Barn House 29

1

Sarsden Halt

CHURCHILL RD. KINGHAM

HASTINGS HILL ROAD

CHURCHILL

B4450 NORTON BESBURY LANE

Chipping Norton OX7

Conduit Farm

2

SIDINGS RD.

MEADOW PLACE

Hall Langston Memorial

CHURCH RD. CHIPPING

Churchill Farm LANGSTON

The Old Rectory

Brook

24 ◄ BELOW

HACKERS LA.

WILLIAM SMITH CL.

ROAD SARSDEN

Haughton House

Sarsden Glebe

3

Mount Farm

Sars

The Lodge

ROAD

Sarsden Glebe Farm

Sarsden

JUNCTION

4

Bledington Heath

DAYLESFORD RD. THE

Manor Farm

ROAD

Moreton-in-Marsh GL56

WEST

Mount Farm

THE GREEN CHURCHILL ROAD

Kingham Prim. Sch.

5

RIVER

WEST OXFORDSHIRE COTSWOLD

Trinder's Farm

MANOR FM. WEST STREET THE GREEN ST. CHAPEL LA.

24

MANOR END Manor Fm. THRESHERS YARD

THE GRANGE

Kingham

Chipping Norton OX7

Far End

WEST END COZENS LA. CHURCH ST.

College Farm

ORCHARD RD. FOWLER'S RD. CHURCH WY.

▲ ABOVE

6

EVENLODE

Oddington Stables

THE FLATS Play. Fld. Pav.

Hall

COTMOR WY.

STATION ROAD

MEADOW WY. NEW

FIELD RD.

STATION ROAD

7

23

University Farm

STREET

Sewage Works

142

Langston Priory Workshops

STOW RD. B4450

MAIN ST. CHAPEL

Bledington

25

Kingham N

26 STATION ROAD B4450

27 Rynehill Fm.

Banks Farm

A B C D E

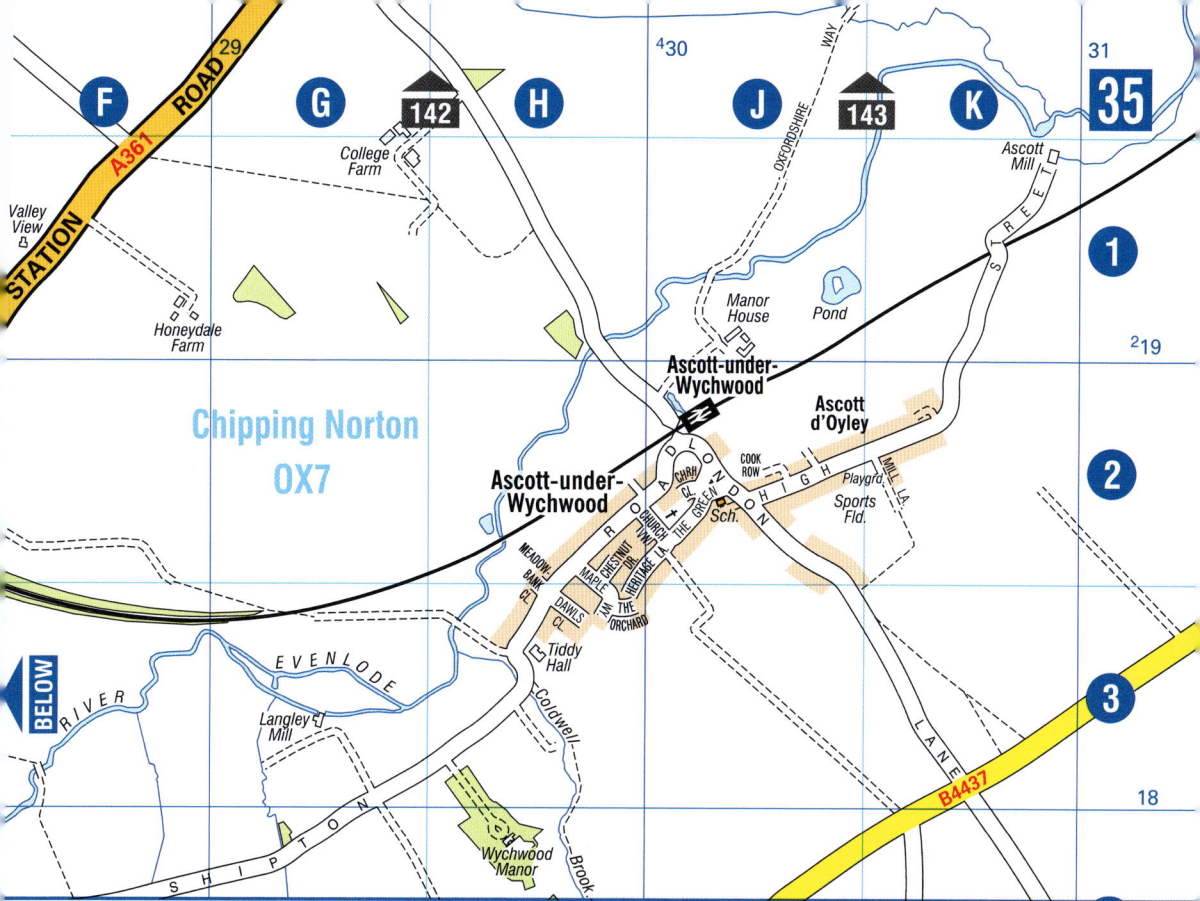

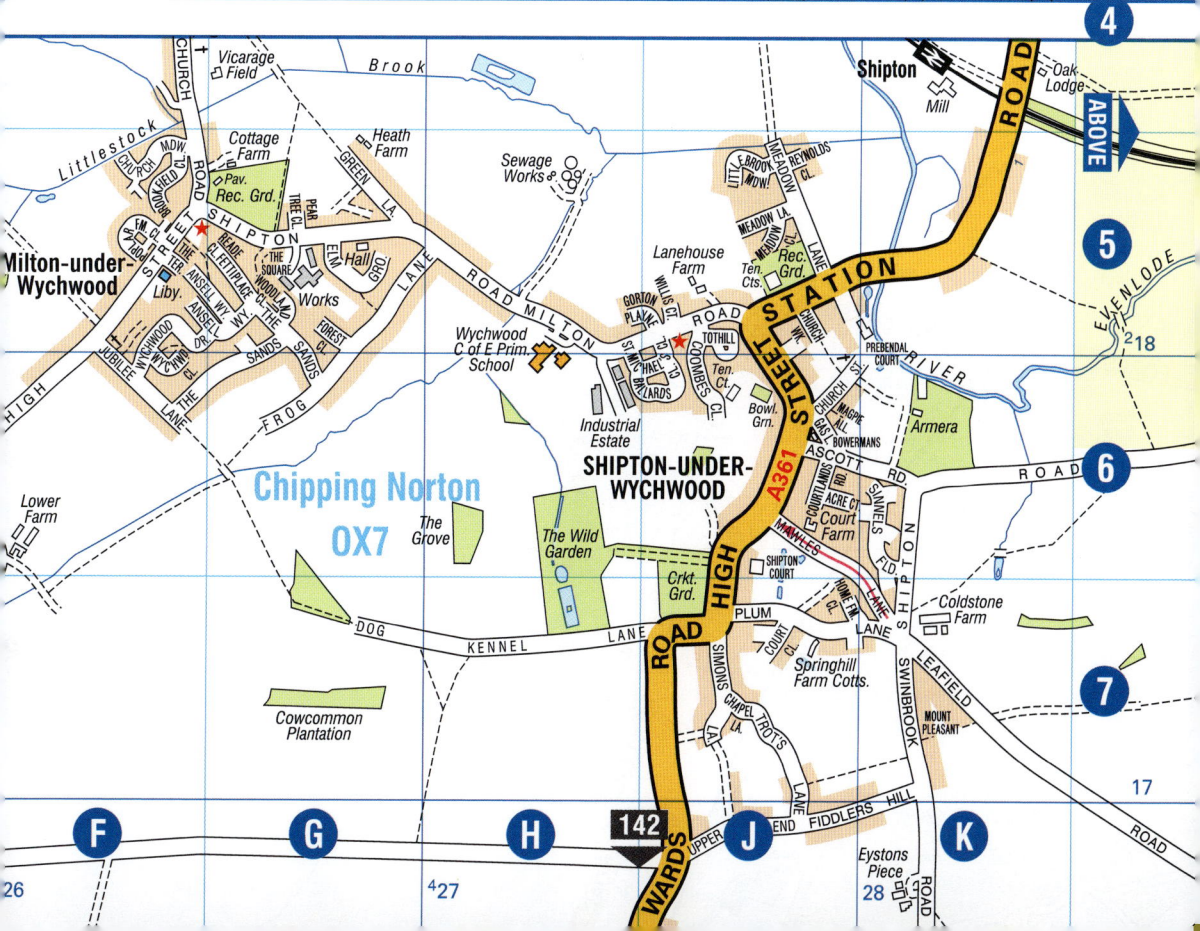

A   **B**   **C**   **D**   **E**

32   33   34

MILL

Up. Court Farm Cotts.

Sycamore Farm

143

CHIPPING

QUARRY

1

Chipping Norton OX7

Blaythorne Cottages

Up. Court Farm

Westend

Lowlands Farm

ORCHARD COTTS.

NORTON

LEIGH CL.

CHURCH

Dulcis Domus

Bowl. Grn.

Manor Farm Cotts.

Langston House

EVERSLEY CL.
RAWLINSON CL.
WEBBS CL.

Ashcroft House

CHADLINGTON

Prim. Sch.

Depot

MANOR CT.

Eastend

Manor Farm

22

CROSS'S

SARSDEN CL.

COLLEGE FARM

Club Hall

Grave Yard

ROADS

Manor Farm

Butts Green

STOCK

Rec. Grd.

2

Blaythorne

Blaythorne Cottages

LANE

Brookend

BULL END

CHURCH

Bull Hill Ho.

HILL

HORSE SHOE LA.

Chadlington Farm

Manor House

CATSHAM LANE

Holybourne House

EAST END LANE

Daisybank Cottages

Greenend

3

GREEN

Lower Court Farm

Sewage Farm

Little Wood

Greenhill Copse

21

Pond

RIVER EVENLODE

4

SPELSBURY RD.

B4026

WATER

220

Spelsbury Villas

Cemy.

EVENLODE CL.

Yth. Cen.

NINE ACRES

B4022

B4022

WAY

Hundley Cottage

HUNDLEY

Ambleside Farm

ROAD

BANBURY HILL

JEFFERSONS PIECE

THE GREEN

NINE ACRES CL.

ELM CRES.

ILEY

5

Walcot Farm

Walcot

POUND HL.

LA.

THE

Playing Fld.

HOST

THE GREEN KIRUP

CHARTNEL

QUARRY

LANE

Pav. Crkt. Grd.

Dyer's Hill Br.

COTSWOLD CL.

DEES

JEFF'S TER.

SPENDLOVE CENTRE

ENSTONE

WYCHWOOD RD.

WYCHWOOD

TICKNELL PIECE RD.

CLUB

Bowls Club

B4437

ROAD

DYER'S HL.

Hall

Mus.

MARKET

BROWNS LA.

THE PLAYING CLOSE

POOLE

CRAWBOROUGH RD.

Sch.

CHARLBURY

FOREST

B4437

Factory

Charlbury

CHURCH LA.

CHURCH

CHURCH S.

SHEEP

LISS TD.

HIXET

HANOVER CT.

SANDFORD CL.

Sandford Mount

Chipping Norton OX7

Rushy Bank

PARK

NELSON

TANNERS CT.

MARLOW CT.

WOODY LA.

LEES HGTS.

Woody La. House

Gordon House

6

19

Bottom Brake

Lee Place

LEE CL.

WOODSTOCK

LEES HGTS.

HUGHES

LITTLE LEES

CLOSE

The Grange

B4437

ROAD

LIGHT

RIVER EVENLODE

Sewage Works

WELLINGTON COTTAGES

SLADE

STURT

B4022

STURT

Whitston House

7

TOWER

North Lodge

STREET

WOOD

FAWLER

Playground

WOODSTOCK

Works

Bevis Farm

BEECH AVENUE

CORNBURY

A

PARK

(DEER PARK)

Lower Park

B

143

B4022

36

C

37

D

E

435

RIVER CHERWELL

OX20

Oxford Canal

WEST CHERWELL OXFORDSHIRE

Wood House

Morar

1

21

FOX

Wood Farm

BANBURY ROAD A4260

TACKLEY HEATH

Kidlington

OX5

Old Man Leys

FOT HILL

HILL BALL

THE BRIDGE

HILL ROAD

ROAD

BALLIOL FARM

Balliol Farm

NETHERCOTE

Nethercott

2

TACKLEY

LWR

Hall

MEDCROFT

ST JOHNS

ST JOHNS RD

Sch.

ST NICHOLAS RD

TW WILLMS

RD

ST JOHNS

BALLIOL CL

Tackley

Play. Fld.

THE GRN.

The Old Barn

Little Manor

HARBOURM'E

CHAUNDY

KILN RD

KILN LANE

ROAD

The Rectory

Court Farm

3

CHURCH

HILL

Hill Court

Park Farm

TACKLEY PARK

²20

4

GLYMPTON ROAD

ROUSHAM ROAD

LANE NEW TEW

21

Blue Barn

River Dorn

5

Hobbard's Hill Copse

River Glyme

Cuckoo Patch

Woodstock

OX20

Balliol Farm

Holly Bank

Lower Dornford Farm

River Dorn

6

Hobbard's Hill

Holly Bank Cottages

Dornford Grove

B4027

Swan's Nest

Slape Bridge

WORCESTER HILL

River Glyme

BURDITCH BANK

CASTLE ROAD

Sports Grd.

Burditch Hall

Burditch House

MARRIOTT

MILFORD PL

MILFORD VW.

Milford Br. Cottage

Milford Bridge

²20

Manor Farm

MANOR CT.

CASTLE RD.

CHURCH CHAPEL HILL

Wootton Place

St. Sch. MILFORD

LANE

7

LAMB'S

WALNUT CL

WOOTTON

Home Farm

River Dorn

Slape Copse

UNION SQ.

HORSESHOE

MILL LA.

The Mill House

END

Williams Hill

Bridge House

River Glyme

Hordley Farm

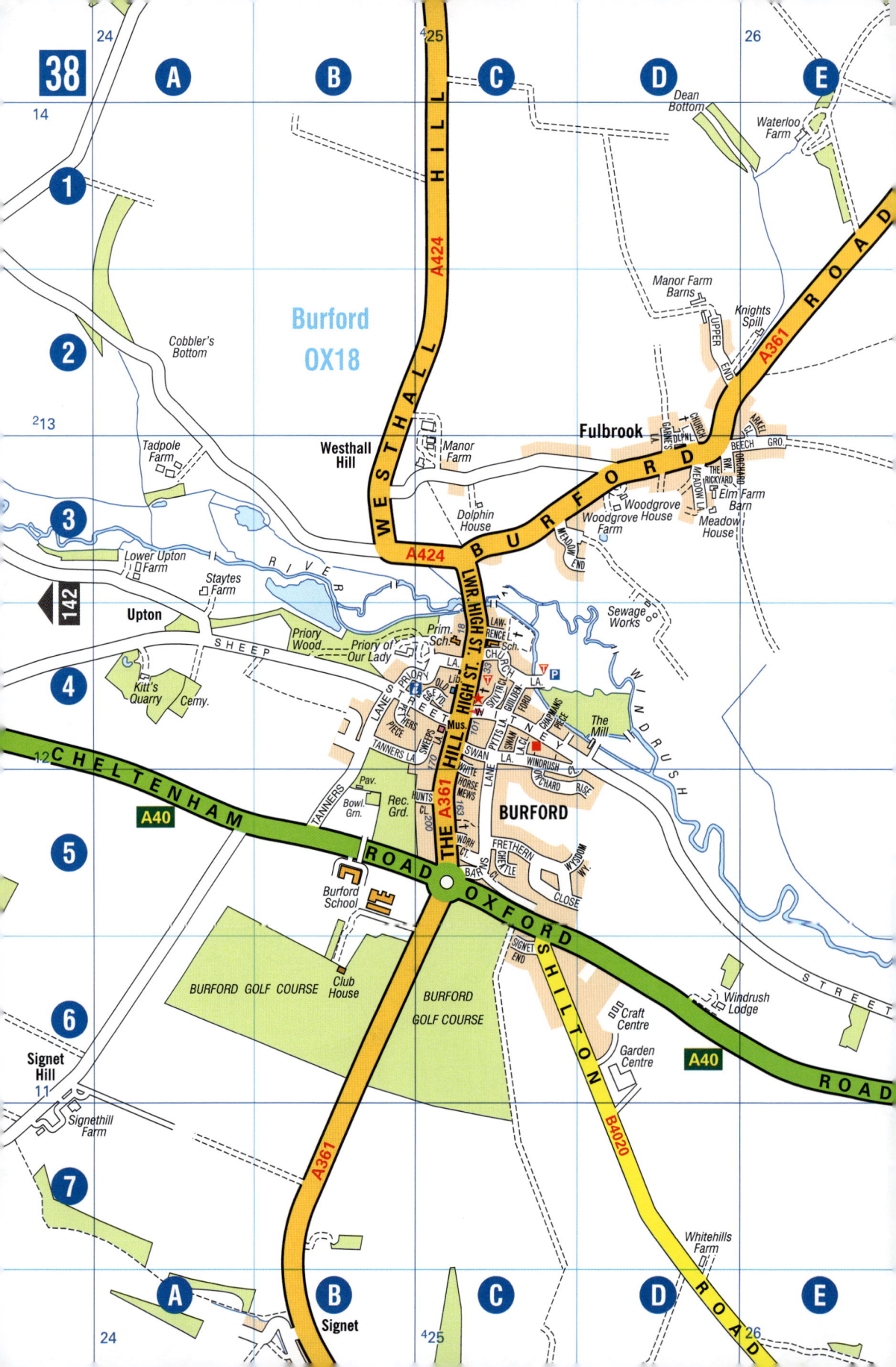

38

24 A 25 B C 26 D E

14

1

Burford
OX18

Cobbler's
Bottom

2

13

Tadpole
Farm

Manor Farm
Barns

Knights
Spill

Dean
Bottom

Waterloo
Farm

**Westhall
Hill**

Manor
Farm

Fulbrook

CHURCH

THE
RICKYARD

BEECH

ORCHARD

ANKEL

GRO.

3

River

Lower Upton
Farm

Staytes
Farm

Dolphin
House

Woodgrove
House
Farm

Woodgrove
Farm

Elm Farm
Barn

Meadow
House

142

Upton

SHEEP

Priory
Wood

Priory of
Our Lady

Prim.
Sch.

Sewage
Works

4

Kitt's
Quarry

Cemy.

Prim.
Sch.

LAW-
RENCE
LA.

Sch.

Lib.

Mus.

The
Mill

WINDRUSH

5

12

CHELTENHAM

A40

ROAD

OXFORD

BURFORD

FRETHERN
CHTTLE

CLOSE

WINDRUSH
CL.

STREET

6

**Signet
Hill**

Burford
School

Burford
Golf Course

Club
House

**BURFORD
GOLF COURSE**

SIGNET
END

SHILTON

Craft
Centre

Garden
Centre

Windrush
Lodge

A40

ROAD

11

Signethill
Farm

7

B4020

Whitehills
Farm

24 A B 25 C 26 D E

Signet

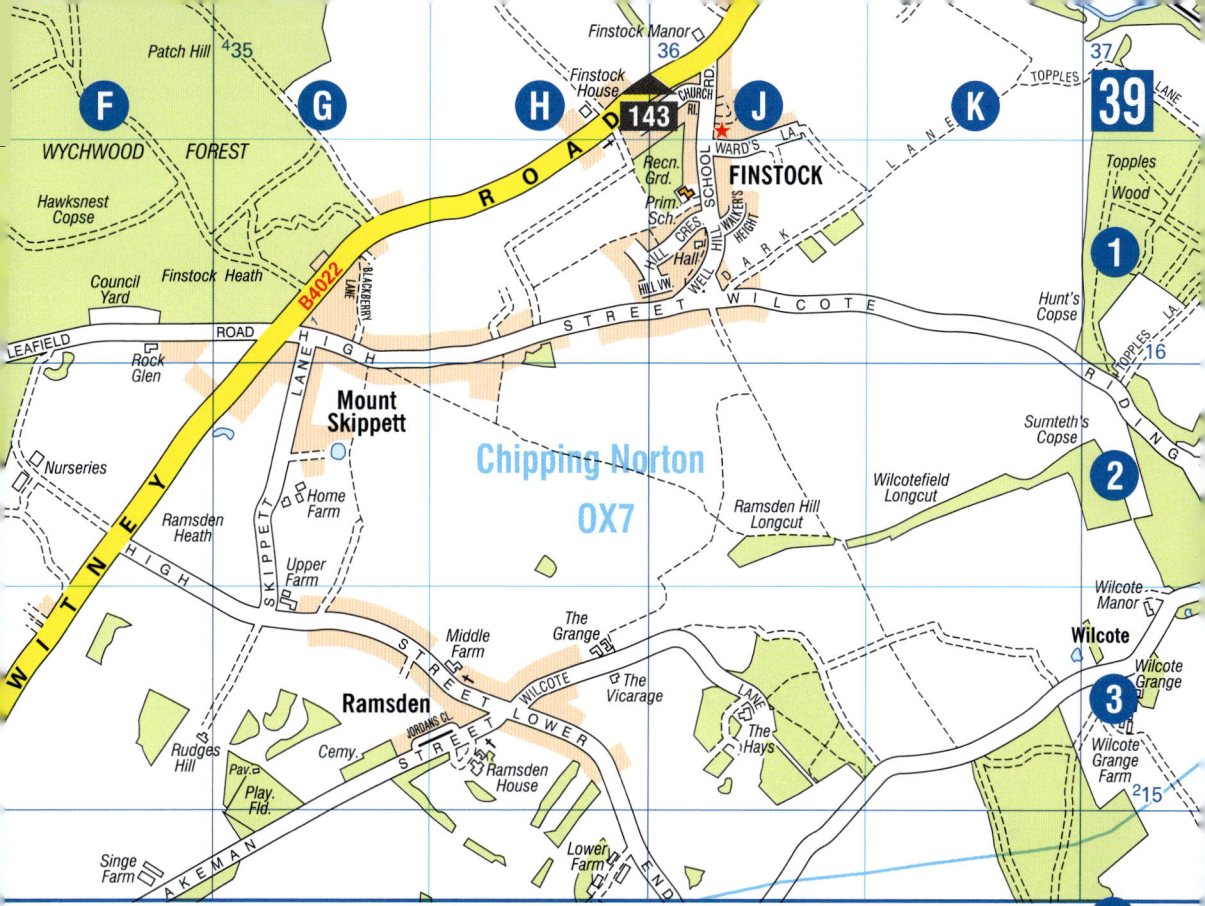
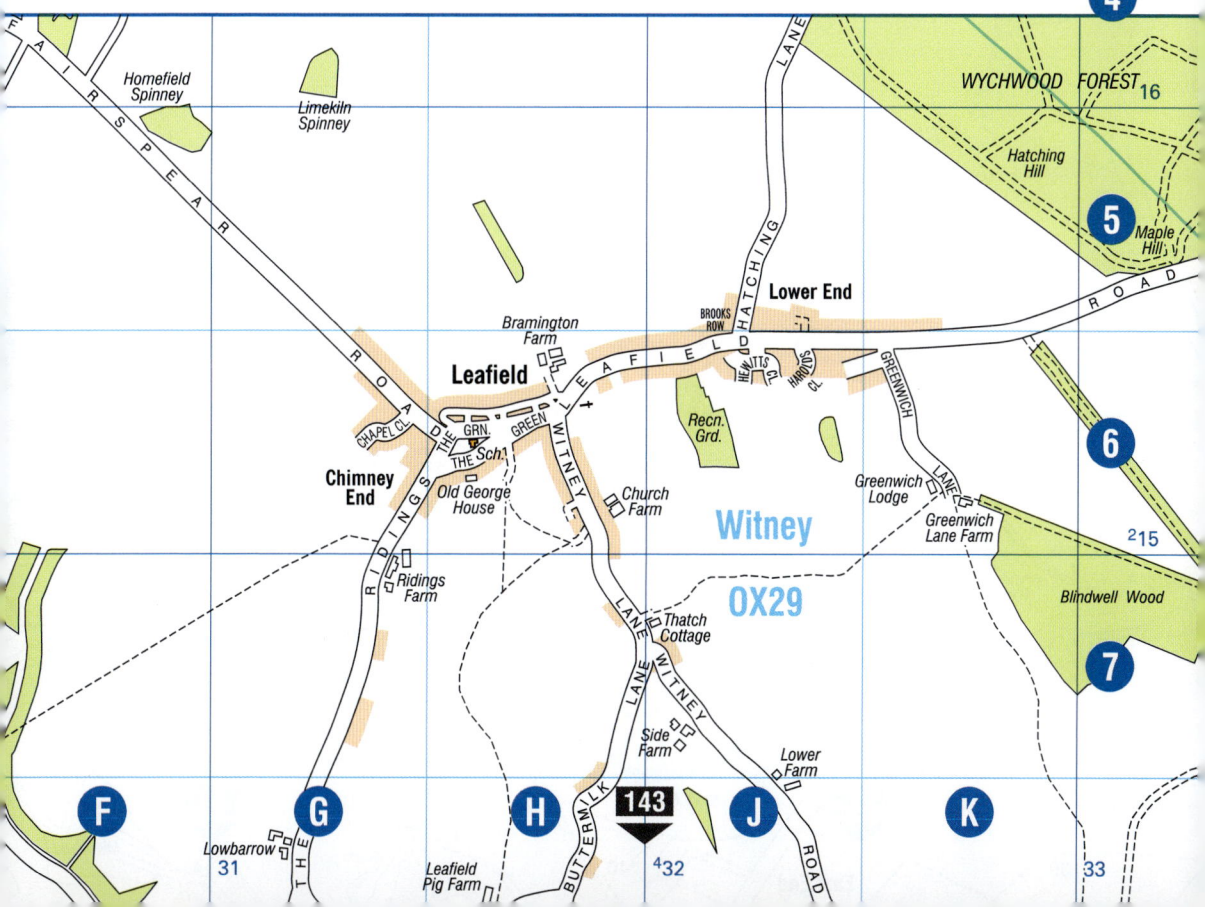

A   B   C   D   E

39   440   Woodstock   41   OX20

1

WOOTTON WOOD

Callow Farm

Limbeck Farm

RIDINGS

18

Littleworth Farm

2

FARLEY LA.
FARLEY LA.   BISHOPS MDW.
WOOTTON
END
FARLEY CL.

North Farm

Tennis Cts.

Highfield Farm

STONESFIELD

Liby. Sports & Social Club

WOODSTOCK

AKEMAN

ROAD

LANE

STREET

Lower Farm

THE TOWER
COCKSHOOT
CL.

POND
LONGORE

THE

PIMBO
RD.

WINLEWELL
CL.
LONGORE
CL.
FENELL
GREENFELD RD.
BOSY CL.

PENDLE CT.
WINLEWELL CL.
JAMES CL.

Charity Farm

Akeman St. Farm

Witney

3

FAWLER

PEAKS
BOOT ST.
FRIEND'S
CL.
Prim. Sch.
HIGH
ST.
BARR'S
STREET

LAUGHTON
WELL RD.

LAUGHTON
CL.

WOODSTOCK

PROSP.

THE CROSS

Spratt's Farm House

Stonesfield Manor

143

17

WALSTERS
WOODLAND RISE
CHURCH ST.
BROOK LA.

Cemy.

Stockey Plantation

Stockey Bottom

ROAD STONESFIELD

Bagg's Bottom

NOTOAKS WOOD

Long Firs

Square Firs

4

THE EVENLODE

5

16

Foxhole Barn

KNOTT OAKS
SQUARE FIRS

CHATTERPIE
ROAD

AKEMAN

ROAD

Chatterpie House

Foxhole Farm

Square Firs

KNOTT OAKS

Lower Riding Farm

West Close Farm

ORCHARD CL.
COMBE GREEN

Play. Fld.

PARK

Combe House

6

Whitehill Bridge

Lower Westfield Farm

Sewage Works

Combe

WEST
END
COMBE GATE
HILL
MIDH'T
CHURCH WK.

Prim. Sch.

RIVER

Higher Westfield Farm

ROBIN

Play. Fld.

Gate Burton

Peagle Wood

7

Whitehill House

Whitehill Wood

North Leigh Roman Villa

Grintley Hill

Cliff Cottage

Combe Cliff

215

Grintleyhill Bridge

EVENLODE

A   52   B   Sturt Copse   C   D   53   E

Upper Riding Farm

East End

39   440   41

Mill Wood

OX5

Wooton Road Cottages

A44

MANOR ROAD

F G H J K

46 18

1

Sewage Works

Glyme Lane

Woodstock OX20

2

The Retreat

VANBRUGH CL.

Pav.

VERMONT DR.

Icehouse Clump

ROSAMUND DR. FARM END

MAX. MY. CL. EVERSON CL.

HILL RISE

Old Woodstock

Cemy.

Depot

Factory

Hensington

The Marlborough School

Swim. Pool

Fishery Cottage

Manor Farm

River

BROOK

HILL GREEN

THE BANBURY ROAD

Column of Victory

Seven Arches

THE CAUSEWAY

OXFORD ROAD

Manor River

UNION ST.

BEAR CL. FLATS

CLOSE

CHURCHILL CL.

Cemy.

KERWOOD CL.

BOUNDARY ROAD

SHIPTON ROAD

HENSINGTON CL.

VERINA CT.

FLEMINGS CL.

DODDS CL.

GRASS

2

17

GREAT PARK

QUEEN POOL

Triumphal Arch

Queen Elizabeth's Island

China Corner

NEW ST.

HIGH ST.

MKTP. MKT.

PARK ST.

RECTORY LA.

COCKPIT

DOWLEY HO.

Hensington Gate

Com. Cen.

Youth Cen.

Old Woodstock Town FC

Pav.

Bowl. Grn.

Ten. Cts.

CADOGAN PK.

RECREATION RD.

GLOVERS CL.

PARSONAGE

PRINCES

BRIAR THICKET

MEADOW

PLANE TREE

RYE GRASS

BELLSWAY

CAMP.

YEW TREE

HEDGE END

Playing Field

RECREATION ROAD

143

WOODSTOCK

BLENHEIM PARK

CHURCHILL GA.

A44

PRINCES

THE COVERT

THE PRIORY

Pest Houses

WEST OXFORDSHIRE

CHERWELL

ROAD

3

4

Blenheim Palace

LOWER PARK

Miniature Railway

Nursery

Maze

The Kitchen Garden

THE LAKE

The Cowyards

Caravan Club Park

Eagle Lodge

Campsfield Wood

ROAD

UP. CAMPSFIELD RD.

A4095

16

5

BLADON RD.

WOODSTOCK RD.

A44

BRIDGE

RIVER GLYME

Bladon Bridge

Playground

Laurel Bank

Springlock Lodge

Bladon Lodge

THE HOMESTEAD

A4095 ROAD

Home Farm

Bladon Pits

The Beeches

ORCHARD FIELD LA.

Rowel Brook

6

15

Springlock Gate

The Lince

EVENLODE

Witney OX29

Lince Lodge

Lince Bridge

The Lince

ST. GROVE

PARK

MANOR RD.

HEATH

CHURCH ST.

LAMB

War Meml.

Sch.

Bladon

Rectory Barn

Withy Clump

Bladon Heath

LANE

7

MAIN

A4095

ROAD PARK

Thatch Cottage

F G H J K

LODGE

BANK HANBOROUGH BUS. PARK

LOWER RD.

CASSINGTON RD.

Hanborough Bri.

44 45 46

49 143 Blakeney 450 PORTWAY C 51 Werghill D 144 E STREE
Copse The Bushes

A B ROAD C D E

CHERWELL
WEST OXFORDSHIRE

AKEMAN

1

Pav. Polo Ground

220

KEMAN CL

Home Farm

Little Cockshot Copse

Washford Pits

FOLK TOWN GRN

THE CHEST. NUTS

Timberyard House

Cockshot Copse

RIVER CHERWELL

Oxford Canal

PARK CL

Works

Pound Cl.

HATCH END

Kirtlington Cof E Primary School

LA NE'S

2

KIRTLINGTON

LA

WY.

HCH

SOUTH WD

RD. HEYFORD

Hall

CHURCH CL

OXFORD CL

CHURCH LA

M I L L

3

Vicarage Farm

Corner Farm

Football Ground

Club House

KIRTLINGTON GOLF COURSE

LANE OXFORD

BLETCHINGDON

GOSSWAY FLDS.

19 KIRTLINGTON GOLF COURSE

Reservoir

Crutchmoor Plantation

Kidlington OX5

Cordle Bushes

4

A4095

Gossway Copse

ROAD SPRINGWELL

L I N C E

Sewage Works

New Barn Farm

Moat Spinney

Ash Wood

5

Dogkennels Spinney

Bletchingdon Park

Springwell Copse

CORNER

18

Ledger's Spinney

TOLLBROOK ROAD

Walker's Copse

B4027

STATION

SANDS CL.

HILL

6

Greenhill Farm

VALLEY

RD. NEW

CAUSE WAY

WESTON

Bletchingdon C of E Prim. School

Manor House

ANNES ST.

GILES ST.

COGHILL

RD. ISLIP

Sewage Works

Bletchingdon

LENTHAL

OXFORD RD.

RD.

B4027

7

Sands Barn

Pav.

Playing Field

17

Village Farm

Diamond Farm

49 143 Knapp's Acre 450 C 51 144 E

A B C D E

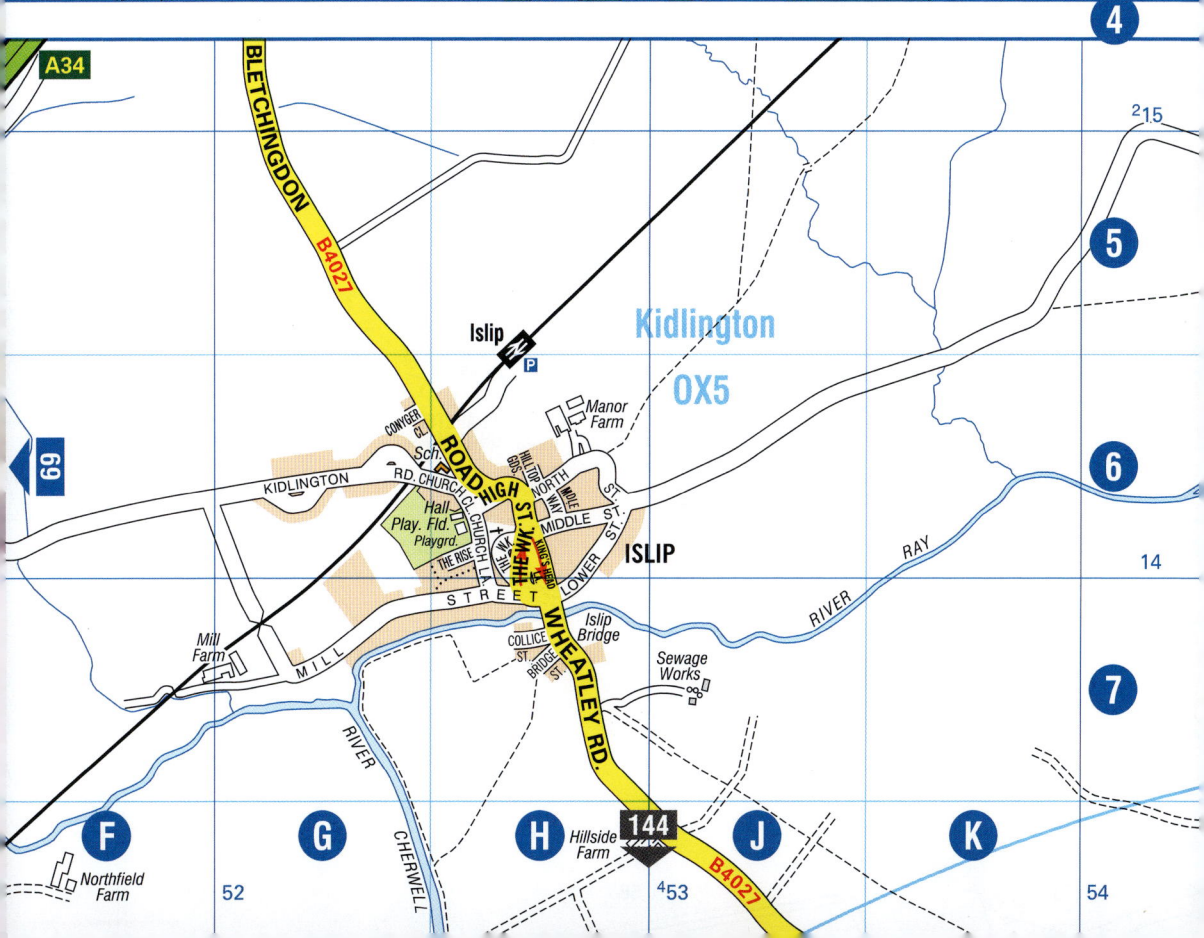

57
⁴58
59

1

Astley
Bridge
Cottage

²18

West End
Farm

MANOR
FARM CL
CHURCH
THE
BUTTS
CHURCH CL
THE
ORCHARD
WEST
END
CROFT
CL

Bicester
OX25

2

M40

Pav.
Rec. Grd.

OTMOOR VW.
GULLEY VW.
FORK

MERTON

Merton
Stud

RAY

Kidlington
OX5

3

RIVER

17

Street Hill

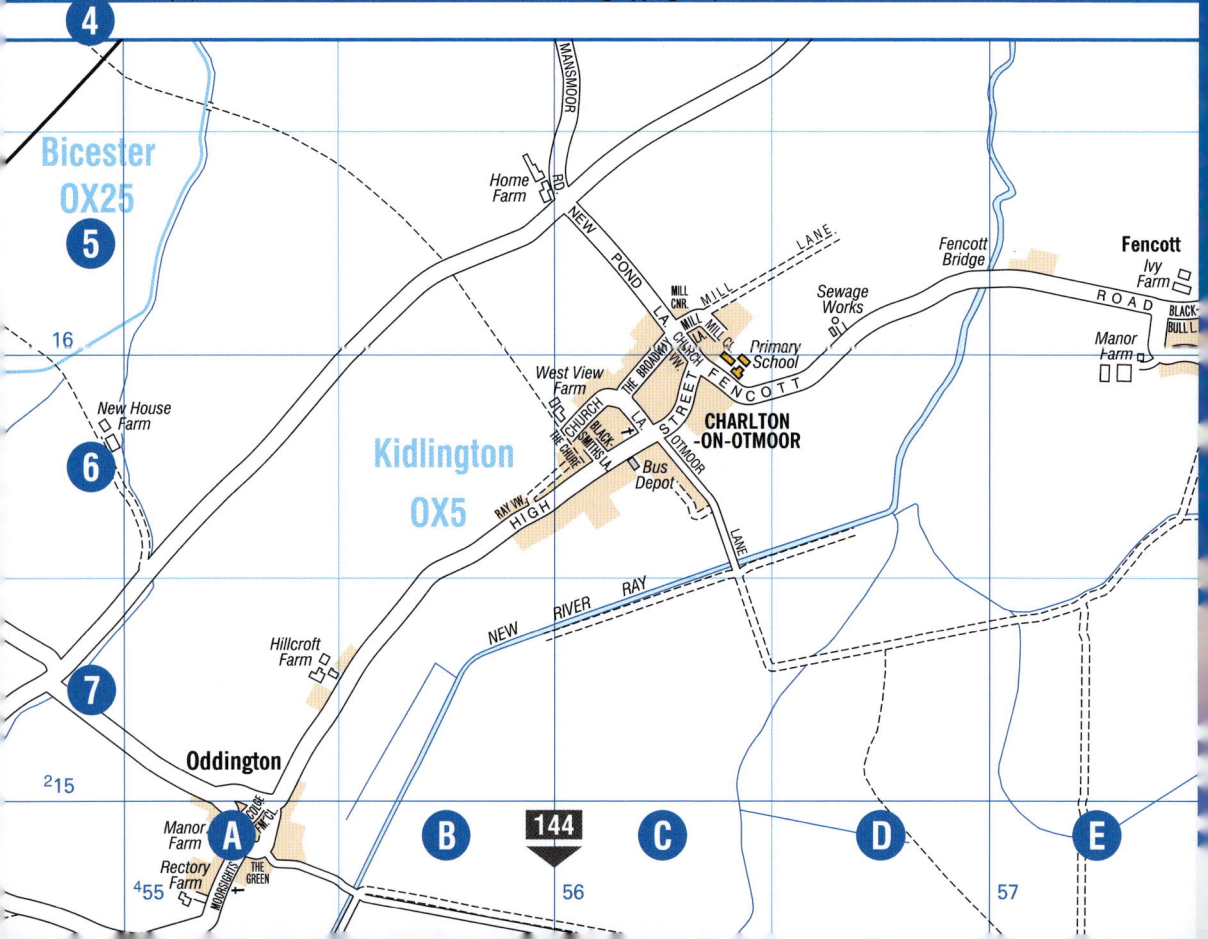

4

MANSMOOR RD

Bicester
OX25

5

Home
Farm

NEW POND LA.

LANE

Fencott
Bridge

Fencott

Ivy
Farm

16

MILL
CNR.
MILL LA.
MILL LA.
MILL

Sewage
Works

ROAD

BLACK-
BULL L.

New House
Farm

West View
Farm

THE BROADWAY
CHURCH VW.
CHURCH LA.
BLACK
THE SHRUBS

Primary
School

FENCOTT

Manor
Farm

Kidlington
OX5

6

CHARLTON
-ON-OTMOOR

RAY VW.
HIGH

ST.
OTMOOR
LA.
STREET

Bus
Depot

LANE

7

Hillcroft
Farm

NEW
RIVER RAY

Oddington

²15

Manor
Farm

MONKSHOLS
LODGE
THE CL
THE GREEN

Rectory
Farm

⁴55

56

57

Blackthorn

Bicester

OX25

AMBROSDEN

Lower Arncott

Upper Arncott

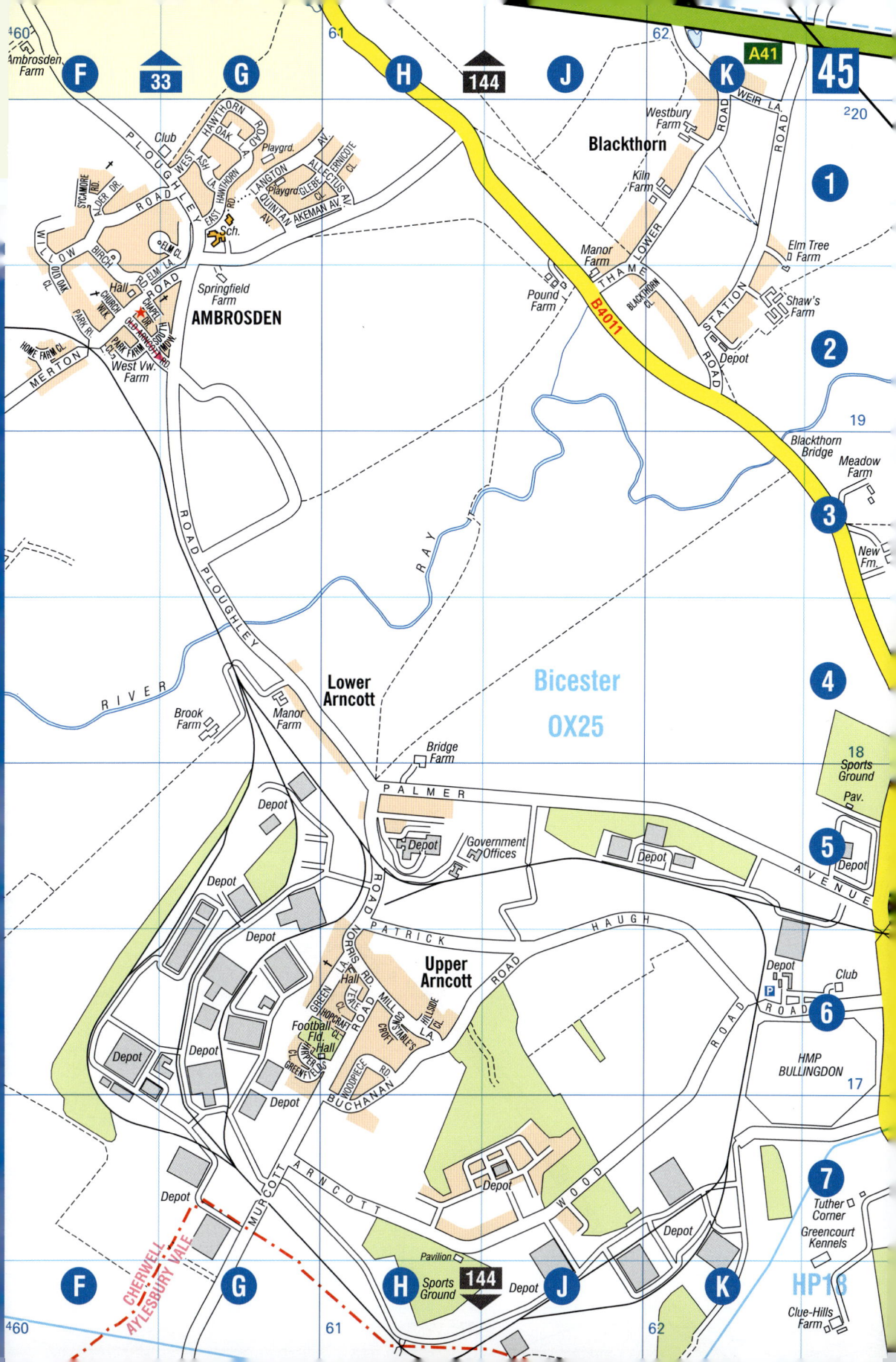

Ambrosden Farm

Westbury Farm

Kiln Farm

Elm Tree Farm

Shaw's Farm

Manor Farm

Pound Farm

Depot

Blackthorn Bridge

Meadow Farm

New Fm.

Club

Playgrd.

Hall

Springfield Farm

Home Farm Cl.

West Vw. Farm

Church

Sch.

Elm La.

Brook Farm

Manor Farm

Bridge Farm

Depot

Government Offices

Sports Ground

Pav.

Depot

Depot

Depot

Depot

Depot

Depot

Hall

Football Fld.

Hall

Club

Depot

HMP BULLINGDON

Depot

Depot

Depot

Depot

Tuther Corner

Greencourt Kennels

Clue-Hills Farm

Pavilion

Sports Ground

Depot

HP18

CHERWELL AYLESBURY VALE

ROADS: PLOUGHLEY ROAD, HAWTHORN ROAD, WEST HAWTHORN RD, EAST HAWTHORN RD, OAK LA, ASH LA, WILLOW CL, BIRCH RD, SYCAMORE RD, ALDER DR, OLD OAK, ELM LA, LANGTON, GLEBE CK, ERNICOTE CL, ALLECTUS AV, AKEMAN AV, QUINTAN AV, PARK RD, PARK CL, MERTON, CHAPEL, OLD ARNCOTT RD, PALMER, PATRICK ROAD, NORRIS RD, GREEN LA, HOPCRAFT CL, MILLS RD, STABLE'S LA, HILLSIDE CL, WOODPIECE RD, GREENFIELDS, CROFT, BUCHANAN, HAUGH, WOOD, ROAD, AVENUE, STATION ROAD, THAME ROAD, BLACKTHORN CL, WEIR LA, ARNCOTT, MURCOTT

RIVER RAY

B4011

460 61 62 460 61 62

220 19 18 17

1 2 3 4 5 6 7

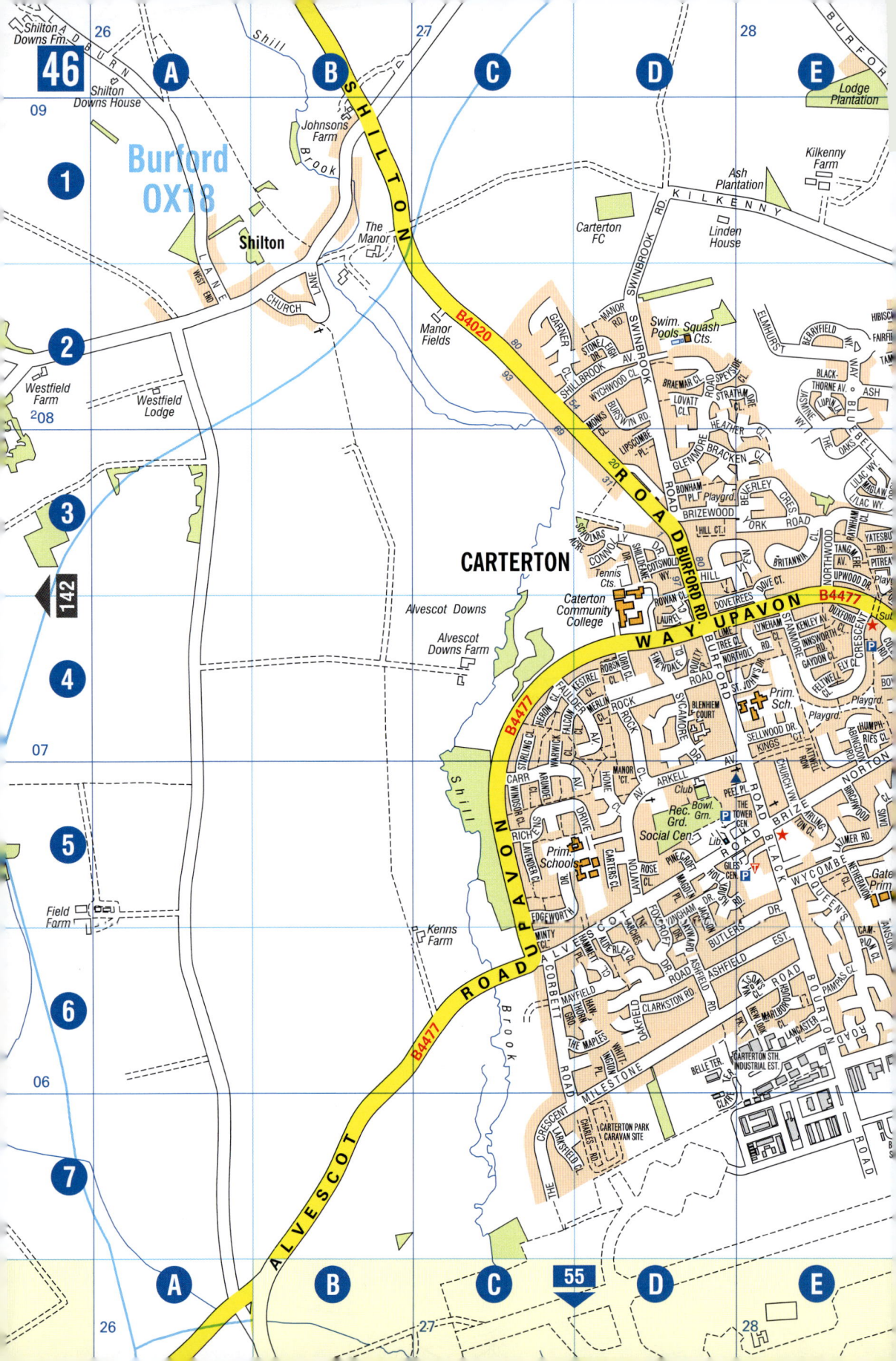

26 | 27 | 28

A **B** **C** **D** **E**

09

Shill

Shilton Downs Fm.

LADBURN

Shilton Downs House

1

Burford OX18

Johnsons Farm

Brook

Shilton

The Manor

SHILTON ROAD

WEST END LANE

CHURCH LANE

2

Westfield Farm

Westfield Lodge

Manor Fields

B4020

08

Carterton FC

Ash Plantation

Kilkenny Farm

KILKENNY RD.

Linden House

SWINBROOK RD.

MANOR RD.

Swim. Pools   Squash Cts.

ELMHURST

BEARYFIELD

HIBISCU

FAIRFIEL

TAM

BLACK-THORNE AV.

ASH

JASMINE

LUPIN CL.

BLUEBELL WY.

GARNER

STONELEIGH

SHILLBROOK

WYCHWOOD AV.

MONKS

BURY N RD.

BRAEMAR CL.

ROSSPEYSIDE

STRATHM

LOVATT CL.

HEATHER

THE OAKS CL.

LILAC WY.

LILAC CL.

LIPSCOMBE PL.

GLENMORE

BRACKEN CL.

BEVERLEY CRES.

WINWHALEY

3

BONHAM PL.

BRIZEWOOD

HILL CT.I

ORK   ROAD

BRITANNIA

YATESBU RD.

PITREAV

PLAY

CARTERTON

BURFORD   ROAD

SHILLBROOK RD.

FRIARS

ACRE

CONVOY LY

COTSWOLD

SHELDANE

HILL

DOVE CT.

NORTHWOOD

TANG MERE AV.

UPWOOD DR.

Alvescot Downs

Tennis Cts.

Carterton Community College

ROWAN CL.

LAUREL

DOVETREES

HILL

B4477

142

Alvescot Downs Farm

WAY UPAVON

B4477

DUXFORD

HENLEY AV.

STANMORE CL.

GAYDON CL.

FELTWELL CL.

ELY CL.

CRESCENT

LYNEHAM

INSWORTH RD.

NORTHOLT

ST. JOHN'S CL.

Sut

ROAD

B4477

ROBSON CL.

ALDER

ROCK

FINCH

HAWK

DALE

DUTY

BURFORD ROAD

LIME TREE CL.

LYNEHAM

Prim. Sch.

ABINGDON CL.

HUMPHRIES CL.

Playgrd.

Playgrd.

NORTON

4

KESTREL

HERON CL.

STIRLING CL.

FALCON

MERLIN

AV.

ROCK

SYCAMORE

BLENHEIM COURT

KINGS

SELLWOOD DR.

ST.

CT.

BOW

07

WARWICK

WINDSOR CL.

ARUNDEL

AV.

SNA

HOME

MANOR CT.

ARKELL

Club

ROAD LW

PEEL PL.

BRIZE

BRIGHWOOD

ARLING TON DR.

5

Field Farm

CARR

RICHE

LAVENDER CL.

LAVENDER CL.

DRIVE

Rec. Grd.

Bowl. Grn.

Social Cen.

P

THE TOWER CEN.

Lib

CHURCH LW.

LATIMER RD.

WYCOMBE

Prim. Schools

CARTERS CL.

ROSE CL.

PINE CROFT

GILES CRN.

P

T

BLACK

QUEENS EST.

Kenns Farm

EDGEWORTH

MINTY

WILT

WINGHAM

JACSON DR.

FOXCROFT

MARGIN

WOLSEY RD.

ROAD

Gate Prim.

6

ALVESCOT

MAYFIELD

THORN

CORBETT

HAWK

RILEY CL.

MARD

HAYWARD

ASHFIELD

BUTLERS

ROAD

CAM.

ANSON CL.

06

THE MAPLES

WHIT.

INGHAM PL.

MILESTONE

OAKFIELD

CLARKSTON RD.

ROAD

MARLBORO

LANCASTER

CLARK

BOURTON ROAD

CRESCENT

BELLE TER.

Carterton Sth. Industrial Est.

CHARLES RD.

LARKSTEAD CL.

PAMPAS CL.

THE

B4477

ROAD UPAVON

Brook

Shill

Carterton Park Caravan Site

7

ALVESCOT

26 | 27 | 28

A **B** **C** **D** **E**

55

Burford

LODGE Plantation

Grove
Farm

ROAD

B4477 NORTON

BRIZE

Foxbury
Plantation

Foxbury
Farm

ROCKY
BANKS

LANE ROAD

BURFORD

MINSTER RD.

MANOR RD.

Grange
Farm

ELM
GROVE

WITNEY

ABINGDON

Astrop
Farm

Wilbro
Farm

2

208

ROAD

LANE

The
Rookery

Manor
Farm

3

Prim.
Sch.

WOODRUSH GDS.

Carterton

OX18

The Sports
Pavilion

Carterton
Leisure
Centre

B4477

ROAD

CARTERTON

Graveyard

BRIZE
NORTON

Prim.Sch.

MOAT CL.

SQUARES
CL.
THE
FOSSEWAY

DALESIDE

143

4

Rec.
Grd.

Pav.
Hall

Ten.
Cts. SOUTH

MERE

CHICHESTER PL.

CHESTNUT CL.

HONEYHAM
CL.

07

Brook

WAY

NGDON
ROAD

WEST OXON
INDUSTRIAL PARK

Highmoor

5

SARUM
CL.

HASTINGS

CRANWELL N.

HALTON RD.

HALTON
RD.

AND-
OVER L.

DRIVE

PLACE

Upper
Haddon
Farm

DEVON

DEVON

Passenger
Terminal

6

Lew
Gorse

RAF
BRIZE NORTON

BRIZE NORTON

AIRFIELD

Fast
are

BELFAST
COURT

VISCOUNT
IND.EST.

06

Ditch

Norton

7

Bampton
OX18

Lower Haddon
Farm

Lower Haddon
Farm Cottages

Lew Heath
House

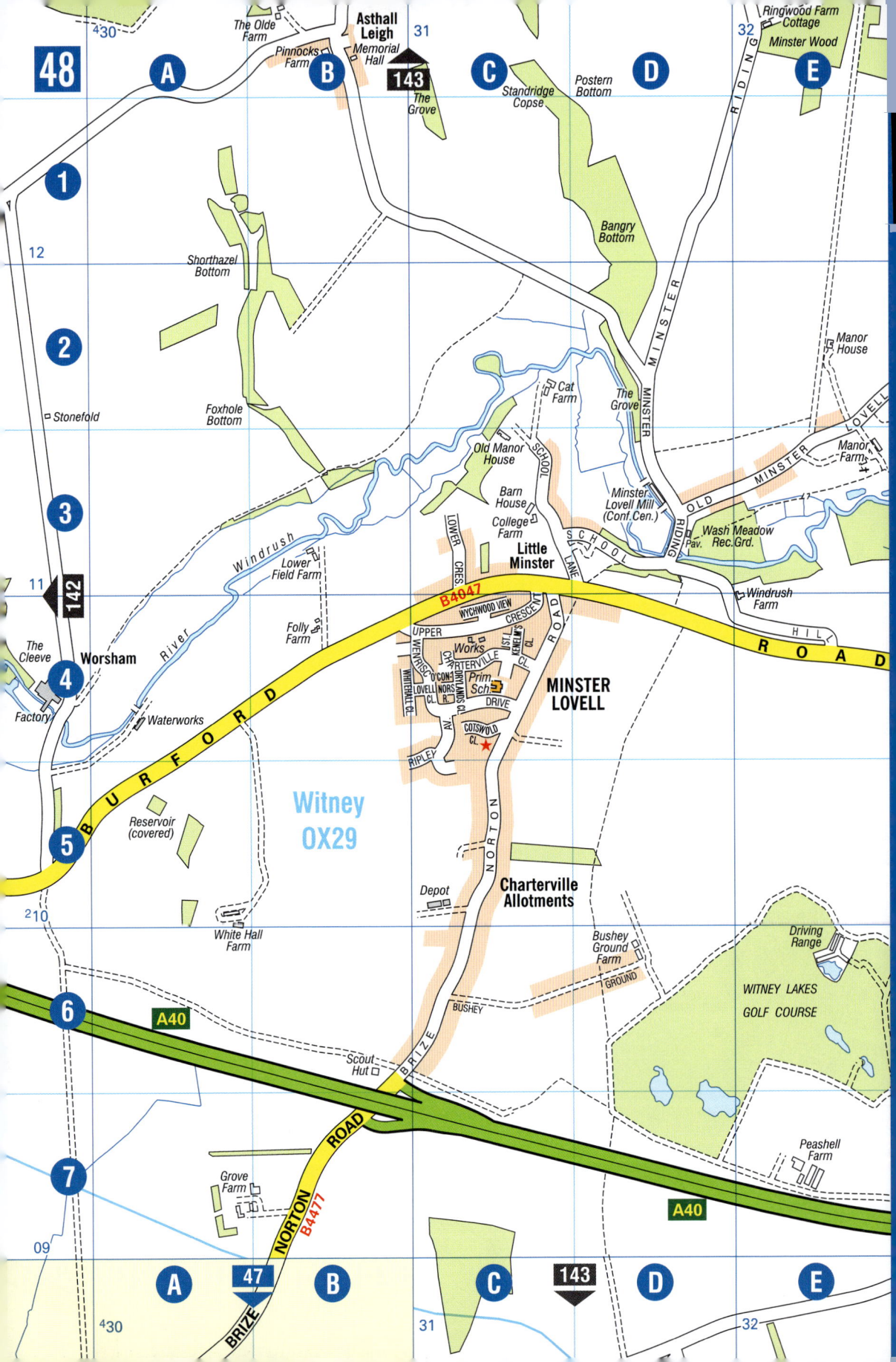

48

Grid references and labels:

A B C D E
1 2 3 4 5 6 7

- The Olde Farm
- Asthall Leigh
- Memorial Hall
- 143
- The Grove
- Pinnocks Farm
- Standridge Copse
- Postern Bottom
- Ringwood Farm Cottage
- Minster Wood
- Shorthazel Bottom
- Bangry Bottom
- Manor House
- Foxhole Bottom
- Stonefold
- Cat Farm
- The Grove
- Old Manor House
- Manor Farm
- Barn House
- College Farm
- Minster Lovell Mill (Conf. Cen.)
- Little Minster
- Wash Meadow Rec. Grd.
- Windrush
- Lower Field Farm
- B4047
- Wychwood View
- Crescent
- Windrush Farm
- Folly Farm
- Upper
- Works
- Charterville
- MINSTER LOVELL
- Prim. Sch.
- The Cleeve
- Worsham
- Whitehall Cl.
- Lovell Cl.
- O Con
- Nors
- Drive
- Factory
- Waterworks
- Cotswold Cl.
- Ripley
- ROAD
- HILL
- BURFORD
- River
- Windrush
- Reservoir (covered)
- Witney OX29
- Norton
- Charterville Allotments
- White Hall Farm
- Depot
- Bushey Ground Farm
- Ground
- Driving Range
- WITNEY LAKES GOLF COURSE
- A40
- Bushey
- Scout Hut
- BRIZE
- Peashell Farm
- Grove Farm
- NORTON
- ROAD
- B4477
- A40
- 47
- 143

142

Coordinate numbers: 430, 12, 11, 210, 09, 31, 32, 30, 31, 32

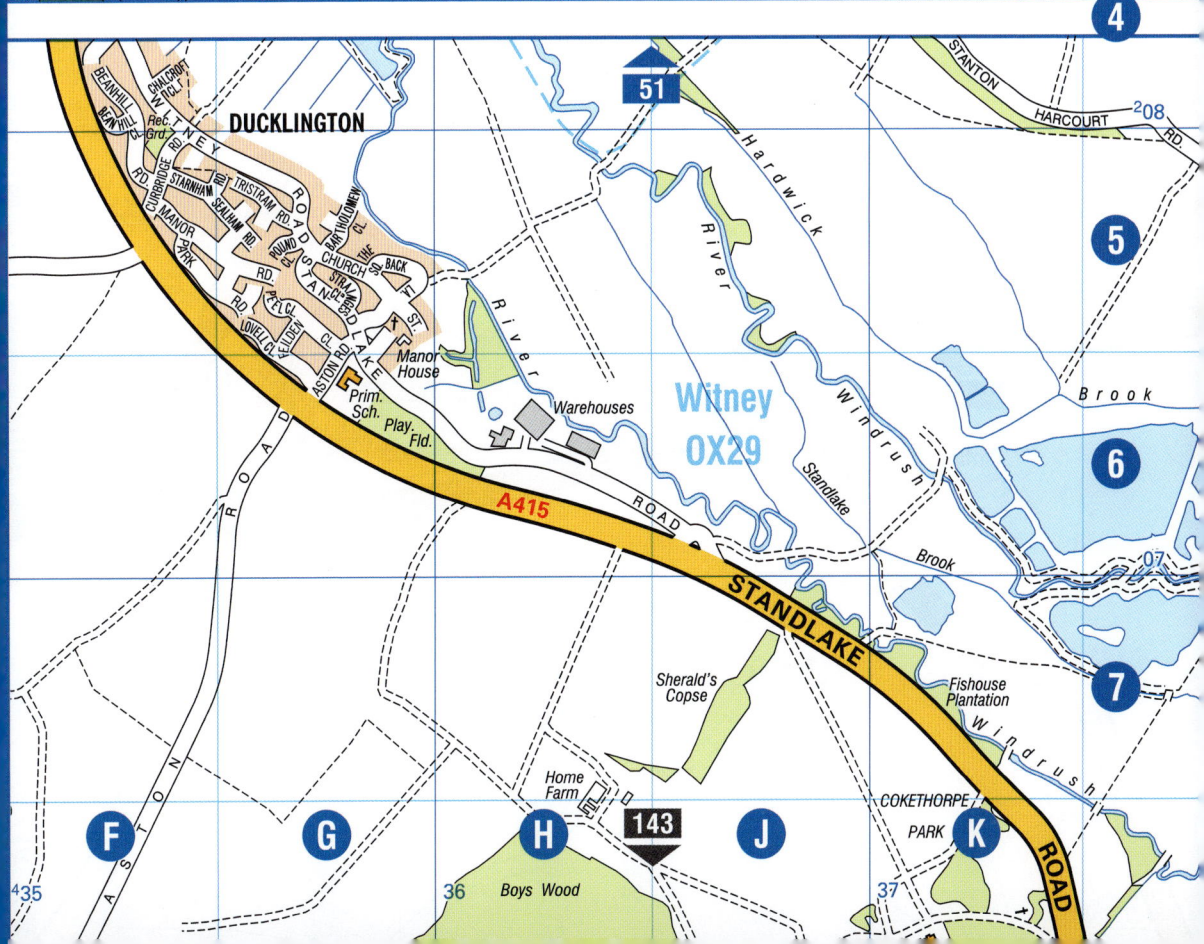

50

33 A B 34 C 49 D 4 35 E

The Workshop

Crawley Mill
INDUSTRIAL ESTATE
Crawley Bri

WITNEY

SCHOOL FIELD GDS

1 Ladywell Pond River Maggots Grove The Horsehoe RIVER Burycroft Farm Southdown Farm MILKING LANE ROAD CRAWLEY QUARRY HOYLE CL ROAD QUARRY

11 Hill Grove Farm WINDRUSH WATER NEWMILL Works NEW MILL Willow Farm WINDRUSH

2 BURFORD B4047 ROAD DRY LANE Depot Bathing Ho. Farm SPRINGFIELD OVAL POPE'S PIECE Witney WOODFORD MILL

WINDRUSH IND. PARK UNXWD RD. PARK RD. Ten. Cts. Club Ho. West Witney Sports Grd. 121 ROAD BURFORD A4095 ROAD MILL Mills

MINSTER IND. PARK NORTHWOOD WINDRUSH Bowl. Grn. Pav. STANWAY CRESN. BRAMSNY CL LANCUT DAVENPORT TOWER CT. 45 PARK ROAD Training Cen. DARK School Witney Comm. Hospital H

3 DOWNS RANGE NWOOD WESTWOOD SOUTH WOOD RD. EAST. GLENMORE BUSINESS CENTRE VALENCE BROADWAY TETBURY DR. CAMPDEN CRESCENT TYNEHAM WINDRUSH VALLEY ROAD APLEY WYCHWOOD CL TOWER 16 UNION ST. BEECH VIZNE RD. WOODLAND CL MOOR AV. WITNEY COMM. HOSPITAL MAG. CT. Liby

2 10 BROOK END RANGE RD. BIRDLIP SAWSHILL EDINGTON TOM SO. School WEX MAN RD. WAY FETTIPLACE Hall Works MORLAND CL PORTLAND DORM. BRK. ASHCOMBE HOLLOWAY RD.

4 DOWNS Witney United Football Club ROAD DEER VALENCE CRESCENT AUSWORTH RISINGHURST STANTON CL FARMING VALE RD. APLEY Cemy. BRMLY HGTS BRAMLEY DUCKLINGTON QUEEN EMMAS ORCHARD DYKE SAXON WEAVERS THE CROFTS TEN. Cts. DX28

DEER ROAD RALEGH CRESCENT WESTCOTE COTSWOLD BOURTON CL ELM CL MARFIELD 50 A4095 WALNUT CL FAIRFIELD FRENCHEN CHURCH TWN RD. School SUB. Sports Arena MARY'S CL. THE SPRINGS THE BOX Ten Cts

5 DOWNS RD. 09 COLWELL PARK RALEGH D'BURY SHERBOURNE CL BARRINGTON CL Play. Fld. Sch. CORNFLD 69 BABBEY BLENHEIM SOUTH LAWN S. LAWN A415 Service Area HENRY BOX CL GORDON Warehouse Bowl. Grn

A40 CURBRIDGE ROAD RD. CURBRIDGE BURWELL DRIVE THORNEY LEYS HOLFORD RD. School Playing Field WILMOT STATION LANE LANE CRANBROOK SWAIN CT.

6 Curbridge Manor Farm Brook THORNEY HARM MDW. MOUNTFIELD RD. BERNHEIM BURWELL COLWELL DRIVE BEESGATE AVENUE ONE

MAIN RD. BAMPTON ROAD Comm. Recn. Grd. THORNEY LEYS IND. PARK MEADOW BURWELL A40 Service Area Sewage Works WITNEY LANE A415 LAKESI DALE BNK MOORS CL

7 A4095 OX29 NEW CLOSE BEANHILL BEAN HILL CHALCROFT TCL Rec. Grd. CURBRIDGE MANOR

08 Duttons Farm

Glebe Farm 33 A B 34 143 C D 4 35 E

51

OX29

36 37 143 38

Osney Hill Farm

F G H J K

Highcroft Farm

Merryfield Farm

1

COGGES WOOD

Middlefield Farm

2

EASTFIELD

AVENUE

FARMERS

WOODSTOCK

Co. Offs.

Co. Offs.

Playing Field

Woodgreen

3

WEST END

BRIDGE ST.

NEWLAND

WEST END IND.EST.

SPINNERS CT.

RIVERSIDE CT.

The Old Warehouse Flats

Woodlands Rd.

Football Grd.

Club Ckt. Grd.

WOODLANDS CLOSE

Wood Green Sch.

Ten. Cts.

Play.Fld.

Northfield Farm

King George's Field

MADLEY

Brook

Pond

10

BRIDGE ST. MILL BUSINESS PARK

WATERSIDE CT.

Newland

GLOUCESTER PL.

The Old Cho.

Mus.

WITAN

Gloucester Ct. Mews

FARRIERS CT.

MEADOW CT.

WITNEY

Langel Common

MILL

IND. EST.

OXFORD

Ind. Est.

STANTON HARCT.

Gibbets Close Farm

HILL

Clementsfield Farm

Wuthering Heights

B4022

A40

4

School

Thtre.

MARKET SQ.

T.H.

WOOLGATE SHOP.CEN.

HIGH ST.

BUTTER CROSS

War Mem.

Co. Offs.

Playgrd.

WADARD'S

CHURCH

MEADOW

Comm. Cen.

Windrush Sports Cen.

Manor Farm

Manor Fm.Mus.

The Blake C of E Prim.Sch.

Cogges

HILL

OXLEASE

STANTON

COGGES

BLAKES

Cogges Hill

High Cogges

High Cogges Farm

5

LANGDALE GA.

EVENLODE CT.

SWINBROOK CT.

OAKFIELD CT.

WINDRUSH

Sch.

WEYS MEAD

FARM MILL

DES ROCHES SQ.

Superstore

Farm Mill

Hardwick

MANOR ROAD

ETON CLOSE

AVENUE

HOLLIS CL.

Old School House

09

The Leys Rec. Grd.

STATION LANE

PARKSIDE

TWO RIVERS IND.EST.

THREE

WESSEX IND.EST.

WITAN PARK

AVENUE

TWO

RIVER

Brook

Hardwick

Spring Hill

Springhill Farm

6

Witney Lake & Country Park

WINDRUSH

HARCOURT

7

08

DUCKLINGTON

F G 49 H J K

TRISTRAM RD.

BARTHOLOMEW

Brook

ROAD

36 37 38

ROAD

WOODSTOCK

A4095

NEWLAND

OXFORD

B4022

215

38

39

40

A B C D E

40

1

Bridewell Farm

Holly Court Farm

Whitening House

Upper Riding Farm

East End

Sturt Copse

THE GREEN

ABEL

2

Riding School

Fish Hill Farm

East End Farm

WILCOTE ROAD

Field Farm

BODDINGTON ROAD

Blackberry Hall

Field Farm

3

End Farm

GREEN

143

CHURCH ROAD

North Leigh Common

Play. Fld.

ROAD

Perrotts Hill Farm

Playing Field

A4095

Saw Mill

CUCKOO

4

NEW YATT BUS. CEN.

NEW YATT LANE

Heath Farm

BRIDEWELL CL.

ROAD

KINGSTON CL.

CHAPEL LA.

PEROT CL.

EVENLODE

NORTH LEIGH

Memorial Hall

Lib.

NURSERY RD.

NORTH LEIGH BUSINESS PARK

WILCOTE WY.

PARK CL.

WOODS CL.

Claypit Clumps

13

CUCKOO LA.

WINDMILL HGTS.

HAZELDENE CL.

Works

LADYWELL CL.

Prim. Sch.

SHAKENOAK

PARKSIDE

ROAD

Pav.

Crkt. Grd.

5

WINDMILL CL.

Play. Grd.

North Gorse

North Leigh FC

Fox Covert

Oval Clump

COMMON CL.

WINDMILL

Blindwell Copse

6

COMMON ROAD

LEIGH

Common Farm

Blindwell Farm

The Strip

The Strip

West Grove

Laurel Clump

EYNSHAM HALL PARK

Eynsham Court

Eynsham Hall

Scott's House

The Lake

DRIVE

The Dells

7

A4095

Osney Hill Farm

Cherrytree Bottom

Monument Clump

Green Wood

Rookery Clump

The Dells

A B C D E

COGGES WOOD

Fletcher's Clump

Hanging Clump

Lodgehill Clump

Little Green Farm

BACK

38 39 40

12

14

Grintleyhill Bridge 41

Combe Cliff

EVENLODE

Combe Mill

Combe

RIVER

Mill Wood

Brook Hill

WOOD

MILLWOOD

Millwood Farm

BOSOVER

ABEL

EVENLODE

BAKER'S CT.

WOOD

SWAN

LONG HANBOROUGH

PARK LA.

Long Hanborough Bridge

153

Myrtle Farm

WASTIE ORCH. RD.

119

ROAD

172

MILLWOOD

VALE

12 Hall

WRITE END

3

75

A4095

130

MAIN

Hanborough

46

ROAD

HILL DESWELL

20

52

14

WITNEY

39

SLATTERS CT.

79

NEW RD.

BECKET

CHURCHILL WY.

GLYME

90

Sch.

RFLY. CL.

Play. grd.

Tennis Cts.

Pav.

2

HARBOROUGH CRES.

CHURCHILL

WY.

ISIS

ROOSE

PINSLEY RD.

PINSLEY RD.

Play. Fld.

WROSLYN

Cook's Corner

PINSLEY WOOD

143

3

WROSLYN ROAD INDUSTRIAL ESTATE

4

13

Witney OX29

OAKLAND CL.

Sch.

PARKLANDS

FREELAND

NASH LA.

HURST

RUSBY CL.

WOODLANDS

THE BLOWINGS

CHURCH VW.

CHURCH LANE

WALKERS

BLENHEIM

Heath Farm

Play. Fld.

Downhills Farm

Nursery

Slatters Farm

Church Hanborough

MANSEL CL.

ROAD

Broad Marsh

BROAD MARSH

Hall

LA.

PIGEON

Cox's Farm

HOUSE

Sewage Farm

Whitehouse Farm

CHURCH LANE

ROAD

Pear Tree Farm

5

ROAD

St. Mary's Convent

Nursery

The Plantation

ROAD

Elm Farm

The Thrift

6

12

Freeland House

THE GREEN

Tanner's Hill Clump

'Lady Grove

Vincents Wood

7

WROSLYN

LANE

CUCKOO

LANE

70

Bowles Farm

41

Castles Copse

Cuckoo Wood Farm

42

43

A   B   142   C   D   E

1

205

2

A361

FILKINS

Peartree
Farm

CROSS TREE LA.

Goodfellows

SONS

BULLS

PL.

Playgrd.

Mus.

THE

GASSONS

HAZELL'S LA.

Filkins
Hall

BURFORD   ROAD

B4477

KING'S

3

Broughton
Poggs

04

4

Manor
Farm

Burial
Ground

Lechlade

GL7

FILKINS

Manor Farm
Buildings

Manor Farm
Buildings

Bowling
Green
Pav.

LANE

BROADWELL

LANE

Manor
Farm

Broadwell
Manor

Broadwell
House

Broadwell

Home
Farm

Kencot

Kencot
Manor

Asthall
Farm

LANE

Hillview
Farm

Dovecote
Barn

5

03

Filkins
Mill

Broadshire
Bridge

KING'S

Broadwell

Club
House

Tennis
Court

Lower
Farm

CALCROFT

6

Broughton
Poggs

Langford   Brook

Ansells
Farm

BROADWELL   ROAD

Langford

CHURCH
ROW

Pav.   Crkt.
Grd.

THE ELMS

St.
Christopher's
C of E Prim.
School

Rectory
Farm

CHURCH LA.

Lower
Farm

HOOKS

LEYS
VIEW

Brook

Broadwell
Mill

Langhat
Ditch

LANE

7

Little
Faringdon
Wood

02

Hulse
Grounds
Farm

LECHLADE

Tillingtons

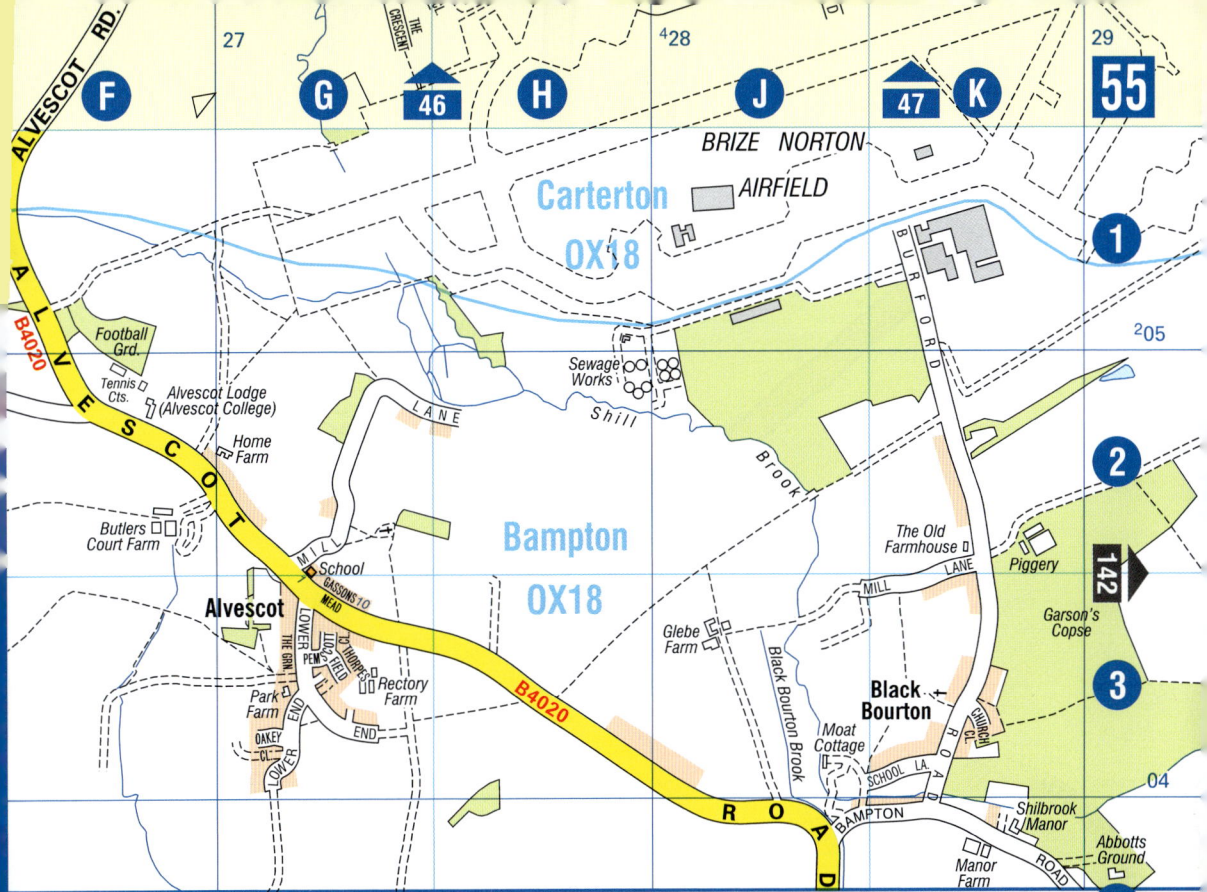
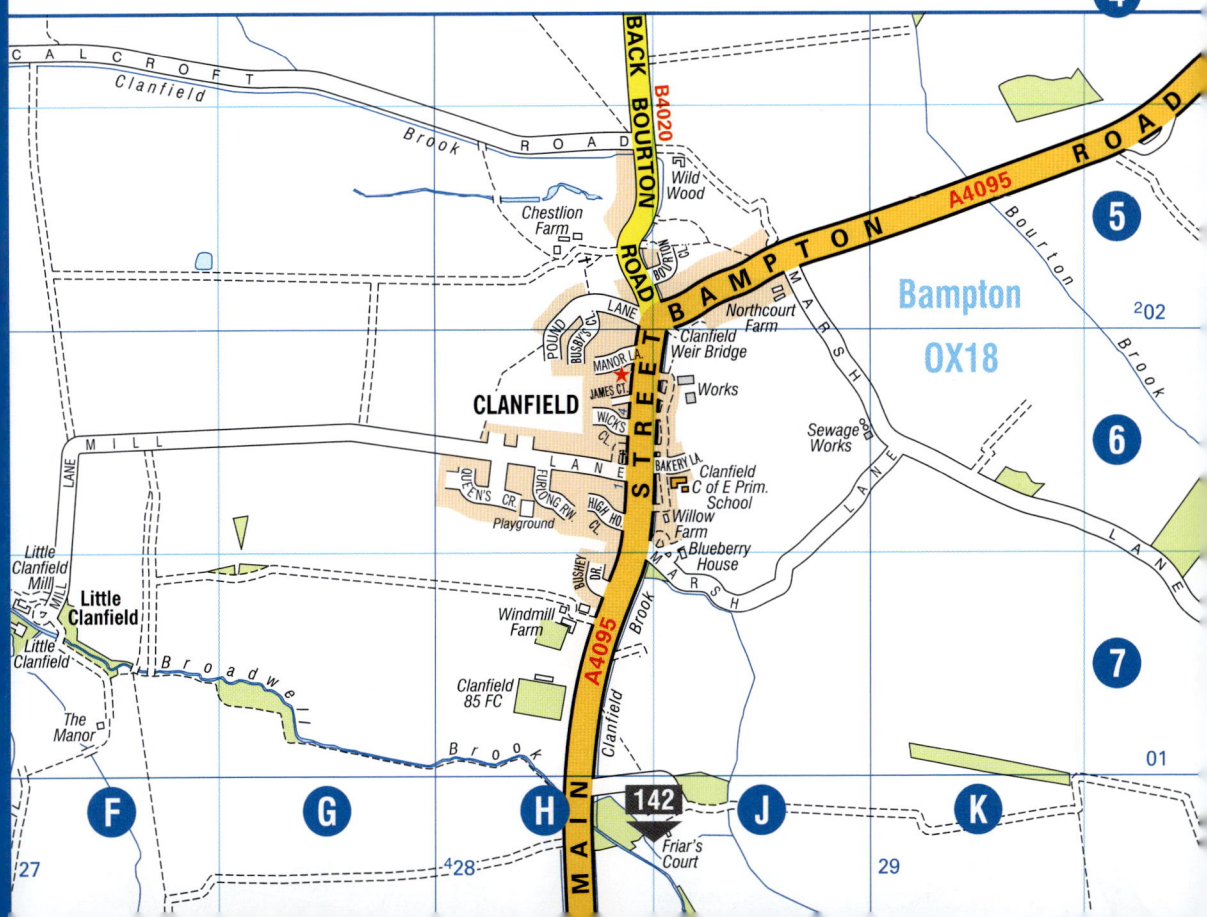

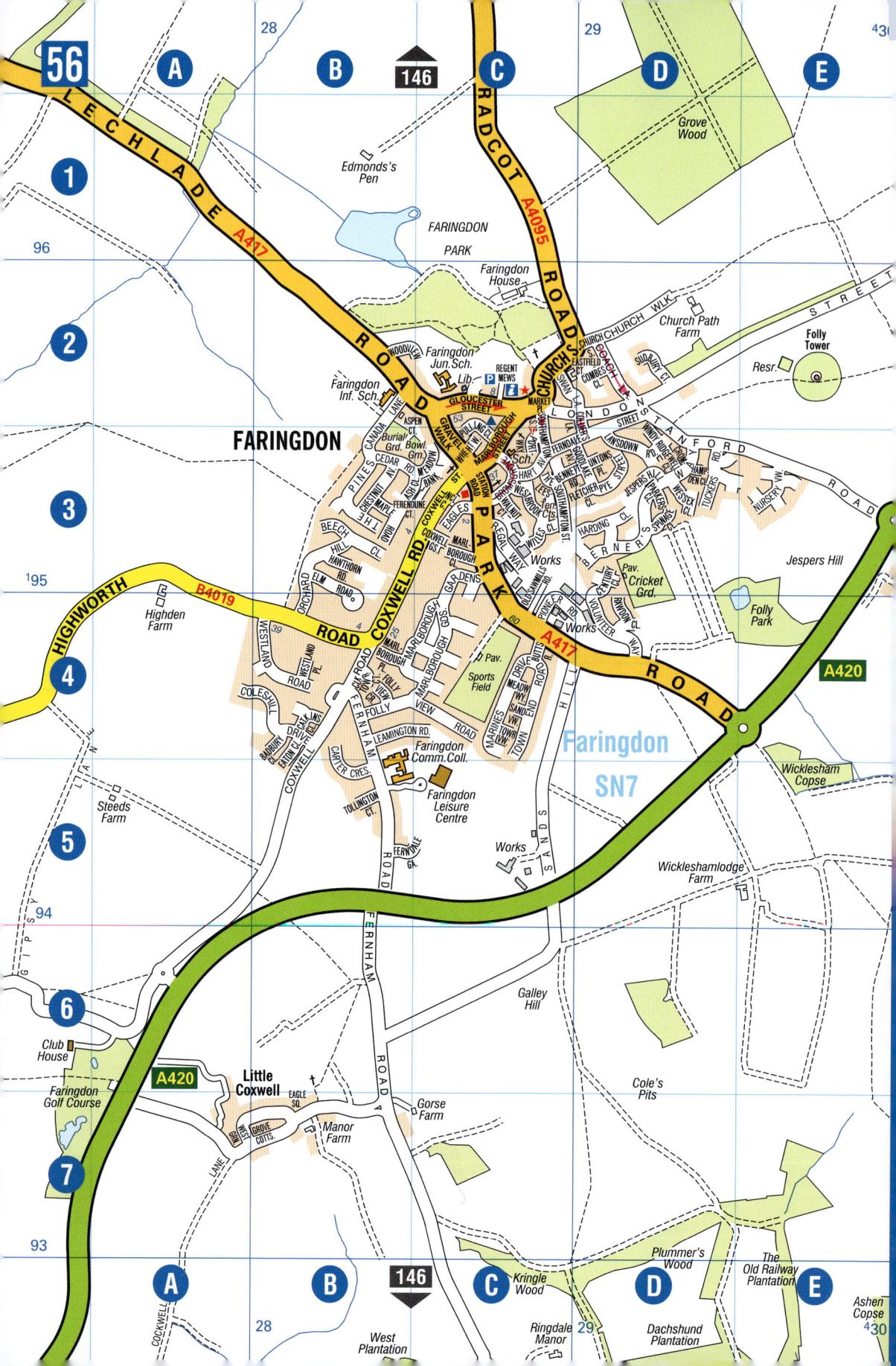

A B 146 C D E

1

28 29 430

96

LECHLADE ROAD A417

Edmonds's Pen

FARINGDON PARK

BRADCOT ROAD A4095

Grove Wood

2

Faringdon House

Faringdon Jun. Sch.

Faringdon Inf. Sch.

Lib.

REGENT MEWS

GLOUCESTER STREET

MARKET PL

CHURCH CHURCH WLK

CHURCH ST

EASTFIELD CT

COMBES CT

SUDBURY CT

Church Path Farm

Folly Tower

Resr.

FARINGDON

PINES CANADA LANE ASPEN CT CEDAR RD FERENDUNE CT CHESTNUT MAPLE THE ROW ASH CL Burial Grd. Bowl. Grn. GRAVEL WALK PULLINGS WHELWHT MARLBOROUGH STREET STATION ROAD COXWELL RD

LONDON STREET STANFORD ROAD

3

195

HIGHWORTH B4019

Highden Farm

BEECH HILL HAWTHORN RD. ELM RD. ORCHARD WESTLAND PL WESTLAND ROAD COLESHILL

COXWELL RD ROAD

COXWELL MARL. BOROUGH GDS.

PARK

GAR. DENS

Works

Works

Pav. Cricket Grd.

Jespers Hill

Folly Park

4

Steeds Farm

BARBURY DRICH CATON CL COXWELL STREET CARTER CRES. TOLLINGTON CT. FERNHAM ROAD FOLLY MARLBOROUGH PL FOLLY VIEW LEAMINGTON RD. ROAD

Pav.

Sports Field

MEADOW WY SANDS MARINES ROXY DRIVE BUTTS TOWN END TOWN VW

Works

A417 ROAD

A420

Wicklesham Copse

Faringdon Comm. Coll.

Faringdon Leisure Centre

FERNVALE GN

Faringdon SN7

5

94

FERNHAM ROAD

SANDS

Works

Wickleshamlodge Farm

6

Club House

Faringdon Golf Course

A420

Little Coxwell

WEST GROVE COTTS.

EAGLE SQ.

Gorse Farm

Manor Farm

Galley Hill

Cole's Pits

7

93

GIPSY LANE COCKWELL LANE FERNHAM ROAD

A B 146 C Kringle Wood D E

West Plantation

28 29 430

Ringdale Manor

Dachshund Plantation

Plummer's Wood

The Old Railway Plantation

Ashen Copse

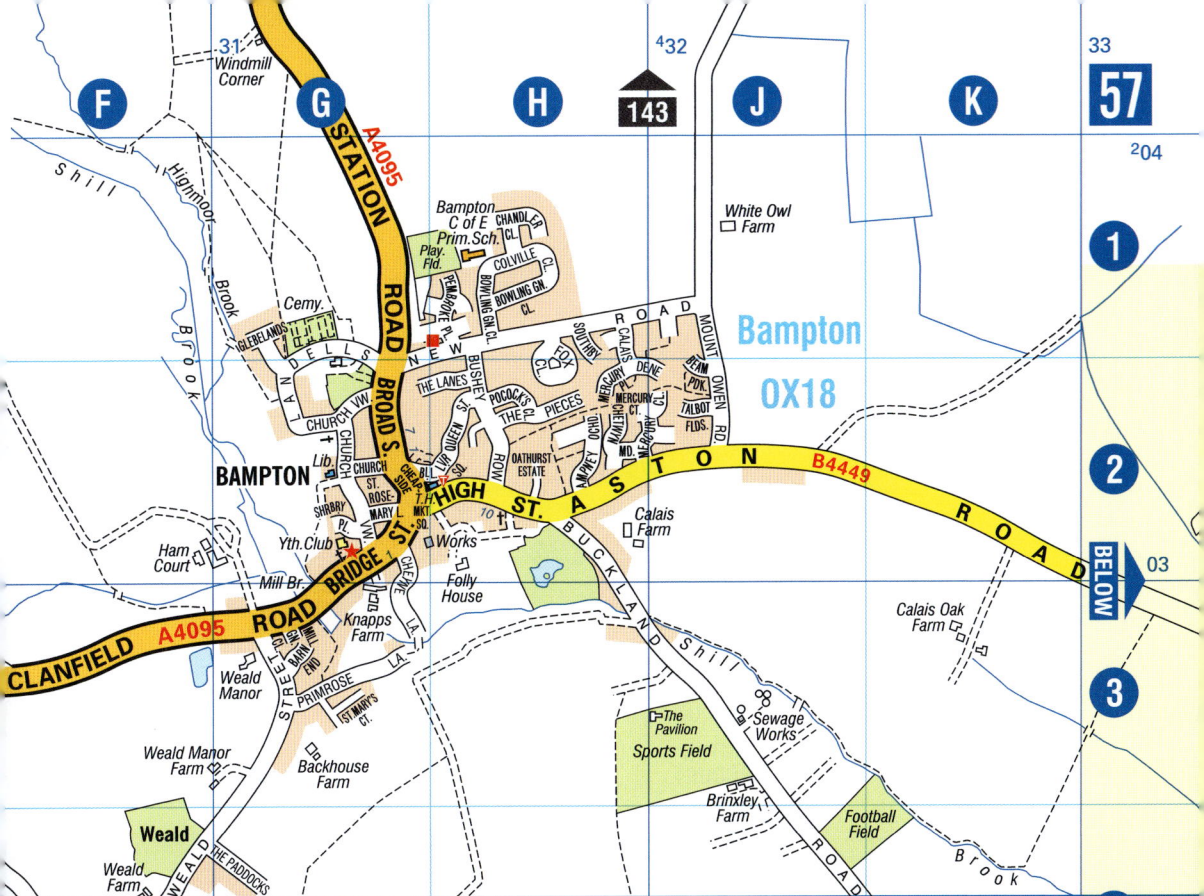

Windmill Corner

Shill

Highmoor

Brook

Brook

STATION ROAD A4095

Cemy.

GLEBELANDS

DELLS LANE

CHURCH VW.

CHURCH ST.

BAMPTON

Lib.

BROAD S

Bampton C of E Prim.Sch.
Play.Fld.
CHANDLER CL
COLVILLE CL
BOWLING GN.CL.
Bowling Gn.
PEMBROKE W

BUSHEY
THE LANES
POCOCKS
THE PIECES
ST.
QUEEN ST.

SIL.

CHGE.

T.H.
MKT. SQ.

SOUTHBY CL
CALAIS DENE
OCHD.
MALTHSE.
MERCURY CT.
MERCURY PL.
OWEN RD.
MOUNT RD.
BEAM
PDK.
TALBOT FLDS.

HIGH ST. ASTON ROAD B4449

Bampton OX18

White Owl Farm

1

2

BELOW 03

3

Calais Farm

Calais Oak Farm

SHBRY
ST. ROSE
MARY.
PL.

Yth.Club
Works
CHENE

CLANFIELD A4095 ROAD BRIDGE ST.

Ham Court
Mill Br.
Knapps Farm

Weald Manor
PRIMROSE LA.

ST. MARY'S CT.

Folly House

BUCKLAND

Shill

The Pavilion
Sports Field

Sewage Works

Weald Manor Farm
Backhouse Farm

Brinxley Farm

Football Field

ROAD

Weald
Weald Farm
THE PADDOCKS

Brook

4

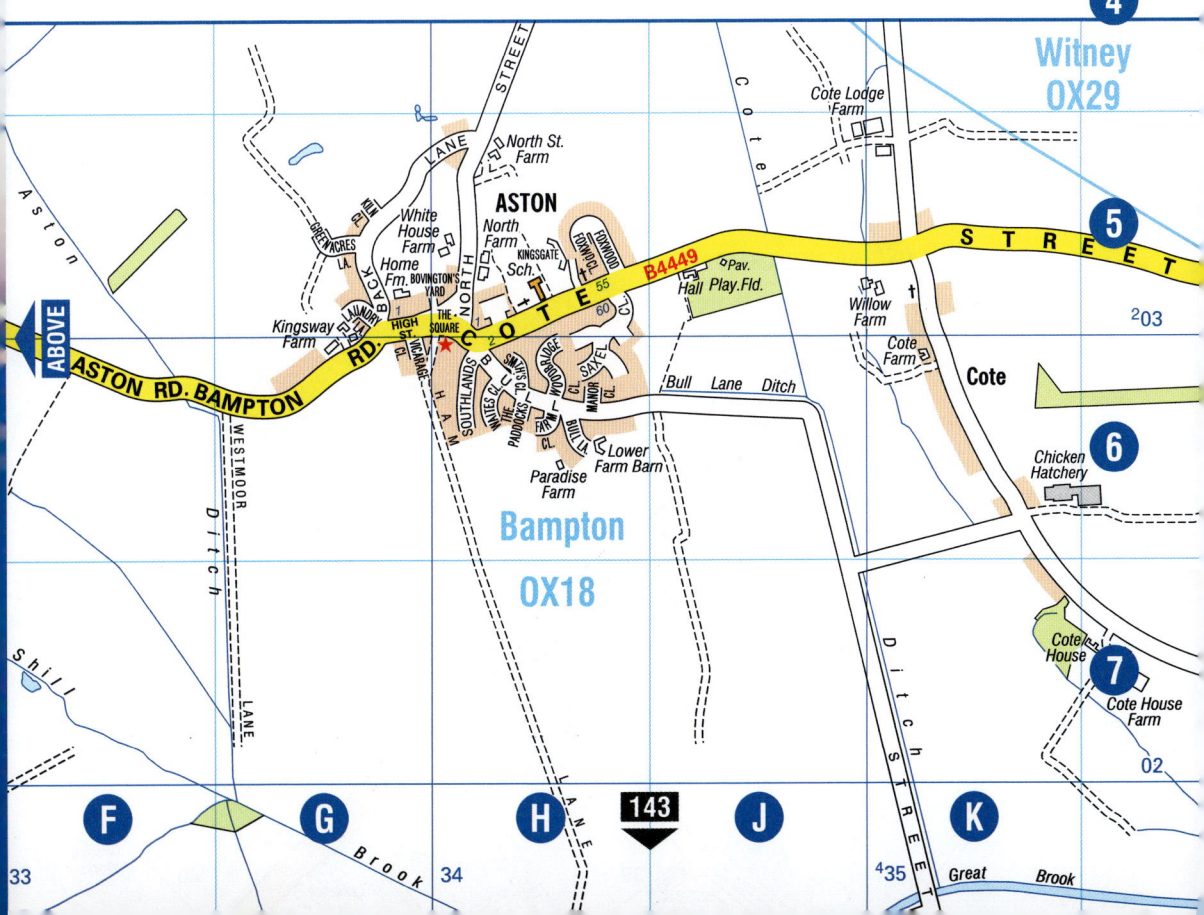

STREET

Cote

Cote Lodge Farm

Witney OX29

5

Aston

LANE

North St. Farm

ASTON

KILN GREEN ACRES LA.
White House Farm
Home Fm.
BOVINGTON'S YARD
North Farm
KINGSGATE Sch.

TOOLWOOD
FOXWOOD CL.

STREET ROAD BACK

Kingsway Farm
LAUNTON RD

THE SQUARE
HIGH ST.
VICARAGE

B4449

Pav.
Play.Fld.
Hall

Willow Farm

Cote Farm

03

ABOVE

ASTON RD. BAMPTON

COTE

SMITHS CL.
WHITE CL.
THE PADDOCKS
WINDRUSH LODGE
MANOR CL.
SAXEL CL.
BUTLER CL.

Bull Lane Ditch

Cote

6

WESTMOOR Ditch

SOUTHLANDS

Lower Farm Barn
Paradise Farm

HAM

Chicken Hatchery

Bampton OX18

Shill

LANE

Cote House

7

Cote House Farm

02

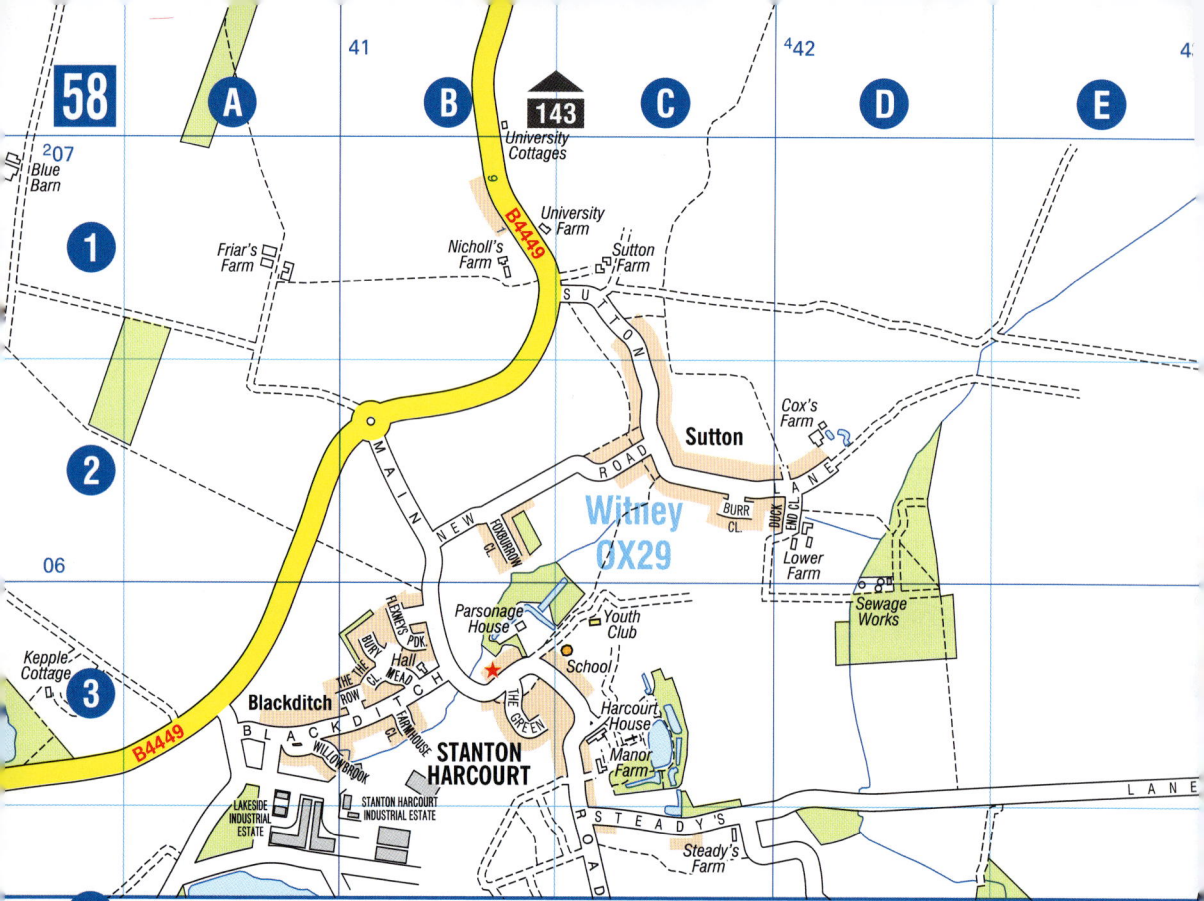

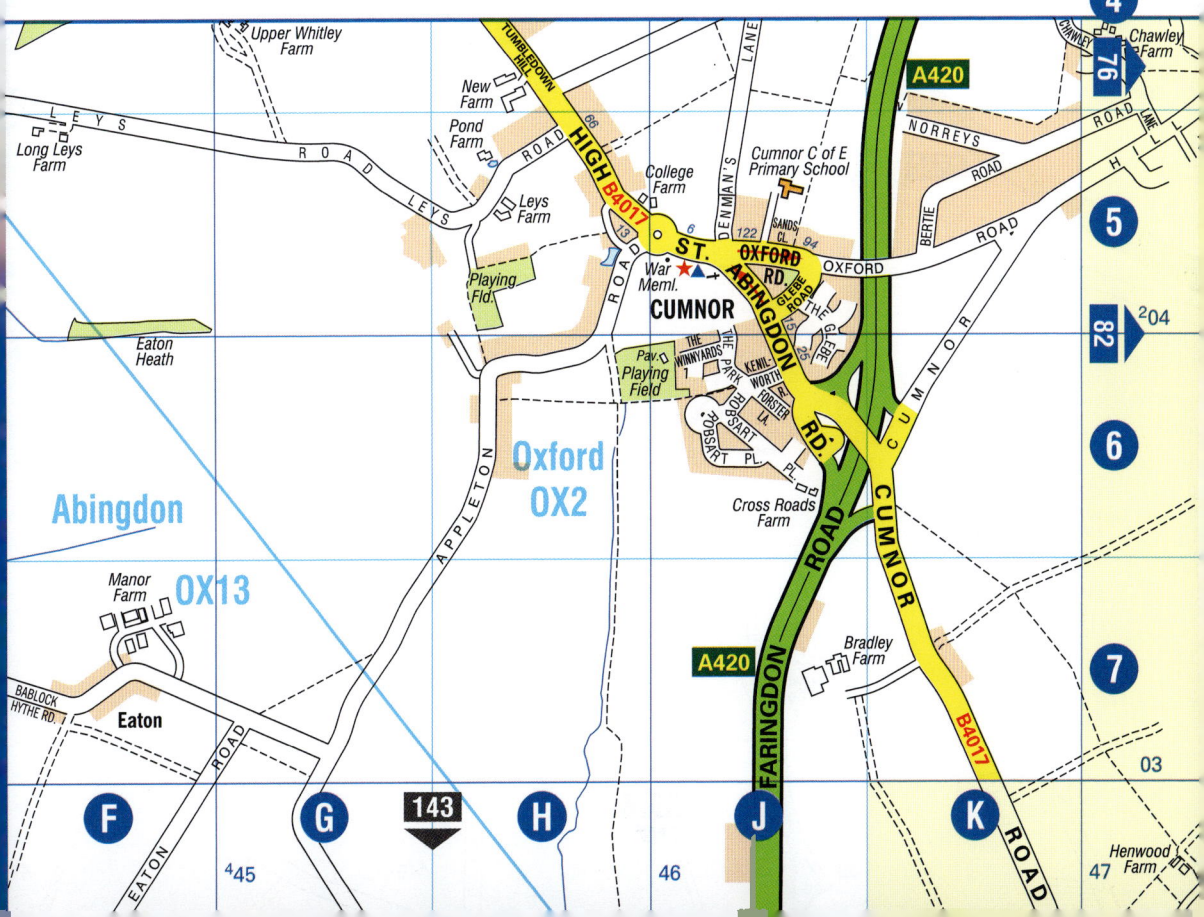

A B 143 C D E

1

200

Longworth Primary School

Draycott Moor Farm

CHURCH LANE
COLLEGE SQUARE
SCHOOL PL. THE SQ.
SCHOOL
COW BANK
SWBANK CL.
SUDBURY LA.
RECTORY LANE

Longworth

2

Northfield Farm

99

HINTON

PINE WOODS LANE

Farmlands

ROAD

GREEN LA.
HARRIS'S LANE
APPLETON

ROAD

DRAYCOTT ROAD

Abingdon OX13

3

A420

A415

FARINGDON RD.

198

AVENUE
LARCH CL.
SCHOOL ROAD
BLANDY ROAD
DRIVE
REDWOOD CL.
Rec. Grd.
Sch.
FIR TREE CL.
Playgrd.

SOUTHMOOR
Hall

LAUREL WY.
GREENHEART WY.
BELLAMY CL.
STONE HOUSE
FRAX...
OXFORD RD.

Church Copse

Kingston Bagpuize Park

Kingston Bagpuize Ho.

KINGSTON BAGPUIZE

4

BEGGARS LANE
WORCESTER PL.
TO THE FELL
PADDOCK WK.
SOUTH PL.
BLACKM...
LIME GRO.
DRAYCOTT CL.
SANDY LANE
NORWOOD AVENUE

Courtclose Copse

5

A420
SPRING ROAD
BULLOCKSPITS LANE

Springfield Farm

CHERRY HAYES AV.

STONEHILL
TOWN POND LA.

LANE

Oakbedding Copse

RECTORY LANE
RACE FARM
Race Farm
Kingston Business Park

6

97

Lower Lodge Farm

Bullockspits Farm

Newhouse Farm

7

Newhouse Cover

CHARNEY

A B 147 C D E

39 440 41

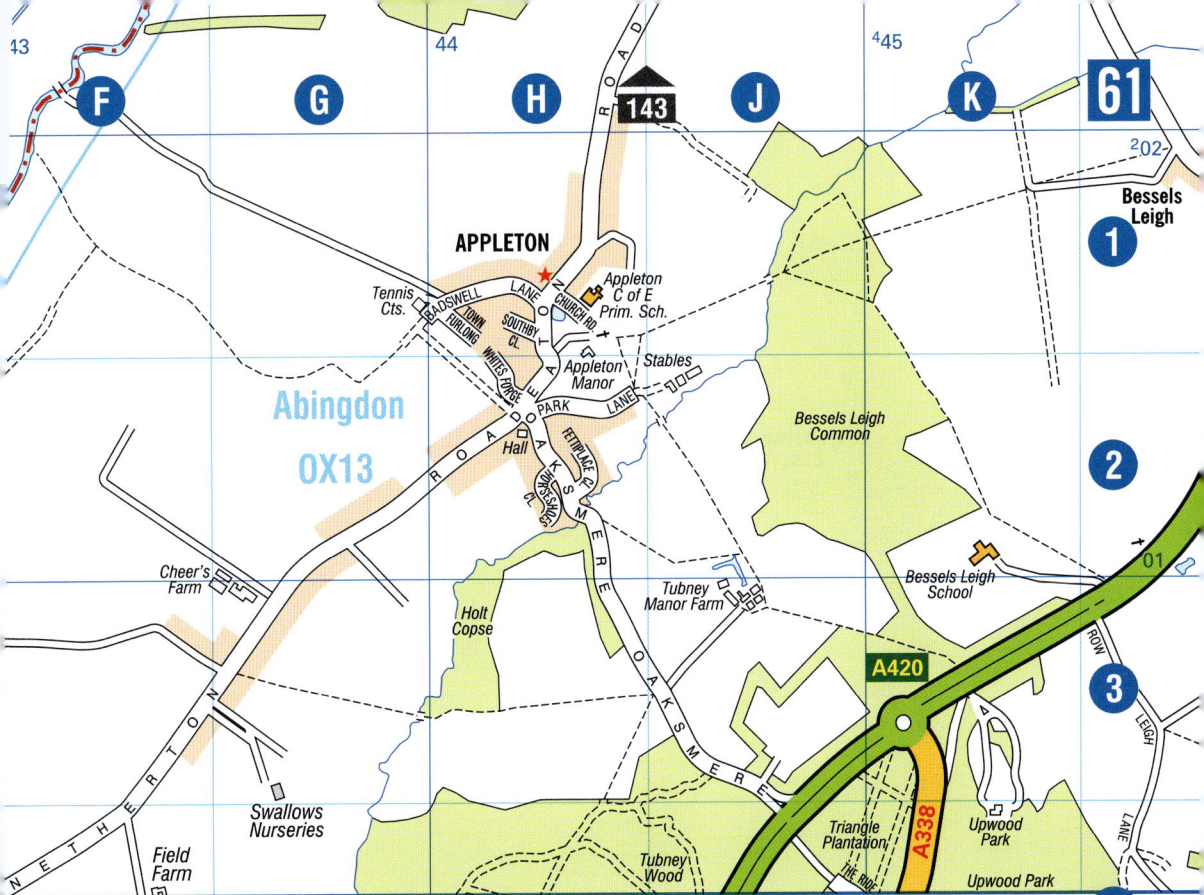

61

43　　　　　　44　　　　45

F　　G　　H　▲143　J　　K

Bessels
Leigh

1

²02

APPLETON

Tennis
Cts.

Appleton
C of E
Prim. Sch.

GADSWELL
TOWN
FURLONG
WHITES VERGE
SOUTHBY CL.
CHURCH RD.
NORTON LANE

Appleton Manor

Stables

Bessels Leigh
Common

2

Abingdon

OX13

PARK

Hall

OAKSMERE

FETTIPLACE PL.

KINGS CL.

EATON ROAD

Cheer's
Farm

Tubney
Manor Farm

Bessels Leigh
School

01

Holt
Copse

A420

3

LEIGH LANE

ROW

NETHERTON

Swallows
Nurseries

Field
Farm

Tubney
Wood

Triangle
Plantation

A338

THE RIDE

Upwood
Park

Upwood Park

4

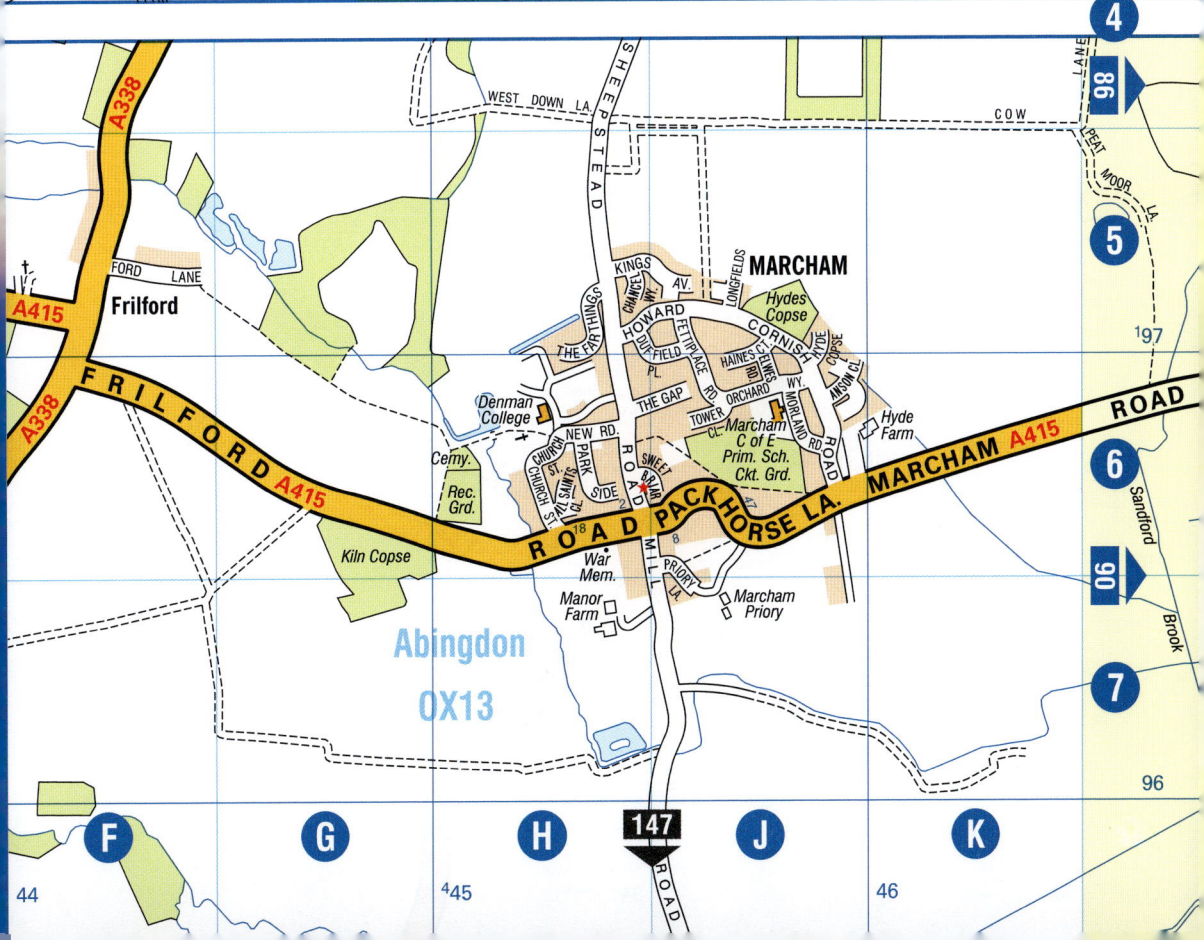

86

A338

WEST DOWN LA.

SHEEPSTEAD

COW

LANE

PEAT MOOR LA.

5

197

FORD LANE

A415

Frilford

A338

FRILFORD A415

KINGS

CHANCEL WY.

LONGFIELDS

MARCHAM

Hydes
Copse

CORNISH

HYDE

HYDE COPSE

ANSON CL.

6

SOUTHILL
THE FIELD
HOWARD
PL.
OUTFIELD
FETTIPLACE RD.
HAINE'S
ORCHARD
ELWES RD.
WY.
MORLAND ROAD

Denman
College

Cerny.

Rec.
Grd.

CHURCH ST.
ALL SAINTS CL.
NEW RD.
PARK
SYDE
ROAD
SWEET BRIAR
TOWER CL.

Marcham
C of E
Prim. Sch.
Ckt. Grd.

Hyde
Farm

MARCHAM A415

ROAD

Sandford

Kiln Copse

War
Mem.

18
8
ROAD PACK HORSE LA.

MILL LA.

PRIORY

90

Manor
Farm

Marcham
Priory

7

Abingdon

OX13

96

44　　　　　45　　　　46

F　　G　　H　▼147　J　　K

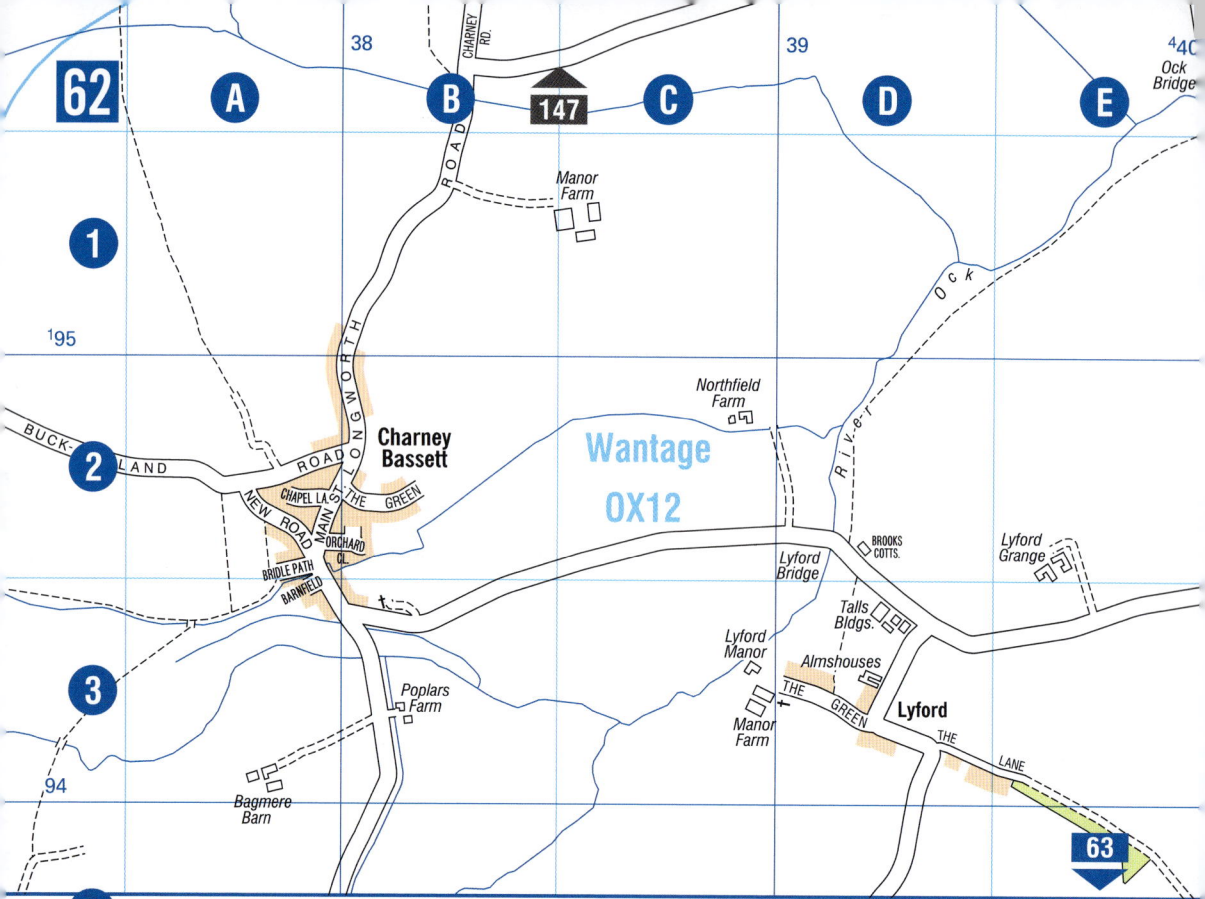

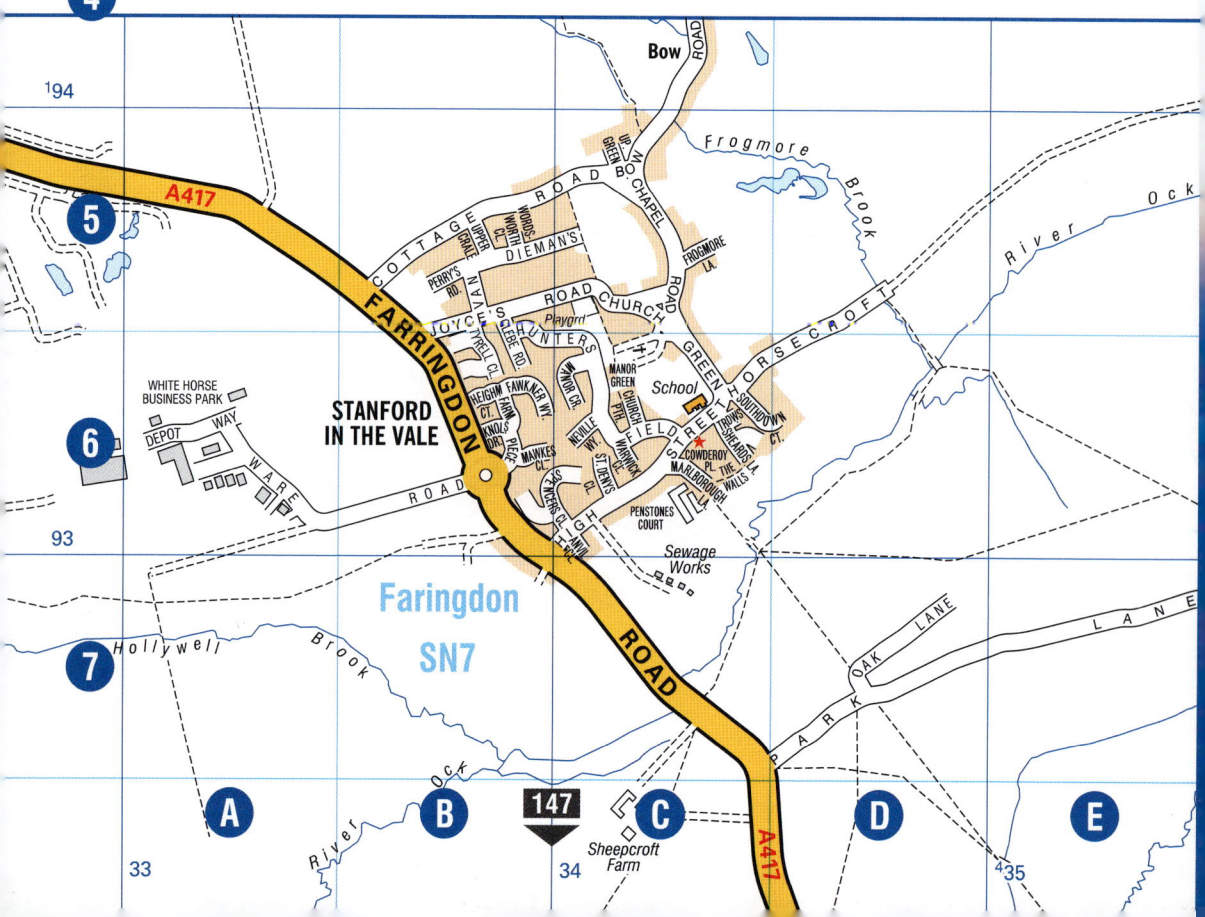

F 62 G H 147 J K 63

Gallows Bridge

94

Brook

1

Letcombe Brook

Childrey

Bailey's Mead Copse

Poughley Farm

EBBES LANE

ASHFIELDS

ALFREDS PL.

Botney Meadows Farm

EAST HANNEY

Ind. Est.

2

HALLS LANE

THE GREEN

MORTON CL.

CROWN

193 RD.

RECTORY FARM CL.

GRN.

NORTH

WINTER

SCHOOL LANE

THE CROFT

STEVENTON

THE MEADS

MAIN STREET

St. James C of E Prim. School

Playing Field

SNUGGS LA.

STREET

Tennis Cts.

Playgrd.

THE PADDOCKS

3

CHURCH STREET

MONKS CL.

ROAD CAUSEWAY

Hall

BROOKSIDE

ALFREY LA.

BLENHEIM ORCH.

BRAMLEY CL.

West Hanney

MILLBRIDGE

MILL ORCHARD

SUMMERTOWN

A338

Wantage

OX12

4

92

OLD MAN'S LANE

Bradfield Barn

5

118

Bradfield Farm Sewage Works

Bradfield Grove Farm

6

Works

Offices

GROVE

91

Grove Wick Farm

PARK

7

Cemetery

Monk's Farm

GROVE

DRIVE

DENCHWORTH ROAD

CHURCHWD

MAPLES

STEPTOE CL.

WICK GRN.

WESTBROOK

DENCHWORTH

THE GRN.

Grove C of E Prim. Sch.

NORTH DR.

TULWICK

Tulwick Farm

NEWLANDS DR.

THE KESTRELS

SHEPHERDS CL.

DRIVE

COLLETT WY.

FLMR HWTH.

OXFORD ROAD

CHURCH VW.

GODINS

ST. JOHN'S RD.

HOWARD AV.

Pill Ditch

LANE

106

F 105 G H J K

Comm. Cen.

Prim. Sch!

Lib.

EASTERFIELD

VICARAGE CL.

STATION ROAD

SHANNON CL.

41

42

40 LA.

BRUNEL CR.

SYCAMORE

HARDWE

OLD MILL

MAIN ST.

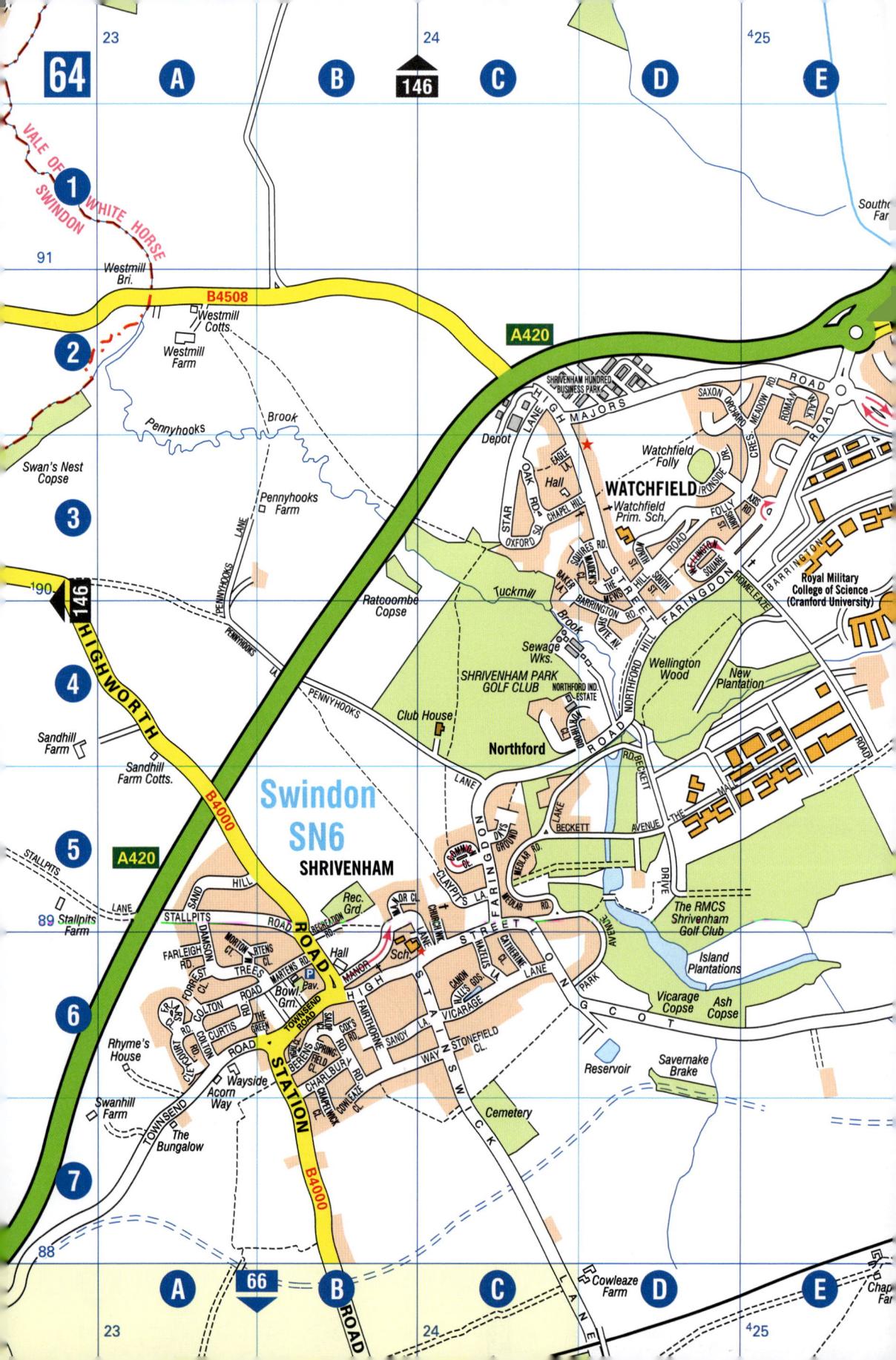

A B C D E

146

1

VALE OF
SWINDON
WHITE HORSE

91

Westmill
Bri.

B4508

Westmill
Cotts.

A420

2

Westmill
Farm

Pennyhooks   Brook

Shrivenham Hundred
Business Park

SAXON

ORCHARD

MEADOW RD.

ROMAN

ROAD

CRES.

FOLLY

Depot

EAGLE
LA.

Watchfield
Folly

HIGH

MAJORS

Southo
Far

3

Swan's Nest
Copse

Pennyhooks
Farm

PENNYHOOKS

LANE

Ratcoombe
Copse

Tuckmill

OAK
RD.

STAR

OXFORD

CHAPEL HILL

SQUARES RD.

BAKER LA.

BARRINGTON

Hall

Brook

WATCHFIELD

Watchfield
Prim. Sch.

THE
MEWS

STREET

WELLINGTON
SQUARE

WHITE AV.

NORTHFORD HILL

FARINGDON

TYE

ROAD

ST.

BARRINGTON

Royal Military
College of Science
(Cranford University)

190

146

HIGHWORTH

Sewage
Wks.

SHRIVENHAM PARK
GOLF CLUB

NORTHFORD IND.
ESTATE

Wellington
Wood

New
Plantation

4

Sandhill
Farm

Sandhill
Farm Cotts.

PENNYHOOKS

Club House

Northford

LANE

ROAD

BECKETT

THE MALL

5

STALLPITS

B4000

A420

SAND

HILL

STALLPITS

ROAD

LANE

Swindon
SN6

SHRIVENHAM

LANE

DAMMS
PL.

FARINGDON

LAKE

MEDLAR RD.

MEDLAR RD.

AVENUE

THE
MALL

DRIVE

The RMCS
Shrivenham
Golf Club

89

Stallpits
Farm

FARLEIGH
RD.

MORTON
CT.

MARTENS
CL.

TREES

Rec.
Grd.

MANOR CL.

CLAYPITS LANE

BECKENTON

CHURCH WK.

Hall

Sch.

CATHERINE

STREET

Island
Plantations

6

Rhyme's
House

COLTON
RD.

CURTIS

FORREST
CL.

COLTON

DAMSON
CL.

ROAD

Bowl.
Grn.

THE
GREEN

Pav.

MARTENS RD.

STAINSWICK

HIGH

MANOR

FAIRTHORNE

SALTH

COX'S
RD.

CANON
RD.

VICARAGE

STREET

STHS.

HILLS GDS.

STANTON

LANE

PARK

AVENUE

LONGCOT

Vicarage
Copse

Ash
Copse

Savernake
Brake

Swanhill
Farm

TOWNSEND

Wayside

Acorn
Way

The
Bungalow

BERENS
FIELD

SPRINGS
RD.

CHARLBURY
RD.

STONEFIELD
CL.

SANDY

WAY

CHAPELWICK
CL.

Reservoir

7

STATION

B4000

ROAD

88

Cemetery

Cowleaze
Farm

Chap
Far

A B C D E

66

BROAD
ROAD

23   24   25

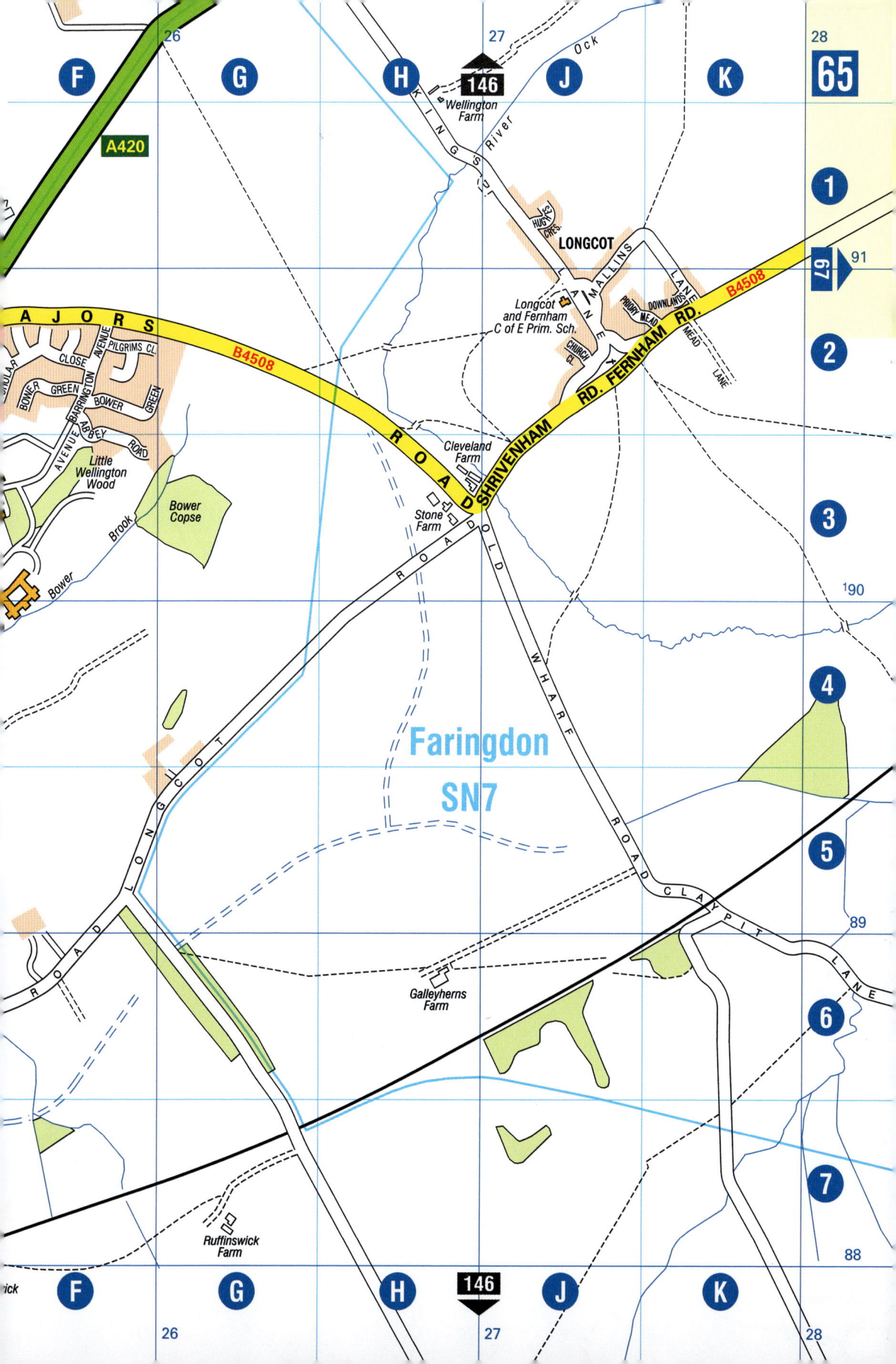

A420

26 27 Ock 28

146

Wellington Farm

KINGSTON ROAD

River

1

HUGS CRES.

LONGCOT

67 →91

B4508

MALLINS LANE

MAJORS

PILGRIMS CL.

CLOSE AVENUE

BOWER GREEN

BARRINGTON

BOWER GREEN

ABBEY ROAD

AVENUE

B4508

Longcot and Fernham C of E Prim. Sch.

CHURCH CL.

DOWNLANDS

PRIORY MEAD

SHRIVENHAM RD. FERNHAM RD.

MEAD LANE

2

Little Wellington Wood

Bower Copse

Brook

Bower

ROAD

Cleveland Farm

Stone Farm

ROAD

3

¹90

WHARF

4

Faringdon

SN7

LONGCOT

ROAD

5

CLAYPIT LANE

89

6

Galleyherns Farm

ROAD

Ruffinswick Farm

7

88

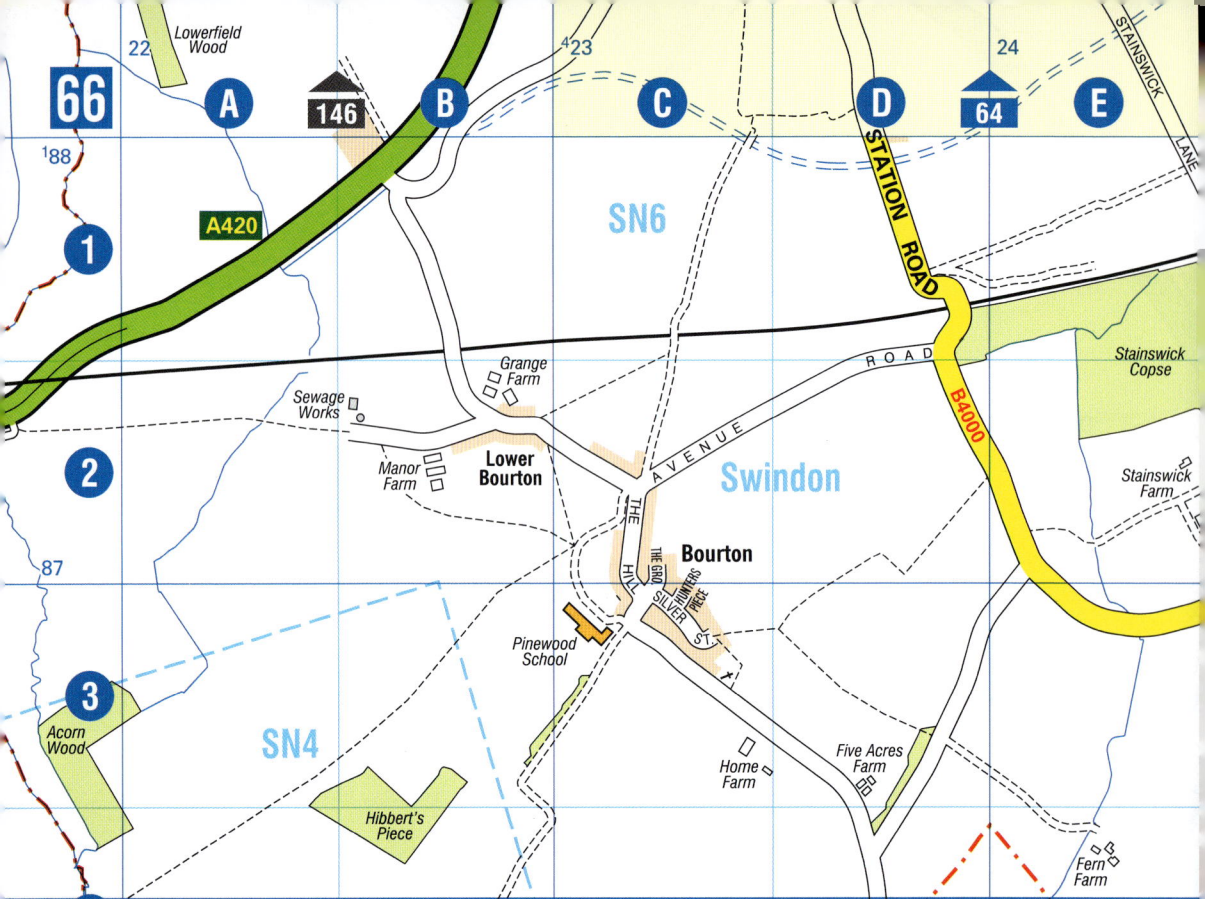
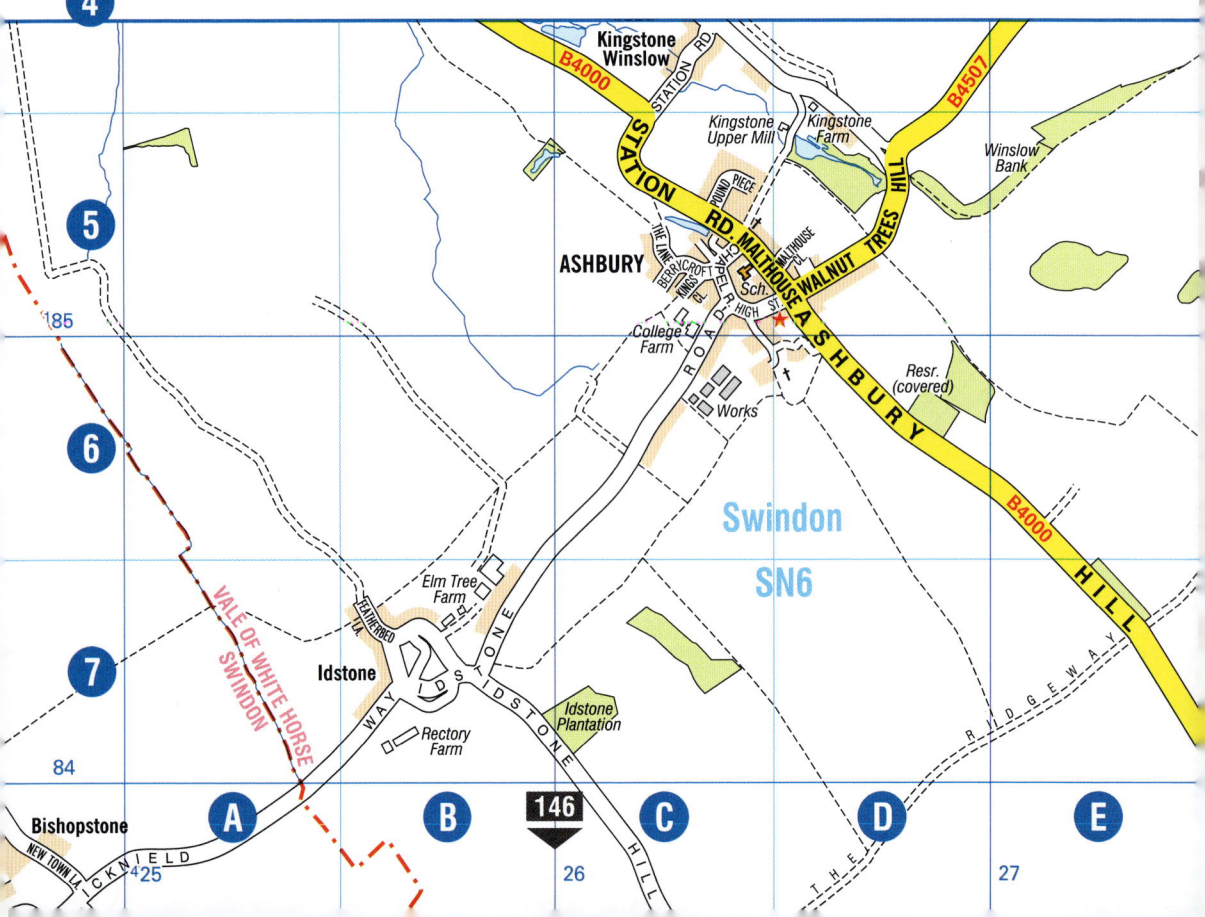

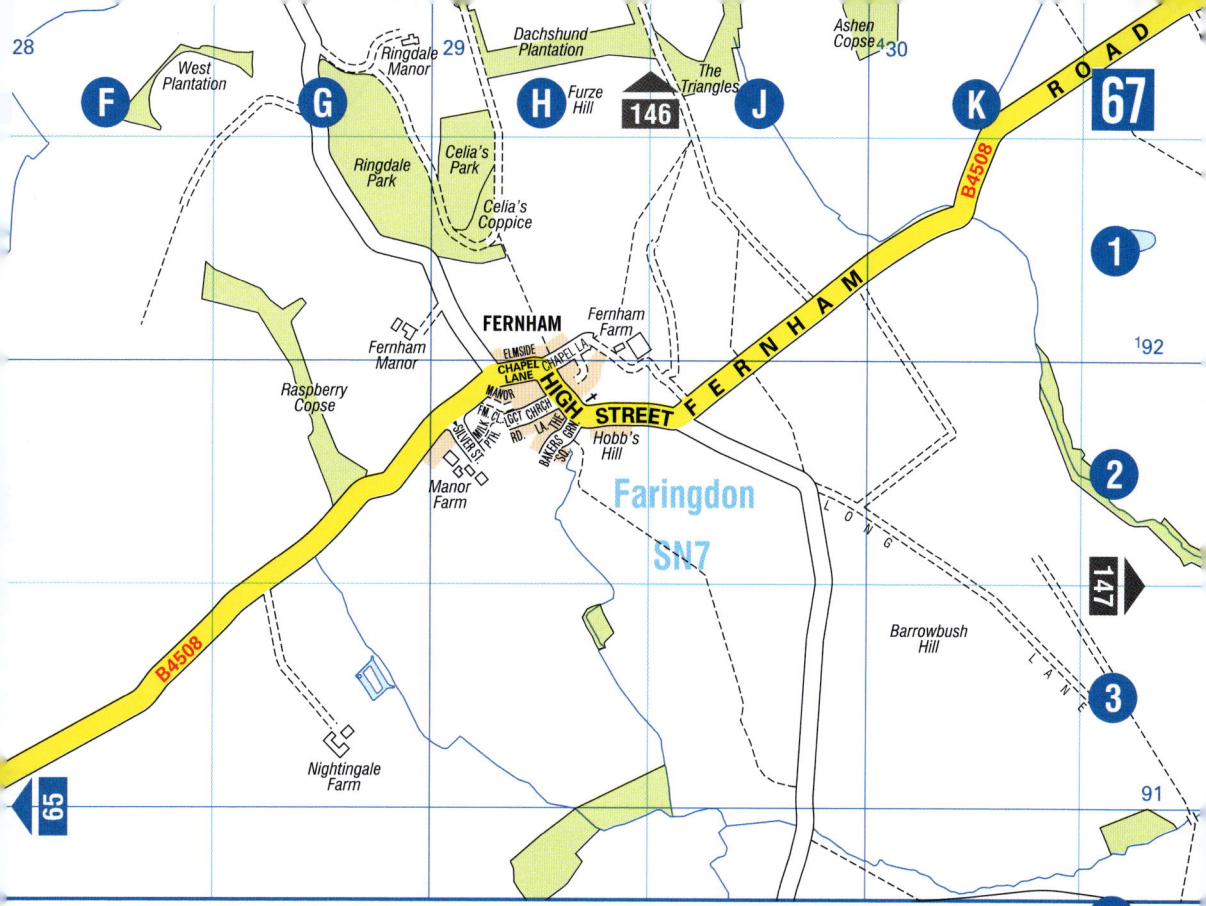

West Plantation

Ringdale Manor

Dachshund Plantation

The Triangles

146

Ashen Copse

4 30

ROAD

B4508

Ringdale Park

Celia's Park

Celia's Coppice

FERNHAM

1

1 92

Fernham Manor

FERNHAM

Fernham Farm

ELMSIDE

CHAPEL LA.

Raspberry Copse

CHAPEL LANE

MANOR

HIGH

2

SILVER ST.

FM. CL.

CHURCH

STREET

Faringdon SN7

Manor Farm

MANOR

BAKERS GRN.

Hobb's Hill

LONG

B4508

147

Barrowbush Hill

3

91

Nightingale Farm

LANE

65

4

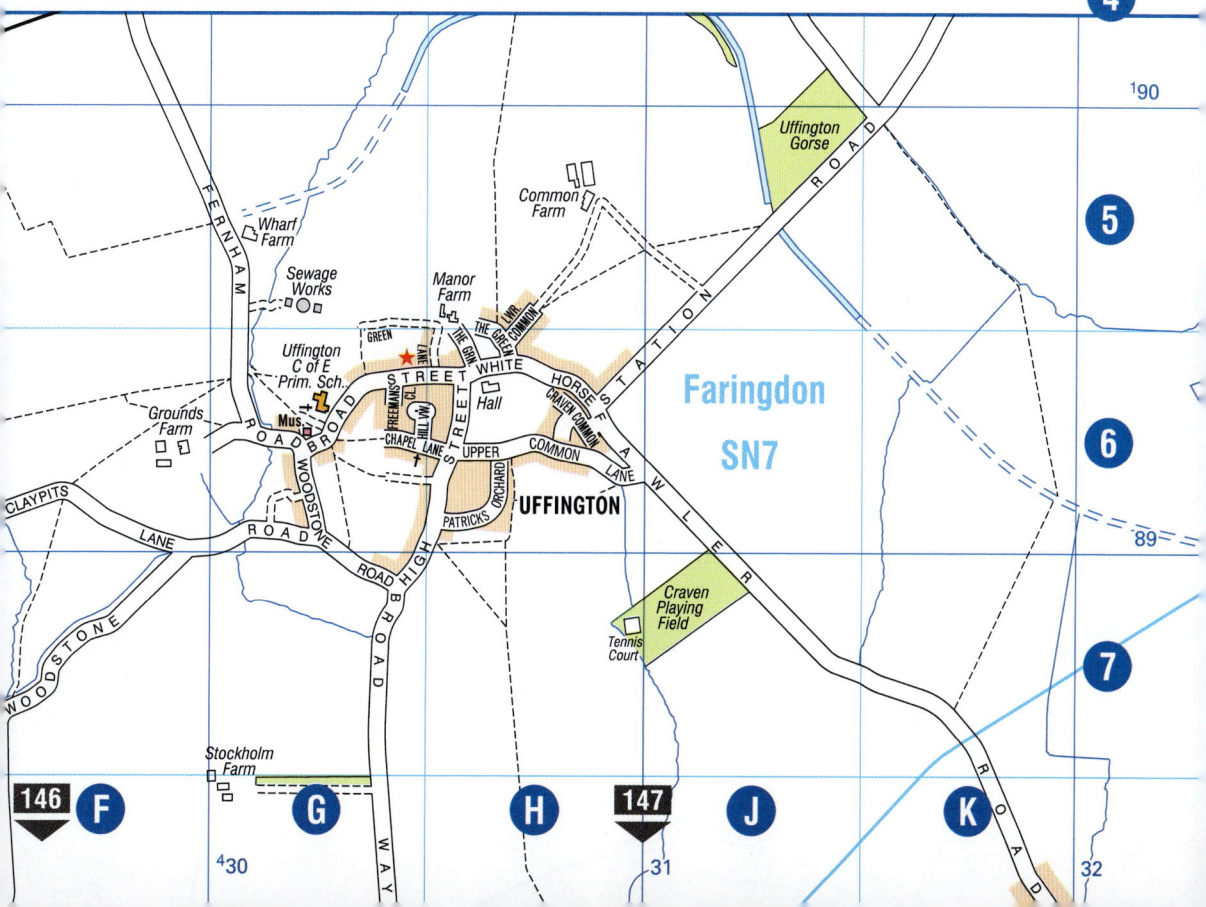

Uffington Gorse

ROAD

5

Wharf Farm

Common Farm

FERNHAM

Sewage Works

Manor Farm

LWR. COMMON

UPR. COMMON

STATION

GREEN

THE GREEN

THE GRN.

Uffington C of E Prim. Sch.

WHITE

HORSE

Faringdon SN7

Grounds Farm

BROAD

STREET

Hall

CRAVEN COMMON

6

CLAYPITS

Mus.

ROAD

FREEMANS CL.

MILL LA.

CHAPEL LANE

UPPER COMMON

LANE

89

LANE

WOODSTONE

HIGH

PATRICKS ORCHARD

UFFINGTON

WALLER

Craven Playing Field

7

WOODSTONE

ROAD

BROAD

Tennis Court

Stockholm Farm

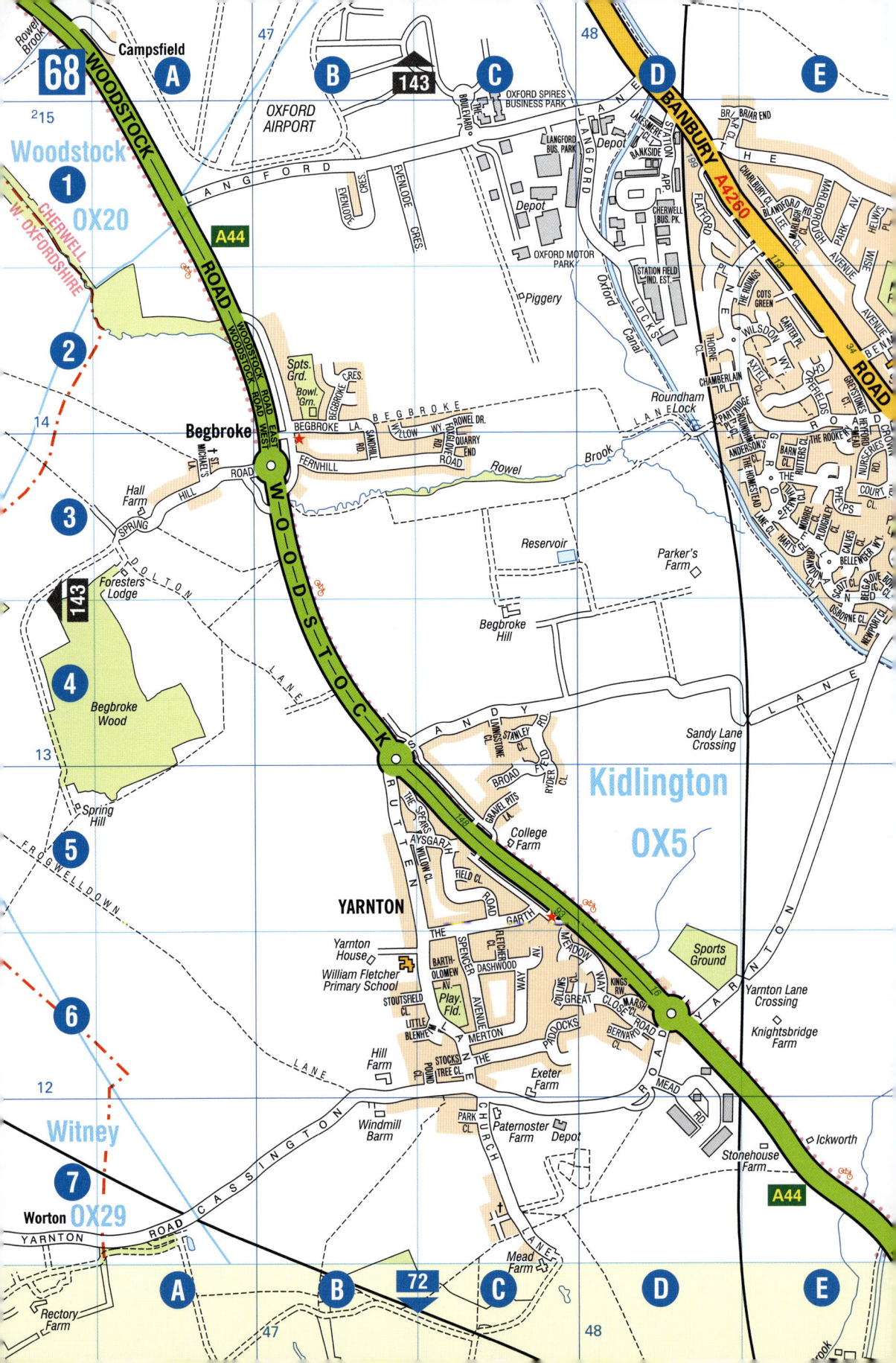

Woodstock

OX20

Campsfield

WOODSTOCK ROAD

A44

CHERWELL
W. OXFORDSHIRE

²15

14

Rowel Brook

47

OXFORD AIRPORT

OXFORD SPIRES BUSINESS PARK

143

THE BOULEVARD

LANGFORD LANE

LANGFORD BUS. PARK

Depot

LANGFORD

EVENLODE CRES.

EVENLODE

Piggery

OXFORD MOTOR PARK

Depot

48

BANBURY ROAD A4260

BR. BRIAR END

THE

STATION APP.

LAKESMERE CL.

BANKSIDE

CHARLBURY CL.
BLANDFORD RD.

CHERWELL BUS. PK.

STATION FIELD IND. EST.

Oxford Canal

LOCKS

MARLBOROUGH

PARK AV.

HELWYS

BEN AVENUE

Roundham Lock

THE ROWNS

COTS GREEN

WILSON WY.

CHAMBERLAIN PL.

THORNE CL.

PARTRIDGE

ROWNHAM'S

ANDERSON'S

THE HOMESTEAD

BARN CL.

THE ROOKERY

BRIDSTONES CL.

OREFELDS

NURSERIES CL.

BELLGROVE RD.

NEWPORT CL.

COURT CL.

CALVES

PLOUGHLEY

MOREL CL.

JOHNSON'S

SCOTT CL.

OSBORNE CL.

BELLEWOR CL.

Begbroke

St. MICHAEL'S CL.

Hall Farm

HILL ROAD

SPRING

DOLTON LANE

143

Foresters Lodge

Begbroke Wood

13

Spring Hill

FROGWELLDOWN

12

Witney

Worton OX29

YARNTON

ROAD CASSINGTON ROAD

Spts. Grd.

Bowl. Grn.

BEGBROKE CRES.

BEGBROKE LA.

FERNHILL

SANDHILL RD.

WILLOW WY.

RADBONE WY.

ROWEL DR.

QUARRY END

ROAD

BEGBROKE

Rowel Brook

W—O—O—D—S—T—O—C—K ROAD WEST
ROAD EAST

Reservoir

Begbroke Hill

Parker's Farm

SANDY LANE

LIMESTONE CL.

STAWLEY CL.

BROAD

RYDER CL.

FYFIELD

College Farm

Sandy Lane Crossing

Kidlington

OX5

THE SPERS

AYSGARTH

WILTON CL.

FIELD CL.

RUTTEN LANE

GRAVEL PITS LA.

GARTH

MEADOW WAY

KINGS RW.

GREAT

SPORTS Ground

Yarnton Lane Crossing

Knightsbridge Farm

Yarnton House

William Fletcher Primary School

BARTHOLOMEW AV.

SPENCER CL.

FLETCHER CL.

DASHWOOD

WAY AV.

CLOSE

MARSH ROAD

BERNARD CL.

COLINS

STOUTSFIELD CL.

LITTLE BLENHE

MERTON

PADDOCKS

Hill Farm

STOCKS CL.

POUND CL.

TREE CL.

THE

Exeter Farm

Windmill Barn

PARK CL.

CHURCH LANE

Paternoster Farm

Depot

Ickworth

Stonehouse Farm

MEAD RD.

A44

Rectory Farm

YARNTON ROAD

Mead Farm

72

47

48

A B C D E

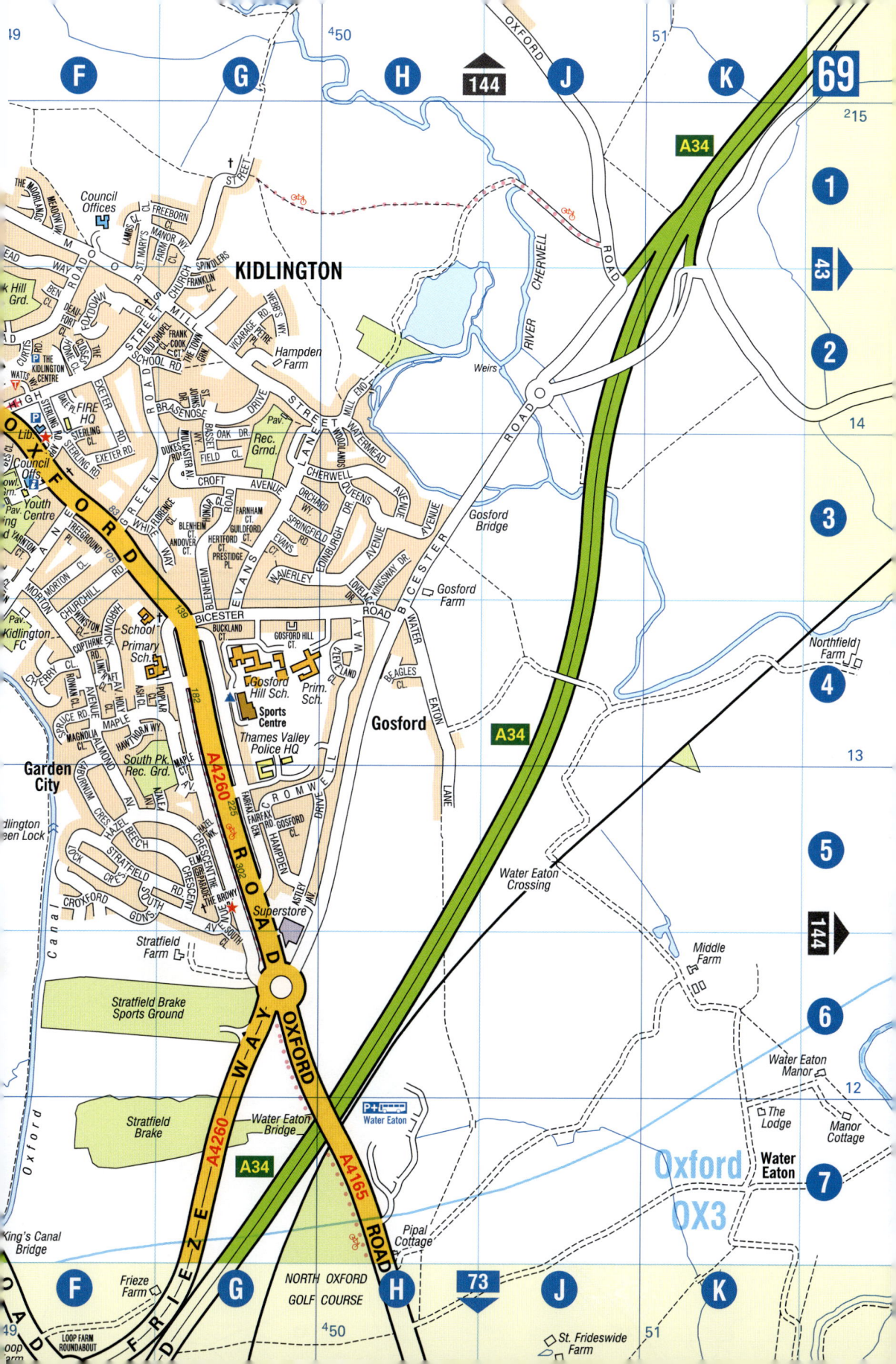

19 450 51 215

A34

1

43

2

14

KIDLINGTON

Council Offices

ST REET

Hampden Farm

River Cherwell

CHERWELL

Weirs

ROAD

Gosford Bridge

3

OXFORD ROAD

THE KIDLINGTON CENTRE

FIRE HQ

Youth Centre

Kidlington FC

Pav.

School Primary Sch.

Rec. Grnd.

Gosford Hill Ct.

Buckland Rd.

Gosford Hill Sch.

Prim. Sch.

Sports Centre

Thames Valley Police HQ

Gosford Farm

Gosford

Northfield Farm

4

A34

13

Garden City

South Pk. Rec. Grd.

BICESTER ROAD

A4260

Water Eaton Crossing

5

144

Stratfield Farm

Superstore

6

Middle Farm

Water Eaton Manor

12

Stratfield Brake Sports Ground

OXFORD

WAY

FRIEZE

Stratfield Brake

Water Eaton Bridge

A4260

Water Eaton

The Lodge

Manor Cottage

King's Canal Bridge

Canal

Oxford

A34

A4165

Pipal Cottage

Oxford OX3

Water Eaton

7

Loop Farm Roundabout

St. Frideswide Farm

19 450 51

A B 53 C D E

Witney OX29

EYNSHAM

1
2
3
4
5
6
7

11
10
09
08

42 43

Bowles Farm

Vincents Wood

Cuckoo Wood Farm

CUCKOO LANE
WROW

Depot

Acre Hill Farm

LANE

City Farm

Eynsham Mill

New Wintles Farm

Evenlode Farm

A40 143 210

A40 NORTHERN BY-PASS ROAD NORTH

ROAD B4449

SPAREACRE
Old Witney Road
WITNEY
TILGARSLEY RD.
SHAKESPEARE
DUNCAN
STRATFORD DR.
FALSTAFF
CL.
FRUITLANDS

Playing Field

BARTHOLOMEW CL.
WILLOWS EDGE
THORNBURY RD.

Corlan Farm

Chil Bridge

CHILBRIDGE

Works

Bartholomew School

Tennis Courts

GREENS
MARLBOROUGH
Wks.
PELCAM CL.
NEWLAND
EVANS CL.
EVANS

JOHN LOPES RD.
Liby.

P

HAN-BOROUGH RD.
MARLBOROUGH PL.
WYTHAM VW.
WYTHAM CL.
DOVEHOUSE CL.

HANBOROUGH ROAD
WYTHAM STREET
MILLMOOR
BECH RD.
HUNTINGTON RD.

Eynsham Prim. Sch.

LITTL.

ST. CASSINGTON RD.

EYNSHAM

NEWLAND
QUEENS
QUEENS LA.
TANNERS LA.
ORCHARD CL.
BITTERELL
Playgrd.

Park House

CHILBRIDGE

Chil Brook

Chilmore Bridge

MERTON RD.
CLOVER ROAD
CONDUIT LA.
ACRE END ST.
GRANGE MILL CT.
BLANDSTONE
THE CL.
HEL ST.
LOMBARD ST.
SWAN ST.
ABBEY
THAMES
MILL ST.
HIGH ST.
THE SQ.
CHCH. LA.
QUEEN ST.
OXFORD ROAD

Abbey Farm

Works
ABBEY PL.
Abbey Park House

ST.

Pav.
Recn. Grd.

OX

Monkswood Close Farm

B4449 ROAD STATION

Oasis Park

PINK HILL

Works
BOTTOM YARD

Moonshine Bowling Alley

STANTON HARCOURT ROAD B4449

Southfield Barn

OAKFIELDS INDUSTRIAL ESTATE

Works

LANE

A B 143 C D E

42 43

1

2

3

4

5

6

7

4 4 45 46

Worton

Battimer
Jericho
Farm

143

R O A D

Rectory
Farm

Tennis
Ct.

Sports
Grd.

Pav.

Depot

Depot

CASSINGTON

Manor
Farm

Grange
Farm

Reynolds
Farm

A40

R O A D

HERN

B Y - P A S S

Cement
Works

Marlborough
Pool

Wharf
Farm

ROAD EYNSHAM

Cassington
Mill House

Caravan
Site

RIVER

EVENLODE

I S I S

72

2 10

Ten Acre Copse

W Y T H A M   G R E A T

W O O D

Common Piece

09

Oxford
OX2

Works

Wharf

Stream

WEST OXFORDSHIRE
VALE OF WHITE HORSE

Great
Plain

Swinford
Bridge

Toll

Swinford
Farm

B4044

Swinford

Water
Works

Wytham
Hill

Lords's
Copse

Rough
Common

Reservoir
(Covered)

59

Woodcroft
Copse

ROAD

RIVER THAMES OR

A 47 B 68 C 48 D WOODSTO E

1

Rectory Farm

11

Kidlington OX5

Mead Farm

CHURCH LANE

Kingsbridge

Brook

Loop Farm

Swing bridge

Wolvercote Junction

Witney OX29

Oxey Mead

2

A40

N O R T H E R N   B Y - P A S S

Weir

Duke's Cut

Duke's Lock House

Duke's Cut Lock

CHERWELL WEST OXFORDSHIRE

Duke's Cut Bridges   Wo Ca

Wolvercote Mill Stream

King's Weir

Kingsbridge Brook

Wolvercote Viaduct

Yarnton or West Mead

RIVER THAMES OR ISIS

King's Lock

Lock House

Pixey Mead

CHERWELL B - Y - P -

OXFORD

Wolvercote

3

210

71

Hagley Pool

Seacourt Stream

or

Wytham Stream

Mill Stream Bridge

HOME CLIFFORD PL.

Paper Mill

MILL STREAM CT.   MILL RD.

HU

CLOSE

4

University of Oxford (University Field Station)

WEBBS CT.

MEADOW

PASSAGE

Wytham Mill

Thames Bridge

Wolvercote Bridge

W - E - S - T - E - R - N

GODSTOW

Boat House

P

Wolvercote Bathing Place

5

Woodview

DUNSTAN LANE

Godstow Bridge

Godstow Abbey (rems.)

09

Common Piece

WYTHAM GREAT WOOD

Overford Farm

Rec. Grd.

Wytham

Linch Farm

Godstow Lock

VALE OF WHITE HORSE

WESTERN

OXFORD

Godstow Holt

RIVER THA

6

Hall

Keepers Cottage

The Mount

Wytham Abbey

Home Farm

A34

Black Jack Hole

7

W Y T H A M

P A R K

B Y - P A S S

Church Farm House

Well

Church Grove

08

A 47 B 76 C 48 D ROAD E

Marley Lodge

BINSEY LA

Eaton

F   G   H   69   J   K

49   450   51

1

11

North Oxford Golf Course

A44   Frieze Farm   A4260   FRIEZE   ROAD   A34

Loop Farm Roundabout

Loop Farm

's Canal Bridge

St. Frideswide Farm

OXFORD ROAD   A4165 BANBURY ROAD

Cutteslowe

2

Peartree Hill

Peartree Hill Farm

Oxford Pear Tree Service Area

P+ Pear Tree

Club House

Sports Ground

JORDAN HILL BUS. PK.

LAKE SIDE   LAKE SIDE   LINKSIDE

HASLEMERE GDNS.

Banbury Road North Spts. Grd.

Ten. Cts.

Cutteslowe Park

Cutteslowe Park House

Sports Ground

A34

Red Barn Farm

A44   A40

Wolvercote Cemetery

Linkside Lake

SOLLERSHOTT

Five Mile Drive Rec. Grd.

HAYWARD   RD.

TALBOT   HARBORD   RD.

Templar   PARK CL.

MARRIOTT CL.   BOURNE   CL.

Tennis Cts.

Bowling Grn.

PEN

Putting Grn.

SPARSEY PL.

PRIORS FORGE   A40   3

PRIORY CT.

DAVID WATER CL.   HOLT WEER CL.

3

ercote al Bri.

WOLVERCOTE ROAD

WOODSTOCK ROAD

TRIGG PL.

FIVE MILE DRIVE   RUTHERFORD   KIRK CL.   36   AVENUE 2   SUNDERLAND

QUEEN'S   GATE   CAREY   ROAD

Wolvercote Roundabout

NORTH   WAY   ELSFIELD

HAREFIELDS

Cutteslowe Prim. Sch.

Sunnymead Recreation Ground

74   210   Cherwell Bri.

WKSMOOR   JACKSON   CUTTESLOWE CT.

Goose Green

RANDOLPH

GOODSTOW

MERE

CHURCHILL

FAIRLAWN END   BLANDFORD   CARLTON   SOUTHDALE   WYATT   RD.   WOLSEY   ROAD

BLADON   QUADRANGLE

St. PETER'S   CHURCH LA.

DAVENANT   UPLAND   CAVENDISH   RD.   WENTWORTH RD.   BODLEY CL.

UPLAND PARK RD.   BUCKLER   SCOTT CL.

WATER EATON ROAD

Sunnymead Bathing Place

OX3   4

4

Lower Wolvercote

PLOUGH

Sch.   CYPRESS

BISHOP   KIRK PL.   McCOMBE   McCOMBIE   HYDE   SALISBURY

SUMMERTOWN HO.

APSLEY   MULBERRY   THE PADDOX   RITCHIE   ISLIP PL.   DREW RD.

HERNES   HERNES RD.   HARPES   ROAD   LUCERNE   RD.

KINGS

Sunnymead

Eaton Lodge

RIVER   CHERWELL

Upper Wolvercote

WOODSTOCK DRIVE   A4144

BLENHEIM   WYNDHAM WAY

PADDOX CL.   SQUITCHEY   LANE   CAPEL CL.   THE FIRS

WEST

SUMMERHILL RD.   HOBSON RD.   VICTORIA

ROAD   HAMILTON   PORTLAND   CROSS

HAWKSWELL GDNS.

5

WOLVERCOTE COMMON

RICHARDS LA.   FIELD WAY   HYDE   OSBERTON CT.

GROVE ST.   ROGERS ST.   LONSDALE   Playing Field

Swimming Pool   Tennis Courts

Oxford   OX2

Playing Fields   Pavilion

WOODSTOCK DRIVE   RIDGE WAY   SOUTH   PARADE

St. EDWARDS AV.   Sch.   Lib.   MARSH   PARMOOR   Summer Fields Sch. Pav.   Northern Meadow Farm   09

St. Edward's School Playing Fields   Pav.

St. Edward's School

SUMMERFIELD   EWERT

Summertown

Nature Park

Canal

OXFORD   Esporta Health & Fitness   THE RUSHES   Bowl. Grn.

Playing Fields   Ten. Cts. Pav.

LARK HILL   CLEAR WATER   BEECH CROFT RD.   BRODLEY

Laundry Cottage   The Cherwell School   Playing Field

Ewert House   P   Ferry Sports Centre   B4495 FERRY   RD.

6

PORT MEADOW

Round Hill

COMPLINS GRD.   ELIZABETH   JENNINGS   FRENCHAY   BAINTON   HORNCLIFFE RD.   DIAMOND   DORCHESTER CT.   MARSTON FERRY CT.   Ten. Cts.

OAKTHORPE RD.   OAK   THORPE   MORETON RD.   Coll.   CHARLBURY

MARSTON   Bowl. Grns.   Oxford High Sch.   The Cherwell School   Playing Field

Wolfson College

7

ISIS   OR   Binsey   Manor Farm

HAYFIELD   LANK HILL   BANTON   CHALFONT   ROAD   LATHBURY   Coll.   BELBROUGHTON RD.   NORTHMOOR   GARFORD RD.   Playing Field

St. John's College Sports Grd.   Tennis Courts

MORETON RD.   STAVERTON   ROAD   THACKLEY END   LINTON   ROAD

University Coll. (annexe)   Coll.   RAWLINSON RD.   Dragon Sch.   CHADLINGTON   Pav.

SS Philip & James C of E Prim. Sch.   MURRAY   BARDWELL   Dragon School   Tennis Courts

08

F   G   H   77   J   K   **Park Town**

Binsey   49   450   WILLOW   ST. MARGARET'S   51   St. Hugh's College   NORHAM END

BURGESS   BRINDLEY   ARISTOTLE   KINGSTON   POLSTEAD   Sch.   RD.   BARDWELL   TOWN   BENSON

A   B   144   C   D   E

Parson's Copse

1

11

2

Sports Ground

SOUTH OXFORDSHIRE
CHERWELL

Sescut Farm

Long Wood

Little Wood

3

lowe Sch. 210
Sunnymead Recreation Grou

RIVER CHERWELL

Cherwell Bri.
New Manor Farm
J C Manor

Hill Farm

Cherwell Farm

Marston Common

Manor Ho.

Pennywell Wood

Church Farm

Sunnymead Bathing Pla

4

ELSFIELD WY NORTHERN A40

Hill Farm

Hill View Farm

5

RIVER CHERWELL

Northern Meadow Farm

wimming Pool

Tennis Courts

09

Cumberlege House

WARDS MOBILE HOME PK.

BRADLANDS

ST. NICHOLAS PARK
NEW TOWN WY.

BY-PASS

SOUTH OXFORDSHIRE
OXFORD

MARSTON FERRY B4495

6

Laundry Cottage
The Cherwell School

Playing Field

OX2

Playing Field

The Cherwell School

RADCLIFFE PL.
PONDS LA.
ELSFIELD ROAD
Cemetery

CHURCH LA.
BUTTS
LITTLE ACREAGE

BACK LANE
OXFORD LANE

BARNS HAY
CANNONS
SOUTHCROFT

Marston

Oxford City FC (Court Place Farm Stadium)

Oxrad Sport & Leisure Centre

Adventure Playground

7

Playing Field

Wolfson College

LINTON RD.
Dragn Sch.
CHARLBURY RD.
GARFORD RD.

Pav.

Playing Field

Dragon School

Park Town
NORHAM END

Tennis Courts

St. Nicholas Prim. Sch.

Pupil Referral Unit
Playing Field

Playing Field
Sub.

ROAD CHERWELL DR.

BOULTS CL.
BOULTS LA.
RIMMER CL.
JESSOPS CL.
CLAYS CL.
HORSEMAN

Playing Field

MARSH LANE B4150

Playgrd.
Peasmoor Piece

New Marston Prim Sch.

Northway Spts. Cen.

BORROWMEAD RD.
STOCKLEYS RD.
DORA CA.
MATFIELD
FOXWEL

08

BARDWELL
OCKHAM CT.
Dragon School
BENSON

A   B   78   C   D   E

St. Catherines Sports Ground

Tennis Courts
Tennis Courts

WELL CT.
RIPPINGTON

Rec. Grd.
OLD MARSTON RD.

52   53

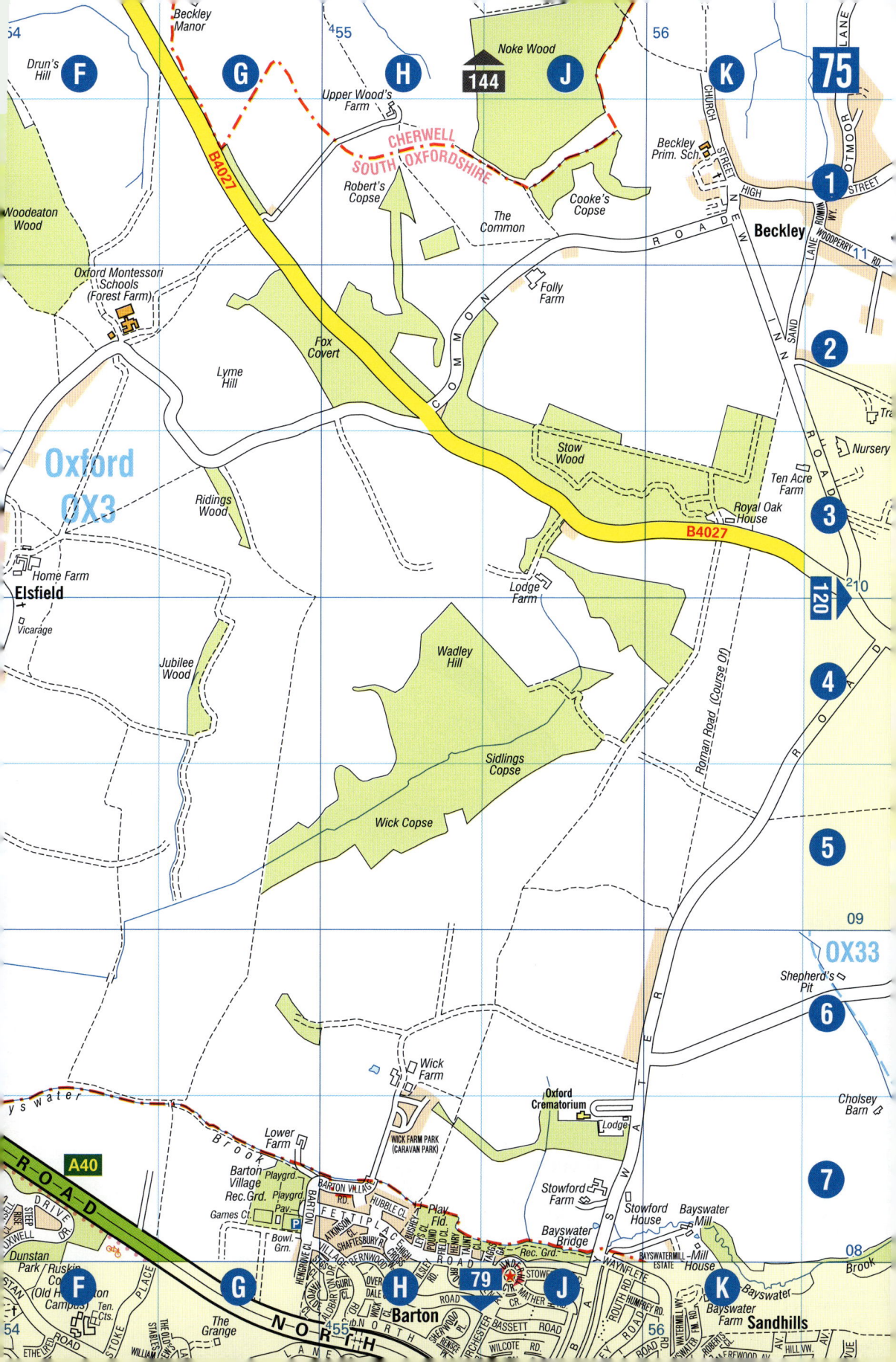

Drun's Hill
F
G
H
Noke Wood
J
K
75
Beckley Manor
455
56
B4027
Upper Wood's Farm
CHERWELL
SOUTH OXFORDSHIRE
Beckley Prim. Sch.
CHURCH STREET
OTMOOR
1
Robert's Copse
Woodeaton Wood
The Common
Cooke's Copse
HIGH
ROMAN WY.
Beckley
WOODPERRY RD.
11
NEW
Oxford Montessori Schools (Forest Farm)
Folly Farm
ROAD
SAND
LANE
INN
2
Tra
Lyme Hill
Fox Covert
COMMON
Nursery
Oxford OX3
Stow Wood
Ten Acre Farm
Royal Oak House
3
B4027
Ridings Wood
ROAD
120
210
Home Farm
Elsfield
Lodge Farm
4
Vicarage
Jubilee Wood
Wadley Hill
Roman Road (Course Of)
5
Sidlings Copse
09
Wick Copse
OX33
Shepherd's Pit
6
WATER
Cholsey Barn
Wick Farm
Oxford Crematorium
Lodge
7
yswater
Brook
Lower Farm
Stowford Farm
Bayswater Mill
Stowford House
Bayswater Mill
08
Wick Farm Park (CARAVAN PARK)
Barton Village Rec. Grd.
Playgrd.
Playgrd. Pav.
Games Ct.
Bowl. Grn.
P
BARTON VILLAS RD.
BARTON
HUBBLE CL.
FETTIPLACE RD.
Play Fld.
ATKINSON CT.
HENRY CL.
SHAFTESBURY RD.
LEYS CL.
POUND CL.
GURL
PIELD CL.
TAWN
Bayswater Bridge
Rec. Grd.
Stowford Bridge
BAYSWATER MILL
ESTATE
Mill House
Bayswater Farm
Brook
A40
Dunstan Park / Ruskin College (Old Headington Campus)
ROAD
DRIVE
STEEP
STREET
DXWELL
Ten. Cts.
F
G
STOKE PLACE
H
79
J
K
Sandhills
The Grange
Barton
NORTH
LANE
54
455
56
ETHE
WILLIAM
ROAD
STABLES
HENWOOD DR.
ALDBRICK RD.
WICK RD.
VILLAGE RD.
BERNWOOD RD.
OVERDALE
SHEPPARD PL.
SND
CHICHESTER
WILCOTE RD.
BASSETT ROAD
MATHER
STOWFORD CR.
ROUTH RD.
HUMPHREY RD.
BRAY
WATERMILL WY.
WATERMILL
ROBERTS CL.
FREWOOD AV.
HILL VW.
VUE

A B C D E

WYTHAM PARK

Church Farm House
Church Grove Well

1

Marley Lodge

MARLEY WOOD

Marleywood Plantation

Bowlingalley Plantation

2 The Plantation

The Plantation

07 **59**

Cowleaze Copse

Hill End (Field Studies Centre)

Higgin's Copse

OX2

Botley Lodge

A34

Seacourt or Wytha

3 Bean Wood

Hill End Farm House

Tilbury Farm

Tilbury Cottages

TILBURY

A420

BOTLEY INTERCHANGE

Playing Field

Botley Primary & Elms Road Nursery Schools

Superstores

SEACOURT TOWER

HINKSEY BUSINESS CENTRE

OLD BOTLEY WALLBRO CT.

Bo Bri

A420

B4044

WA

Cammoor Copse

Stimpson's Copse

Stimpson's Cottages

HILL BY-PASS

STIMPSONS CL.

STONE CL.

FOGWELL ROAD

POTTLE CL.

HOMESTALL

BUSHY CL.

DEANFIELD RD.

OWLINGTON LANE

BROAD CL.

SEACOURT ROAD

HAZEL RD. POPLAR RD. ELMS RD.

ELMS CT. CHURCH

BOTLEY

Li

THE SQUARE

Cerny.

CONIFER CL.

E 4 EYNSHAM

B4044

Red House Farmhouse

Noble's Farm Cotts.

EYNSHAM RD.

NOBLES RD.

TUDOR COURT PARK

CT.

GRANGE CT.

FOGWELL RD.

LODGE CL.

100

ROAD WEST

EVELYN RD.

ELMS RISE

GOINGS

11

SPRINGFIELD RD.

HUTCHCOMBE RD.

CONN RD.

ARTHRAY

PAUL'S CL.

FINMORE RD.

ROAD GARTH

CRABTREE RD.

THE

MAPLE CL.

THE CRO

06 205

5 Dean Court

CUMNOR

ORCHARD RD.

DEAN TON

STURDE

BROWNS CL.

GREENLA CL.

PINNOCKS

PINNOCKS

SONGERS

QUEENS CL.

THIRD ACRE RISE

ARNOLDS WAY

STANVILLE RD.

HUTCHCOMBE FARM CL.

CUMNOR RISE

HUTCHCOMB RD.

MONTAGU CL.

TOYNBEE CL. CL.

HAWTHORN RD.

CEDAR

CHESTNUT

LABURNUM

LARCH CL.

CHERRY

BEECH ROAD

SYCA RD. MORE RD.

YARNELLS ROAD

SWEE

Denman's Farm **143**

Hid's Copse

DEAN COURT RD.

Hutchcomb's Copse

Play. Fld.

LIME WAY

6 Ash Copse

Hid's Brake

HID'S COPSE RD.

CUM

DELAMARE WY.

THE CEDARS

HURST RISE

SCHOLAR PL.

BARN CL.

HALLS

Matthew Arnold Sch.

Cumnor Hill

Tennis Cts.

Pav.

Play. Fld.

Playing Field

Dene House

(Oxford Westmin of E

Tennis Cts.

Harcourt Hill Leisure Centre

Playing Field

Well Yard Copse

7 **A420** **59**

CHAWLEY

Bornholm Farm

Chawley

Chawley Farm

Long Copse

COLEGROVE DOWN

HILLSIDE

CUM

COTSWOLD RD.

TURNPIKE

CLOVER

HURST LANE

Mills

Timber Yard **82**

NORREY

CUMNOR C of E Primary School

SANDS CT.

ERTIE

ROAD CUMNOR

HURST HILL

Hurst

A B C D E

47 48

OXFORD

Oxford

OX1

Binsey

Manor Farm
Binsey Green
The Limes
The Grove
The Lodge
Boat Houses
Medley Manor Farm
Rainbow Bridge
Port Meadow
Fiddler's Island
The Golf Driving Range
Trading Estate
New Botley
King George's Field
Oatlands Rec. Grd.
Playing Field
Osney
North Hinksey Village
North Hinksey Prim. Sch.
Manor Farm
Raleigh Park
The Fold
Conduit House
Harcourt Hill
Sports Ground
Sports Ground
Nature Reserve

RIVER THAMES or ISIS

Castle Stream
Mill Stream

BOTLEY ROAD
A420

BY-PASS
A34
ROAD

VALE OF WHITE HORSE

SS Philip & James C of E Prim. Sch.
University Coll. (Annexe)
School
St. Margaret's
Walton Manor
St. Hugh's College
Norham Manor
University Parks
Observatory
Laboratories
Radcliffe Infirmary
Somerville College
Green College
Keble Coll.
St. Anne's Coll.
St. Antony's Coll.
St. Benet's Hall Coll.
Jericho
Oxford Uni. Press
Worcester College
Ruskin College
Beaumont St.
Balliol College
Trinity College
St. John's College
Rhodes Ho.
Nuffield Coll.
Manchester Coll.
The Music Room
St. Giles
Banbury Road
Woodstock Road
A4165
A4144

Oxford
Park End Street
New Osney
Hythe Bridge Street
Oxford Castle
Westgate
Pembroke College
Christ Church College
Corpus Christi College
The Bate Collection
Oxford Business College
Grandpont
Grandpont Park
Grandpoint Nurs. Sch.
Cricket Ground
Tennis Courts
Sports Ground
Tennis Cts.
Hinksey Park
Swim. Pool
Lady Margaret Hall
Soc. of the Sacred Heart
Dept. of Educ. Studies
Oxford University Cricket Club (The Parks)
Pitt Rivers Museums
R. THAMES
Oxford Ice Rink
Oxford Business Centre
Littlemead Bus. Pk.
Kings Meadow Ind. Est.
The Kings Centre
Osney Mead Industrial Estate
Bulstake

ABINGDON ROAD
A4144 ROAD
A205

South Hinksey
Hinksey Hill Farm
HINKSEY HEIGHTS GOLF COURSE
Club House
Raleigh Park

P+ Seacourt

78

OXFORD

OX1 · OX2 · OX4

Park Town
Dragon School
Lady Margaret Hall
Norham Manor
Soc. of the Sacred Heart
Dept. of Educ. Studies
Oxford University Cricket Club (The Parks)
UNIVERSITY PARKS
Observatory
Laboratories
Keble Coll.
University Museum & Pitt-Rivers Museum
Rhodes Ho.
Mansfield Coll.
Wadham Coll.
St. John's College
Trinity College
Balliol
Linacre Coll.
New College Sports Ground
Music Meadow
Great Meadow
St. Catherine's College
St. Cross College
Magdalen Grove
Magdalen Coll.
Deer Park
Angel & Greyhound Meadow
HIGH STREET
A420
Merton College
Christ Church Cathedral
Corpus Christi College
The Bate Collection
CHRIST CHURCH MEADOW
Oxford Business Coll.
Botanic Gardens
Merton Field
St. Hilda's Coll.
Magdalen College Sch.
Christ Church Sports Ground
Oxford University Sports Complex
Rugby Football Ground
Greyfriars
Cricket Ground
Sports Ground
ABINGDON ROAD
A4144
Hinksey Park
Eastwyke Farm
Boating Club
Astons Eyot
Iffley Fields
Boat House
Long Bridges Bathing Place
University College Sports Grd.
New Hinksey
DONNINGTON BRI. RD.
B4495
WEIRS LA.
Boat House
Donnington Spts. Cen.
St. Gregory

New Marston
St. Catherines Sports Ground
Exeter College Sports Grd.
Hertford College Sports Ground
Park Farm
Rec. Croft Grd.
Playing Field
Tennis Courts
Trinity College Sports Ground
Magdalen College Sports Ground
Fellows Garden
Long Meadow
King's Mill La.
River Cherwell
Addison's Walk
MARSTON
Bathing Place
Mesopotamia
Holywell
CHERWELL DR.
74

CHERWELL

HEADLEY WAY
Oxford Children's Hospital
Northway Spts. Cen.
New Marston Prim. Sch.
Peasmoor Piece
Prim. School
Jack Straw's Lane
Headington
Cotuit Hall
Rye St. Antony School
St. Michael's C of E Prim. Sch.
Pullens Field
Pollock House
Richard Hamilton Bldg.
Government Buildings
Halls of Residence
Headington Sch.
Student Centre
Headington Hill Hall
Headington Hill Park
Harcourt House
Cheney Student Village
Headington Hill
SOUTH PARK
Oxford Brookes University
OBU Cen. for Sport
Cheney Sch.
Playing Field
A420 HEADINGTON ROAD
MORRELL AVENUE
Warneford
WARNEFORD HOSPITAL
Cricket Ground
Southfield Park
Oriel College Sports Ground
Southfield Golf Course
Barracks La.
Oxford Comm. Sch.
COWLEY ROAD
ST. CLEMENT'S ST.
East Oxford Prim. Sch.
Pembroke St.
St. Stephen's Ho.
St. James's Ho.
Hughes
Convent
Hospices
Conv.
Larkrise School
St. Gregory The Great Catholic Sch.
Florence Park
Bowl. Grns.
B480
IFFLEY ROAD
COWLEY ROAD
HENLEY ROAD
A4158 IFFLEY ROAD
Renault
DONNINGTON BRI. RD.
Thtre.
Comm. Cen.
Playgrd.
RADCLIFFE RD.
CORNWALLIS RD.

OXFORD

OX4

Florence Park

A40 NORTH WAY

Barton

LONDON ROAD

EASTERN

Sandhills

Risinghurst

JOHN RADCLIFFE HOSPITAL

Ruskin College (Old Headington Campus)

Dunstan Park

Bury Knowle Park

A420

A40 Thornhill

Nielsen House

Rowlands Ho.

Headington Quarry

Quarry Recreation Ground

Windmill Prim. Sch.

Nature Reserve

NUFFIELD ORTHOPAEDIC CENTRE

Reservoir (covered)

The Oaks Oak Apple

Monk's Wood

Monk's Farm

Oxford

PARK HOSP.

New Headington

Wood Farm Prim. & Slade Nursy. Schs.

Shotover Edge

Shotover Hill

SHOTOVER COUNTRY PARK

CHURCHILL HOSPITAL

Hospice

The Fulbrook Centre

Open Magdalen Wood

Open Magdalen Wood

Nature Pk.

Shotover Cleve

Westhill Farm

FIELD GOLF COURSE

SLADE

A4142

Brasenose Wood

Open Brasenose

HOLLOW WAY

B4495

Cowley Marsh

Horspath

SOUTH OXFORDSHIRE OXFORD

Brasenose Farm

Bullingdon Green

Temple Cowley

St. Francis C of E Prim. Sch.

Superstore

BY-PASS

HORSPATH ROAD INDUSTRIAL ESTATE

ISIS BUSINESS CENTRE

Horspath Athletics Grd.

OXFORD ROAD

Cowley

Tennis Courts

Sports Ground

Bowling Green

A   Brook   B   ▲ 144   C   58   D   Minchin Court Farm   E

08   Baywater   STANTON   END
r   Bayswater   Polecat La.
 Farm   Rec. Grd.   Sewage Works
MICKLE WY.

Sandhills
1   HILL VW.   Sandhills Primary School   Forest Hill
EREWOOD   BURDELL   AVENUE   MILTON CR.   RD.   WHEATLEY
MEREWOOD   DELBUSH   SWEET   Manor Farm   BADGER CL.   POWELL CL.
HOSTER   BURSILL   ELTON   TERRACE   GRN. CL.   Cemy.
DARLINGTON   CL.   L O N D O N   A40   Forest Hill House   B4027
Nielsen House   Sub.   Thornhill   Sun Trap
2   ROWLANDS   P+   Red Hill Farm   R
HO.   Tennis Courts   Swilly   Thornhill Farm   O
Risinghurst   A

07   Sports Ground   D
Pav.

OX3   Thorn Hill   Obelisk   Shotover House   Fish Ponds

3   Monk's Wood   The Spinney   Greenlane Clump   **Oxford**
0   ◄ 79   Home Farm
Monk's Farm   Forest Farm   Wheatley Pr
4   Shotover Hill   John Watson & Wheatley M Schools
P   Shotover Plain   Ochre Pits   The Common
06   Shotover Cleve   R O A D   O L D   R O A D   LITTLEW
hotover Cleve   SHOTOVER COUNTRY PARK   KEYDALE   BARR OW
5   Piggery   ACREMEAD   ROAD   ROW   LITTLEW & BUS. CEN.
KELLY'S   LITTLEWORTH
Westhill Farm   Horspath Common   SANDY   **Littleworth**
6   S   A
BLENHEIM WY.   **Horspath**   N
SPRING   LANE   PROSPECT PARK   D   Y   W A Y   WINDMILL
COLLEGE WY.   Sch   BUTTS   L   CENTRE   Green Gates
MANOR RD.   FORDS CL.   WRIGHTSON   COLCUTT CL.   A   HILL RISE
CHURCH RD.   CL.   MANOR   ROAD   N   SUNNY RISE   VALLEY RD.
7   Cycle Track   THE GREEN   E   HORSEPATH PARK CARAVAN SITE   COWPER CL.
Horspath Athletics Grd.   Football Grd.   Rec. Grd.   BUTLER CL.
OX4   Hall   ROAD   C U D D E S D O N
O X F O R D   R O A D   Brook

A   Sewage Works   B   ▼ 144   C   D   R O A D   E   Old Horspath Farm
57   Hollow   58   Hill Farm

Parson's Farm

Holton Wood

Warren Farm

Warren Wood

Pond Farm

Buryhook Corner

Holton

Cottage Copse

Rec. Grd.

A40

Wheatley Park School

Barns Close

The Rectory

Holton Place

Church Farm Barns

Lib.

The Park Sports Cen.

John Watson Sch. (Sen. Site)

Old House

Church Farm House

4

06

Tennis Courts

Games Courts

Oxford Brookes University (Wheatley Campus)

Garden Copse

Playing Field

Ten. Cts.

COLLEGE CLOSE

Playing Field

...Jun. ...rsy.

BLENHIEM... Youth Cen.

WESTFIELD RD. PARK HILL WESTFD RD. GARDNER LA. HOLLOWAY

ST. MARY'S HO.

ST. MARY'S CL. THE GLEBE

FAIRFAX GA.

WHEATLEY BUS. CEN.

BISCOE CT.

SUNNY-SIDE

TYWOOD CL.

Holton Mill Bungalow

Holton Mill House

Holton Mill Cottage

5

121

CL.

WHEATLEY

HIGH STREET

Lib.

HATHWY'S WREN

CROWN SQ.

THE OLD TRIANGLE

ANSON CL.

AMBROSE PL.

AMBROSE RISE

CULLUM HO.

CULLUM RD.

LETSOM WY.

MILLER RD.

THE AVENUE

LONDON ROAD

A40

Littleworth Park Caravan Site

SIMON'S CL.

FARM CL.

STATION RD.

CHURCH RD.

CL.

KELHAM HALL DR.

HOWE CL.

KIMBER BEECH CLOSE

FRIDAY LA.

NEW BERRY DR.

CROWN

ORCHARD CL.

JACKIES LA. ELM CL.

ROMAN ROAD

ELTON CRES.

HILLARY WY.

WINDOWS CT.

THE ROAD

Wheatley Bridge

Wheatley Bri. Fm.

Amilla House

The ...undout

OX33

BISHOPS CL.

Dymock

Coombe House

Castle Hill Farm

Builder's Yard

Sewage Works

New Barn

Castle Hill

D205

ASHURST CT. L.

SWORFORD LANE

RIVER

6

6

7

LADDER LANE HILL

Coombe Wood

THAME

A   **B**   **C**   **D**   **E**

1   **2**   **3**   **4**   **5**   **6**   **7**

Chawley

47   48

Bornholm Farm
Chawley Farm
Long Copse
Leisure Centre
Playing Field

76

Mills
Timber Yard

Cumnor C of E Primary School

NORREYS ROAD
BERTIE ROAD
OXFORD
OXFORD RD
ABINGDON
SANDS CL
GLEBE ROAD

04

A420

59

CUMNOR ROAD

OX2

HURST HILL
Hurst Cottage
Cumnor Folly

Camp HQ
Powder Hill Copse
Hen Wood
Powder Hill House
Chilswell House (Carmelite Priory)
Birch Copse

YOULBURY WOOD
Youlbury Scout Camp
Youlbury

Cross Roads Farm
KENIL WORTH FORSTER LA
PL

Bradley Farm

203

WHITEBARN
Youlbury House

Oxford

FARINGDON

A420

Henwood Farm

RIDGEWAY LANE

Signal Elm House

BEDWELLS

Henwood
B4017
WHITE HILL LA
White Hill Farm
Little Bradley Farmhouse
HILL VIEW LA

Mayo's Farm
Stone's Farm

SANDY LANE
ORCHARD LA
BOARS HILL

Jarn Mound
Jarn Wild Gardens
Boars Hill Heath
Blackthorn
Foxco He

02

143

Wootton Village
Wootton C of E Prim. Sch.
Reservoirs (Covered)
Middle Farm

JARN WAY

BESSELSLEIGH
ROAD

Depot
149
132

Wootton Business Park
DEERHURST PK
LEIGH CFT
BEECH CL
MANOR RD

WOOTTON
52 A9D

ROAD

OLD BOARS HILL

Pav. Play Fld.
P
Plygrd.
HOME CL
HOME

Abingdon
OX13
LASHFORD LANE
Nature Reserve
Playing Field Plygrd.
SANDLEIGH RD
BERRYMERE RD
COUP
WATSON
MITCHELL
LAMBOROUGH HILL
Comm. Cen. Sports Ten. Cts.
LANSDOWNE RD
ARTHUR
MATHEWS

86

THE
SAV
SMITH

FOX

47   48

01

A   **B**   **C**   **D**   **E**

F Harcourt Hill
G
H SOUTHERN
77
J
K
1 Cold Harbour

Nature Reserve
Hinksey Hill Farm
Club House
A34
South Hinksey
THE DEVIL'S BACKBONE
VALE OF WHITE HORSE
OXFORD
Pav.
Bowl. Grns.
SUNNINGWELL RD.
LINCOLN RD.
MONMOUTH RD.
NORTHAMP RD.
JOHN TOWLE CL. STH.
Playt

HINKSEY HEIGHTS GOLF COURSE
Hinksey Hill Cottages
MANOR CL. CHURCH CL. ST. LAWRENCE RD. SILVER RD. JOHN LL. PRINCES RD. BAILEY COTT LA.
ABINGDON
2
RED BRIDGE HOLLOW CARAVAN SITE
RED BRIDGE
SOUTHERN BY-PASS RD.

Chilswell Lodge
PATH
BY-PASS ROAD
HINKSEY HILL INTERCHANGE
A423
Egrove Cottage
A34
84
203
Rec. Grd.

Chilswell Copse
CHILSWELL
Chilswell Farm
BETTY LANE
HILL LANE
SPRING COPSE
BADGER LANE
Bagley Croft
3 Templeton College
Spring Copse
ABINGDON

Limekiln Copse
CHILSWELL LANE
HINKSEY HILL ROAD
OXFORD ROAD
Westwood House
Hangman's Bottom
BAGLEY WOOD
Bottom Copse
Colley's Ladder West
Colle
4
BY-PASS

Chilswell Farm Cottages
RED COPSE LA.
WEST WOOD
Middle Hill
5 Watery Brake
Und

OX1
Yatscombe Copse
FOXCOMBE LA.
HAMELS LANE
BAYWORTH LANE
Cow Hall Bottom
Watery Brake Gate Piece
Three Corner Piece
West Middle Copse
East Middle Copse

Foxcombe Hill
BERKELEY ROAD
FOXCOMBE LANE
Brumcombe Copse
Duckling Copse
Woodcraft Wood
Laud's Copse
Bagley Wood Sawmill
Farringdon Gap
6
Old Peg

Boars Hill
Foxcombe Hill
LINCOMBE LA.
BAYWORTH MOBILE HOME PARK
Manor Farm
Old Man's Piece
Bagley Wood
Milestone Piece
Sunningwell Bottom
WOOD ROAD
7 Lower Sug Copse

Oxford Preservation Trust
Bayworth
OX13
SUNNINGWELL RD.
QUARRY RD.
BRUMCOMBE LANE
GREEN LANE
Chandlings Manor School
BAGLEY WOOD ROAD
Upper Sugworth Copse
A34
ABINGDON

F
G
H
87
J
K
Sunningwell
SUGWORTH

84

A **B** **78** **C** **D** **E**

University College Sports Grd.

Long Bridges Bathing Place

Iffley Fields FAIRACRES

St. Gregory The Great Catholic Sch.

1

New Hinksey

ABINGDON DONNINGTON BRI. DONNINGTON

WEIRS LA. B4495

Florence Park

Bowl. Grns. Playgrd.

Cold Harbour

Boat House

Donnington Spts. Grd.

St. Gregory The Great Catholic Sch.

Iffley Mead Sch.

CORNWALLIS

LYTTON ROAD

OUTRAM RD.

Mus.

TURN LEFT

CHURCH COWLEY RD. B4495

2

Red Bridge Hollow Caravan Site

RED BRIDGE

Red Bridge

KENNINGTON ROUNDABOUT

Boat House

Iffley Lock

Bakers

ABBERBURY

Iffley

Rose Hill Cemetery

Oxford

Rose Hill

WESTBURY CRES.

WESTBURY CR.

KELBURNE

MAYFAIR

FAIRLIE

SOUTHERN

A423

Egrove Cottage

HINKSEY HILL INTERCHANGE

EAST CHURCH

Playing Field

Rose Hill Primary School

LITTLEMORE ROUNDABOUT

EASTERN

NEWMAN

3

ABINGDON

83

A423

Templeton College

Kennington Junction

BY-PASS ROAD

SOUTH

Sewage Works

EASTERN BY-PASS ROAD

A4142

Superstore

HEYFORD HILL ROUNDABOUT

E-A-S-T

OXFORD

Prim. Sch.

4

BAGLEY WOOD

A34

Colley's Ladder West

Colley's Ladder East

BLACKMAN CL.

EDWARD RD.

Rose Isle

VALE OF WHITE HORSE

RIVER

HEYFORD HILL

OXFORDSHIRE

SANDFORD

LITTLEMORE MENTAL HEALTH CEN.

Yamanouchi Research Institute Sports Grd.

Littlemore Park

THE OXFORD SCIENCE P

5

Watery Brake

Under Woods

COW LANE

RIVER VIEW

OTTERS REACH

THAMES

Fiddler's Elbow

ARMSTRONG

Orchard House

6

Three Corner Piece

West Middle Copse

East Middle Copse

St. Swithun's C of E Prim. Sch.

MEADOW VIEW ROAD

KENNINGTON

SIMPSONS WAY

Sandford Pool

Sandford-on-Thames

LINK

A4074

7

Lower Sugworth Copse

Old Peg Brake

BAGLEY WOOD ROAD

Sports Ground

Recreation Ground

THE PADDOCK

Cemetery

SANDFORD

CHURCH LANE

ISIS

Abingdon OX14

Woodlands Park

PEBBLE HILL MOBILE HOME PARK

Sandford Lane Industrial Estate

Lower Farm Cotts.

A **B** **88** **C** **D** **E**

Radley Large Wood

52   53

Map grid references

F · Cowley · G · H · 79 · J · K

Temple Cowley Prim. Sch.
Temple Cowley Pools
B480
B4495
Oxford Business Park North
Cowley
HOLLOW WAY
GARSINGTON ROAD
Templars Retail Park
A4142 WAY
Oxford Business Park
David Lloyd Leisure
Oxford Business Park South
BY-PASS
ROAD WATLINGTON
OX4
Church Cowley C of E Prim. Sch.
Recreation Ground
Ambassador
Oxford Retail Park
Works
Oxford Stadium
Chiltern Bus. Cen.
County Trading Estate
Cowley Bus Centre
TRANSPORT
OXFORD ROAD
MOTOR WORKS
Works
144 Warehouse 04
WAY
Horspath Road Industrial Estate 56
Isis Business Centre
Horspath Athletics Grd.
ROAD
Tennis Courts
Sports Ground
Bowling Green Pav.
Northfield Farm
Guydens Farm
B480
Sandy Lane Rec. Grd.
Indoor Bowl. Cen.
Peers Sports Cen.
Peers School
Nuffield Industrial Estate
Littlemore
Depot
Tennis Courts
Playing Fields
SANDY LANE
BLACKBIRD
Schs.
Blackbird Leys Pre-Sch.
Blackbird Leys Park
College
Blackbird Leys
Lib. Blackbird Leys Leisure Cen.
Evenlode Tower
Windale Ho.
Pegasus Prim. Sch.
SORREL ROAD
BLACKBERRY ROAD
JUNIPER DRIVE
Northfield Sch.
Spindlebury Nature Park
Northfield
Windale Brook First Sch.
Ozone Leisure & Entertainment Park
Oxford United FC (Kassam Stadium)
GRENOBLE ROAD
Sewage Works
Tenacre Caravan Site
Works
Depot
126
Northfield 203
OX44
Sandford Brake
Sandfordbrake Farm
Bushy Copse
Manor House
Toot Baldon

F · G · H · 89 · J · K
54 · 55 · 56

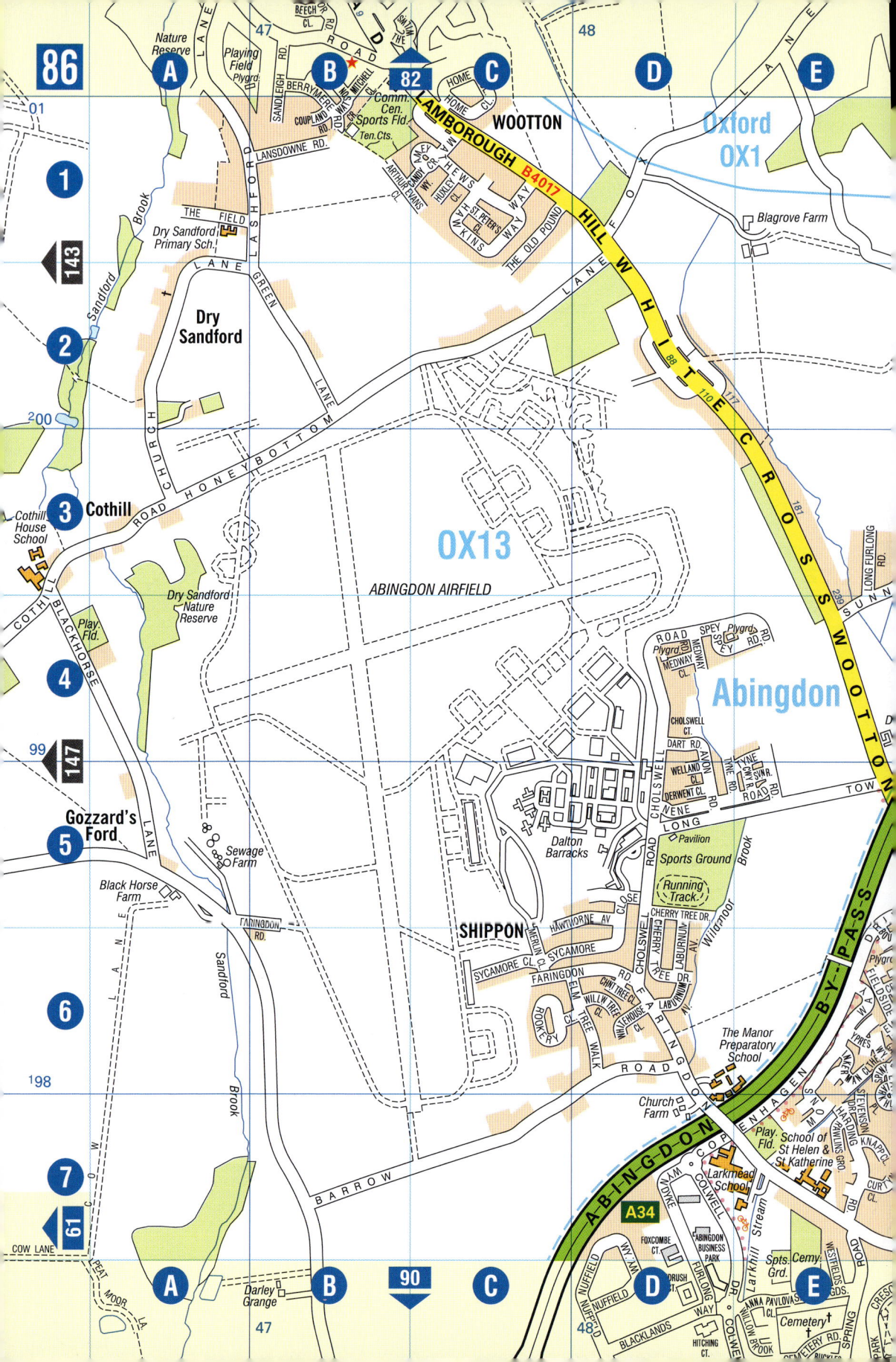

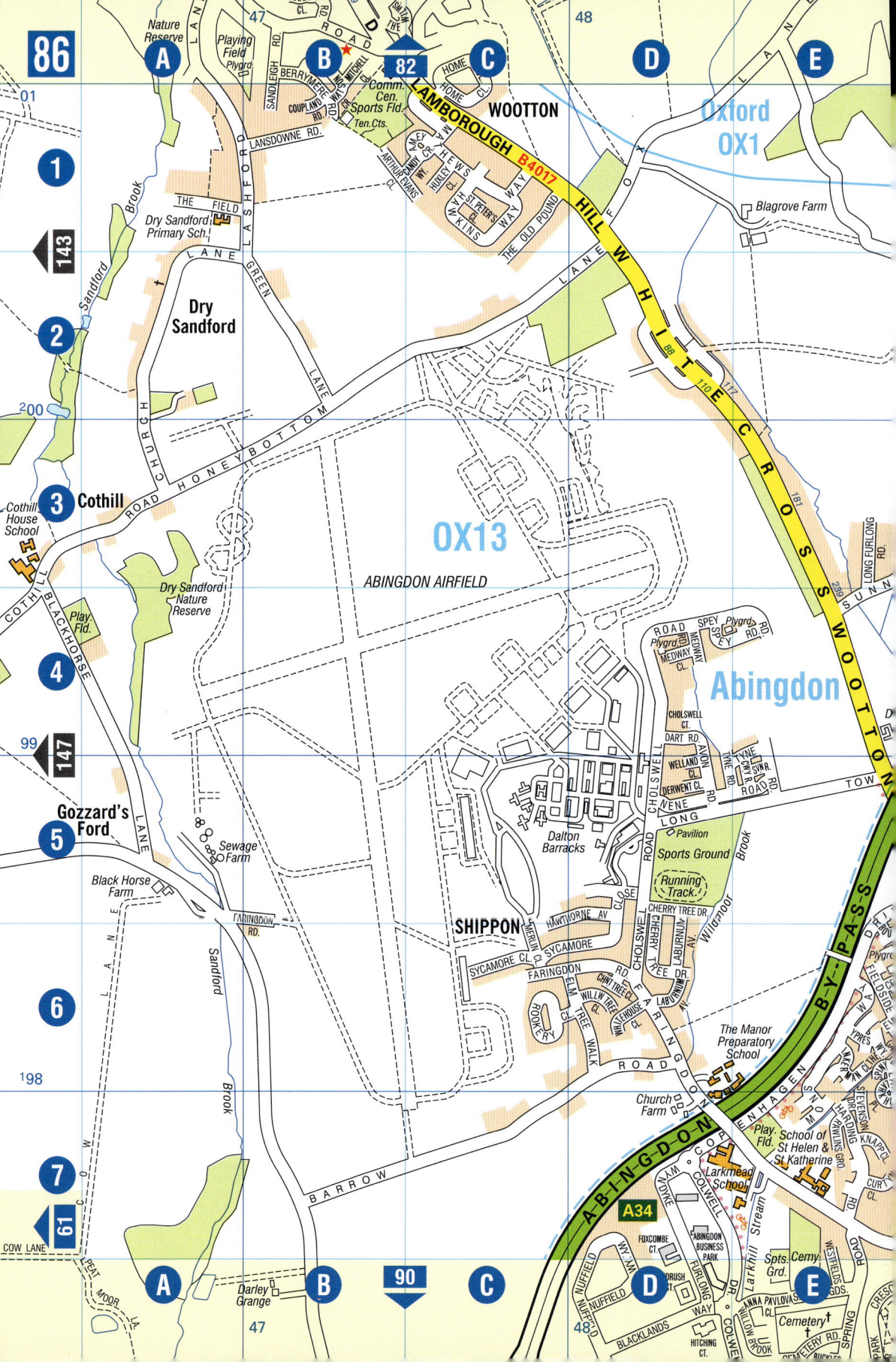

A B C D E

47
48

Nature Reserve
Playing Field
Plygd

BEECH CL.
ROAD
SANDLEIGH RD.
WAY
MITCHELL
WAYS
COUPLAND RD.
BERRYMERE RD.

82

HOME CL.
HOME CL.

WOOTTON

Oxford OX1

01

1

◄ 143

LANSDOWNE RD.

Comm. Cen.
Sports Fld.
Ten. Cts.

LAMBOROUGH
B4017

HILL

ARTHUR EVANS CL.
ST PETER'S RD.
HAWKINS WY.
ANDY HUXLEY WAY
MATHEWS
ANDY
HAWKINS
THE OLD POUND

FOX LANE

WHITE

Blagrove Farm

THE FIELD
Dry Sandford Primary Sch.

LASHFORD

GREEN LANE

CHURCH

LANE

Dry Sandford

2

200

LANE

HONEYBOTTOM

86

110

117

CROSS

3 Cothill
Cothill House School

ROAD

OX13

ABINGDON AIRFIELD

181

WOOTTON

COTHILL

BLACKHORSE

Dry Sandford Nature Reserve
Play Fld.

ROAD
SPEY
SPEY
RD.
Plygrd
Plygrd
MEDWAY CL.
MEDWAY

Abingdon

4

99
◄ 147

CHOLSWELL CT.
DART RD.
WELLAND CL.
AVON CL.
TYNE RD.
SWN R.
TYNE

DERWENT CL.

CHOLSWELL ROAD
NENE

ROAD

LONG

TOW

Gozzard's Ford

5

Sewage Farm

Dalton Barracks

Pavilion
Sports Ground

Running Track

Wildmoor Brook

Black Horse Farm

BY-PASS

6

FARINGDON RD.

SHIPPON

HAWTORNE AV.
SYCAMORE
MERLIN CL.
CLOSE
CHERRY TREE DR.
CHERRY TREE DR.
CHERRY TREE DR.
LABURNUM AV.

SYCAMORE CL.
FARINGDON
ELM TREE CL.
WILLOW TREE WALK
CHNT TREE CL.
ROOKERY

LANE

COW

Sandford Brook

ROAD

FARINGDON

The Manor Preparatory School

FIELDSIDE

PRES
WY
AM
NFLUE
NUFFIELD
STEVENSON RD.
HARDING RD.
PAWLINS GRO.
KNAP CL.
CURT CL.

198

Church Farm

Play Fld.
School of St Helen & St Katherine

7

61 ◄

COW LANE

BARROW

COPENHAGEN

Larkmead School

Foxcombe CT.
NUFFIELD WY.
AM DYKE
COLWELL

A34

ABINGDON BUSINESS PARK

ANNA PAVLOVAS
DR.
Larkhill Stream

DRUSH
FURLONG

Spts. Grd.

Cemy

PEAT MOOR

Darley Grange

90

Cemetery

WY AM
NUFFIELD

BLACKLANDS
WAY

HITCHING CL.

ANNA PAVLOVAS
COLWELL BROOK

CEMETERY RD.
SPRING

WESTFIELDS
ROAD
RD.
GDNS.
CRES.

A B C D E

47
48

OX1

Bayworth
Preservation Trust
Upper Sugworth Copse
Lower Sugworth Copse
Chandlings Manor Sch.
Piece

1

SUGWORTH LANE
OXFORD ROAD
A34
BY-PASS

Sunningwell
Sunningwell C of E Prim. Sch.
Pav.
Ckt. Grd.
BILL SMEAD
BEAULIEU COURT
DARK LA.
PEN LANE
GREEN LANE
QUARRY RD.
LINCOMBE LANE

Lodge Hill Interchange

2
200
RADLEY PARK
RADLEY GOLF COURSE

ABINGDON ROAD
A4183
OXFORD ROAD

PEN LA.
Depot

3

88

Long Furlong House
A34

4
Peach Croft Farm

Tilsley Park (Sports Park)
Multi-Purpose Sports Pitches

ABINGDON
OX14

99

Prim. Sch.
Spts. Fld.

PRINCE GRO. DRIVE
LOVELACE
BALLARD CHASE
HANSON RD.
ROSE GN.
KNOLLY'S CL.
GIBSON CL.
CULLERNE CL.
BOULTER
ALEXANDER
HANSON RD.
ROSE GN.
LANGLEY
FRANKLIN
SPENLOVE
ELDRIDGE
KYSBIE CL.
EATON RD.
HILLVIEW RD.
SOUTH AVENUE
WEST AV.
NORTH AVENUE
EDEN CL.
NORTHFIELD CL.
LLOYD CL.
MANDE-VILLE CL.
WHEATCROFT CL.
PICKLERS HILL
SUMMER
MATTOCK WAY
TWELVE ACRE
HUNTER
FIELDWAY
CHILDREY WY.
COMPTON
THISTLE
BOXWELL
TIFFORD
CARSE
FELTON
BOREFORD RD.
PEACHCROFT

PEACHCROFT CEN.
Rec. Grd.
Northcourt
ELIZABETH AV.
BROOK
STOCKEY END
RADLEY DRIVE
BARROW HILL CL.
NORRIS CL.
CHAMPS CL.
CORN
HOUND
REGISTERS LA.

5

ABINGDON
OX14
A4183
OXFORD ROAD

DUNMORE
FARM
AUSTIN
BENSON
PARSONS
BEVERLEY
BOXHILL
NORTHCOURT RD.
SELLWOOD RD.
HOLLAND RD.
PICKLERS HILL
WELFORD
BUSCOT DR.
KENNET
UPTON
CHILTON CL.
HENDRED
WINDRUSH
ISIS CL.
ME CL.
HAMBLE CL.
ST. PETER'S RD.
HEDGEHOG CL.
THE COPSE
CHESTNUT
HENSON
Football Fld.
Cycle Track
RADLEY

6

B4017
Fitzharrys School
Jun. Sch.
Dunmore Infant Sch.
Wildmoor
Abingdon & Witney College
Comm. Cen.
Northcourt
Football Grd.
APPLEFORD
RUSH COMMON PRIM. SCH.
CHERWELL
CAM
Radley Road Industrial Estate
SEWELL
GARDINER

198

Wick Hall

John Mason School
Ind. Est.
Depot
BRAMPTON CL.
THORNHILL WK.
SPRINGFIELD DR.
SOUTHMOOR WY.
FULWELL
St. Nicholas C of E Sch.
CHEYNEY WK.
STANILAND
BOXHILL
GEOFFREY BARBOUR RD.
Rec. Grd.
ABBOTT RD.
FOUNTAIN CT.
NORMAN AVENUE
SWINBURNE
WARWICK
BAILEY
DAISY
SAFFRON
RAMSONS
THE MARES
MARCHAM
PORTWAY
DUNMORE
BROADWAY
OLD FARM CL.
MINCHIN
MERTON

7

Industrial Estate
Thrupp House

Playing Flds.
Pav.
FITZHARRYS RD.
CLIFTON DR.
KINGSTON
WERNHAM
WILLIAMS
St. Edmund's Catholic Prim. Sch.
Rec. Grd.
Conv. Schs.
Ten. Cts. A
Schs.
Comm. Cen.
HADLAND
DEXTON
LEY
AUDLETT
HERMITAGE
WELLS
HOBBS
ELWES
DUNDAS
HAMMERS
WITTENHAM
White Horse Leisure & Tennis Centre
Science Park
THE QUADRANT
NAPIER CT.
THE PENTAGON
LANE

VINEYARD
BATH ROAD
B4017 ST.
OXFORD A4183
STERT ST.

Abingdon School
Albert Park
Pav.
Bowl. Grn.
Supermarket
Works
Thames View Industrial Park
Abbey
Crazy
Works
Playground
Crabtree
Barton
Sherwood
Farriers
Abbey Close
Library
Broad St.

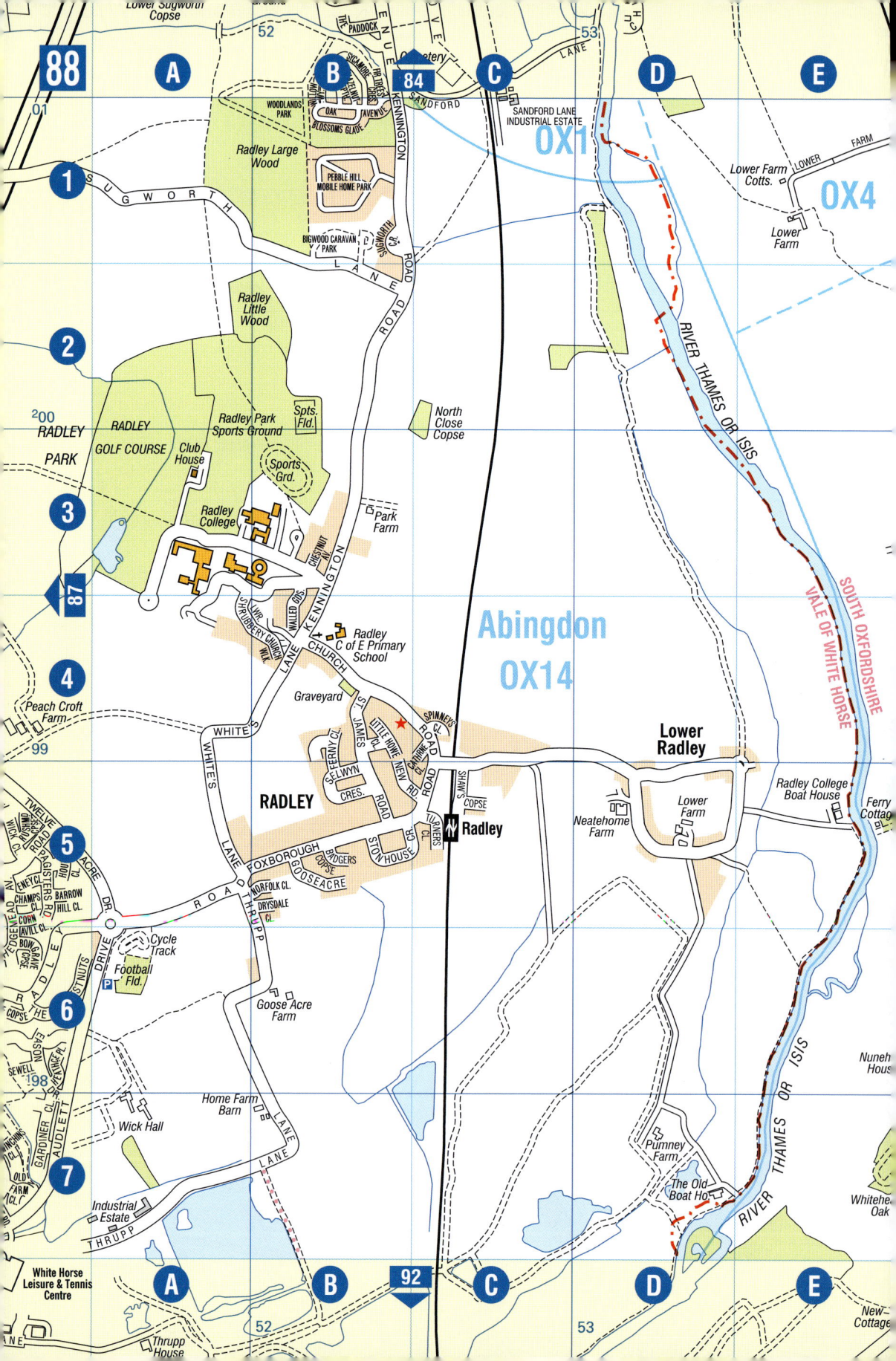

A **B** **C** **D** **E**

OX1

Lower Sugworth Copse

THE PADDOCK

Cemetery

SANDFORD

Sandford Lane Industrial Estate

Lower Farm Cotts.

Lower Farm

OX4

LOWER FARM

WOODLANDS PARK

SYCAMORE CL

OAK BLOSSOMS GLADE

AVENUE

KENNINGTON

SUGWORTH LANE

SUGWORTH CR.

PEBBLE HILL MOBILE HOME PARK

Radley Large Wood

BIGWOOD CARAVAN PARK

ROAD

Radley Little Wood

200 RADLEY PARK

RADLEY GOLF COURSE

Club House

Radley Park Sports Ground

Spts. Fld.

Sports Grd.

North Close Copse

RIVER THAMES OR ISIS

Radley College

Park Farm

CHESTNUT AV

KENNINGTON

87

SHRUBBERY WLK

LWR. WALLED GDS.

LANE

CHURCH

Radley C of E Primary School

Abingdon OX14

SOUTH OXFORDSHIRE

VALE OF WHITE HORSE

Peach Croft Farm

99

Graveyard

ST JAMES

LITTLE HOME

SPINNEY'S

CL

NEW RD.

ST JAMES CL

SEFERNY CL

SELWYN CRES.

ROAD

CATHRINE CL

ROAD

SHAW'S COPSE

Lower Radley

Lower Farm

Radley College Boat House

Ferry Cottage

WHITE'S

RADLEY

FOXBOROUGH CL

GOOSEACRE

BADGERS COPSE

STONE HOUSE CL

TANNERS CL

Radley

Neatehome Farm

TWELVE ACRE DR.

WICK HALL RD.

REGISTERS RD.

ENCYCLOPEDIA

CORN

CHAMPS CL

BARROW HILL CL.

AVILL CL.

NORFOLK CL.

DRYSDALE CL

BOW GRANE

THRUPP

HEDGEVEAR

CHESTNUTS

RADLEY ROAD

DRIVE

Cycle Track

Football Fld.

Goose Acre Farm

SEWELL CL

JOHNSON CL

'98

GARDNER CL

PRENTICE PL

AUDLETT

Wick Hall

Home Farm Barn

LANE

Pumney Farm

Nuneham House

The Old Boat Ho

RIVER THAMES OR ISIS

Whiteheath Oak

LANCHING CL

OLD FARM CL

R COPSE

HE

Industrial Estate

THRUPP

White Horse Leisure & Tennis Centre

A **B** 92 **C** **D** **E**

Thrupp House

New Cottage

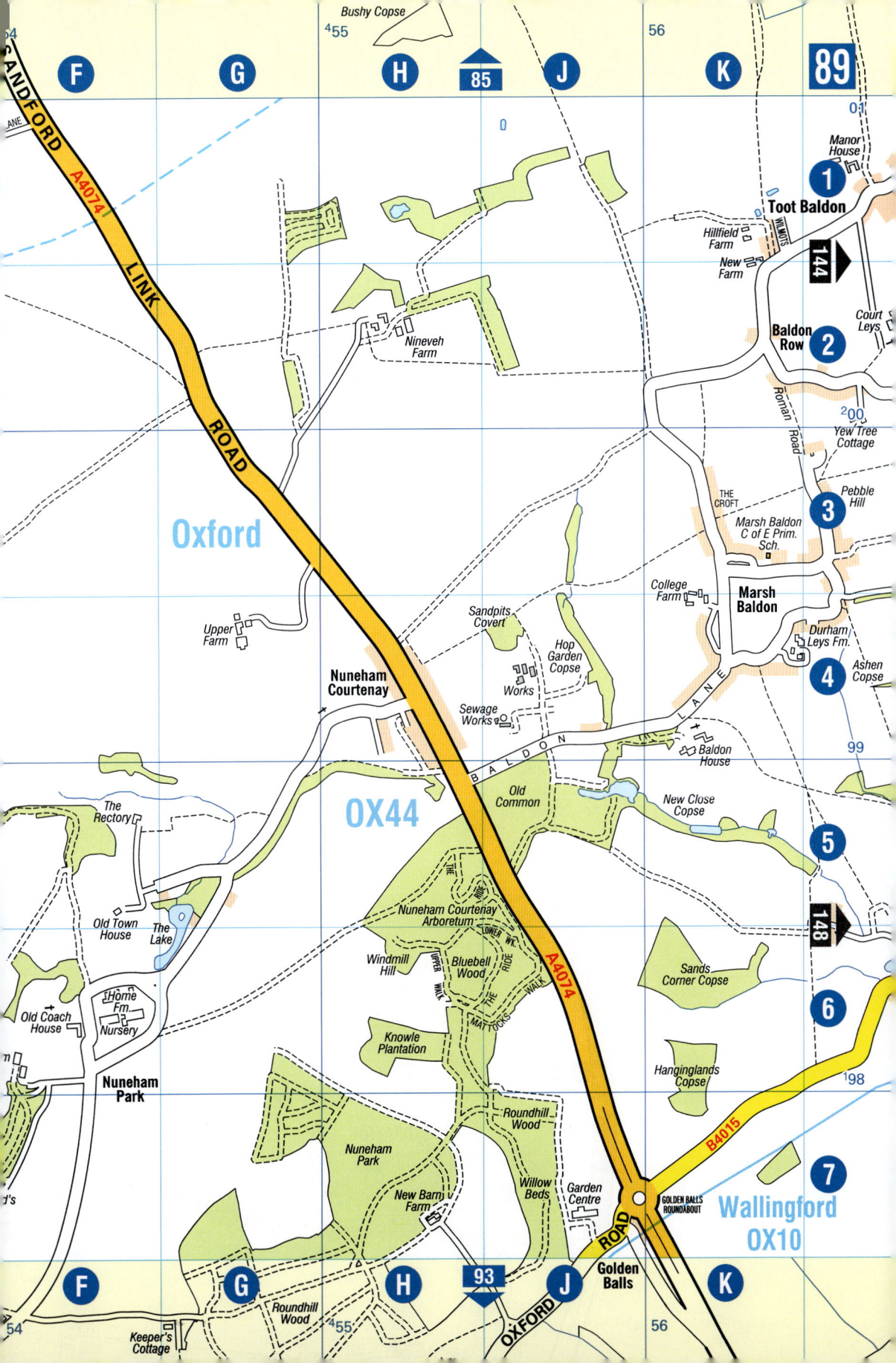

Bushy Copse
455
56
01

Manor House

1

Toot Baldon

Hillfield Farm

New Farm

144

Court Leys

Baldon Row **2**

Nineveh Farm

Roman Road

Yew Tree Cottage
200

THE CROFT

Pebble Hill **3**

Marsh Baldon C of E Prim. Sch.

Oxford

Sandpits Covert

College Farm

Marsh Baldon

Hop Garden Copse

Durham Leys Fm.

Works

Ashen Copse **4**

Nuneham Courtenay

Sewage Works

99

BALDON LANE

Baldon House

OX44

Old Common

New Close Copse

The Rectory

5

Old Town House

The Lake

Nuneham Courtenay Arboretum

THE RIDE

LOWER WK.

148

Windmill Hill

Bluebell Wood

UPPER WALK

THE WALK

Sands Corner Copse

6

Old Coach House

Home Fm. Nursery

MATTOCKS WALK

Knowle Plantation

Hanginglands Copse

198

Nuneham Park

Roundhill Wood

B4015

Nuneham Park

New Barn Farm

Willow Beds

Garden Centre

Wallingford **7**

OX10

GOLDEN BALLS ROUNDABOUT

Golden Balls

OXFORD ROAD

Roundhill Wood

Keeper's Cottage

454
455
56

A **B** 86 **C** **D** **E**

1

97 ◄ 61

2

3

OX13

4

Abingdon

5

195 ◄ 147

6

7

94

A **B** 96 **C** **D** **E**

BARROW

47   48

MARCHAM ROAD A415
A415
Sandford Brook
River Ock

BY-PASS
A34
Marcham Road Interchange
MARCHAM
Superstore

ABINGDON ROAD
A34

DRAYTON ROAD B4017
Sutton Wick
Stonehill
Stonehill House
Wick Lane
Preston Lane

Larkmead School
FARINGDON
Colwell
Nuffield
Abingdon Business Park
Foxcombe Ct.
Windrush Ct.
Blacklands
Furlong Way
Hitching Ct.
Willow Brook
Colwell Dr.
Anna Pavlova
Spring Gds.
Cemetery
Cemetery Rd.
Buckles
Police HQ
Abingdon Hospital H
Kimber Rd.
Eyston Wy.
Fairacres
ROAD OCK
Ock Mill Cl.
River Ock
Jenyns
Plygrd.
Potenger Wy.
Lady Grove
Paddock
Ladygve
Caldecott
Caldecot
Caldecott Prim. Sch.
Orpwood Wy.
Nash
Unterell Wy.
Shepherd Gds.
Medlicott Dr.
Francis Little Dr.
Suffolk Wy.
Burton Cl.
Ely Cl.
Byron Cl.
Serley Cl.
B4017 ROAD
Lady Eleanor Ct.
Saxton
Gainsborough
The Hyde
Turner
Nichol
Prim. Sch.
Mill
Tennyson Dr.
Wordsworth Dr.
Bridges
Longfellow Dr.
Masefield
Coleridge
Preston
Lucca
Coromsa
Virginia
Playing Fld.

CORNEVILLE RD.
CLOSE
Drayton Prim. Sch.
B4017 ROAD
NEWMAN
CRABTREE LA.
MEAD
L'ESPARRE
HILLIAT FIELDS
HILLIAT FIELDS
SUTTON WICK LANE
GREEN
FYFORD CLOSE
MANOR CL.
THE GREEN
ABINGDON ROAD
HENLEYS
DRAYTON
CAUDWELL CL.
GRAVEL
Grave Yard
CHURCH LA.
FISHER WY.
MARCHAM WY.
WHITEHORN'S WY.
WHITEHORNS
LYNTON RD.
STEVENTON RD.
HIGH STREET DRAYTON
B4016
HALLS
BYERS
Gilbourn's Farm
MILTON
Wks.
Council Depot
Little Smiths Farm
EAST WY.
DRAYTON EAST WY.
EAST
ROAD
Hall
Pav.
Rec. Grd.

Darley Grange
PEAT MOOR LA.

47   48

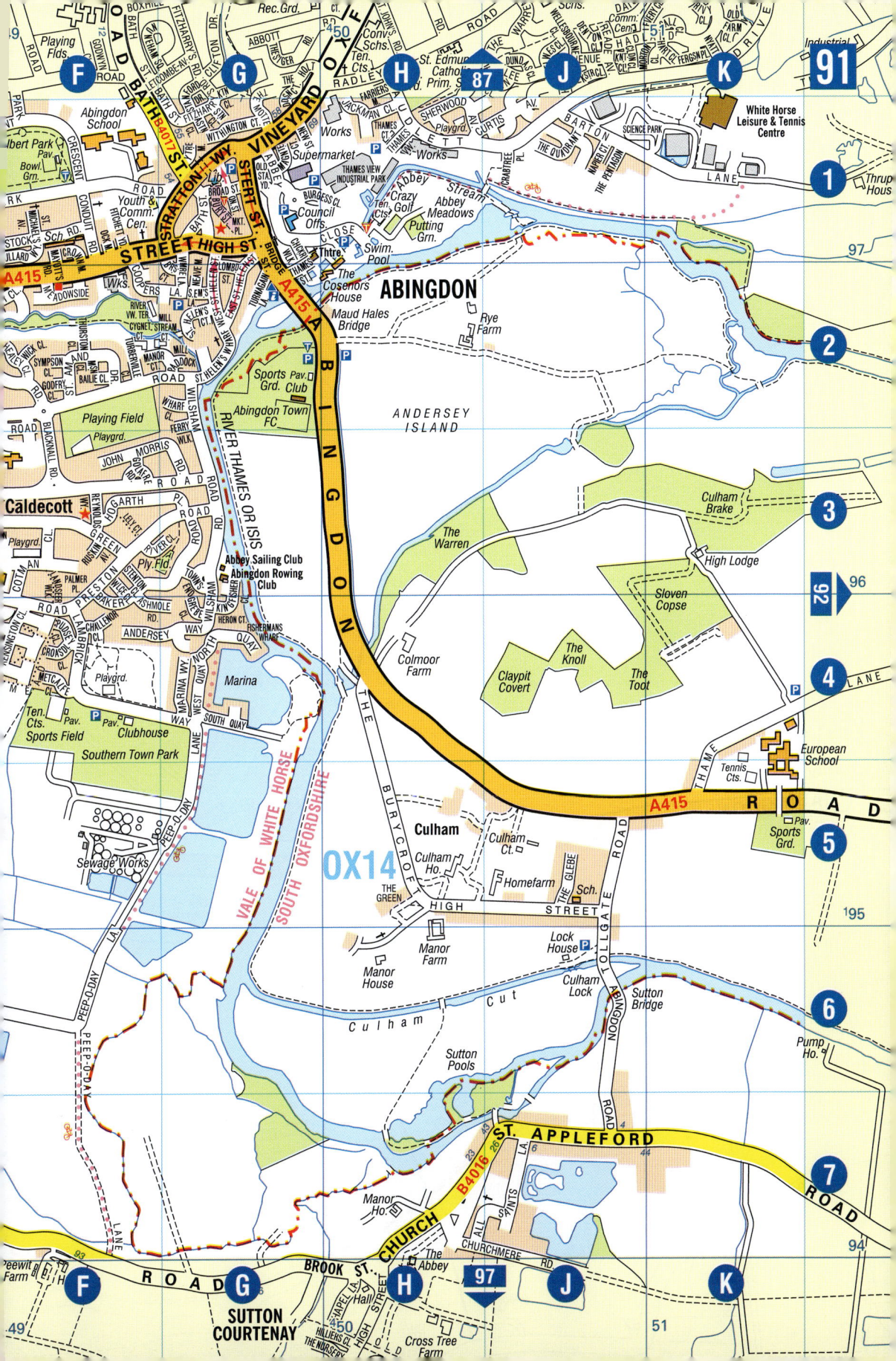

F G H 87 J K

Playing Flds.
Industrial
Thrup Hous
1

BATH ST STRATTON WY STERT ST VINEYARD
Abingdon School
Albert Park Pav
Bowl Grn
Youth & Comm. Cen.
STREET HIGH ST
A415
MEADOWSIDE
Wks.

White Horse Leisure & Tennis Centre
SCIENCE PARK
BARTON
THE QUADRANT
NAPIER CL
THE PENTAGON
LANE

St. Edmund Catholic Prim.
FARRIERS
SHERWOOD
CURTIS AV.
CRABTREE PL
Works
Supermarket
THAMES VIEW INDUSTRIAL PARK
Abbey Stream
Abbey Meadows
Crazy Golf
Putting Grn.
Swim. Pool
Thtre.
Council Offs.
MKT. PL.
The Coseners House
Maud Hales Bridge
ABINGDON
Rye Farm
2
97

RIVER THAMES OR ISIS
Sports Grd. Club
Abingdon Town FC
Playing Field
Playgrd.
JOHN MORRIS ROAD
WHARF
WILSHAM
FERRY
A
B
I
N
G
D
O
N

ANDERSEY ISLAND

The Warren
Culham Brake
High Lodge
3
92 96

Caldecott
Playgrd.
PRESTON
BAKER
ASHMOLE
ANDERSEY WAY
HERON CT.
FISHERMANS WHARF
Abbey Sailing Club
Abingdon Rowing Club
NORTH QUAY

Sloven Copse
The Knoll
The Toot
Claypit Covert
Colmoor Farm
Colmoor Farm

LANE
P
4
European School
Tennis Cts.

Ten. Cts.
Sports Field
Clubhouse
Southern Town Park
Pav.
MARINA WY
WEST QUAY
SOUTH QUAY
Marina
THE
BURYCROFT

A415 R O A D
Pav.
Sports Grd.
5
195

Sewage Works
PEEP-O-DAY
VALE OF WHITE HORSE
SOUTH OXFORDSHIRE
OX14
Culham
Culham Ho.
THE GREEN
Culham Ct.
Homefarm
HIGH STREET
Sch.
TOLLGATE ROAD
ABINGDON ROAD

Manor Farm
Manor House
Lock House
Culham Lock
Culham Cut
Sutton Bridge
6
Pump Ho.

PEEP-O-DAY LA.
Sutton Pools
Manor Ho.
CHURCH ST APPLEFORD
B4016
ALL SAINTS
CHURCHMERE RD.
7
ROAD
94

Peewit Farm
F ROAD G BROOK ST H 97 J K
SUTTON COURTENAY
Cross Tree Farm
The Abbey
51

A · B · 88 · C · D · E

1

White Horse Leisure & Tennis Centre

Industrial Estate

THRUPP

OLD FARM CL.

52 · 53

The Old Boat Ho.

Whiteh. Oa

Thrupp House

LANE

New Cottag

97

VALE OF WHITE HORSE
SOUTH OXFORDSHIRE

Viaduct

Lock Wood

Water Treatment Works

Ewer's Copse

2

RIVER THAMES OR

ISIS

RIVER THAMES

Furze Brake

ham ake

3

Warren Farm

gh Lodge

96 · 91

4

LANE THAME

LANE THAME

Ten. Cts.

Culham Science Centre

THAME

Spts. Grd.

Sewage Works

THAME

Vehicle Driving Test Centre

European School

Tennis Cts.

5

ABINGDON · Pav. ts

A415

ROAD · STATION RD.

Culham

CULHAM NO.1 SITE

A B I N

195

Zouch Farm

Fullamoor Farm

6

Pump Ho.

SOUTH OXFORDSHIRE
VALE OF WHITE HORSE

7

APPLEFORD RD. B4016

RIVER THAMES OR ISIS

94

A · B · 98 · C · D · E

Bridge m Ho.

52 · 53

SCHOOL LA. · MANOR CL. · REET

F G H **89** J K

1

Oxford
OX44

Keeper's
Cottage

Roundhill
Wood

Blacklands
Plantation

Clifton
Heath

New Barn
Farm

Willow
Beds

Garden
Centre

GOLDEN BALLS
ROUNDABOUT

56

Golden Balls
ROUNDABOUT

Golden
Balls

A4074

97

2

New
Covert

The Coppice

B4015

Burcot
Farm

3

A415

Burcot
Grange

Burcot
House

BALFOUR
COTTS.

94

96

Abingdon
OX14

COURTIERS
GRN.

Ten.
Ct.

Sports
Grd.

Pav.

Clifton
Hampden

WATERY LA.

OXFORD

RIVER THAMES OR ISIS

BURCOT PK.

The Close
(Nursing Home)

Burcot

LINNET
CL.

John Mason
Cheshire H.

4

Sch.

Butts
Furlong

HIGH

STREET

Clifton Hampden
Bridge

BRIDGE HOUSE
CARAVAN PK.

P

ABINGDON

Warren Farm
Cottage

Northfield
Farm

195

5

Clifton
Lock

Weir

Clifton Cut

New Barn
Farm

6

Home
Fm.

Lower
Farm

Sewage
Works

Bodkins
Sports
Grd.

Pav.

Wks.

7

Weir

Long
Wittenham

54

F

College
Farm

G

FIELD ST.

LITTLE

STREET

HIGH

H **99** WITTEN- HAM

J

ROAD

56

K

94

A B 148 C D E

57 58

1

97

2

A4074

BARRINGTON CL.
PRITCHARD CL.
TOWER RD.
Works
RUSSELL CL.
JACKSON CL.
CRUTCH FURLONG
EVENLODE DR.
CHERWELL RD.
GLYME DR.
COLNE DR.
ROAD
Roman
LAY
CHWELL RD.
AVENUE
COLT
WEST
CHWELL RD.
OCK DR.
CHERWELL RD.
BERINSFIELD
LEACH RD.
Cemy.
DR.
Lib.
Comm. Cen.
GREEN FURLONG
GLEBE
BERINSCOURT HO.
SHADWELL RD.
Abbey Sports Cen.
ABBEY WOODS CL.
WEY RD.
WEY CL.
Mount Farm
The Copse

3

BALFOUR COTTS
96
93
ouse Home)
BULLINGDON CL.
Wks.
Coin Offs.
Wks.
Berinsfield Prim. Sch.
CHILTERN AV.
LODDON AV.
WINDRUSH CL.
KENNET RD.
Berinsfield Adult Learning
STRAW

ABINGDON A415 ROAD
BERINSFIELD ROUNDABOUT

4

Burcot
LINNET CL.
John Masefield Cheshire Home
ROAD
BURCOT
LANE
Wally Corner
DORCHESTER ROAD

5

195

RIVER THAMES OR ISIS
ABINGDON
Dorchester Sailing Club
OXFORD
DRAYTON ROAD
Queonford Farm
Queenford Bri.

6

Abingdon OX14
ROAD
THE LIMES
HIGH
Minchin Rec. Grd.
Pav.
DRAYTON
Cemy.
PAGE FURLONG
ROAD
Bishop's Court
BELCHER CT.
BARRING GATE
MARTIN'S LANE
ST.
QUEENS CL.
MANOR FARM RD.
MONKS RD.
Thame
Monk's Bri.
Abbey Bri.
PRIEST'S

7

DORCHESTER ON THAMES
JAMES ST.
CROWN
SCH.
BEECH CROFT
MALT-HOUSE LA.
MALTHOUSE LA.
QUEEN ST.
WATLING
ROTTEN ROW
HENLEY BRIDGE
Dorchester Abbey Mus.
River
Sub.
Overy Mill
Overy Farm
Overy Manor
Priest's Moor Bri.
A4074

94

A B 100 C D E

Bridge End
WATLING LANE
ORCHARD LA.
WITTENHAM LA.
SAMIAN
Overy
ROAD
Irrig Lag

57 58

Oxford
OX44

61

97

96

195

94

Hayward
Bri.
60

Chequers
Cottage

Lower
Covert

127

Hill
Farm

Great
Holcombe

Great
Holcombe
Farm

A329

HOLCOMBE LA.

Beauforest
House

Newington
House

Newington

RIVER THAME

Drayton
View

Sports
Field

Manor
Farm

STADHAMPTON RD.

LANE

FORD

THE OSIERS

CHURCH LA.

HIGH ST.

WATER LANE

GRAVEL WALK

**Drayton
St. Leonard**

R O A D

Drayton
Ho. Fm.

Heathercombe
Ho.

Ford

Upper
Grange

**Wallingford
OX10**

148 96

Ewe
Farm

Lower
Grange

Lane End
Farm

W A Y

A M M E R

M O O R   L A N E

P A I N   W A Y

Piggery

A329

THAME

MOOR

Catcharm
Corner

L A N E

ST. LAWRENCE CL.

NURSERY

Court
Farm

R O A D

WARBOROUGH

60

61

59

Lower B
Far

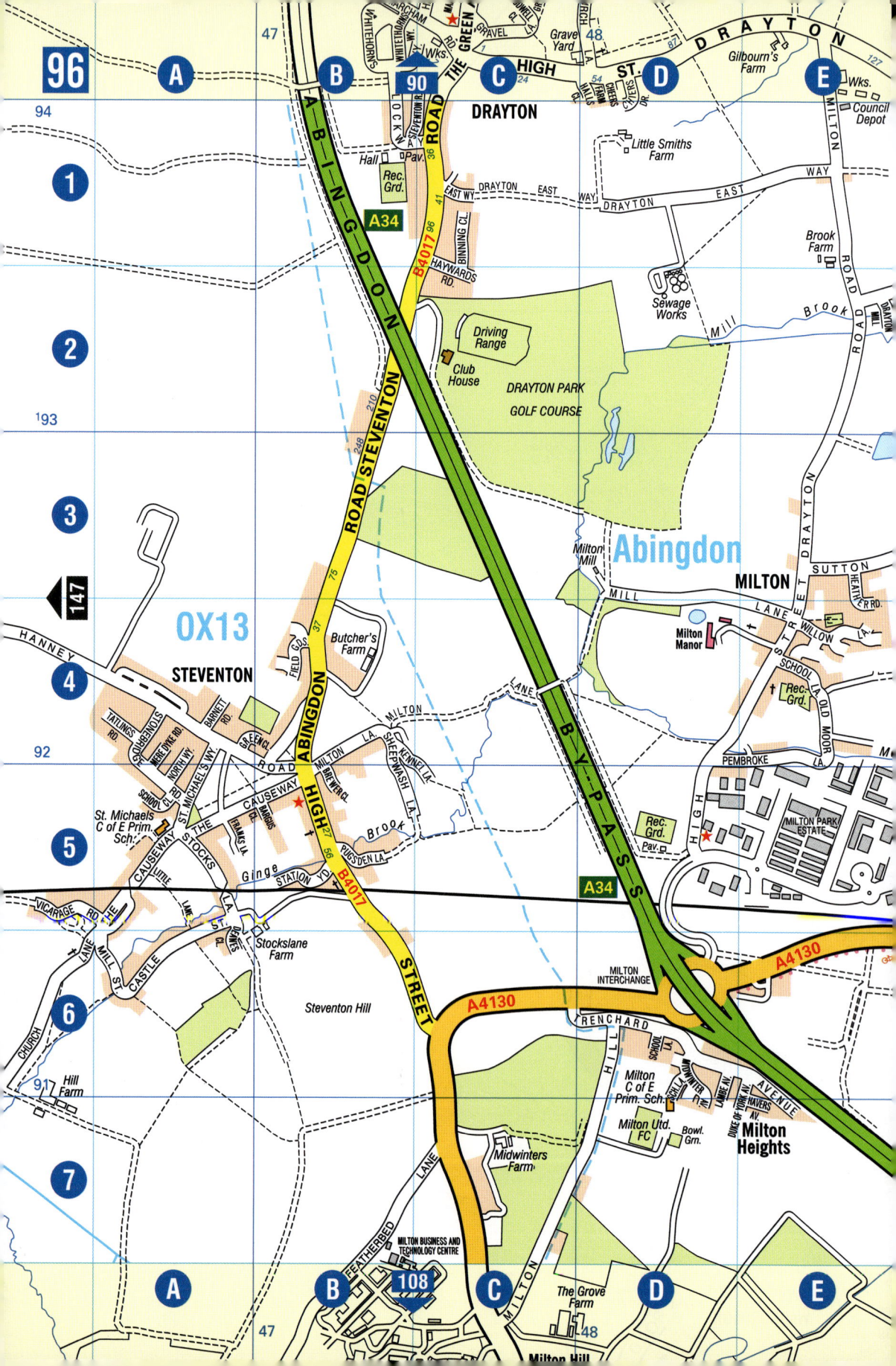

94

47

193

147

92

91

48

DRAYTON

HIGH ST

DRAYTON

THE GREEN

ROAD

A34

B4017

Hall

Rec. Grd.

Pav.

EAST WY

DRAYTON EAST WAY

DRAYTON EAST WAY

HAYWARDS RD.

BINNING CL.

Little Smiths Farm

Gilbourn's Farm

Wks.

Council Depot

MILTON ROAD

DRAYTON

Brook Farm

Brook

MILL

Sewage Works

Driving Range

Club House

DRAYTON PARK GOLF COURSE

Abingdon

Milton Mill

MILL

MILTON

SUTTON

HEATHER RD.

WILLOW LA.

STREET DRAYTON

OLD MOOR LA.

SCHOOL LA.

Milton Manor

Rec. Grd.

PEMBROKE LA.

OX13

HANNEY

STEVENTON

ROAD STEVENTON

ABINGDON ROAD

HIGH STREET

B4017

FIELD GDS.

Butcher's Farm

MILTON LA.

SHEEPWASH LA.

KENNEL LA.

BREWER CL.

Brook

FUG'S DEN LA.

LANE

B-Y-P-A-S-S

A34

Rec. Grd.

Pav.

HIGH

MILTON PARK ESTATE

TATLINGS RD.

CROUGENOLS

MERE DYKE RD.

NORTH WY.

BARNETT RD.

GREEN CL.

SCHOOL LA.

St. Michaels C of E Prim. Sch.

ST. MICHAEL'S WY.

THE CAUSEWAY

FRANKS LA.

STOCKS

Ginge

STATION YD.

Brook

A34

A4130

A4130

MILTON INTERCHANGE

MILTON

TRENCHARD

Stockslane Farm

Steventon Hill

VICARAGE RD.

MILL ST.

CASTLE

CHURCH

Hill Farm

Midwinters Farm

FEATHERBED LANE

MILTON BUSINESS AND TECHNOLOGY CENTRE

SCHOOL LA.

Milton C of E Prim. Sch.

Milton Utd. FC

Bowl. Grn.

LAMBE AV.

DUKE OF YORK AV.

MINSTER AV.

NAVERS AV.

AVENUE

Milton Heights

The Grove Farm

MILTON

Milton Hill

90

108

A B C D E

PEEP-O-DAY LA.

Manor Ho.

CHURCH ST.

ALL SAINTS

91

94

1

ROAD

B4016 ROAD BROOK ST.

The Abbey

CHURCHMERE RD.

Hulgrove Farm

CHAPEL LA.

OLD STREET

Hilliers Hall

Cross Tree Farm

WALLINGFORD

HILLIERS CL.

THE NURSERY

HILLY RD.

BARNS

LADY PL.

Pav.

Recreation Ground

WAY

2

MILL LANE

TULLIS CL.

LADY PL.

COURTENAY CL.

TOWN CL.

FRILSHAM ST.

Village Hall

193

SUTTON COURTENAY

HIGH ST.

HOBBYHORSE

LANE

HILLIS FIELD

MILTON RD.

ROAD

KATCH'S DE

Gravel Pit

3

ROAD MILTON

BRADSTOCKS

TYRRELL'S WY.

BARRETTS WY.

WAY

ROAD HARWELL

98

TYRRELL'S PL.

TYRRELL'S WY.

Sutton Courtenay All Saints C of E Primary School

OX14

4

Ditch

92

COURTENAY

Warehouse

Nature Study Reserve

MILTON PARK ESTATE

Sutton Courtenay Environmental Educ. Cen.

Didcot Power Station

Pav.

5

MILTON PARK ESTATE

SUTTON

Didcot OX11

Club

Durnells Bridge

Works

Wareho

New Farm

MILTON

LANE

A4130

ROAD

BASIL

6

A34

VALE OF WHITE HORSE
SOUTH OXFORDSHIRE

LYNDENS
OXBU 91
DR.

Foxhall Manor Park

B4493

BRENDON

HEIGHTS

MALVERN CL.

COTSWOLD

NORTH

HENLOCK CL.

ROAD

7

Didcot Field

QUANTOCK

MENDIP PK.

THE OVAL

FIRST AV.

WORTHAM

RD.

L. Va
Ba

ORDNANCE

SECOND

VAU

Play. Fld.

Stephen Freeman Primary School

MAN

WILLS CL.

MERRITT

ROAD

MORRELLS CL.

BRASENOSE

49

450

51

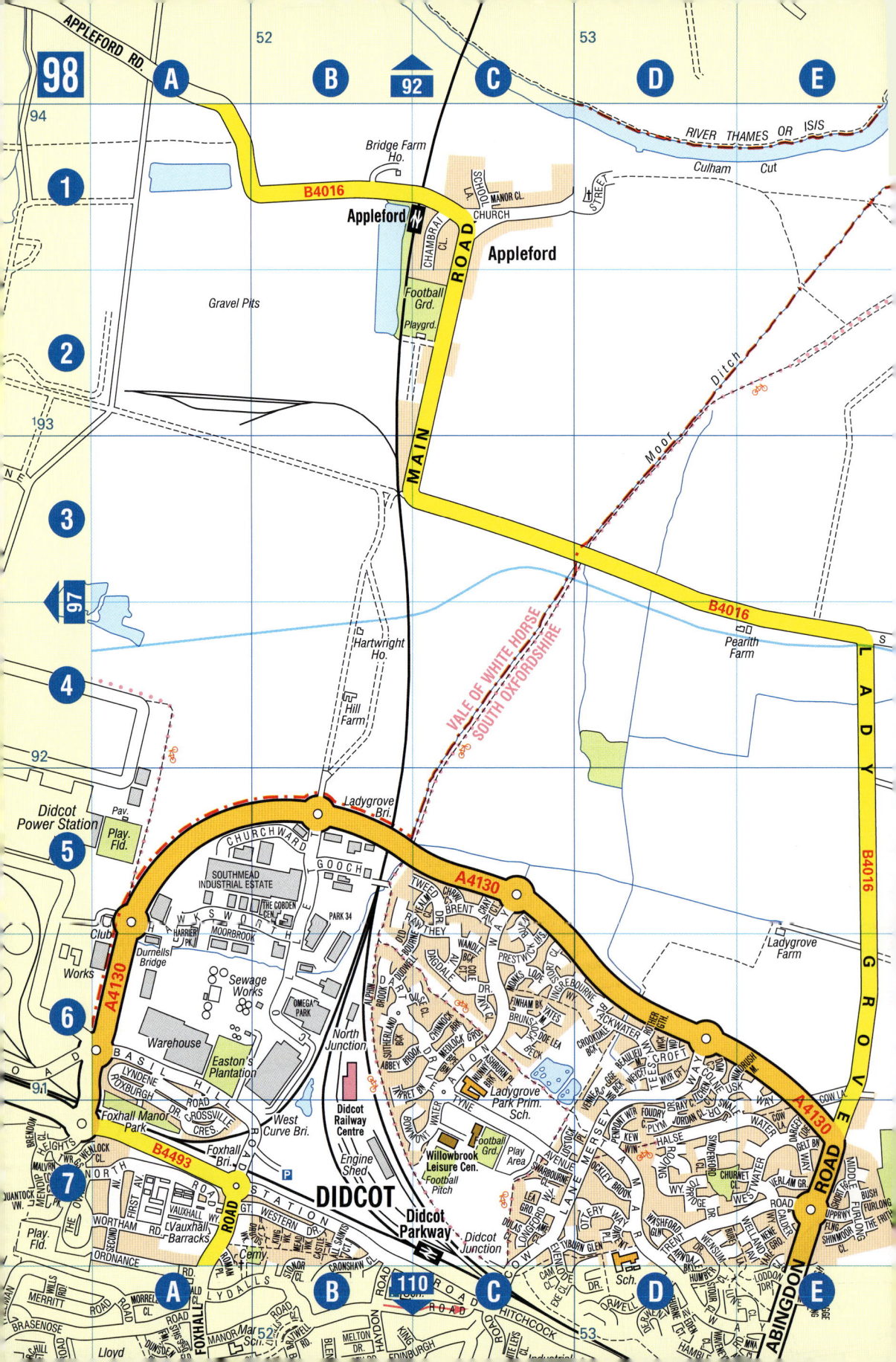

A · B · C · D · E

APPLEFORD RD.

52 · 53

94

92

RIVER THAMES OR ISIS

Culham Cut

Bridge Farm Ho.

B4016

Appleford

1

SCHOOL

MANOR CL.

STREET

ROAD

CHURCH

CHAMBRAI CL.

Appleford

Gravel Pits

Football Grd.

Playgrd.

2

193

MAIN

Moor Ditch

3

97

B4016

Hartwright Ho.

VALE OF WHITE HORSE
SOUTH OXFORDSHIRE

Pearith Farm

4

Hill Farm

92

Didcot Power Station

Pav.

Play. Fld.

Ladygrove Bri.

5

CHURCHWARD

GOOCH

SOUTHMEAD INDUSTRIAL ESTATE

THE COBDEN CEN.

PARK 34

A4130

TWEED

CHASE

BRENT

CRAY

WAY

LADYGROVE

B4016

Ladygrove Farm

Club

HARRIER PK.

MOORBROOK

WINSWORTH

RAWTHEY

OLD BOURNE

DUDDEL

DART

BOURNE

DUDDEL

WANDLE

DENE

PRESTWICK CL.

MAW

INGSBOURNE WK.

Works

Durnells Bridge

Sewage Works

OMEGA PARK

ALPHIN BROOK

SUTHERLAND

ABBEY BROOK

CHINNOCK

MEDLOCK

AVON

FINHAM BK.

BRUNS

DOE LEA

CROOKDALE BCK.

BEAULIEU

ROTHER

WYCK

CROFT

6

A4130

Warehouse

Easton's Plantation

North Junction

BASIL HILL ROAD

LYNDENE

ROXBURGH

CROSSVILLE CRES.

West Curve Bri.

Didcot Railway Centre

Engine Shed

TRENT

DARENT

WATER

TYNE

AVON

ASHBURN CL.

BOWMONT WATER

Ladygrove Park Prim. Sch.

BECK

LOSTOCK

MERSEY

COLNE

USK

TEES

WYR CT.

WYCK

BRUSH

WAY

TEME

DRAY CT.

KEW

FOUDRY CL.

CITCHEN

SWAL

HALSE

COW LA.

A4130

Foxhall Manor Park

Foxhall Bri.

ROAD

B4493

7

MENLOCK CL.

NORTH

HEIGHTS

WR

MENDIP

MALVERN

QUANTOCK VW.

BRENDON

FIRST AV.

WORTHAM

ORDNANCE

VAUXHALL WY.

L.Vauxhall Barracks

STATION

WESTERN

DR.

KINGS

SAINTS

Cerny

FOXHALL ROAD

MELTON DR.

HAYDON

NOR CL.

CRONSHAW CL.

DR.

EDINBURGH

KING

WILLERS

ROAD

ROAD

DIDCOT

Didcot Parkway

Didcot Junction

P

Willowbrook Leisure Cen.

Football Grd.

Football Pitch

Play Area

LEA

SWARBOURNE

AVENUE

DULAS

LONGFORD

YBURN GLEN

COW LANE

CAM

OTTER WAY

WASHFORD

CHURNET CL.

WELLAND

WENSUM

WESTWATER

LODDON

BUSH FURLONG

THE FRITH

SHINWOOD CL.

ABINGDON ROAD

Sch.

ORWELL

HUMBER

CALDER

VERLAM GR.

MIDDLE FURLONG

UPPRWY

FLNG.

Play. Fld.

MERRITT

WILLS

ROAD

MORREL CL.

MANOR

BRASENOSE

Lloyd

52

LYDALLS

53

110

HITCHCOCK ROAD

A · B · C · D · E

F **G** **H** 93 **J** **K**

94

Weir

Clifto

Pav. Bodkins
Sports
Wks. 455

Long Wittenham
C of E Prim.
Sch.

College
Farm

LITTLE

WITTENHAM

ROAD

1

Pendon
Mus.
THREE POPLAR
MOBILE HOME PARK

**Long
Wittenham**

Church Farm
Cottage

The
Manor Ho.

Wittenham
Ho.

**Abingdon
OX14**

Westfield

HIGH
WILSONS CL.
ST. JOHN'S RW.
FIELDSIDE
THE CR.
SADDON CL.
SAXONS
DIDCOT
HEATH
STREET

Paradise
Wood

War
Mem.

**Little
Wittenham**

The
Nursery

2

193

ROAD

Westfield
Barn

Rose Hurst
Farm

Wittenham
Hill

Hill
Farm

Sinodun
Hills

LITT
NAT

3

100

P

Westfield
Farm

SHIRES

4

Willington
Down Farm

Long Wittenham
Wood

Folly
Farm

Fir Trees
Nurseries

Haddon Close
Orchard

White Lees

Haddon
Close

HILL

SHIRES

HILL

92

5

**Didcot
OX11**

White Lees
Farm

91

6

HADDEN HILL
GOLF COURSE

A4130

WALLINGFORD RD.

7

F **G** **H** 111 **J** **K**

54

Golf
Range

Hadden
Farm

455

LONG WITTENHAM RD.

56

DORCHESTER ON THAMES

A B 94 C D E

1

94
57 58

Priest's Moor Bri.

Overy Mill

Dorchester Abbey Mus

Overy Farm

Overy Manor

Overy

Irr
La

Church Farm Cottage

The Manor Ho.

Weir

Day's Lock

Bridge End

Sewage Works

Meadside

2

Wittenham Ho.

Little Wittenham Bridge

River

A4074

War Mem.

Little Wittenham

193

The Nursery

RIVER THAMES OR ISIS

ROAD

HE

Abingdon OX14

LITTLE WITTENHAM NATURE RESERVE

Little Wittenham Wood

Wallingford OX10

3

Sinodun Hills

Castle Hill

99

Hi
Far

Wittenham Clumps

North Farm

P

4

92

Sinodun Hill

S I R E S

Didcot OX11

5

Style Acre

H I G H

6

Highlands Farm

A4130

91

GREENMERE

DIDCOT

Beauchamp Grange

KING'S ORCHARD

GREENMERE ROAD

Prim. Sch.

Play. Fld.

Wellsprings

DATCHET COR.

Nursery

7

A4130

Frog's Island Farm

WEST END

BAKERS

MONKS MES.

PENN. GREEN LA.

WALLINGFORD ROAD

CHURCH ROAD

Brightwell Manor

BRIGHTWELL

BRIGHTWELL-CUM-SOTWELL

STREET

BELL

MACKNEY LANE

SOTWELL LANE

Pumping Station

Pavs. Rec. Grd.

Slade Far

A B 112 C D E
57 58

F
Catcharm Corner
Court Farm
G
H
▲ 95
J
K

94
Lower Fa
1

*460
61

WARBOROUGH

SNODUN CL
ST LAWRENCE CL
HENFIELD VW.
THE QUAKER LA.
THE GREEN LA.
GREEN LA. SOUTH
GREEN NORTH
Pav.
The Green
2

A329

OATLANDS CL
GRAVEL LA.
St. Laurence
C of E Prim. Sch.

SHILLINGFORD

THAME ROAD
NEW RD.
CHERRY CL
WARBOROUGH RD.
ORTL CALDOG CL
PLOUGH CL
193

3

Shillingford Farm

ROAD
WHARF
SHILLINGFORD CT.
COURT
DR.
THE MEWS
WALLINGFORD ROAD

Hale Farm
◄ 102 HALE

4

A4074

BENSON
92
THE CLOSE

Elm Bridge
OXFORD RD.
LITTLEWORTH RD.
Littleworth
Prim. Sch.
WATL

ELM BRIDGE ROUNDABOUT
B4009
A4074
CHURCHFIELD LA.
FIRST FLD
5

Shillingford Hill

THE AV.
GREEN VW.
RIVER VW.
BEECH
Caravan Park
Brightwell Vineyard
Rush Manor
Rush Court Gardens
Rush Court Nurseries
Rush Court
RIVER THAMES
or
ISIS
CHURCH LA.
ST HELEN'S
CHURCH CL
CHURCH RD.
GRAVEL CL
CASTLE SQ.
CASTLE
Lib.
CASTLE
AV.
6

Severalls Farm

Benson Lock
Preston Crowmarsh
91

Lower F
Orcha

Sotwell Hill House
(Retirement Home)

7

SLADE END ROUNDABOUT

Crowmarsh Battle Farm

Slade End
BOSLEY VW.
F
WANTAGE ROAD
G
H
▼ 113
J
K

Riverside

459
*460
61

Playground
ST GEOR
DR.
DOYLE

94

A B C D E

1

Parsonage Farm
Lower Berrick Farm
Berrick Salome
WELLER CL.
148
Hare Hall
Parson Piece
Scald Hill

62 63

2

CHAPEL LA.
Roke
Roke Farm

¹93

3

Rokemarsh
Works
B4009
S A N
LANE
COTTESMORE

101

Hale Farm
HALE
PORT HILL RD.
THE WEIR
SANDS END
SANDS WY.
RUMBOLD'S
SIDE
ROAD
ST ANN'S
BRAZE LANE
THE CEDARS
STREET
Cottesmore Farm Barns
Prospect Farm
COTTESMORE
Win F

4

THE CLOSE
Hall
ROAD
CHILTERN
NORTHFIELD
GREENS END
BLACKLANDS
BLACKLANDS WY.
GREEN CL.
ROAD
THE CEDARS
Benson Veteran Cycle Mus.
Fifield Manor
Fifield Farm Barns

92

Littleworth
LITTLEWORTH RD.
WATLINGTON
ROAD
Prim. Sch.
CHAPEL END
CROMWELL
WEST
ALDRIDGE CL.
FIELD
BROOK ROAD
WYCHWOOD
DRY LEAS
BARN CL.
ROSSER'S CT.
JOSEY CRES.

OXFORD
CHURCHILL CL.
ROAD

5

HORSESHOES
CASTLE
COLLEGE
HIGH STREET
CASTLE CL.
MILL CT.
GRACE'S CT.
COACH WY.
THE LANE
B O L D
LONDON ROAD
PADDOCK CL.
Control Tower

Wallingford
OX10

CHURCH CL.
CHURCH RD.
ST HELEN'S CRES.
ST HELEN'S AVENUE

6

Benson Lock
A4074
BENSON
BENSON AIRFIELD
ANDOVER
BELFAST RD.
ARGOS
WHIRLWIND WY.
CHIPMUNK
ROAD
LANCASTER
AVENUE WEST
JAVELIN WY.
BATTLE ROAD
GREEN LANE
EYRES
CL.
Brownin

91

Preston Crowmarsh
Lower Farm Orchard
VIKING TER.
RAF Benson Prim. Sch.
Barracks
RAF BENSON

7

Crowmarsh Battle Farm
Riverside
RIVER THAMES or ISIS
BENSON LA.
Sewage Works
148
ALISTER TAYLOR
GEORGE TUTTLE
ANTHONY
HILL RD.
BULLDOG CL.
HUDLESTON
BEGGARSBUSH
FIELDEN
Pav.
SQUARE
KOCHRANE AVENUE
FREDRA CL.
BAKER ROAD
BAKER CL.
BENSON HILL

A B C D E

62 63

F G H **Brightwell Upperton** J K **103**

Silos

Uppertown Farm

94

Uppertown Croft

1

School House

Watlington OX49

Heath Plantation

Ashley's Wood

2

Rumbold's Copse

Brightwell Grove

193

LANE

D S GROVE LANE

Refuse Tip

B4009

LANE

3

148

Britwell Salome House Brockholes Covert

BROCKHOLES

Hyde Shaw

4

92

LANE

FIREBRASS HILL

Huntingland

MARTYN'S WY.

BRITWELL RD.

HAMPDEN WY.

CHAUCER CT.

5

PARSON'S

WINGFIELD CL.

BURROWS

EWELME

Grave Yd.

The Rectory

The Copper Ho.

Warren Bottom

WAY

Icknield Fld.

Ewelme Farm

Manor Ho.

Sch.

THE CLOISTERS

HILL

STREET

6

Play. Fld.

Fords Farm

P Pav. Sports Grd.

P

91

HENLEY

Cow Common

FIELD

Down Farm

Rabbits Hill

DAY'S

LANE

GROVE

WAY

KNIGHTSBRIDGE

POTTERS LANE

GRINDON

Littleworth Hill

7

F G H J K

64

465

66

A B 147 C D E

1

²90

Hill
House

2

147

Childrey

A417

3

89

4

Coppice
Leaze Farm

West
Challow

Manor
Farm

THE
GLEBE
ORCHARD

GDNS

SILVER

LANE

5

West Challow
Bridge

88

Godfrey's
Farm

6

WAY

LAWRENCE

TOWH

118

7

87

Childrey Brook

ROAD

Brook

147

CIRCOURT

MARSH

LANE

Woodhill

Little
Woodhill

WOODHILL

WOODHILL
LA.

Woodhill
Farm

LANE

GROVE
TECHNOLOGY
PARK

WAYLAND
AV.

FARADAY RD.

RIDGE

WAY

EUSTON
WAY

DOWNSVIEW

Sewage
Works

Brook

Club

Driving
Range

Factory

WOODHILL

LANE

CORNHILL

Works

Canal
Farm

Wise's
Farm

Challow
House
Farm

East
Challow

ST.
NICHOLAS
PL.

PARK

CANAL WY.

THE
ORCHARD

Park
Farm

SAXON PL

OSBORNE

SIDG

ST

KING

SEGS
BURY

LYDSEE
GA.

SEGSBURY CT. LA

CHALLOW

A417

WARMANS
CT.

LAHAM

King Alfred's
Comm. Spts. Coll.
(West Site)

OLD
SCHOOL LA.

Play
Fld.

Playgrd.

Prim.
Sch.

REYNOLDS
WY.

F.
H.
FIELD GDS.
SARAZAC
WY.

OLD FLD. RD.

CHICHESTER
WY.

LETCOMBE
HILL
CL.

HILL
PL.

VICARAGE

Cemy.

Pav.
Cricket
Grd.

Townsend

Cornhill
Farm

CORNHILL

LANE

HIGH

WINDMILL

LANE

B4507

Kirklands

Windmill
Hill

ICKLETON

147

A B C 119 D E

37 38

Oblakes
Farm

MILL
PADDOCK

KINGS
CL.

FIELD

REGS RD.

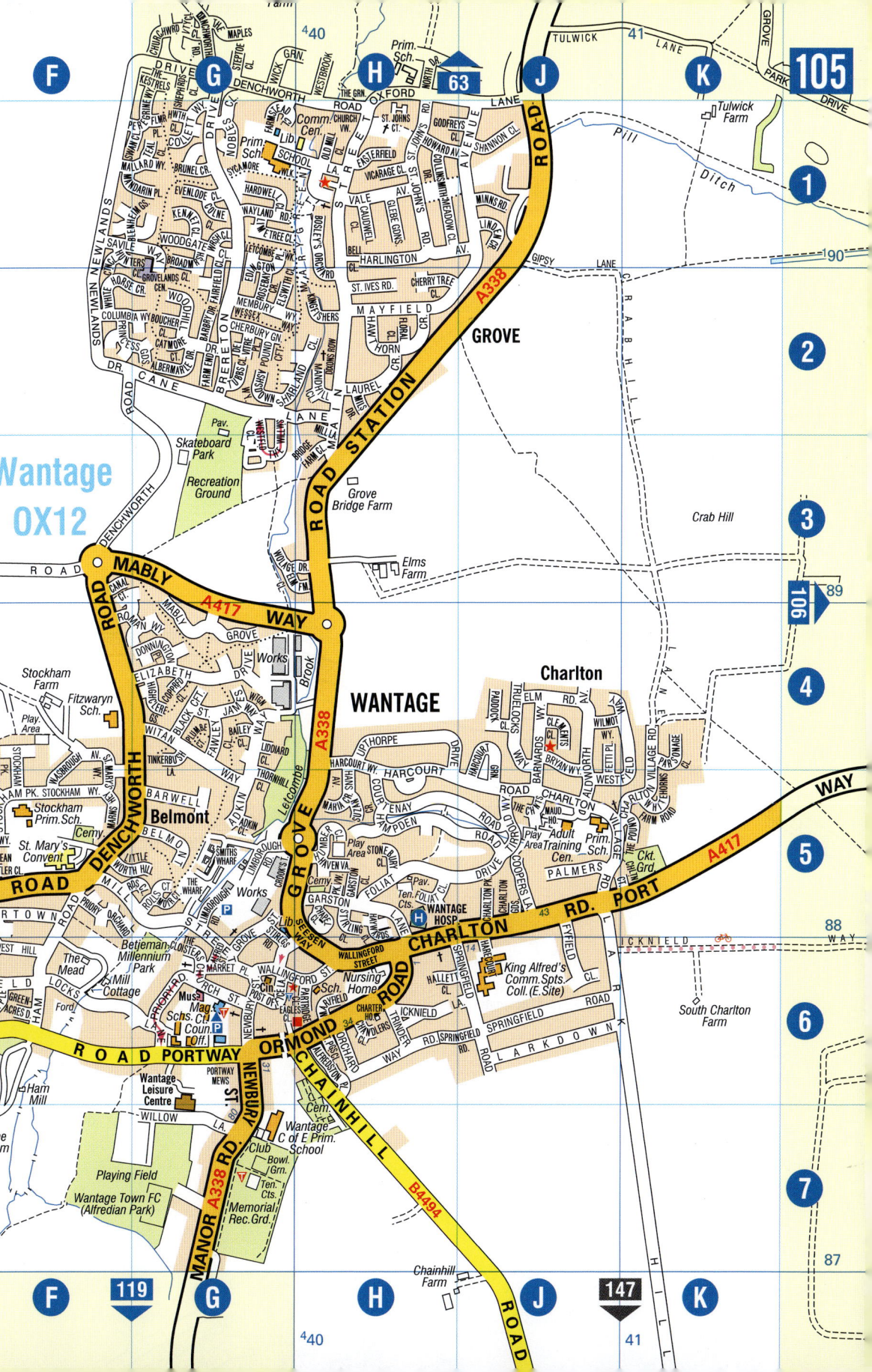

Wantage OX12

F G H J K

63

119 147

GROVE

WANTAGE

Charlton

Belmont

Tulwick Farm

Crab Hill

Stockham Farm

South Charlton Farm

Chainhill Farm

Grove Bridge Farm

Elms Farm

Fitzwaryn Sch.

St. Mary's Convent

Stockham Prim. Sch.

Betjeman Millennium Park

Mill Cottage

The Mead

Ham Mill

The Ham

Playing Field

Wantage Town FC (Alfredian Park)

Wantage Leisure Centre

Portway Mews

Wantage C of E Prim. School

Memorial Rec. Grd.

Skateboard Park

Recreation Ground

Wantage Hosp.

Nursing Home

King Alfred's Comm. Spts. Coll. (E. Site)

Adult Training Cen.

Prim. Sch.

Charlton Road

Springfield

Larkdown

Icknield

Wallingford Street

Market Pl.

Mus. & Mag. Schs. Ct.

Coun. Off.

Comm. Cen.

Prim. Sch.

Lib.

Prim. Sch.

St. Johns Ct.

Vicarage Cl.

Oxford

TULWICK LANE

GROVE PARK DRIVE

Pill Ditch

Crabhill Lane

A338 ROAD STATION ROAD

MABLY WAY A417

DENCHWORTH ROAD

GROVE

A338

NEWBURY ST.

MANOR RD. A338

ORMOND ROAD PORTWAY

CHAINHILL

B4494

CHARLTON ROAD

RD. PORT WAY A417

ICKNIELD WAY

90

89 106

88 WAY

87

1 2 3 4 5 6 7

39 40 41

Tulwick
Farm

GROVE

1

Pill   Ditch

¹90

2

PARK

Crab Hill

3

Field Barn
Farm

Lains
Barn

89   **105**

DRIVE

4

Ardington
Wick

P O R T   W A Y

A417

5

MASON'S
CT.
THE CLOSE
WELL ST.
SCHOOL   ROAD   HIGH   STREET
CHURCH ST.
THE RICKYARD
ARDINGTON

Ardington   Brook

Giggers
Wood

88

ICKNIELD   WAY

Playing
Field
Pav.

Pav.

Sheephouse
Farm

th Charlto
Farm

6

**West
Lockinge**

Res.
(Covered)

VIEW

Rounda
Hill

**East
Lockinge**

Flagstaff
Hill

7

PARK   LA.   PARK   LA.

Arn
Hill

Road

Arnhill
Park

Betterton   Brook

87

BITHAM

44   45   46

1

190

2

Quab Hill

WOODS

FARM ROAD

Ludbridge Mill

Brookleys Fish Farm

Greensands

FEATHERBED LANE

3

A417

Lud Bridge

ALLIN'S LANE

VINEYARD

COULING'S CL.

WHITE

ORCHARD ROAD

OLD RD.

108   89

Wantage OX12

WEST HENDRED

THE BANKSIDE

Mill Farm

MILL LANE

MILL LANE

ORCHARD STREET

CAT LANE

Mus.

CHURCH STREET

ST. MARY'S RD.

EAST HENDRED

Bowling Alley Row

4

GREENWAY

Playgrd. Rec. Grd.

Ten. Cts.

THE MILLHAM

MANOR LA.

FORDY

THE SPINNEY

The Hendreds C of E Prim. School

CHURCH STREET

HIGH STREET

NEWBURY

St. Amand's Catholic Prim.Sch.

Ambling Way North

5

Red Barn

THE LYNCH

HORN LANE

88

Ambling Way South

Goldbury Hill

Park Hill Row

Park Hill

Icknield Row

ROAD

Holloway Plantation

Icknield Plantation

6

Co.

Aldfield Common

Stoney Row

Ginge Brook

Black Mills Row

Skeets Bush Cottages

7

Stoney Henge Row

STILEWAY ROAD

87

Lower Farm

West Ginge

East Ginge   Manor Farm

Elmtree Plantation

Ellaway's Barn

44   45   46

A B C D E

1

2 Quab Hill

3 Greensands A417 Rowstock

4

5 Wantage OX12

6

7

A B C D E

OX13

96 MILTON BUSINESS AND TECHNOLOGY CENTRE

Milton Hill House (Training Centre)

Cricket Grd.

The Grove Farm

OX14

Milton Hill

Abingdon

A4130

GROVE

Middle Farm

Rowstock Farm

Horn Down

Golden Mile Row North

Golden Mile Row South

Lydebank Plantation

Ambling Way North

Chimney Corner Plantation

Ambling Way South

Common Row

Icknield Plantation

Aldfield Common

Windmill Row

Aldfield Farm

Old Down Row

Picked Common Row

Redlands Row

HILLSIDE

HILLSIDE

WEST DRIVE

VALE RD.

COLN RD.

CURIE

MAXWELL

THAMES

EIGHTEENTH ST.

SIXTEENTH ST.

TENTH ST.

TWELFTH ST.

SIXTH ST.

FOURTH ST.

FARADAY AV.

HARWELL INTERNATIONAL BUSINESS CENTRE

SECOND AVENUE

AVENUE

NORTH DRIVE

NORTH DR.

Winaway Farm

WINAWAY

Harwell Primary School

WESTFIELD WAY

THE STYLES

ORCHARD

Rec. Grd. Pav. Playgrd.

Ten. Cts. Club

WANTAGE

A417

READING

Sports Field

HARWELL FIELD

A4185

STREET

SOUTH

AVENUE

DRIVE

THIRD ST.

FIRST ST.

SECOND ST.

THIRD

Pav.

Sports Field

147

119

LIBRARY AV.

STILLEWAY

RUTHERFORD

TWENTIETH ST.

SEVENTEENTH

FIFTEENTH

HIGH ST.

DALTON AV.

FARADAY

STREET

QUEREL

ELEVENTH ST.

THIRTEENTH ST.

ROAD

HUNGERFORD ROAD

HUNGERFORD ROAD

FEATHERBED LANE

MILTON HILL

47 48

190

89 107

88

87

47 48

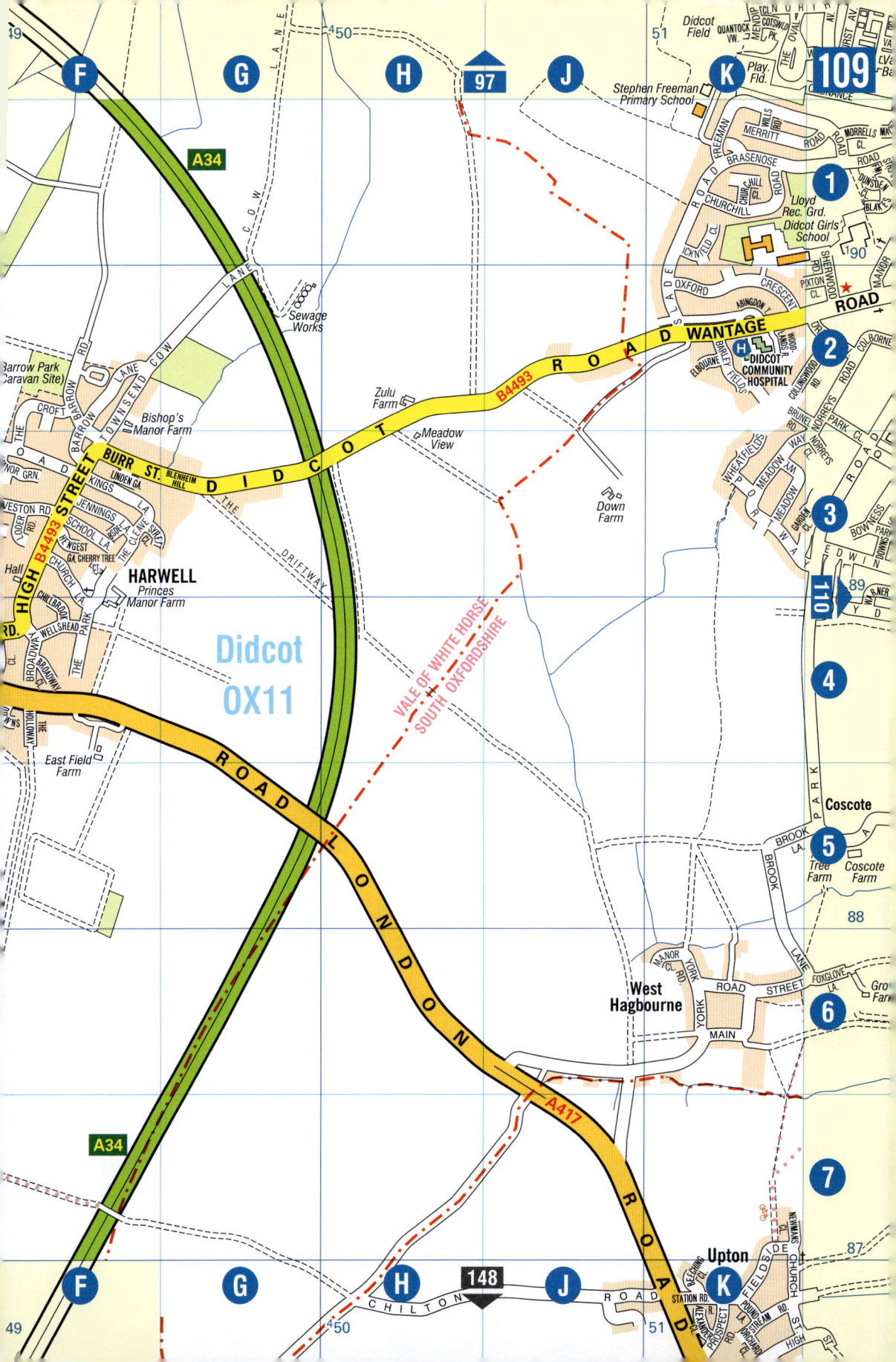

F G H 97 J K 1

49 50 Didcot Field 51

Stephen Freeman Primary School

QUANTOCK VW.
MENDIP
COTSWOLD
THE OVAL
NORTH AV.
HURST AV.

Play. Fld.

MERRITT
WILLS RD.
MORRELLS MA.
CL.
DUNSDEN CL.
BLAKE'S CL.

BRASENOSE

FREEMAN ROAD
CHURCHILL
CHURCHILL CL.
ROAD
SHERWOOD RD.

Lloyd Rec. Grd.
Didcot Girls' School

ICKNIELD CL.
OXFORD
CRESCENT
PIXTON CL.

90

ROAD 1

MANOR RD. 2

ABINGDON T.
WANTAGE ROAD
COLBORNE RD.

A34

BARLEY
FIELDS
ELBOURNE

DIDCOT ROAD B4493

DIDCOT COMMUNITY HOSPITAL H

BRUNEL RD.
NORRES PARK CL.
NORRES RD.

ROAD 2

COLLINGWOOD RD.

WHEATFIELDS
MEADOW WAY
GARDEN CL.
MEADOW WY.
MEADOW WAY
BOWYERS PARK RD.

EDWIN ROAD 3

89

WY. NER.
CL.

110 3

4

Zulu Farm

Meadow View

Barrow Park Caravan Site

THE CROFT
BARROW RD.
COW LANE
TOWNSEND
COW LANE
COW LANE

Bishop's Manor Farm

Blenheim Hill

BURR ST.
BURR STREET

LINDEN GA.
KINGS LA.
SCHOOL LA.
JENNINGS
HENGEST GA.
CHERRY TREE CT.

THE CLEAVE

THE DRIFTWAY

Down Farm

Sewage Works

HARWELL
Princes Manor Farm

HIGH STREET B4493

WESTON RD.
CODER RD.
Hall
CHURCH
CHILBROOK CL.
WELLSHEAD
THE PARK
BROADWAY
BROADWAY
THE PARK

Didcot OX11

VALE OF WHITE HORSE
SOUTH OXFORDSHIRE

Coscote 5

BROOK LA.
BROOK LANE
Tree Farm
Coscote Farm

88

A34

East Field Farm

HOLLOWAY
SNS.

LONDON ROAD

West Hagbourne

MANOR CL.
YORK RD.
YORK ROAD
STREET
FOXGLOVE LA.
Gro. Farm

YORK RD.
MAIN ROAD 6

A417

7

Upton
RECTORY
NEWMANS LA.
CHURCH ST.
PROSPECT RD.
FIELDS
ALEXANDER RD.
POUND CL.
STATION RD.
CHILTON
ROAD

87

F 148 G H J K

49 50 51

DIDCOT

Didcot Parkway

98

WANTAGE

Didcot Community Hospital

Lloyd Rec. Grd.
Didcot Girls' School

Manor Sch.
Manor Sch.
Civic Hall

Nursy. Sch.

Industrial Estate

Gas Works

All Saints C of E Prim. Sch.

ABINGDON RD.
A4130

BROADWAY

Comm. Cen.
Market Pl.
Mag. Ct.

Cemy.

Greenmere Prim. Sch.
Laburnum Gro.

St. Birinus Sch.
Edmunds Park
Didcot Cen.
The Didcot Wave
Leisure Cen.

Royal Berkshire Court

JUBILEE WAY

Fleet Meadow Comm. Hall

Northbourne
Prim. Sch.

Playing Field

The Crescent

Rec. Grd.

Cherry Tree Farm

GREAT MEAD

East Hagbourne

HIGGS

NEW ROAD
B4016

BLEWBURY

Coscote
Yew Tree Farm
Coscote Farm

West Hagbourne

Hagbourne C of E Prim. Sch.

Bowl. Grn.

Grove Farm

Hagbourne Mill Farm

SOUTH OXFORDSHIRE
VALE OF WHITE HORSE

B4016

BESSEL'S WAY

Upton
Frogalley Farm

114

Sewage Works

109

89

88

87

52

53

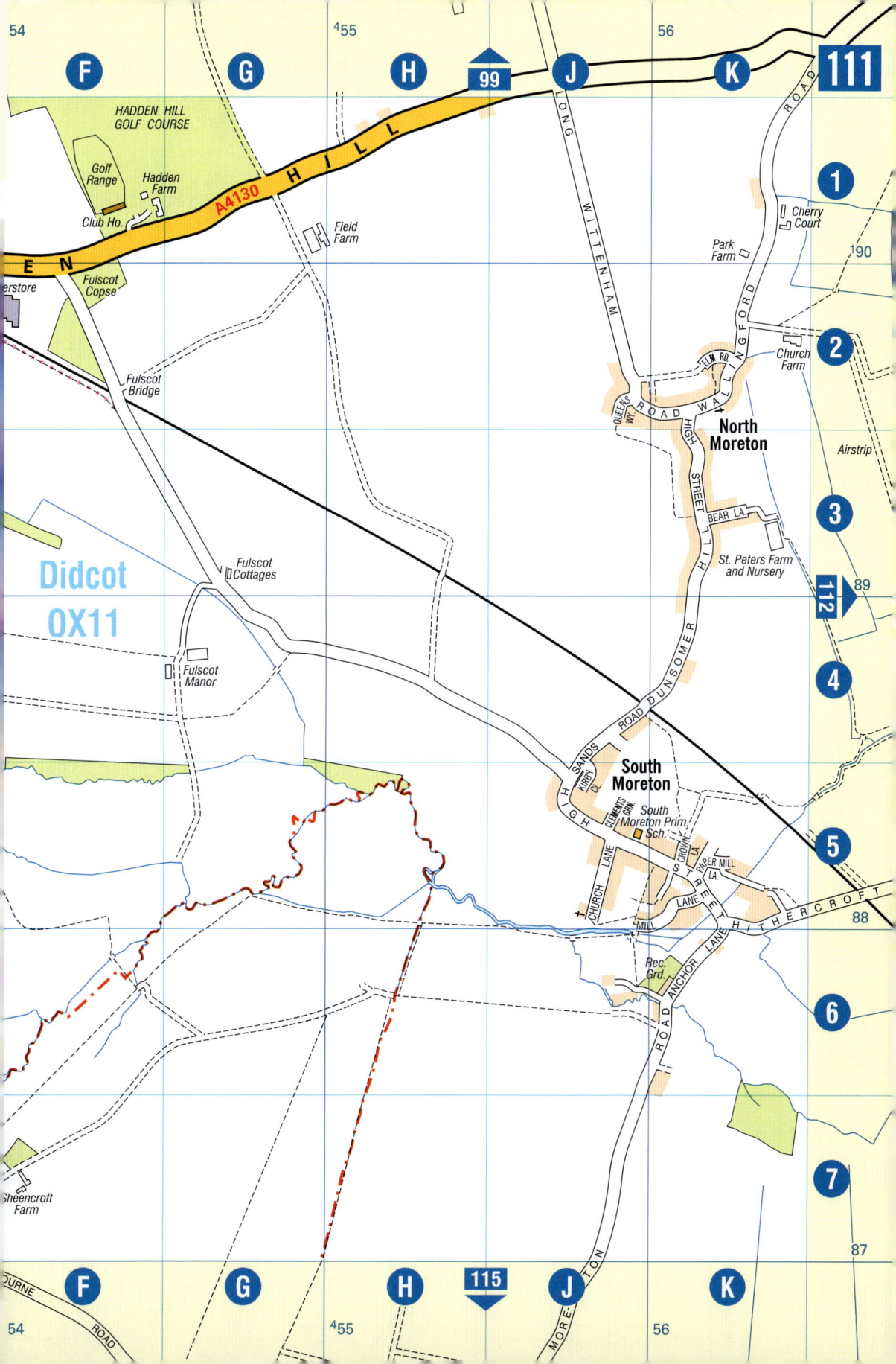

F G H J K

54 ⁴55 56

99

HADDEN HILL GOLF COURSE

Golf Range

Hadden Farm

Club Ho.

A4130 HILL

EN

Fulscot Copse

...erstore

Field Farm

LONG WITTENHAM

WALLINGFORD ROAD

Cherry Court

Park Farm

ELM RD

Church Farm

QUEENS WY

HIGH STREET

ROAD

North Moreton

Airstrip

BEAR LA.

St. Peters Farm and Nursery

Fulscot Bridge

Fulscot Cottages

Didcot OX11

Fulscot Manor

ROAD DUNSOMER

HIGH STREET

SANDS

KIRBY CL.

CLEMENTS GRN

South Moreton

South Moreton Prim. Sch.

CHURCH LANE

S CROWN LA.

PAPER MILL LA.

STREET HITHERCROFT

MILL LANE

Rec. Grd.

ANCHOR LANE

ROAD

MORETON

Sheencroft Farm

...OURNE ROAD

1

2

3

112 89

4

5 88

6

7 87

F G H J K

54 ⁴55 56

115

A4130

ROAD

A   B   100   C   D   E

Brightwell Manor

BRIGHTWELL-CUM-SOTWELL

WELL STREET   SOTWELL ST

PENN LA   Nursery

Pumping Station

Slade E Farm

1

Cherry Court

WALLINGFORD

190

Pavs. Rec. Grd.

Mackney Court Farm

MACKNEY LANE

2

Kibble

North Moreton

Airstrip

Ditch

Sherwood Ho.

Mackney

Sherwood Farm

3

LA

St. Peters Farm and Nursery

89 ◄ 111

Brook

4

Mill

HITHER C R

Hithercroft Farm

Old Hithercroft House

Didcot

5

HERCROFT C

CHURCH

88

OX11

Cholsey Hill

6

7

87

A   **B**   116   **C**   **D**   **E**

The Manor

Karanga

Sewage Works

The Hazels

Manor Farm

ROAD

MARYMEAD

Cholsey Prim. Sch. Day Cen.

57 The Lees

58

57

58

W CROSS F

BUL LA

Crowmarsh
Riverside

SLADE END
ROUNDABOUT
Slade End

1

Howbery Park
Hydraulics Research
Station
90

WALLINGFORD

Playground
WILDING
Blackstone
Cemy.
Wallingford
School
Castle
Leisure
Centre

Queen's Av.
Inf. Sch.
COOPERS PIECE
ROWLAND FLD.
Comm. Cen.
CLAPCOT WY.
Bull Croft Park
Pav.
Bowl. Grn.
Castle (rems of)

2

Institute of
Hydrology
Playing
Field
Council
Offs.
WINTER'S FLD.
HOWBERY FM.

Fir Tree
Jun. Sch.
Play Fld.
STATION RD. IND. EST.
Comm. Cen.
Lib.
Mus.
County Offs.
BEAR LA.
Tennis Cts.
Riverside Park
& Pools
Pav.

AFC
Wallingford
Rugby Pitch
Club Sports Ground
HITHERCROFT
Hithercroft Ind. Est.
KINECROFT
Goldsmiths
Wallingford
Bridge

3

Caravan
Park
NEWNHAM GN.
NEWNHAM GN.
MURREN CFT.
89
Sch.

HITHERCROFT
ROUNDABOUT
LESTER RD.
WHITLEY RD.
Hithercroft Industrial Estate
HITHERCROFT CT. RD.
Brook
Wallingford
THE SIDINGS
Prim. Sch.
FLUDGER
St. John's Road
St. Leonard's
Lower Wharf
Boat Yard

CROWMARSH
GIFFORD
130

Bradford's
A4130

WALLINGFORD
COMMUNITY
HOSPITAL
Bradford's Bridge
THE MURREN
ORCHARD CL.
St. Leonard's Ct.
Newnham
Farm

4

Wallingford
OX10

International Agricultural
Information Centre

WINTERBROOK LANE
Winterbrook
WINTERGREEN LA.
Winterbrook

Cox's
Farm
WINTERBROOK LANE
Cholsey and Wallingford Railway

5

White Cross
(Nurses Home)
Ten. Cts.
NOSWORTHY
A4130
WAY
88

Winterbrook
Bridge
North Court
Flat
The
Lake
Mongewell

PORT WAY

READING ROAD
A329
Brook
House

6

Mongewell
Park Fm.
HILL
148
B4009

MONGEWELL
PARK

7

Field
Cottage
Mill
Court
Blackall's
Farm
Blackall's
House

WALLINGFORD ROAD
87

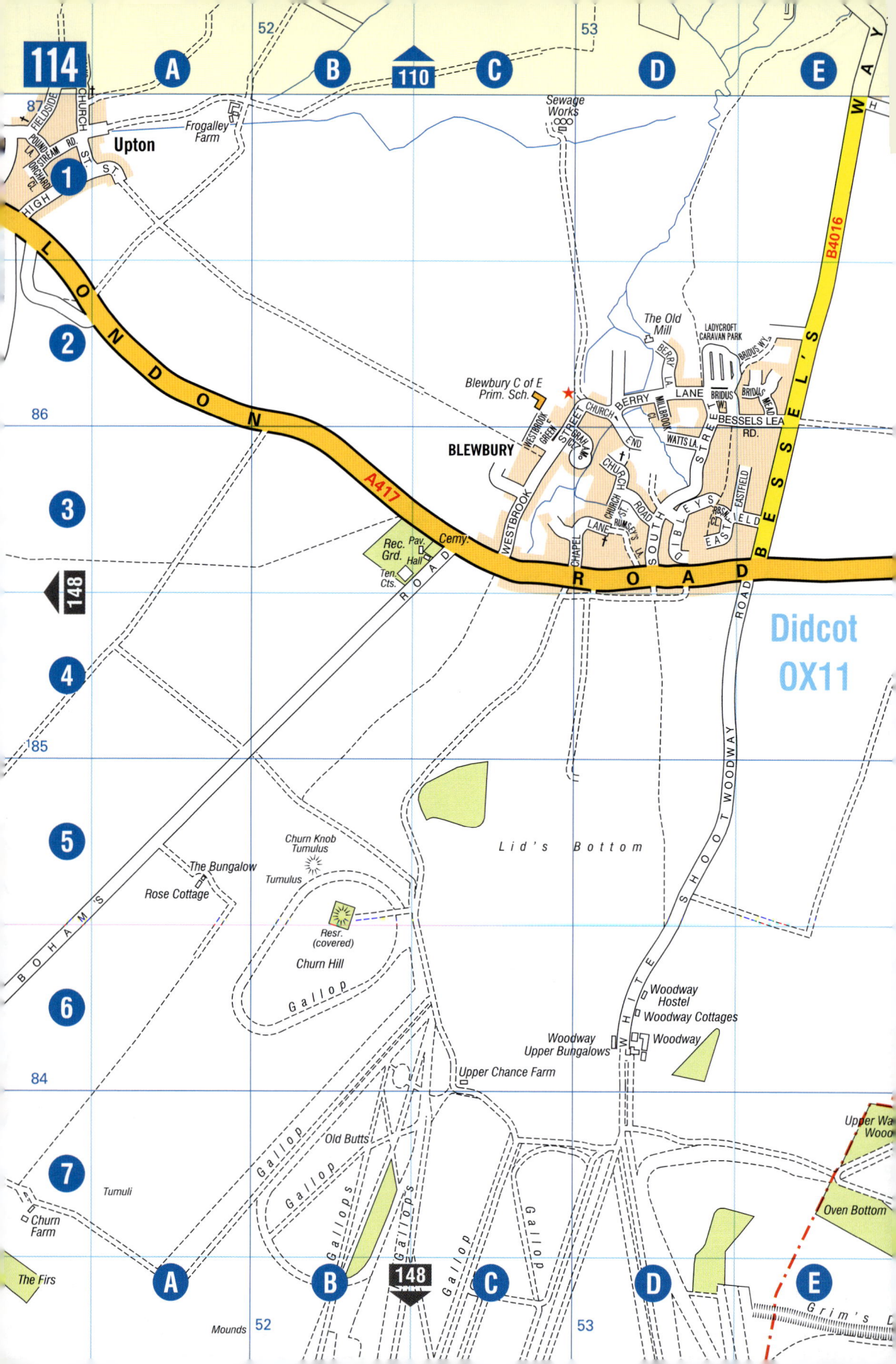

114

A B **110** C D E

Upton

Frogalley Farm

Sewage Works

The Old Mill

Ladycroft Caravan Park

Blewbury C of E Prim. Sch.

BLEWBURY

Berry Lane

Bridus Wy.

Bessels Lea Rd.

Church End

Berry Lane

Westbrook Green

London Road

A417

Church Street

Millbrook

Watts La.

Bridus

Didcot OX11

Cemy.

Westbrook

Chapel Lane

Church Lane

South St.

Rumsey's La.

Ibley's Cl.

Eastfield

Easthill Cl.

Rec. Grd.

Pav. Hall

Ten. Cts.

ROAD

148

Lid's Bottom

Woodway

White Shoot

Woodway

The Bungalow

Rose Cottage

Churn Knob Tumulus

Tumulus

Resr. (covered)

Churn Hill

Gallop

Woodway Hostel

Woodway Cottages

Woodway

Woodway Upper Bungalows

Upper Chance Farm

BOHAMS

Gallop

Old Butts

Gallop

Gallops

Gallops

Gallop

Gallop

Tumuli

Churn Farm

The Firs

Upper Wa Woo

Oven Bottom

Grim's D

Mounds 52

53

A B 148 C D E

CHURCH ST.

HIGH ST.

FIELDSIDE

PRIOR

STREAM

ORCHARD

87

86

185

84

54 455 455 56

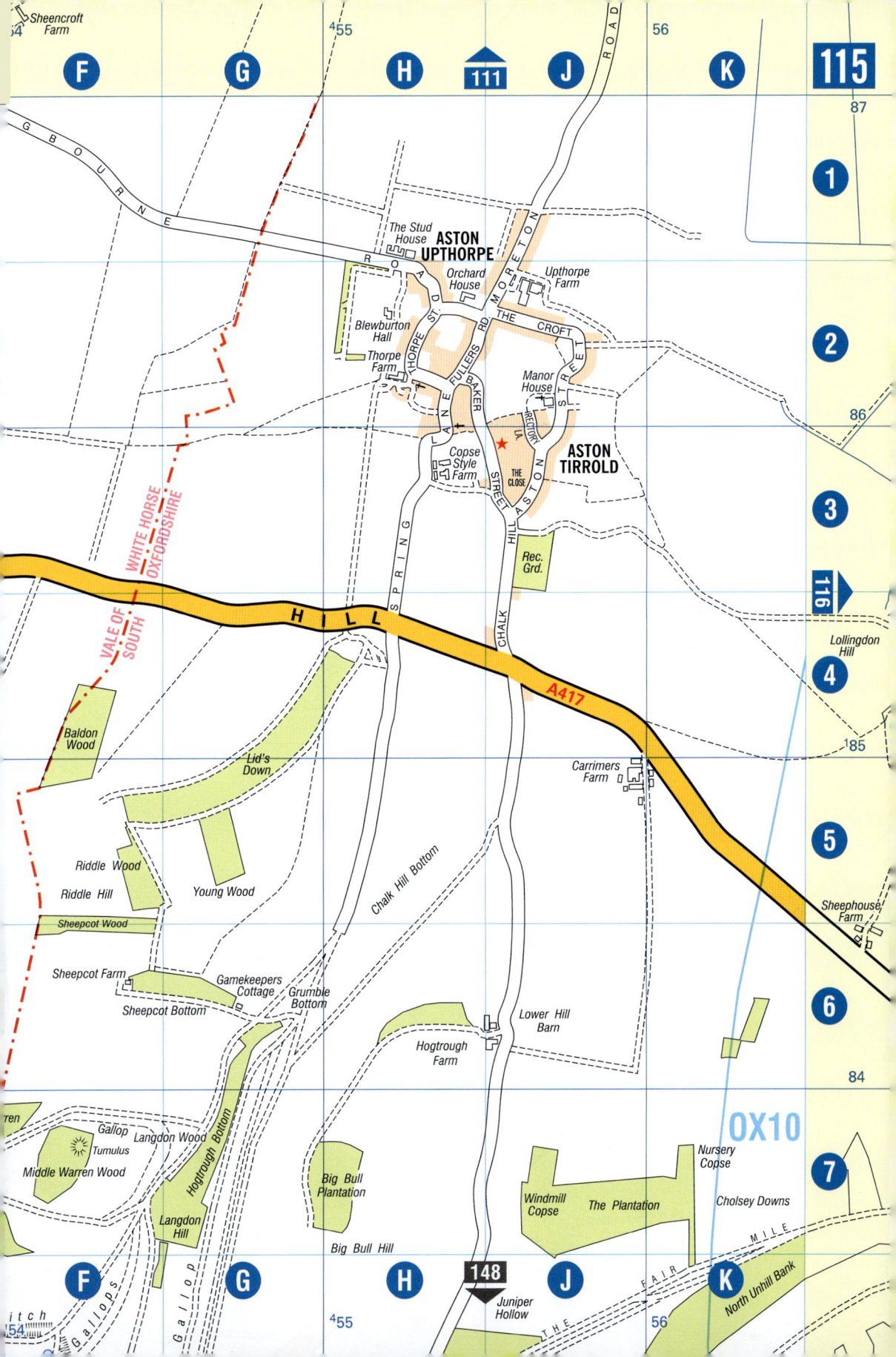

Sheencroft Farm

1

GBOURNE

ROAD

The Stud House

ASTON UPTHORPE

Orchard House

Upthorpe Farm

MORETON

THE CROFT

2

86

Blewburton Hall

THORPE ST

FULLERS RD

BAKER

Thorpe Farm

Manor House

ASTON STREET

RECTORY LA.

ASTON TIRROLD

3

Copse Style Farm

THE CLOSE

★

LANE

WHITE HORSE
OXFORDSHIRE

Rec. Grd.

SPRING

116 ►

VALE OF SOUTH

HILL

CHALK

Lollingdon Hill

4

185

A417

STREET

Baldon Wood

Lid's Down

Carrimers Farm

Sheephouse Farm

5

Riddle Wood

Young Wood

Chalk Hill Bottom

Riddle Hill

Sheepcot Wood

Sheepcot Farm

Gamekeepers Cottage

Grumble Bottom

Lower Hill Barn

6

84

Sheepcot Bottom

Hogtrough Farm

OX10

Gallop

Langdon Wood

Tumulus

Hogtrough Bottom

Big Bull Plantation

Nursery Copse

7

Middle Warren Wood

Windmill Copse

The Plantation

Cholsey Downs

Langdon Hill

Big Bull Hill

MILE

North Unhill Bank

itch
54

GALLOPS

Gallop

Juniper Hollow

THE FAIR

116

A B 112 C D E

87

1

The Lees

Manor Farm

The Hazels

Sewage Works

CHURCH

Karanga

Cholsey Prim. Sch.
Day Cen.
Playing Field
Rec. Grd.
Pav.

MARYMEAD
WALLING
LITTLE
CROSS
CHECKERS
PL
THE
POUND
PL
ROAD
HONEY
POUND LA
LA
COLLEGE
FAIRFIELD
DROVESIDE
BROOKSIDE
CRESCENT
ST. GEORGE'S
BEEHIVE CL
BUCKTHORN LA.
SANDY LA.
KENNEDY
ANN
ELL
CL
KENTWOOD CL
KENTWOOD WAY
STATION
PAPIST

2

Pancroft Farm

The Elms

Cholsey

The Paddocks

WEST END

WEST END.

BRENTFORD CL

WOMANS

ROAD

Kentwood Farm

86

3

Westfield

115

Wallingford
OX10

Lollingdon Farm

4

Lollingdon Hill

Lollingdon Copse

LANE

OFFLANDS COURT

185

5

A417

Sheephouse Farm

Breach House

Breach Farm

BREACH FM COTTS

WILLOW COURT LANE

Manor Cottages

Cranford House School

GLEBE CL

6

Westfield Nursery

Vernlil Kennels

WEST

HALFPENNY

The Old Vicarage

Recreation Ground

84

Downs Farm

SHORTLANDS HILL

Badger Bank

NORTH

ROAD

MOULSFORD

7

Cholsey Downs

Kingstanding Hill

Starveall Farm

148

Moulsford Bottom

WANTAGE RD.

North Unhill Bank

A B C D E

57

58

Lower Lodge

Walnut Bank

59 | 460 | 61 | 87

CHOLSEY

ROAD
OLD BLACKALLS DR
Blackall's Farm
Field Cottage
Mill Ct.
Mill Court Farm

East End Fm.
Blackall's House
Larkmead
SOUTHWELLS CL
ROWLAND RD
ROAD

ILGES LANE
LANE

WEDHAM CL
CHELSEA PL
CHARLES RD.

THE SPRINGS HOTEL
GOLF COURSE

Play. Fld.

The Springs Hotel & Golf Club

B4009

1

2

Rectory Farm Ho.
CHURCH LA.
THE STREET
POLLOCKS LA.
North Stoke
COOK LANE
WHITE HOUSE RD. 86

A329
WAY
ABBOTS MEAD
PAPIST WAY

Pav. Sports Fld.

Cholsey Marsh Nature Reserve

RIVER THAMES

Little Stoke Ho.

Littlestoke Manor Farm

Barracks Farm

148

3

4

185

Moulsford Prep. Sch.

THE READING
A329

WALLINGFORD

White Hill

5

6

84

Moulsford Manor

Lower Farm
FERRY LANE
FERRY LA.
THE FERRY

WOODCOTE ROAD
WALLINGFORD B4009

Reading
RG8

Ivol Barn

ROAD

7

South Stoke Prim. Sch.
Playing Field

South Stoke

CROSS KEYS RD.
CHAPEL DRAINS
THE COTTAGES
SOUTH BANK
STREET
ROAD

Lower Cadley's

A329
STREET
HILL
FERRY LA.
WALL

59 | 460 | 61

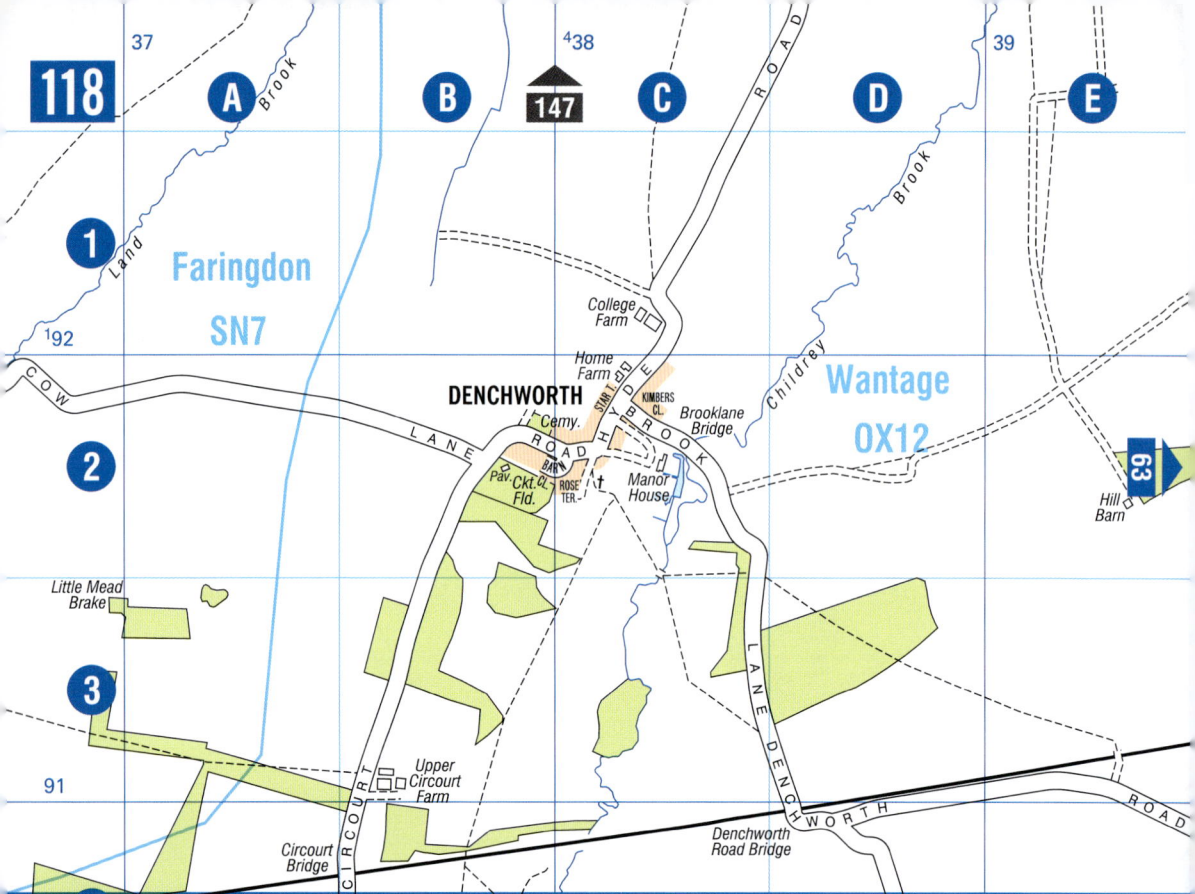
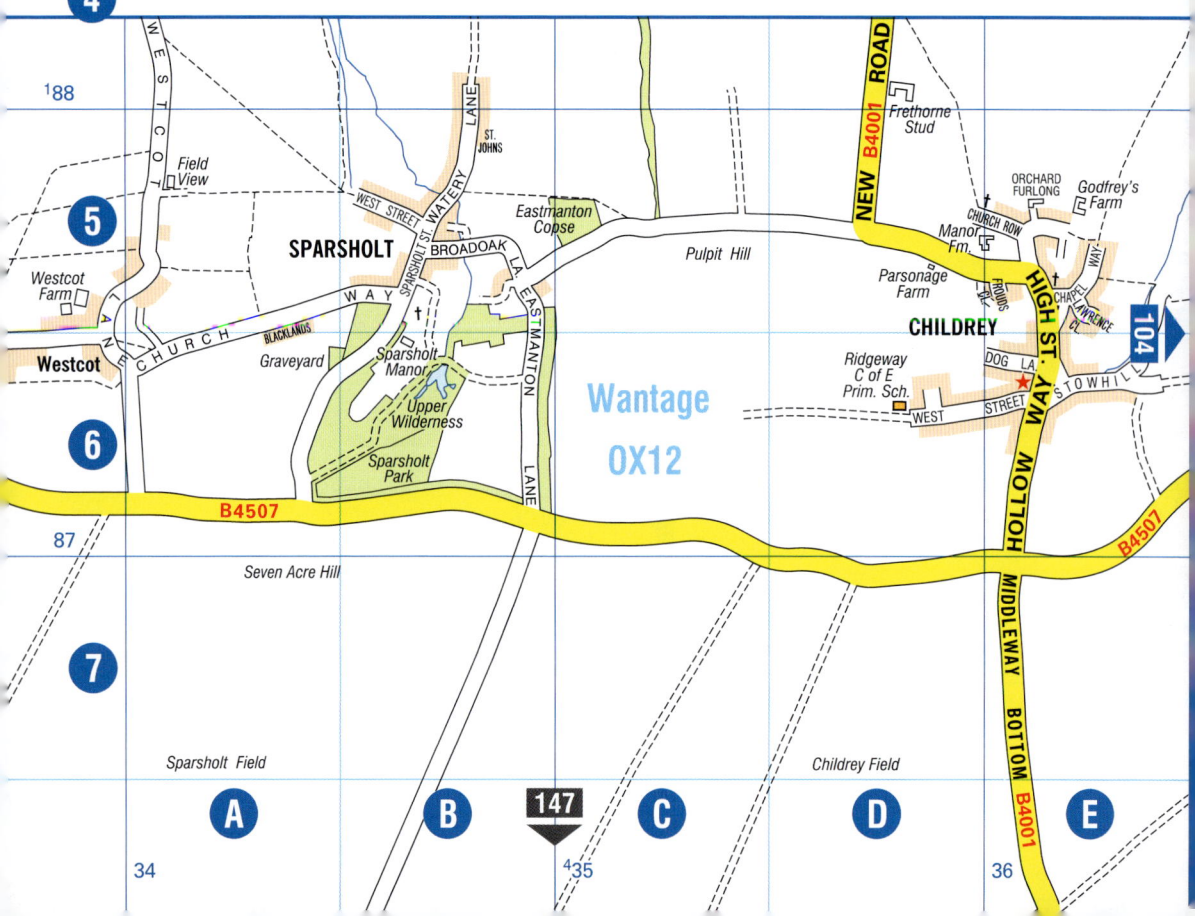

1

147 ▶ Wantage Field

Wantage
OX12

2

86

3

Bablakes Farm

MILL PADDOCK

KINGS CL. REGIS CL. MANOR

OLD MANOR CT.

LETCOMBE REGIS

Recreation Ground
Letcombe FC
Pav.

Letcombe Manor

MARBAERY

POST OFFICE LA.

Court Hill

OLD STABLES RD.

ST. TINNY WARBOROUGH

BASSETT

HILL ROAD

Warborough Farm

A338 ROAD

A338

MANOR ROAD

4

187

Spts.Fld.

AVENUE
FARADAY AV.

Sports Field

Pav.

A34

SOUTH OXFORDSHIRE
VALE OF WHITE HORSE

5

86

THAMES RD.

SIXTEENTH ST.
SIXTH
TWELFTH
TENTH ST.
NINTH
FARADAY AVENUE
THIRD STREET
FIRST ST.

EIGHTEENTH ST.

RUTHERFORD RD.
ROENTGEN
FIFTEENTH ST.
DALTON AV.
BECQUEREL
ELEVENTH

FARADAY AVENUE

LIBRARY AVENUE

LIBRARY AV.

SEVENTEENTH ST.

NINETEENTH ST.

Ridgeway House

P

P

HARWELL INTERNATIONAL BUSINESS CENTRE

FERMI ROAD

DIAMOND SYNCHROTRON

Play. Fld.

EIGHT

Diamond Cho.

RD. THIRTEEN

P

AVENUE

FROME ROAD

KENNET ROAD

A4185

Didcot
OX11

PERIMETER ROAD

DOWNSIDE ROAD

6

86

Limetree Farm

MANOR CL.
LIMETREES
ORNE
TOWNSEND
HOLLOW

RD. TWO

FIVE

Rutherford Laboratory

ROAD NINE
ROAD FIFTEEN
EIGHTI

SEVERN ROAD
WAYLAND ROAD
AVON ROAD

CRESCENT ROAD

Chilton Prim. Sch.

Jubilee Bridge

CHILTON

STREET
MAIN
CRAFTS

THE LANE

LANGDON LA.
SHELL DR.
PREE

DIDO ROAD

A34

THE PADDOCK
THE ORCHARDS
SOUTH
LOWER RD.
MANOR
LANGDON
SELDE
GR.
EVEN
VIEW

7

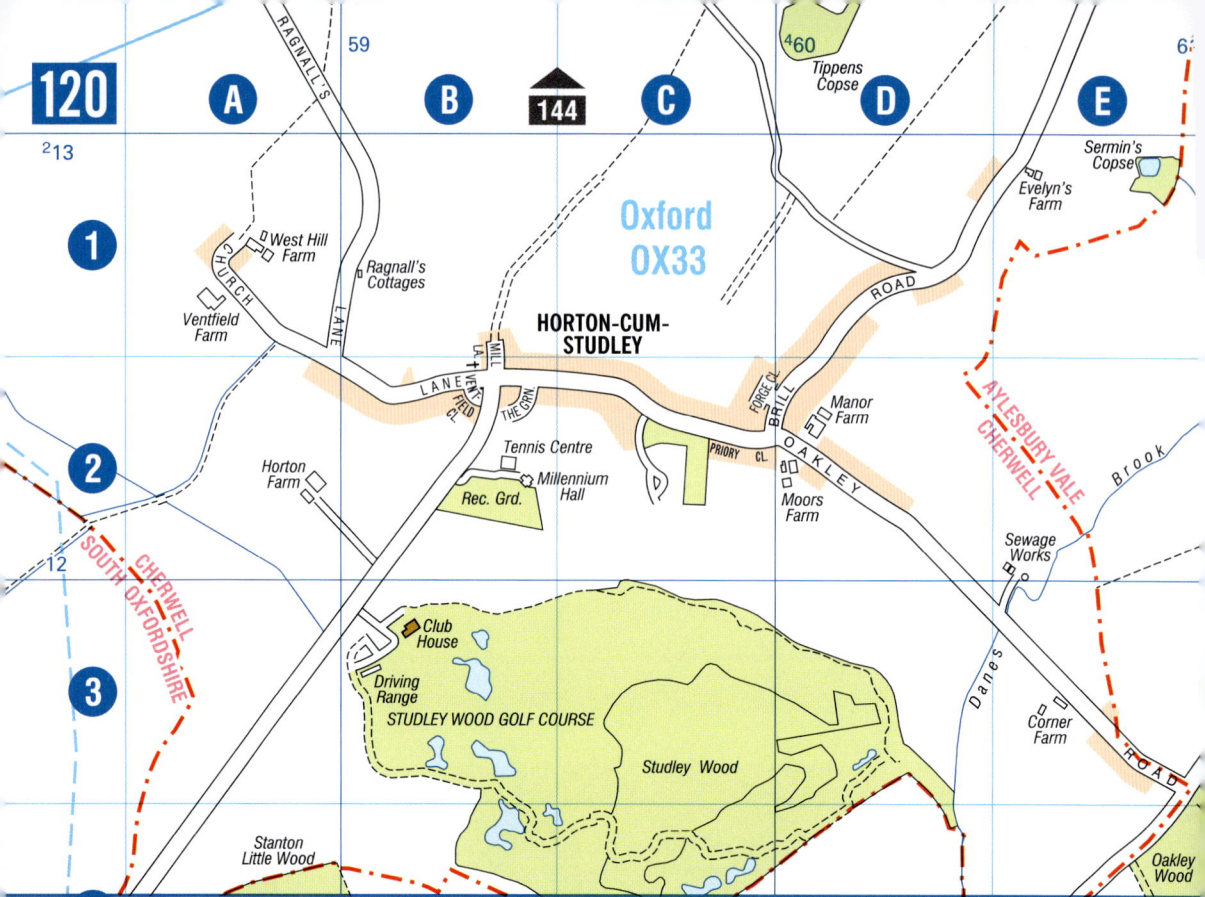
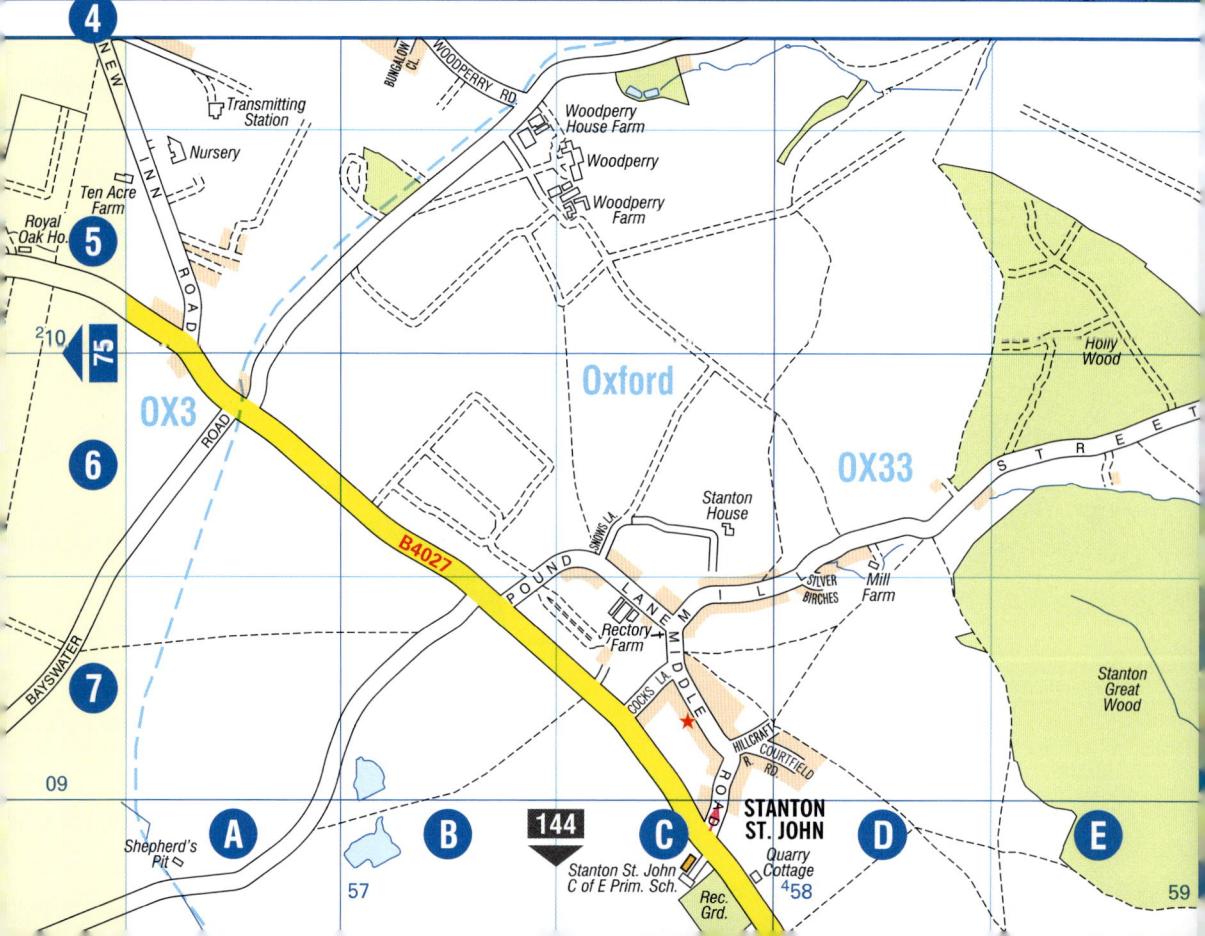

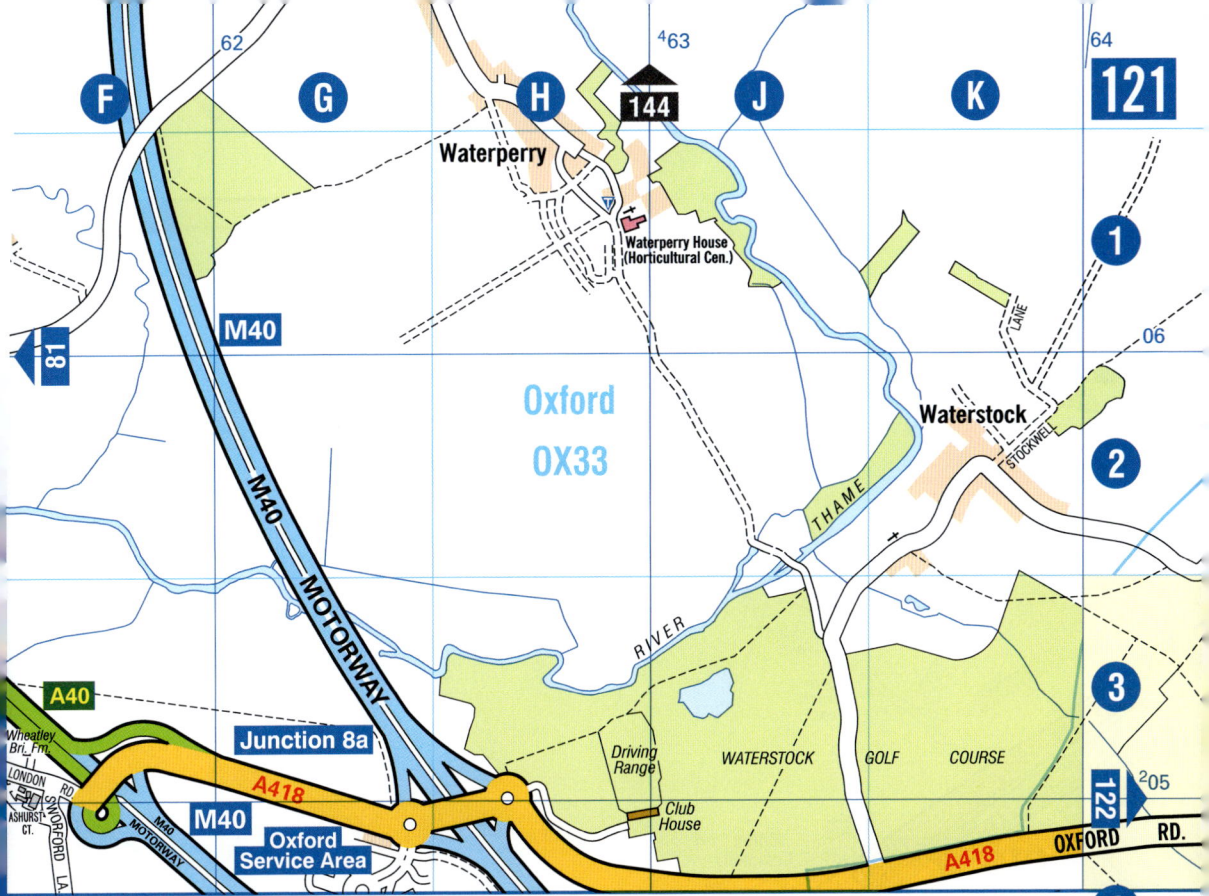
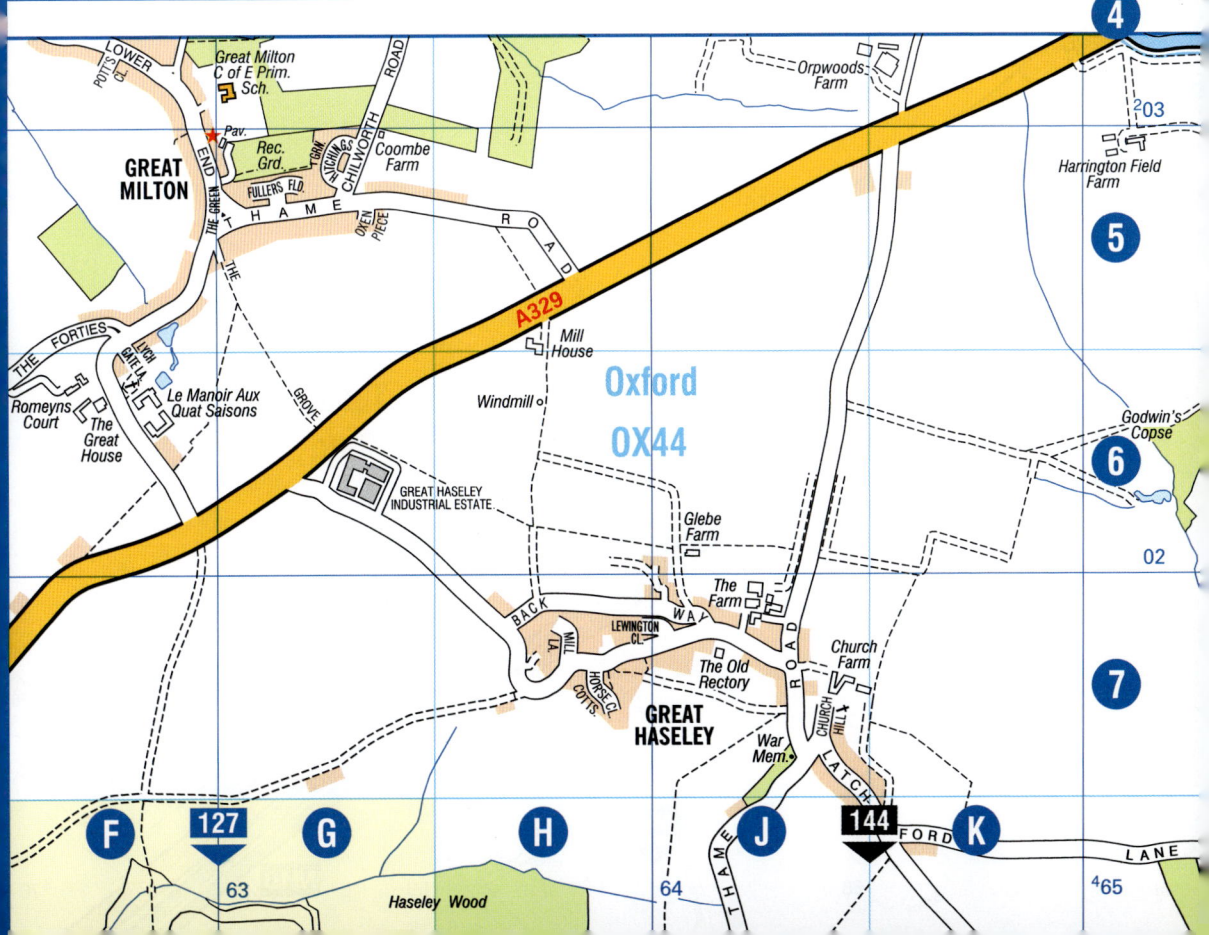

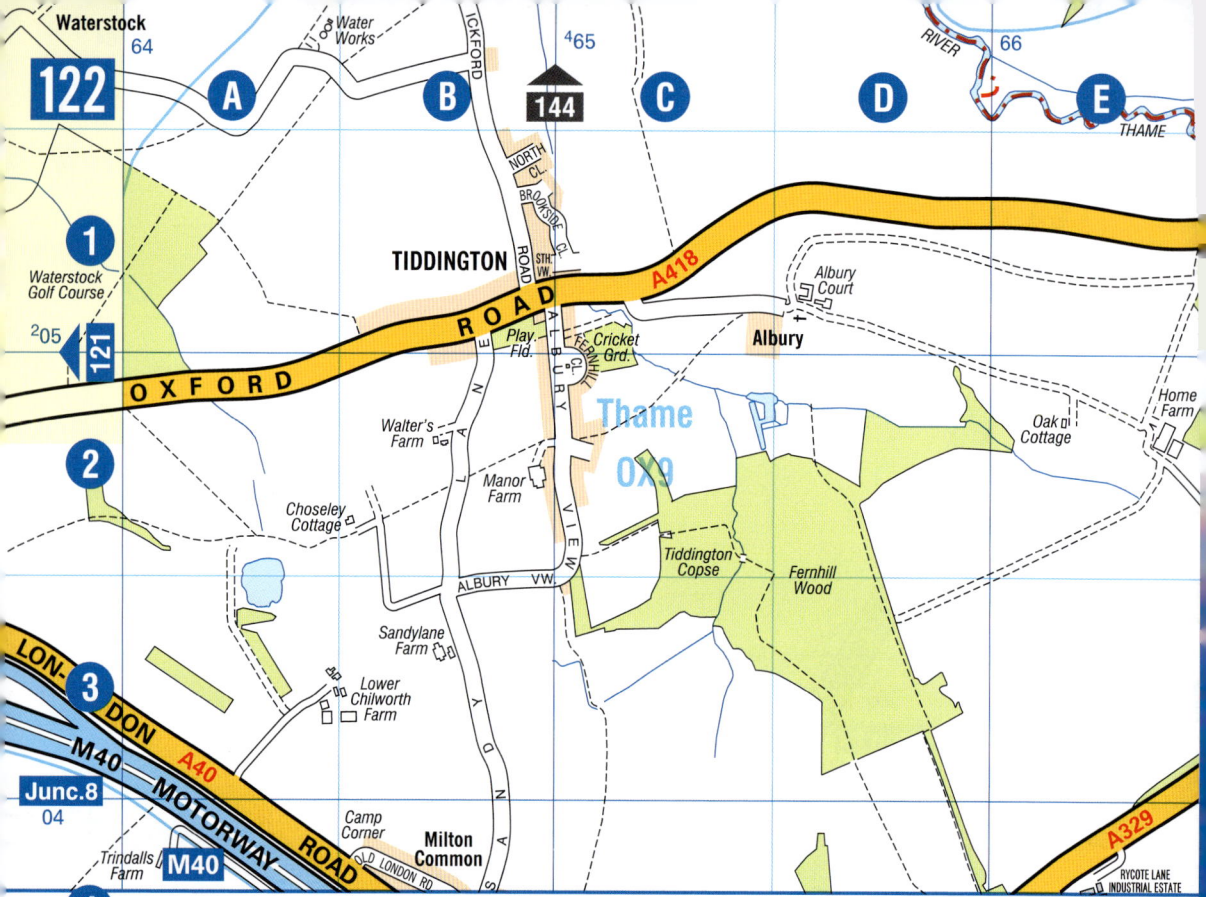
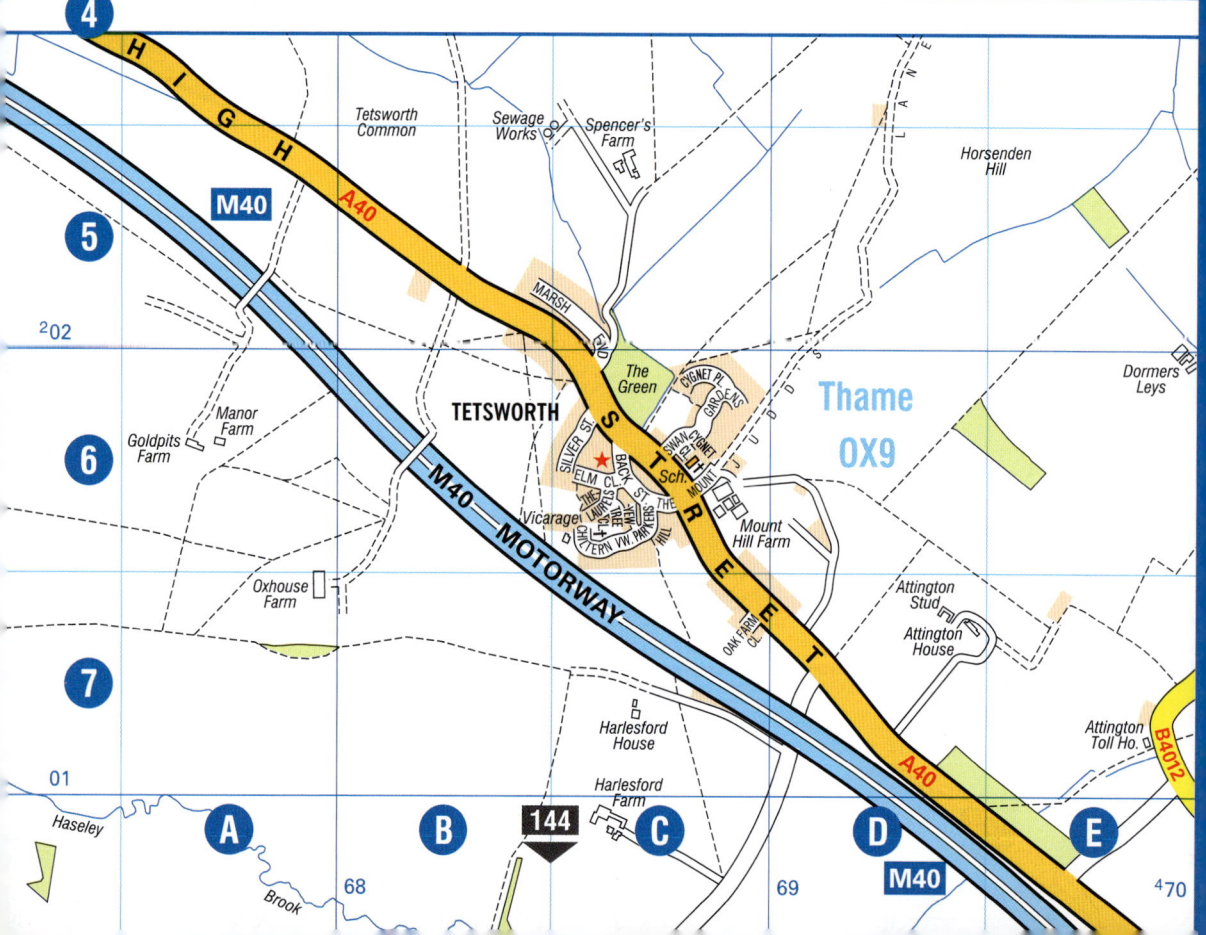

Mottymead

F G H J K

123

Lopemede Farm

Grove End Cott.
Grove End Farm
Fieldings

THAME

Scotsgrove Farm
Scotsgrove Cotts.
Scotsgrove House
Scotsgrove Hill

145

ROAD
THAME

1

07

Rose Cottage
Scotsgrove Mill

Golf Driving Range Southfield

B4011

Clacken Arches

AYLESBURY

A418

AYLESBURY VALE
SOUTH OXFORDSHIRE

Thames Mead Farm

ROAD

Motel

KINGSEY

2

LANE

A418

RIVER THAME

Mill Ho.

Depot

Thame Bridge

Warehouse

B4445 RD.

QUE
EBERHILL
FLTWD. WY.
SKIPPON RD.
LAMBERT WY.
BROOK SIDE
YEATES CL.
WILLOW RD.
ASHLAKE RD.
MEADOW WY.
GREENWY.
MOREND
PARLIAMENT
CL.

Sewage Works

LANE

MOOREND

POUNDHEAD
CARDWELL

IRETON CL.
RUSHALL RD.
BERKELEY
CAVALIER RD.
CLARKSON
DEMO

CRANMERE
A4129

RD.

Rugby Football Grd.

3

HINTON
DUNBAR
PELHAM RD.
GRENVILLE
ONSLOW DR.
PEMBROKE

Whites Farm
06

Town Farm

OXFORD

Lord Williams's Upper Sch.

BELL LA.
PRIEST END
HIGH ST.
CHURCH RD.
HOMESTEAD
MASTERS CT.

Ckt. Grd.

Pav.

NORTH
CHERITON

Mkt.

Superstore
FRIDAY CT.

Racquets
Fitness Centre

The Red Gallery

STREET

WELLINGTON

MOAT'S CRES.
KING'S
FAIRFAX
AYRES RD.
STUART WY.
LANGDALE RD.

KINGSEY
Road

KINGSEY RD.
A4129

4

St. Joseph's Catholic Prim. Sch.

BEECH
SYCAMORE
CHESTNUT
HAZEL
CEDAR
MAPLE

Theatre

UP. HIGH ST.

PARK

The Red Gallery

ST. ANDREWS
GASLEY

Thame Community Hospital

Thame Tennis Club
Tennis School

MEADOWCROFT
Play. Fld.
Youth Centre

TOWERSEY

HUNT RD.
CHESHAM
B4012

Towersey
Rd.

Thame Sports & Arts Centre
Playing Field

OXFORD GS.

HAWTHORN
COMBE HILL
CONDUIT

Recreation Ground

Cuttle Brook Nature Reserve

HOLLIERS
MORETON
ELLIOTT CL.
PEARCE CT.

NELSON ST.
ELMS RD.
SHMN LA.
LIB. RD.

War Meml.

Rec. Grd.

CHOWNS RD.

John Hampden Prim. Sch.

HORSECROFT
CHILTERN GRO.
HORTON CL.

QUEENS

CHINNOR
B4445

CROFT
PROFT

COTMORE

TOWERSEY
DRIVE

PICKENFIELD

5

B4012

Cotmore Wells Farm

124
205

Field View

Batesleys Farm

WINDMILL
HAMPDEN AV.

Thame Utd. FC (Hithercroft Stadium)

THAME

Meadow Brook House

DIEMAN'S RD.
John Hampden Nursy. Sch.

Warehouses

YOLE NS
BLMRE
MORBEY RD.
LIMM RD.

NEWBARN
STATION

Thame Park Business Centre

JEFFERSON WAY
UPTON RD.

YARD

Works

Depot

Factory
Works

CHINNOR
HOWLAND

6

Thame OX9

Park Meadow Cottage
Park Meadow Farm

ROAD
WENMAN

Oakfield

ROAD

ROAD
CHIN.

B4445 RD.

Blackditch Farm

Moreton
Chestnut Farm
Leys Farm

Meadowbrook Farm

Bow Bridge

Greys Mead

B4012

Brook

Cuttle

PARK

Lodges

Highclere

Thame Park

Sydenham Hurst

04

7

F G H J K

Parkgrange Farm

THAME ROAD

145

71

72

THAME PARK

Thame Park (remains of Abbey)

Weir

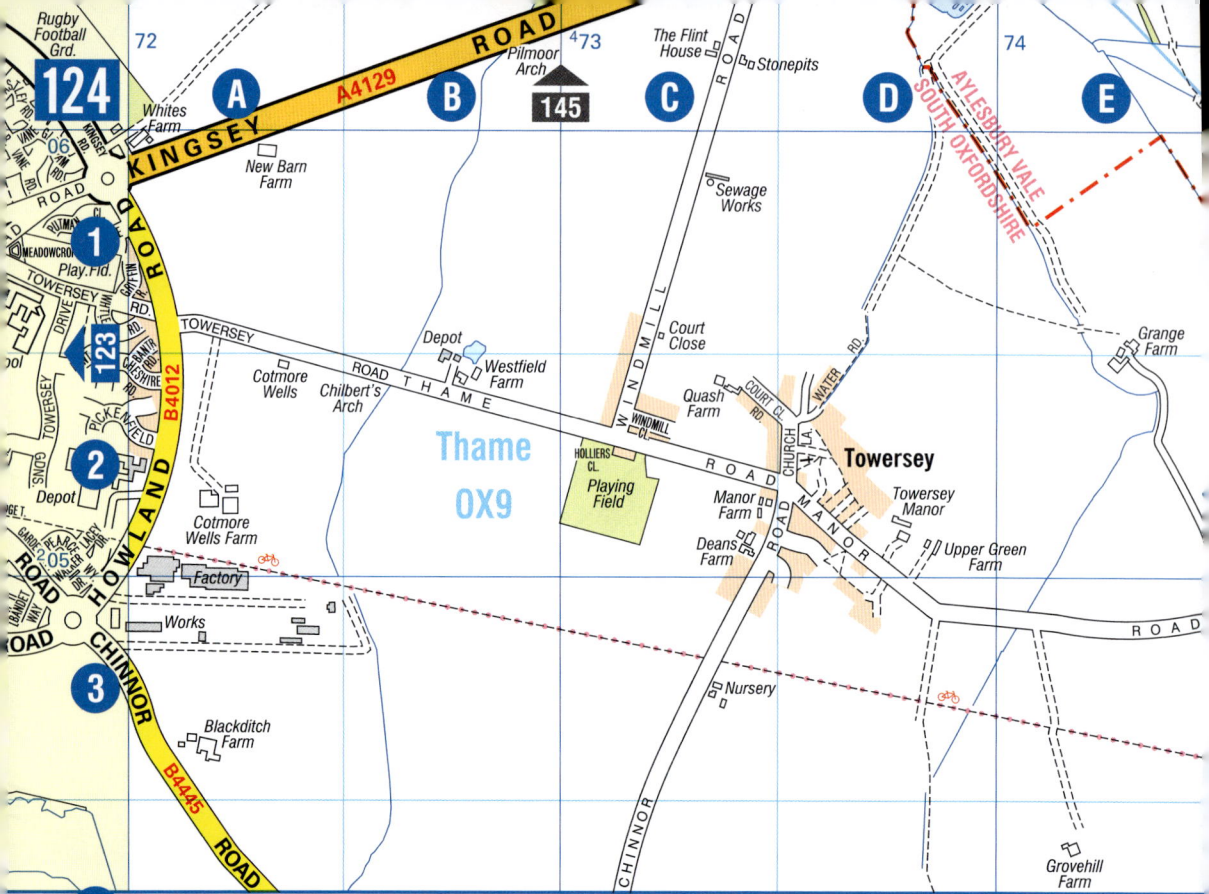
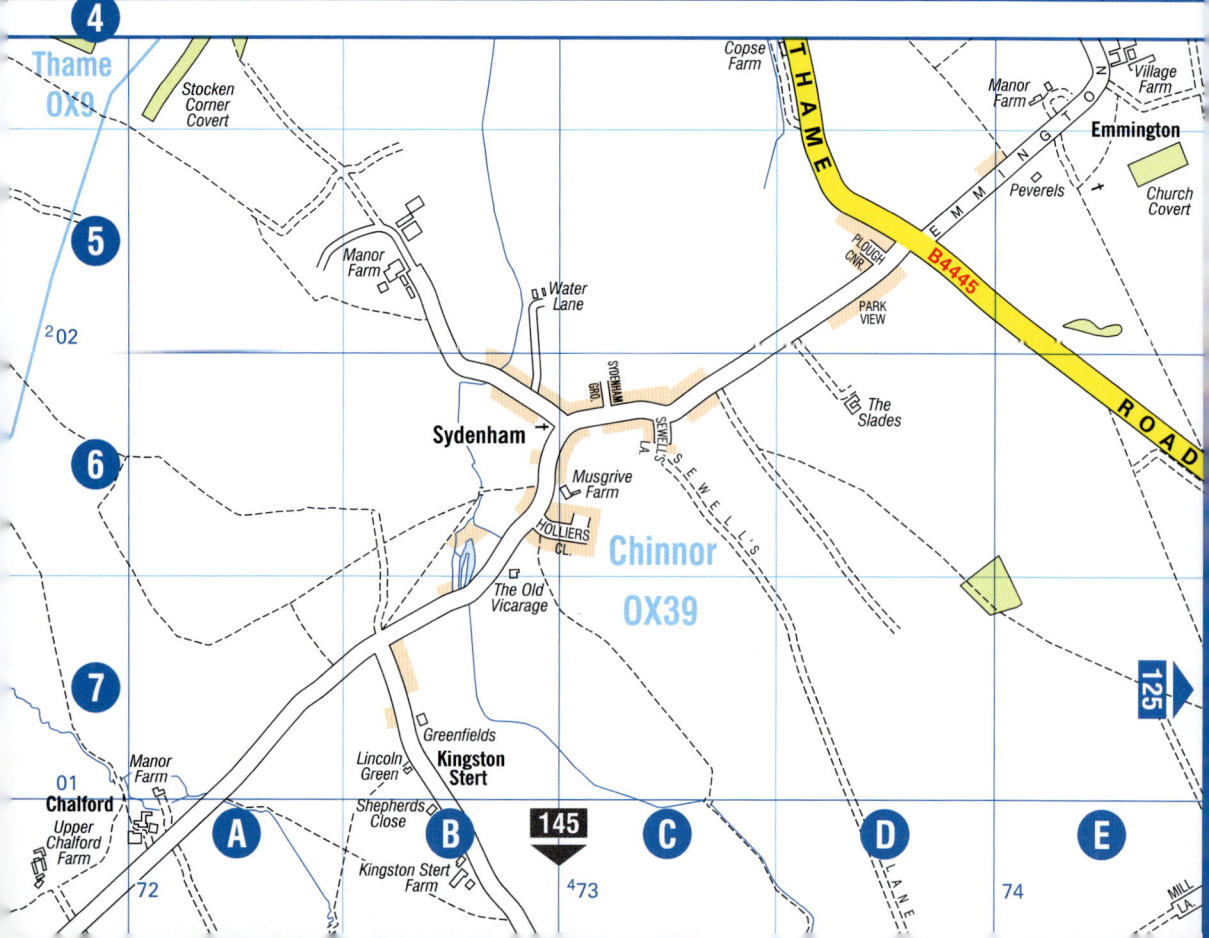

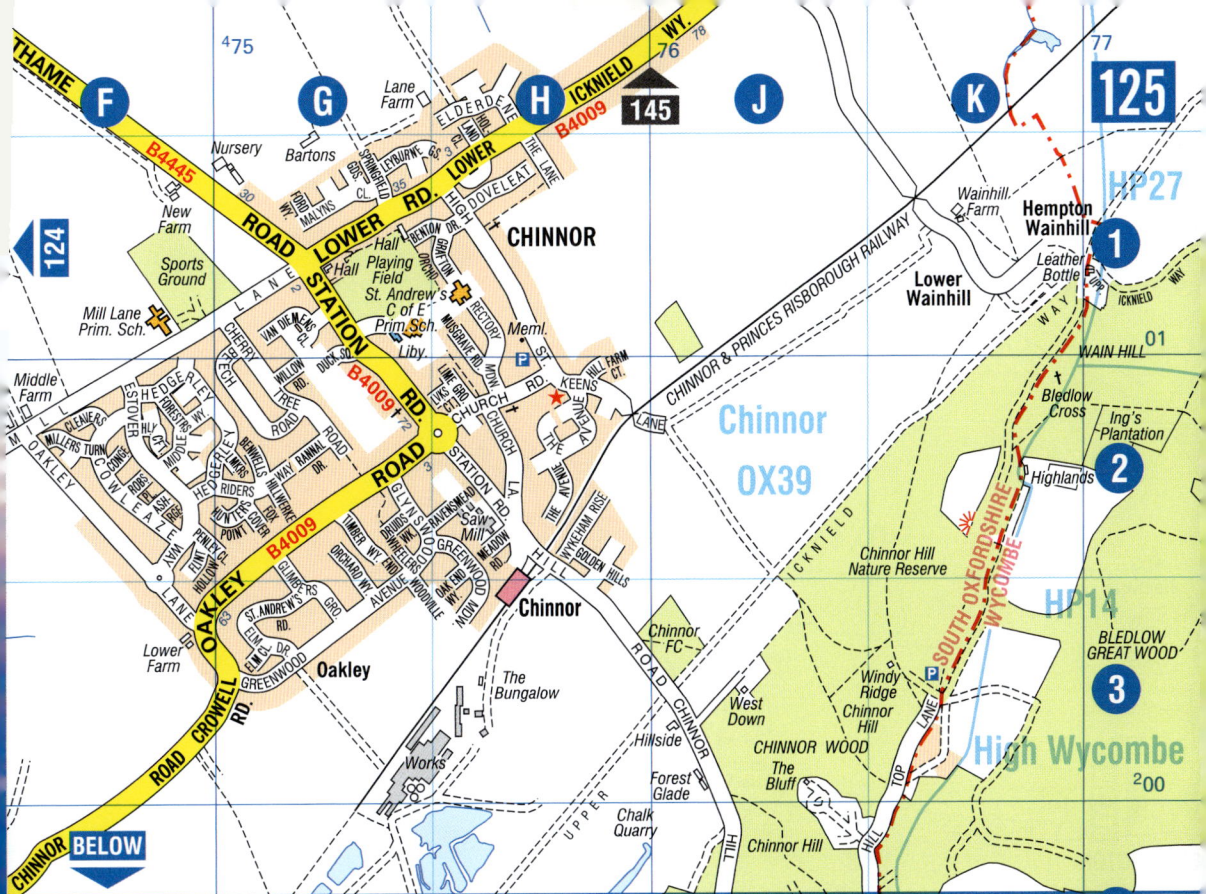

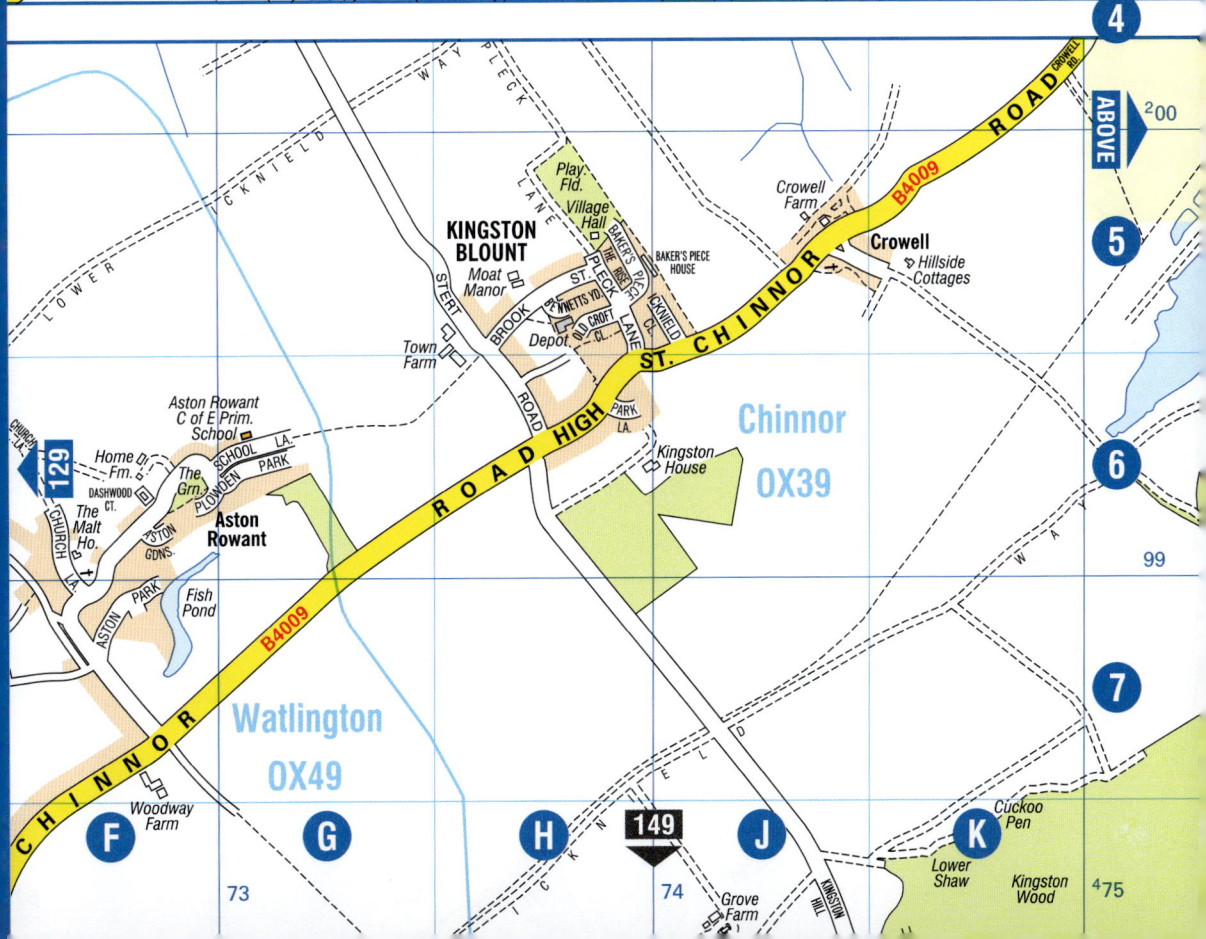

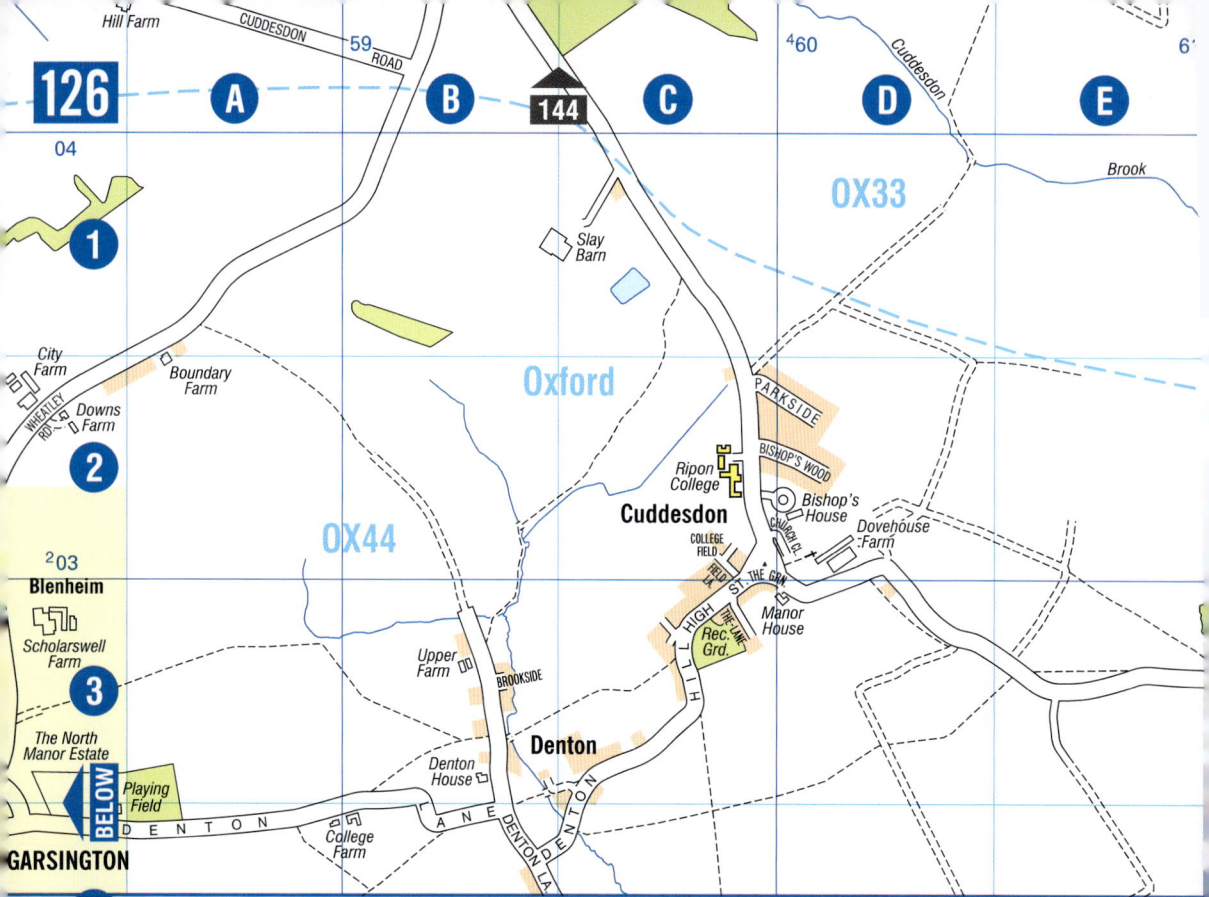
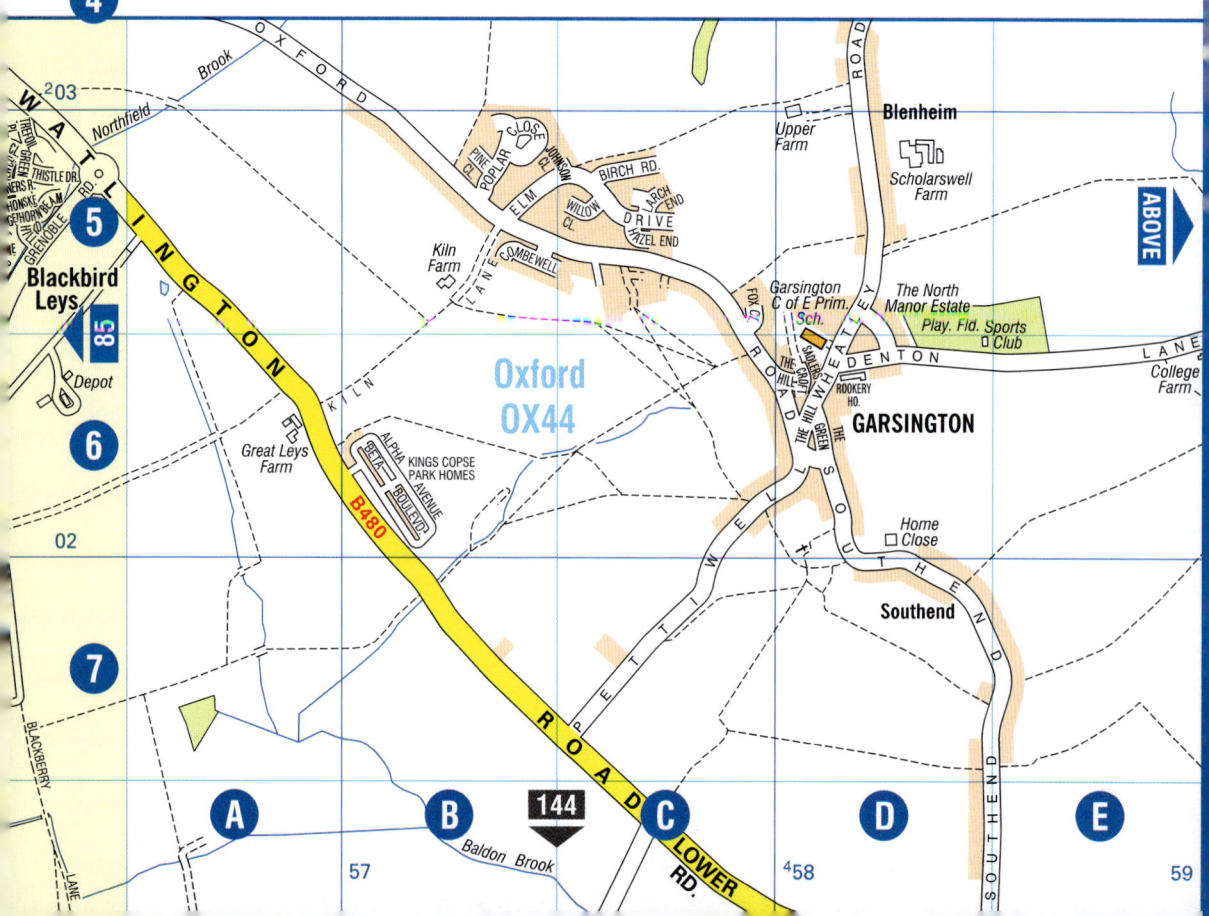

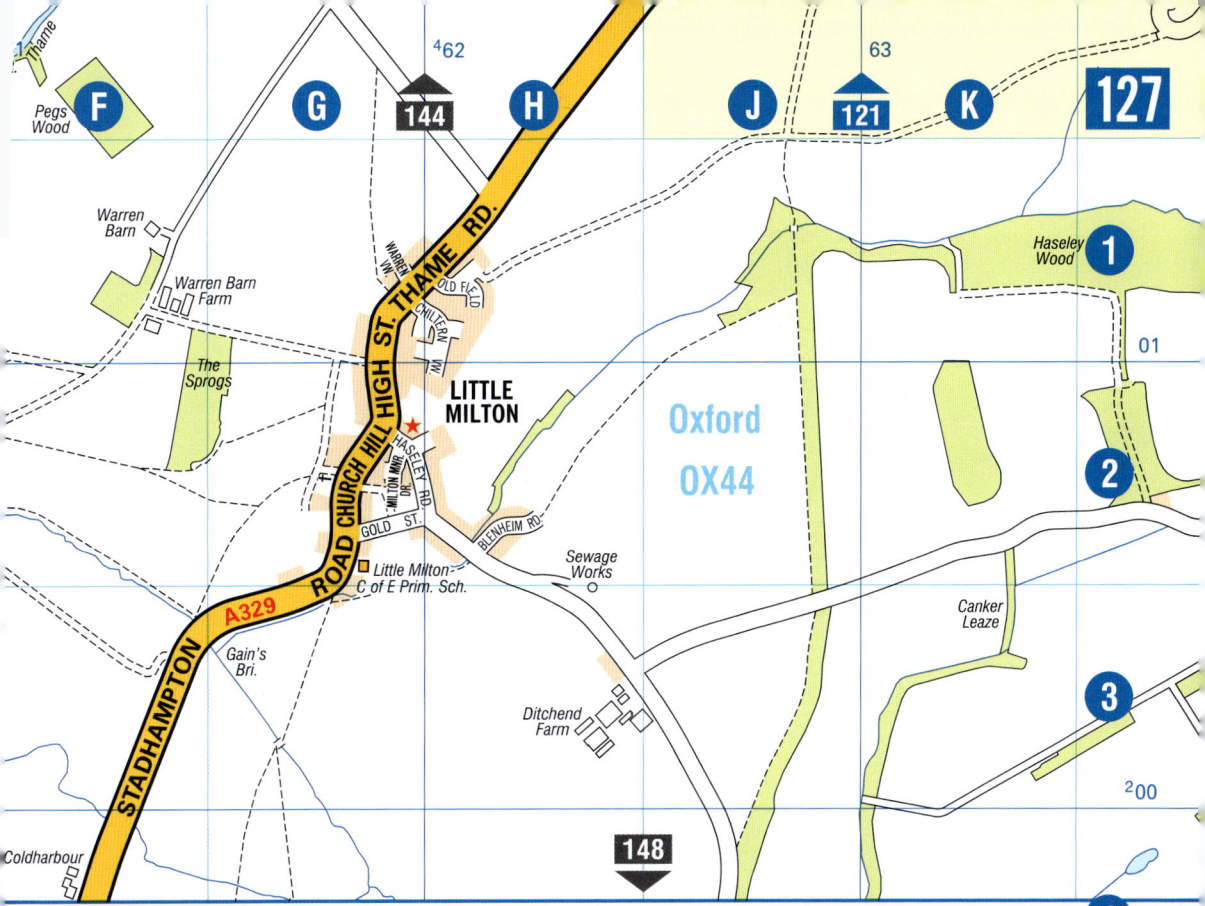
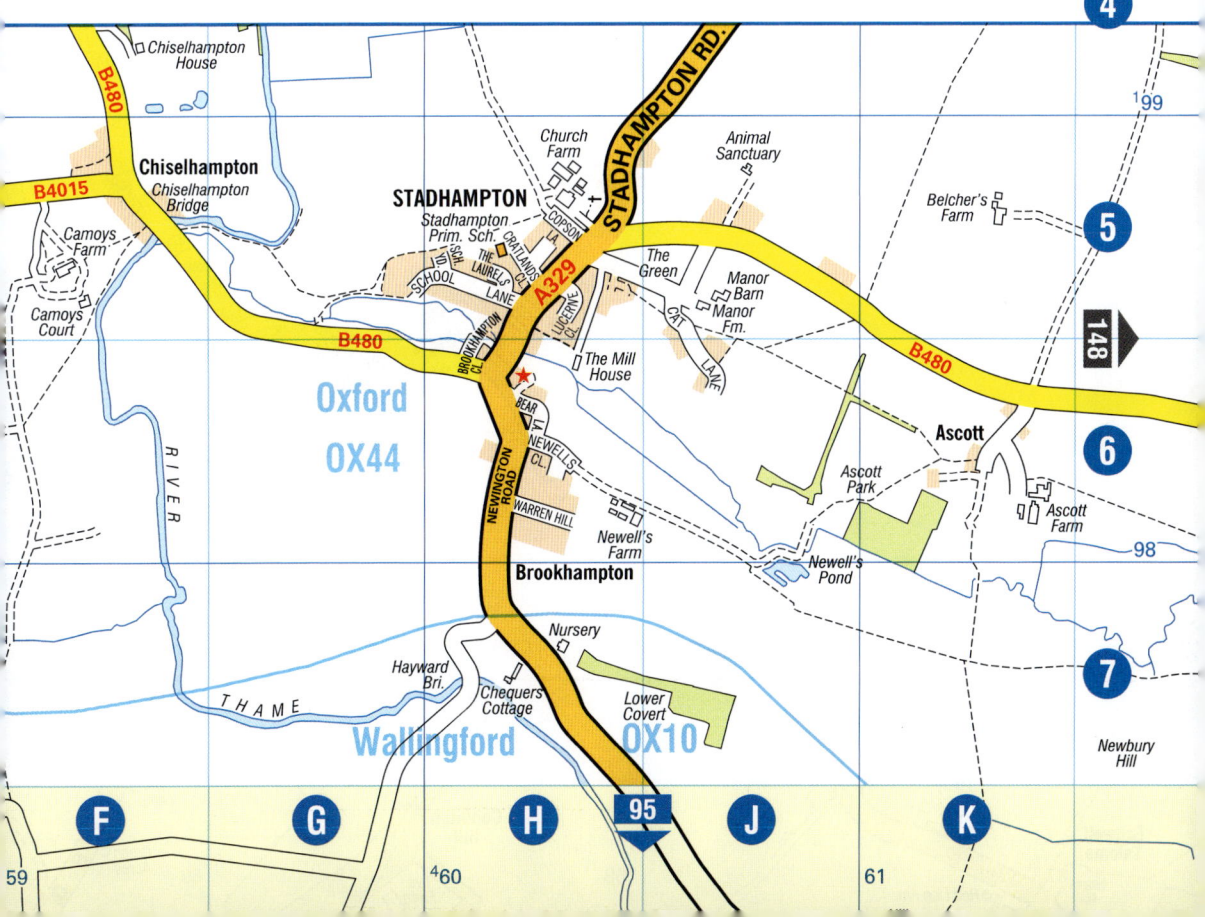

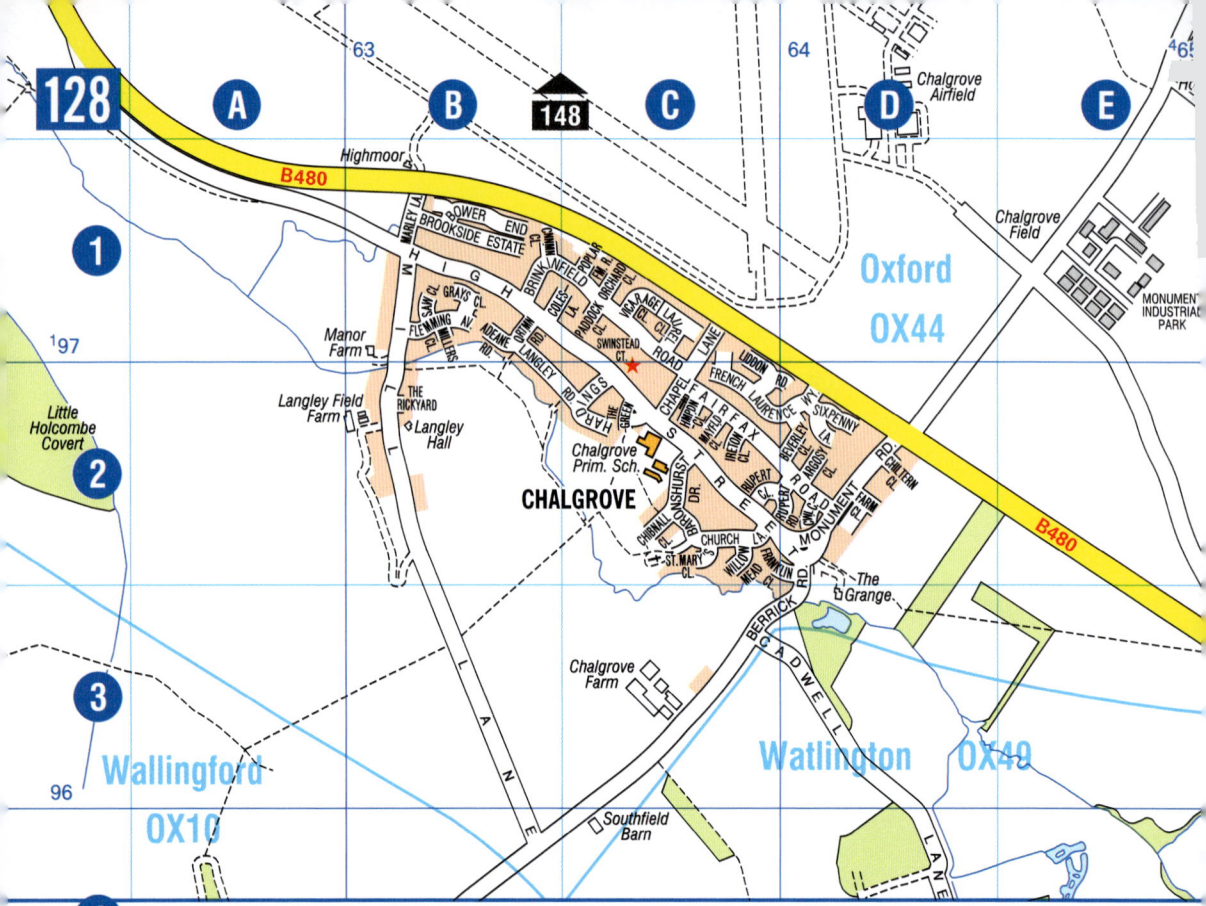
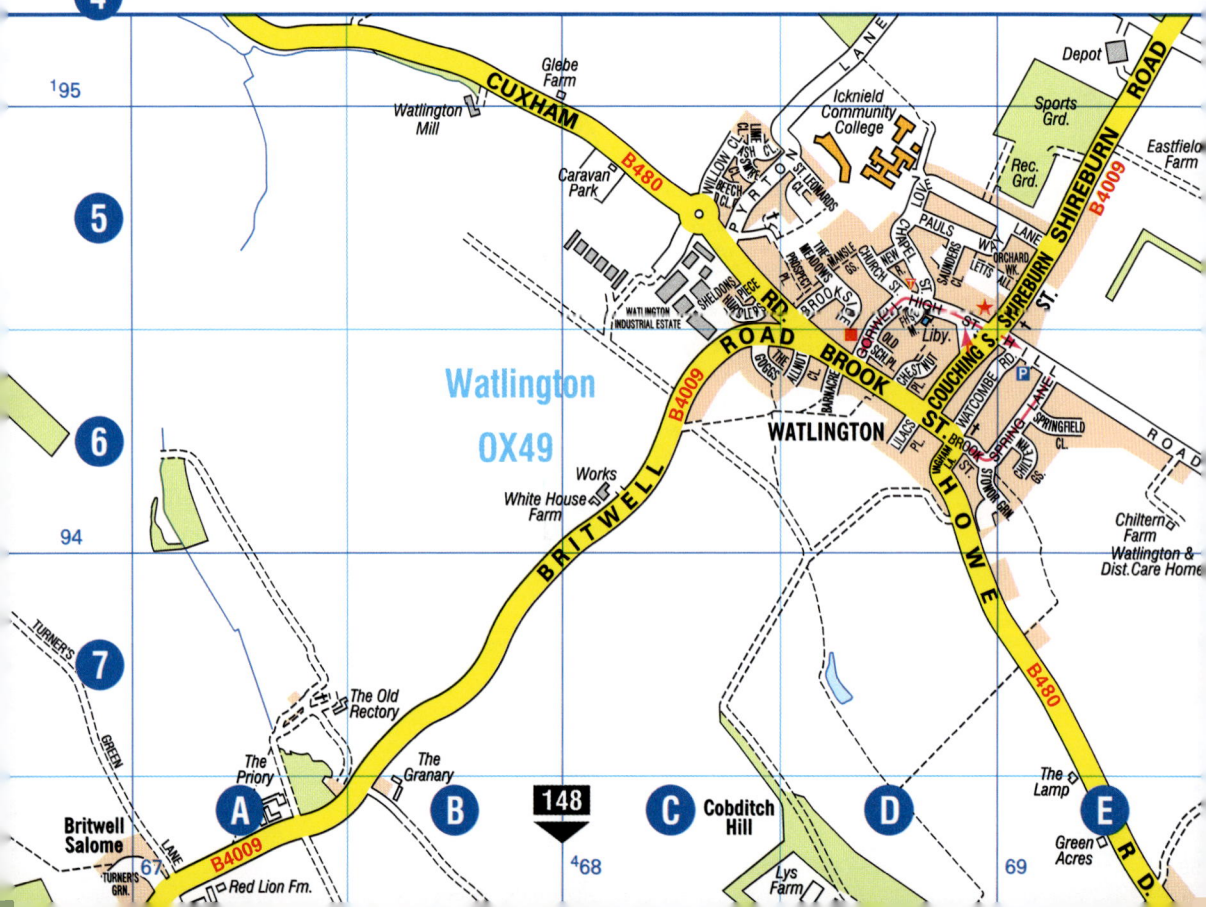

F G H 145 J K 129

OX39 472 73 71

B4102

Lower Farm

Blenheim Farm

BOX TREE LANE

LOWER RD.

Adwell Farm

Postcombe

CHALFORD ROAD

Thame OX9

A40

M40 MOTORWAY

SALT LANE

Beech Farm

1

125

200 WAY

Aston Rowant C of E Prim. School

Home Fm.

The Grn.

DASHWOOD

The Malt Ho.

CHURCH CT.

CHURCH LA.

SCH. LA.

PLOWDEN GDNS.

UPTON

Aston Rowant

2

99

M40

LOWER

ROAD

Hope Lodge

Aston Park Stud

ASTON PARK

Fish Pond

ROAD

3

B4009

Woodway Farm

Nethercote

NETHERCOTE LANE

Sewage Works

Moor Court

Moat

NESTON

Manor House

LEWKNOR

Church Farm

Knapp Farm

Church Ho.

Sch.

BARLEY CLOSE

CHURCH LA.

LEWKNOR RD.

HILL RD.

TOWN CL.

HIGH STREET

BUTTS WY.

CHINNOR ROAD

Watlington OX49

A40

4

198

B4009

5

ASTON HILL

149

WAY

Junction 6

Cuckoo Pen

Beacon Hill

Little London Wood

6

97

WATLINGTON ROAD

B4009

Field Farm House

Resr. (covered)

HILL

M40

M40 MOTORWAY

ICKNIELD WAY

Hill Farm

7

Nature Reserve

F G H 149 J K

ICKNIELD WAY ROAD

Old Cricketground Plantation

71 472 73

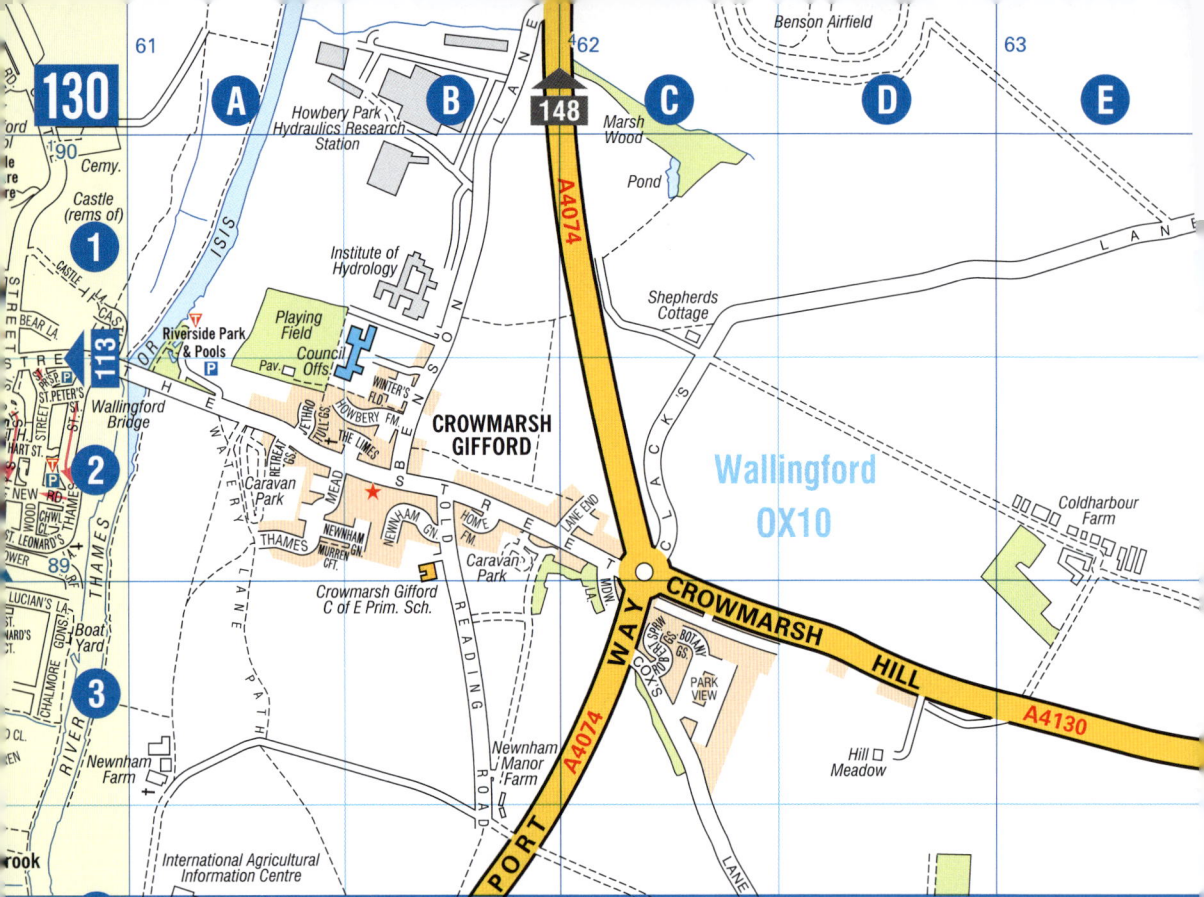

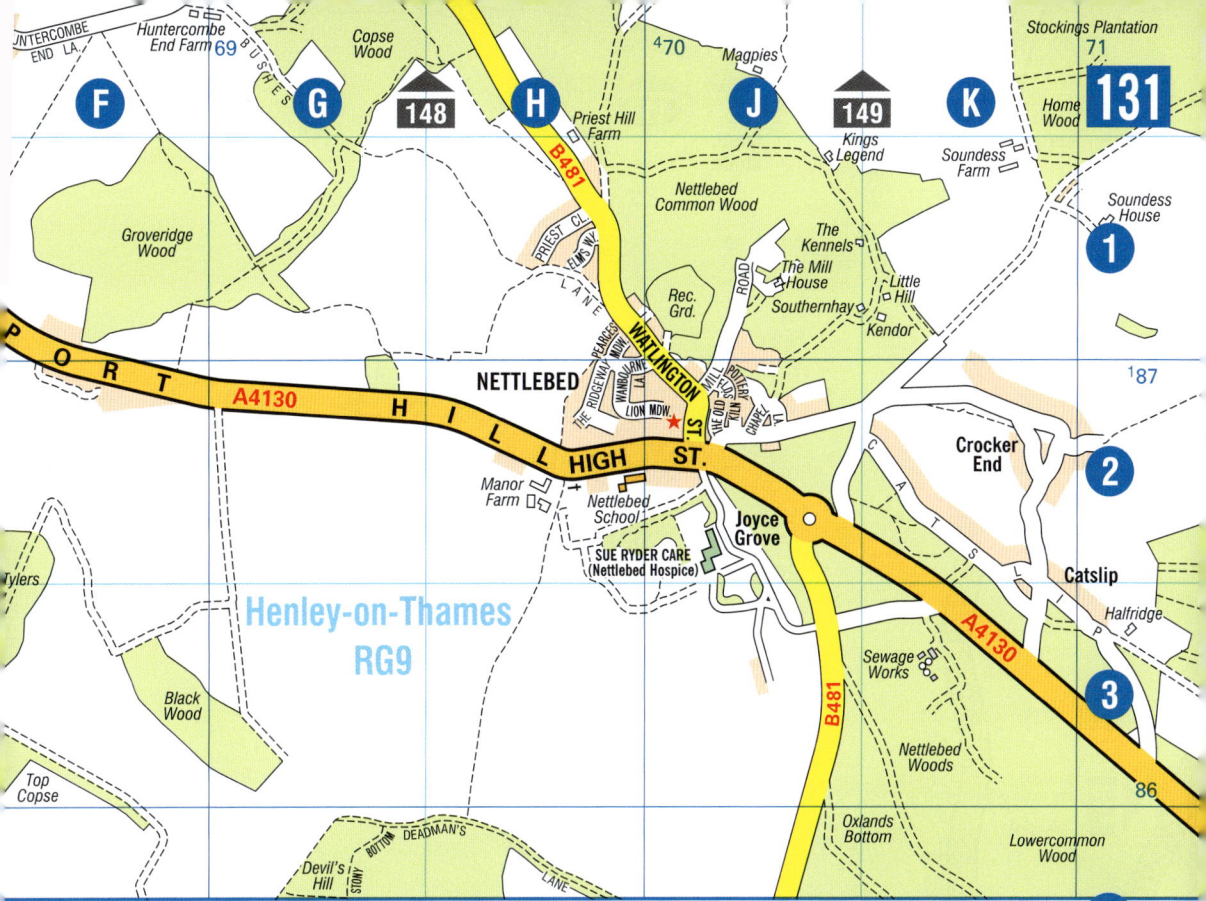

F **G** **H** **J** **K**

Stockings Plantation

Huntercombe
End Farm **69**

Copse
Wood

Magpies

148

Kings
Legend

149

Soundess
Farm

70

71

Home
Wood

K

Soundess
House

1

UNTERCOMBE
END LA.

BUSHES

Groveridge
Wood

Priest Hill
Farm

B481

PRIEST CL.

ELMS WK.

Nettlebed
Common Wood

The Kennels

The Mill
House

Southernhay

Little
Hill

Kendor

87

2

Crocker
End

PORT

A4130

HILL

HIGH
ST.

WATLINGTON
LION MDW.

THE RIDGEWAY
PEARCES MDW.
WANDARNE LA.

NETTLEBED

Rec.
Grd.

ROAD

THE OLD
KILN POTTERY
KILN
CHAPEL

Catslip

2

Manor
Farm

Nettlebed
School

Nettlebed

**SUE RYDER CARE
(Nettlebed Hospice)**

Joyce
Grove

B481

A4130

Halfridge

3

Tylers

**Henley-on-Thames
RG9**

Sewage
Works

Nettlebed
Woods

86

Black
Wood

Top
Copse

STONY
BOTTOM
DEADMAN'S

Devil's
Hill

LANE

Oxlands
Bottom

Lowercommon
Wood

4

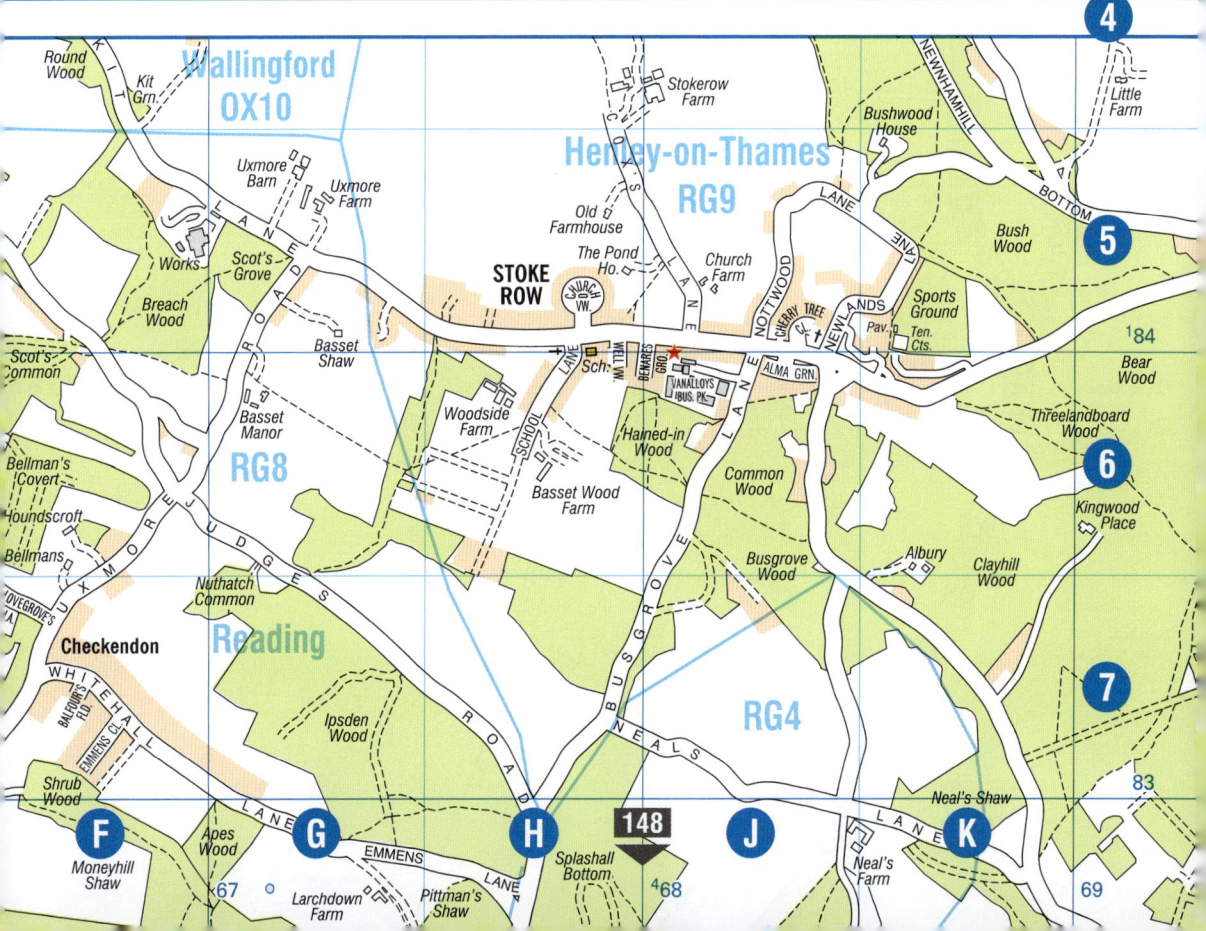

Round
Wood

Kit
Grn.

**Wallingford
OX10**

Stokerow
Farm

Bushwood
House

NEWNHAMHILL

Little
Farm

4

KIT

Uxmore
Barn

Uxmore
Farm

**Henley-on-Thames
RG9**

Old
Farmhouse

The Pond
Ho.

Church
Farm

LANE

BOTTOM

Bush
Wood

5

Works

Scot's
Grove

UXMORE

**STOKE
ROW**

CHURCH
VW.

NOTTWOOD

CHERRY
TREE

NEW
LANDS

Sports
Ground

Pav.

Ten.
Cts.

84

Bear
Wood

Breach
Wood

Basset
Shaw

Sch.

WM HELM

BENIMRS
GRO.

VANALLOYS
BUS. PK.

ALMA GRN.

Threelandboard
Wood

6

Scot's
Common

Basset
Manor

RG8

Woodside
Farm

Woodside
Wood

SCHOOL

Basset Wood
Farm

Hained-in
Wood

Common
Wood

LANE

Kingwood
Place

Bellman's
Covert

Houndscroft

Bellmans

UXMORE

JUDGES

Nuthatch
Common

Reading

ROAD

Busgrove
Wood

Albury

Clayhill
Wood

LANE

7

GROVEGROVE'S LA.

Checkendon

WHITEHALL

BUSGROVE

RG4

83

BALDON'S RD.

EMMENS CL.

Ipsden
Wood

NEALS

Neal's Shaw

Shrub
Wood

LANE

Apes
Wood

148

Neal's
Farm

LANE

69

F **G** **H** **J** **K**

Moneyhill
Shaw

67

Larchdown
Farm

EMMENS

Pittman's
Shaw

Splashall
Bottom

68

MOULSFORD
OX10

Walnut Bank
Res.
COW

THE STREET

WALLINGFORD ROAD A329

UNDERHILL

FERRY LANE
FERRY
FERRY LANE
FERRY LA.
FERRY ROAD
WOODCOTE ROAD

South Stoke
117

Playing Field
Cross Keys Rd.
CHAPEL SQUARE
DEACON'S CLOSE
SOUTH
CLEEVE COTTS.
THE GARDENS
BANK

WALLINGFORD ROAD

Sewage Works

Grove Farm House
Grove Farm Cottages
Grove Farm

RIVER THAMES

Runsford Hole
Boat House

SOUTH OXFORDSHIRE
WEST BERKSHIRE

Reading RG8

Spring Farm Stables
Spring Farm House
Spring Farm Cottages

B4009

Streatley Farm Cotts.
148
Streatley Farm

82

WANTAGE

A417

RECTORY RD.
TOWNSEND RD.
THREE GABLES LA.

Cleeve Lock

Tullsclose Shaw

Sheephouse Shaw
Weir

Cleeve Mill
Fish Pond

Lough Down

Lodge

Pav. Play. Fld.

Works

STREATLEY

Lardon Chase
LARDON COTTS.
CHESTNUT COTTS.

The Ridgeway

Cleeve CT.

PENNY PIECE
MILL RD.
CLEEVEMEDE
CLEEVE RD.
MOUNT FIELD
ELVENDON ROAD
SPRINGHILL
WESTWAY
SPRINGFIELD END
MIDDLE SPRINGS
ICKNIELD PL.
ICKNIELD
ROAD

Cleeve
Goring C of E Prim. Sch.
CLEEVE DOWN
CLEEVE

Battle Farm
BATTLE ROAD

SUMMERFIELD RI.

Battle Plantation

MILLDOWN RD.
MILLDOWN AV.
HERON SHW
LYCROFT CL.
FERNE CL.
MEADOW CL.
FAIRFIELD
LOCKSTILE MEAD
LOCKSTILE WAY
LOCKSTILE RD.
MEADOW CL.
VALLEY CL.

GORING

COURT GDNS.
CARIAD WK.
HOWGATE DR.
MILLERS
NUN'S ACRE
ELMHURST WK.
ELMHURST RD.
CROSS RD.
LYNDHURST RD.
GLEBE RIDE
RECTORY
FARM
THE BIRCHES
UPPER RED CROSS RD.
B4009

Thames Bank Nursing Home
Withy Eyot
Goring Lock
Weir
Streatley & Goring Bri.

B4009
HIGH STREET
WALLINGFORD STREET
READING

B4526 READING ROAD

Whitehill Plantation
Cricket Grd.
Burntwood

Coombe Bottom Fm.
The Coombe
Streatley C of E Prim. Sch.
Coombe Bottom
STREATLEY HILL
THE BULL HILL
HILL MDW.
GDS.
THE OLD FORGE

WALNUT TREE CT.
WALNUT TREE
YEW TREE
FERRY LANE
LOCK
STATION
LIMETREE RD.
GATEHAMPTON ROAD

Goring
Lib.
148

Rec. Gnd.
GATEHAMPTON
RAILWAY
Cottages
THE HILLS GRN.
QUEENS CT.

Playing Field

Green Hill
Common Wood

The Grange
GRANGE CL.
RIVER LANE
Long Meadow
The Beeches
LONG MEADOW
LITTLE CROFT RD.
CROFT RD.
REMCROFT
ELM GRN.

GATEHAMPTON ROAD
Gatehampton Farm
Gatehampton Ho.
Gatehampton Manor
Gatehampton Lodge

Papist Bushes

RIVER THAMES

Boat House

A329 WALLINGFORD ROAD READING ROAD

Holies Walk Wood

Ash Copse
Hollies Hanging

148

RG8

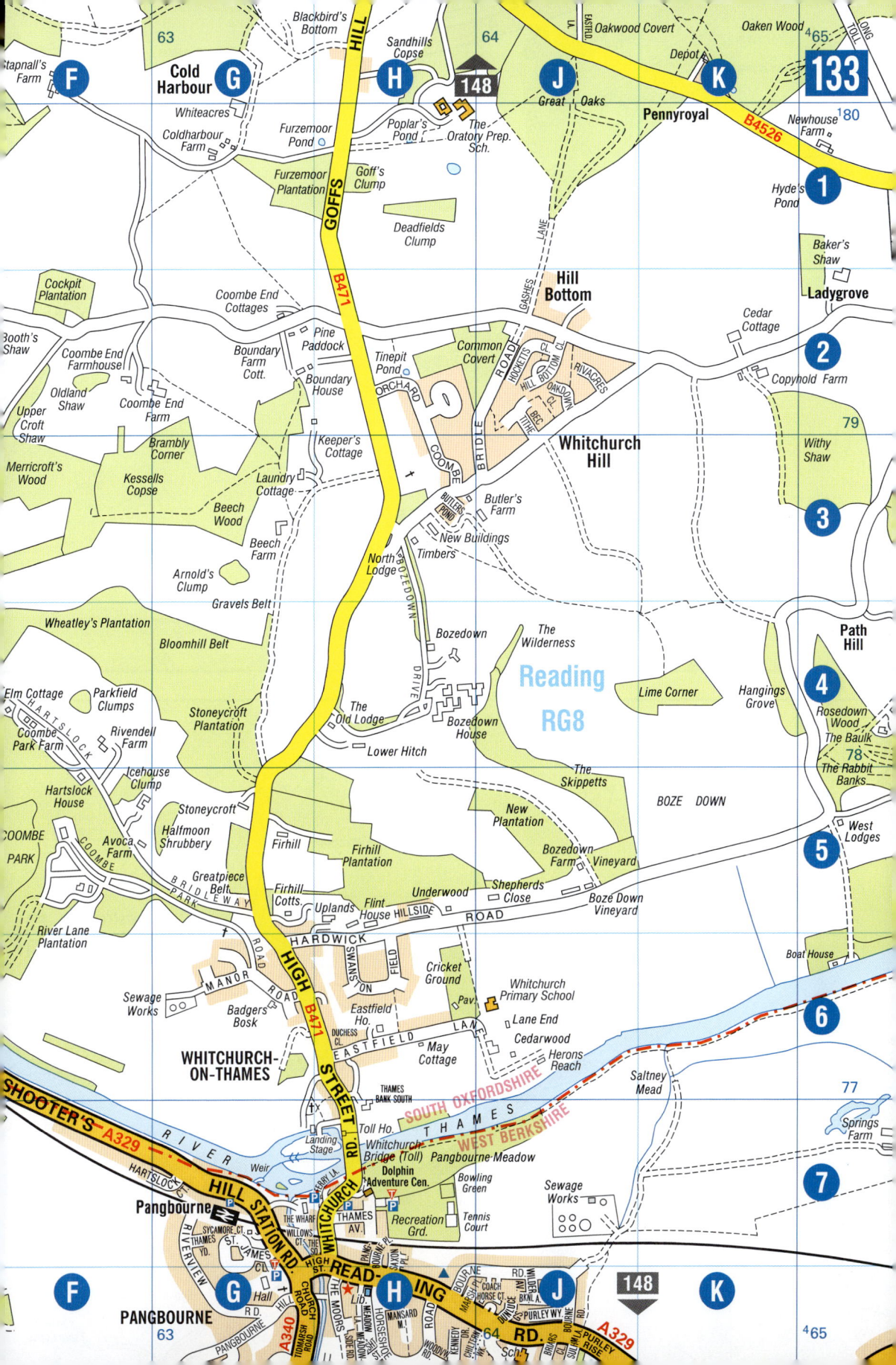

F **G** **H** **J** **K**

63 · 64 · 65

Stapnall's Farm

Cold Harbour

Blackbird's Bottom

Sandhills Copse

148

Oakwood Covert · Oaken Wood

Depot

Whiteacres

Furzemoor Pond

Poplar's Pond

The Oratory Prep. Sch.

Great Oaks

Pennyroyal

B4526

Newhouse Farm · 180

Coldharbour Farm

Furzemoor Plantation

Goff's Clump

Hyde's Pond

1

Deadfields Clump

Baker's Shaw

Ladygrove

Cockpit Plantation

Coombe End Cottages

Pine Paddock

Boundary Farm Cott.

Boundary House

Tinepit Pond

Common Covert

Hill Bottom

Cedar Cottage

Copyhold Farm

2

Booth's Shaw

Coombe End Farmhouse

Oldland Shaw

Coombe End Farm

Keeper's Cottage

Whitchurch Hill

79

Withy Shaw

Upper Croft Shaw

Merricroft's Wood

Brambly Corner

Kessells Copse

Laundry Cottage

Butler's Pond

Butler's Farm

3

Beech Wood

New Buildings

Beech Farm

Timbers

North Lodge

Arnold's Clump

Gravels Belt

Bozedown

The Wilderness

Path Hill

Wheatley's Plantation

Bloomhill Belt

Lime Corner

Hangings Grove

4

Elm Cottage

Parkfield Clumps

Stoneycroft Plantation

The Old Lodge

Bozedown House

Reading RG8

Rosedown Wood

The Baulk

78

The Rabbit Banks

Coombe Park Farm

Rivendell Farm

Lower Hitch

The Skippetts

Hartslock House

Icehouse Clump

Stoneycroft

Halfmoon Shrubbery

Firhill

Firhill Plantation

New Plantation

Bozedown Farm Vineyard

BOZE DOWN

West Lodges

5

COOMBE PARK

Avoca Farm

Greatpiece Belt

Firhill Cotts.

Uplands

Flint House

Underwood

Hillside Road

Shepherds Close

Boze Down Vineyard

Boat House

River Lane Plantation

BRIDLEWAY PARK

HARDWICK ROAD

SWANSTON FIELD

Cricket Ground

Pav.

Whitchurch Primary School

Lane End

6

Sewage Works

MANOR ROAD

Badgers Bosk

Eastfield Ho.

DUCHESS CL.

May Cottage

Cedarwood

Herons Reach

Saltney Mead

77

Springs Farm

WHITCHURCH-ON-THAMES

HIGH STREET RD. B471

EASTFIELD LANE

THAMES BANK SOUTH

Toll Ho.

SOUTH OXFORDSHIRE

WEST BERKSHIRE

THAMES

Sewage Works

7

SHOOTER'S A329

RIVER

HILL

HARTSLOC

STATION RD.

Landing Stage

Weir

FERRY LA.

Whitchurch Bridge (Toll)

Dolphin Adventure Cen.

Pangbourne Meadow

Bowling Green

Tennis Court

Pangbourne

THE WHARF

WILLOWS

THAMES AV.

Recreation Grd.

RG

READING

148

F **G** **H** **J** **K**

PANGBOURNE

63

SYCAMORE CT.

JAMES CL.

Hall

RIVERVIEW

THAMES YD.

CHURCH ROAD

A340 TIDMARSH RD.

PANGBOURNE RD.

HILL

STATION RD.

Lib.

THE MOORS

MANSARD M.

BOURNE RD.

COACH HORSE CT.

KENNEDY DR.

HORSESHOE

PURLEY WY.

BRIARS CL.

SULHAM LA.

PURLEY RISE

Sch.

A329 READING RD.

64 · 65

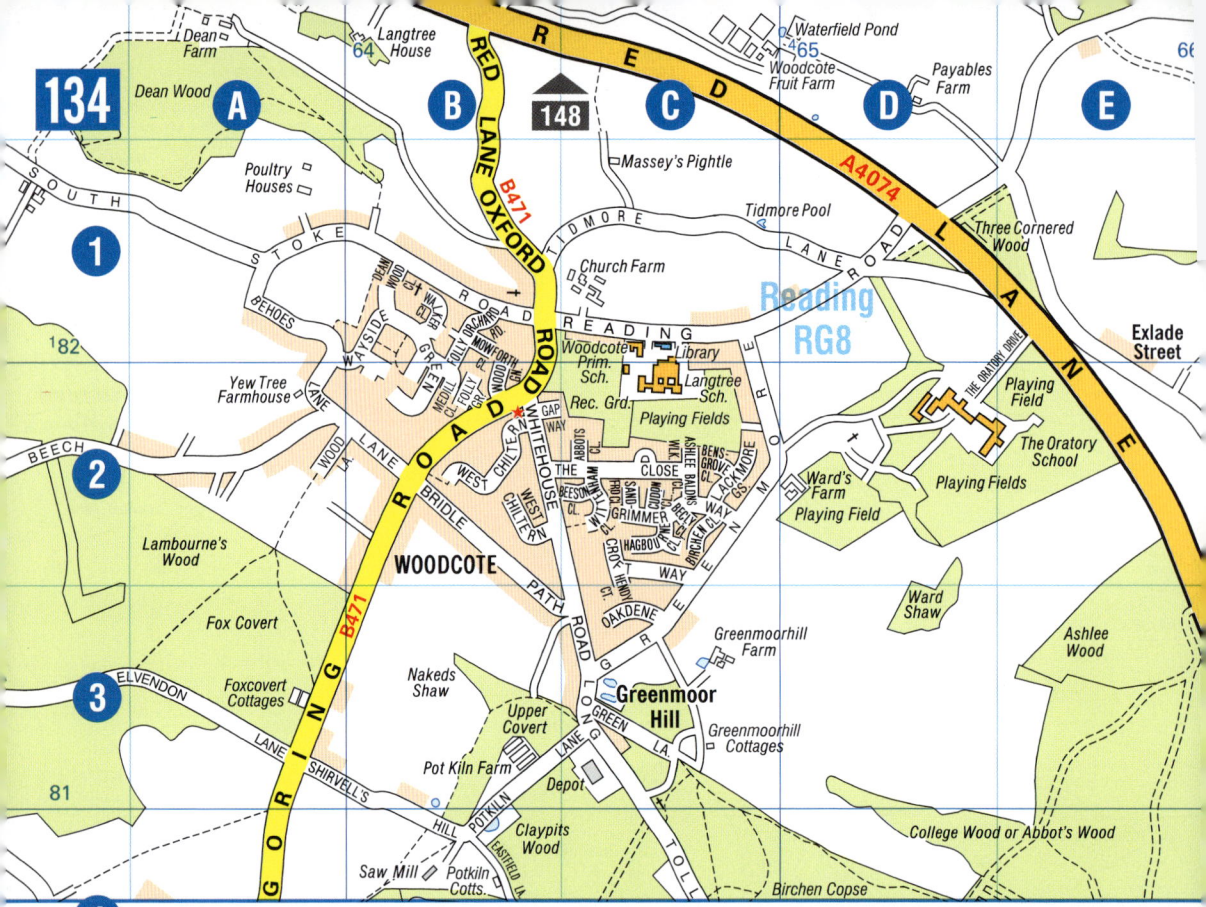
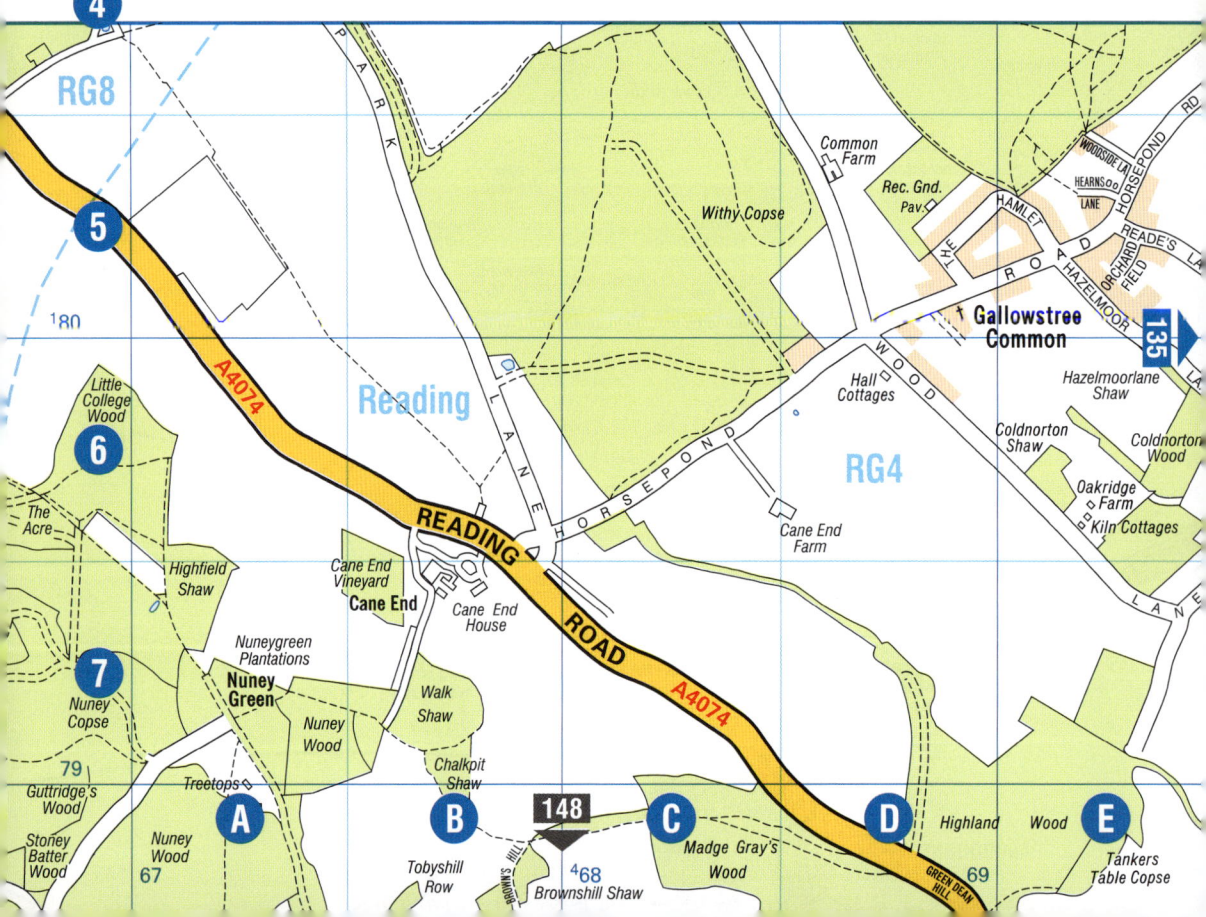

Henley-on-Thames

RG9

Kingwood

135

F 148 G 149 H J 137 K

Bow Gannark Bolts Cross House

GREYS GREEN GOLF COURSE

Kingwood Common Kingswood Kennels Greatbottom Wood

Colts Desscot

Cherry Croft

Kingwood Common The Flint Barn

Sadgrove Barn Manor Farm Cotts. Peppard Farm

DOG LANE

Peppard C of E Prim. Sch.

Peppard Common

COLLIERS LA COLLIERS LANE

Peppard Common

Pavilion Playing Field

B481 PEPPARD HILL CHURCH HILL

GRANGE AV.

Springwood

Arundel

Rectory Cott.

Chiltern Bank Shiplake Farm Cottage

Rotherfield Peppard

Springwood Court

Stoney

GREYS GREEN GOLF COURSE

Beechwood House

Spring Wood Sedgehill Spring

Bottom Barn

Bottom

149 81

STEVENS LANE DOVE LANE ESTER LANE CARLING LA COLMORE LANE STOKE ROW ROAD CHILTERN ROAD SHIPLAKE ROAD

Old Copse

PEPPARD GRAVEL HILL

Home Farm Cottage

Blounts Court

Blounts Farm

HORSEPOND ROAD GALLOWSTREE ROAD

Pavilion

Playing Field

Field Cottages

Slade's Wood

SONNING COMMON

Crosscroft

Blackmore Farm Pond Farm

COURT ROAD BLACKMORE LANE

Bishopswood Farm

134

READE'S

Lib.

Prim. Sch.

Chiltern Edge Community School

Bottom Ho

The White Cottage

Frieze Farm

Frieze Cott.

Well Ho.

Hall

Coldnorton Wood

HAZELMOOR

The Herb Farm

B481

Young Wood

Works

Holly Tree Farm

Reading

RG4

Hag Pits

Hagpits House

Sewage Works

Filter Beds

Morgan's Wood

Vicarage

Kidmore End

Emmens Cottage

Pond House

Rudgings Plantation

Bird Wood

PEPPARD ROAD

Curtis's Farm

School Cemy.

Vines Farm

Bur Wood

F 148 G H 149 J K

Long Copse

Farm Cottages

Kidmore Road House

Cucumber Plantation

Bishoplands Farm Cotts.

The Old Thatched Cottage

470 71 72 79 80 180 82

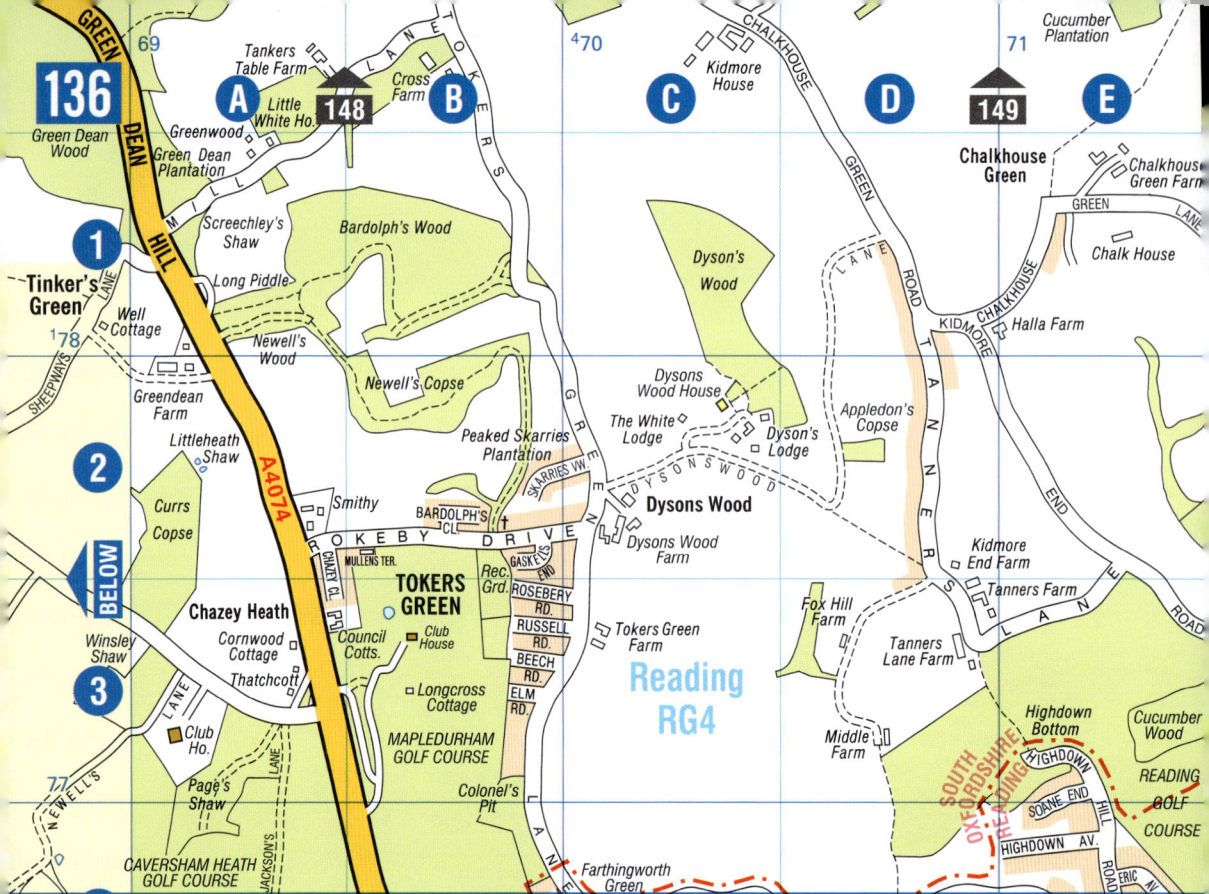
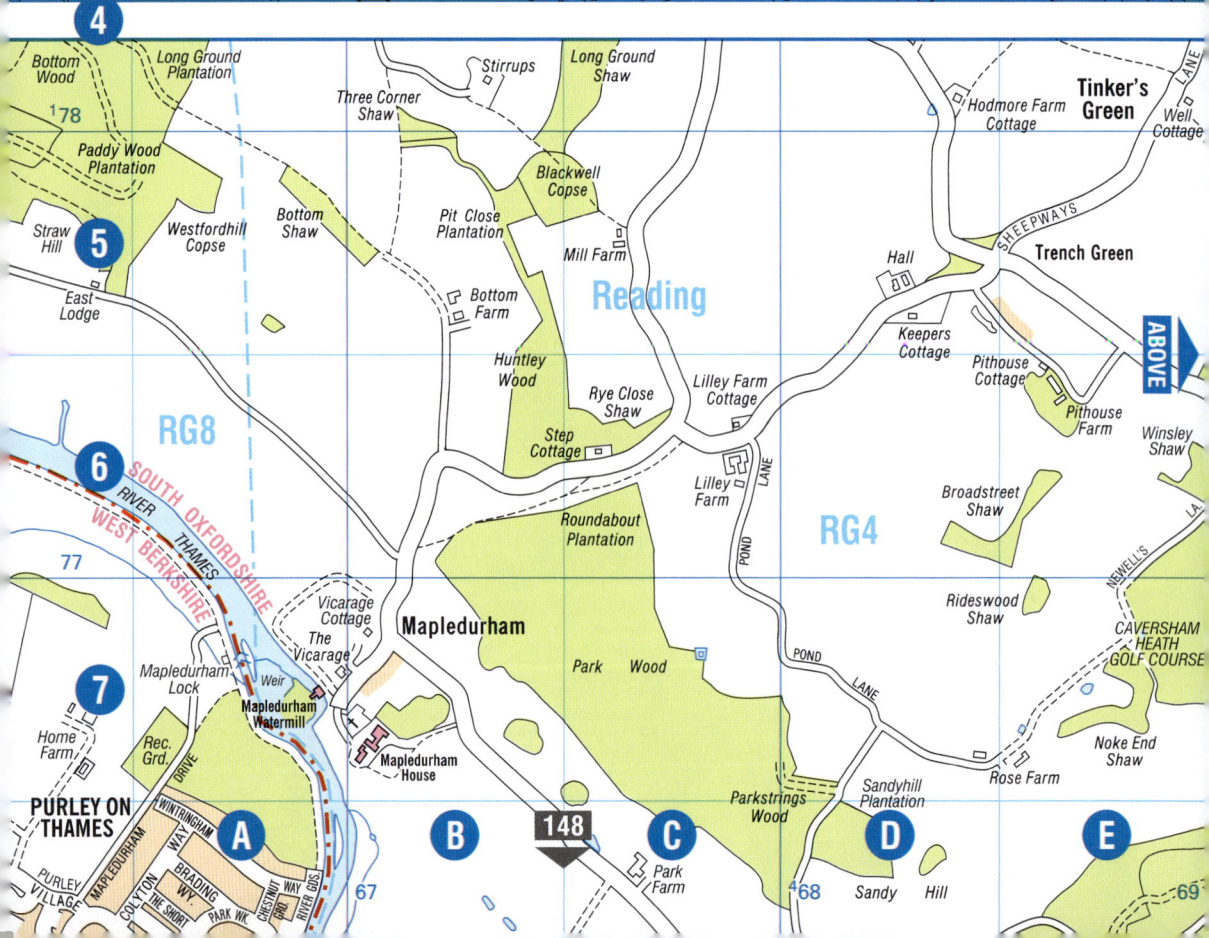

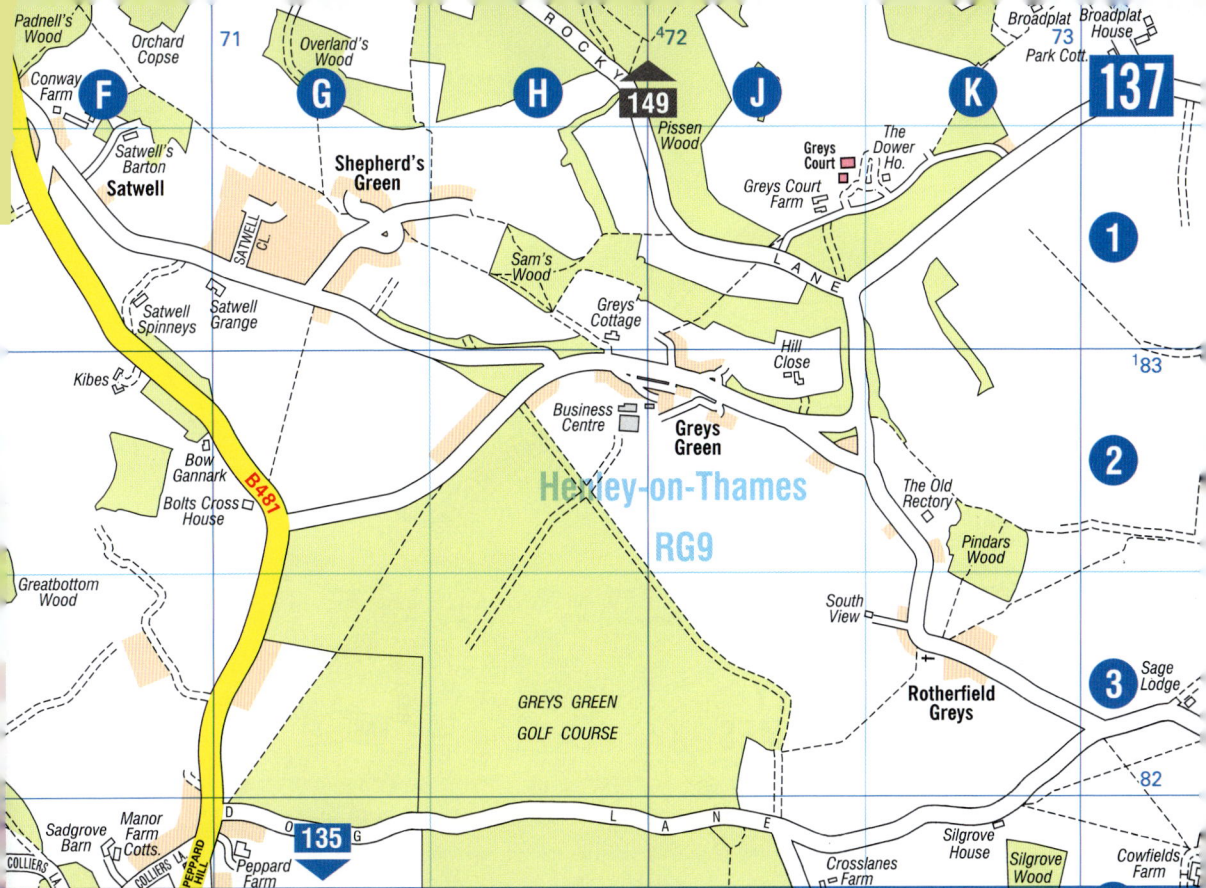

Padnell's Wood

Orchard Copse

71

Overland's Wood

149

Broadplat
Park Cott.

73

Broadplat House

Conway Farm

Shepherd's Green

Pissen Wood

Greys Court

The Dower Ho.

Satwell's Barton

Satwell

Greys Court Farm

LANE

Sam's Wood

Satwell CL.

Greys' Cottage

Hill Close

Satwell Spinneys

Satwell Grange

Kibes

Business Centre

Greys Green

The Old Rectory

Bow Gannark

B487

Bolts Cross House

Henley-on-Thames

RG9

Pindars Wood

South View

Greatbottom Wood

Sage Lodge

Rotherfield Greys

GREYS GREEN

GOLF COURSE

¹82

Sadgrove Barn

Manor Farm Cotts.

135

Peppard Farm

PEPPARD HILL

D O G

L A N E

Crosslanes Farm

Silgrove House

Silgrove Wood

Cowfields Farm

COLLIERS LA.

COLLIERS LA.

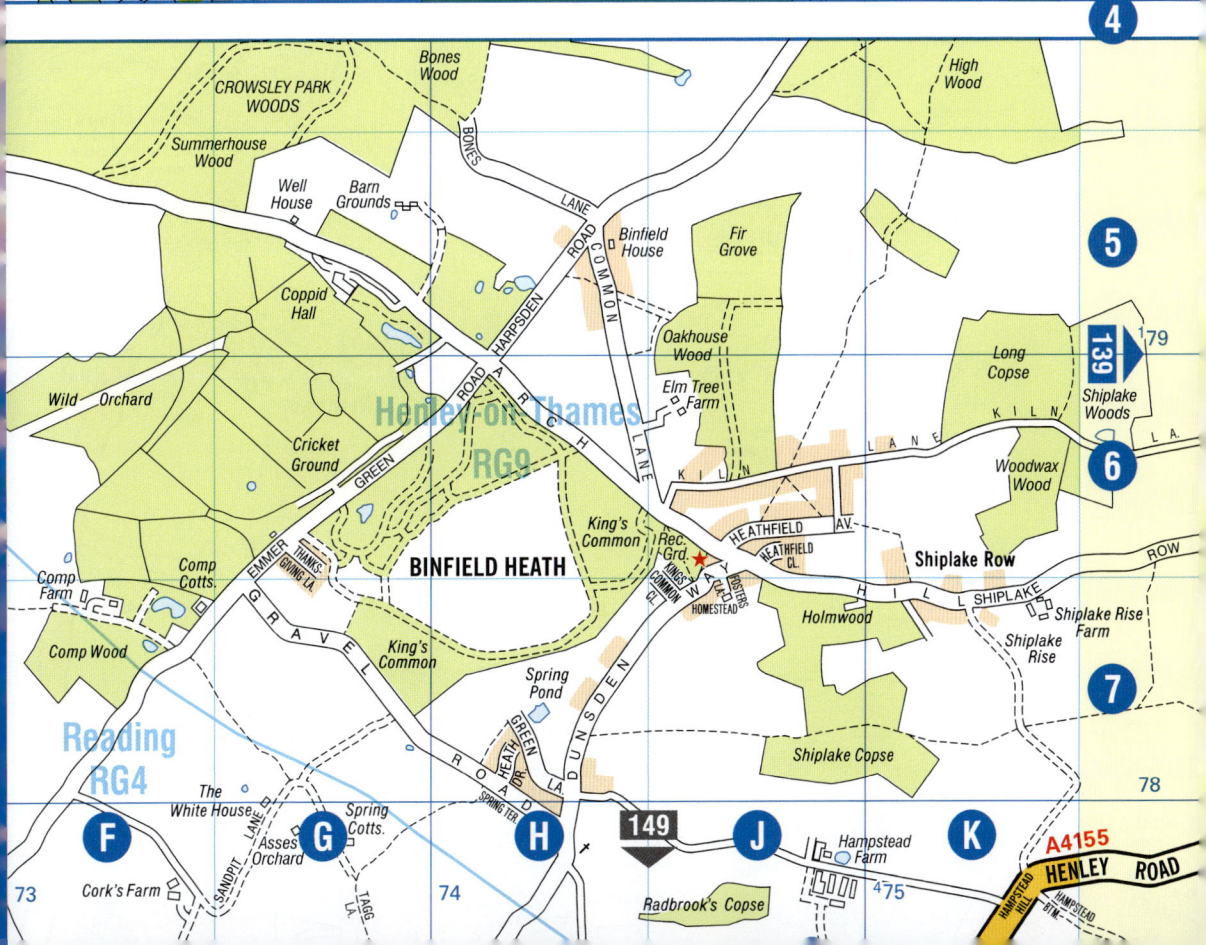

Bones Wood

High Wood

CROWSLEY PARK WOODS

BONES LANE

Summerhouse Wood

Well House

Barn Grounds

Binfield House

Fir Grove

Coppid Hall

HARPSDEN

COMMON

Oakhouse Wood

Long Copse

139

¹79

Wild Orchard

ROAD

Elm Tree Farm

Shiplake Woods

Cricket Ground

GREEN

LANE

KILN

Woodwax Wood

6

Henley-on-Thames

RG9

KILN

Comp Farm

Comp Cotts.

EMMER

THAMES GIVING LA.

King's Common

Rec. Grd.

HEATHFIELD

HEATHFIELD AV.

Heathfield CL.

Shiplake Row

ROW

SHIPLAKE

Reading

RG4

BINFIELD HEATH

DUNSDEN

COMMON

HOMESTEAD

FOSTERS

HILL

Holmwood

Shiplake Rise Farm

Shiplake Rise

Comp Wood

GRAVEL

King's Common

Spring Pond

Shiplake Copse

The White House

ROAD

GREEN LA.

78

Asses Orchard

SANDPIT LANE

Spring Cotts.

SPRING TER.

HEATH

149

Hampstead Farm

A4155

73

Cork's Farm

TAGG. LA.

74

Radbrook's Copse

⁴75

HAMPSTEAD HILL

HAMPSTEAD BTM.

HENLEY ROAD

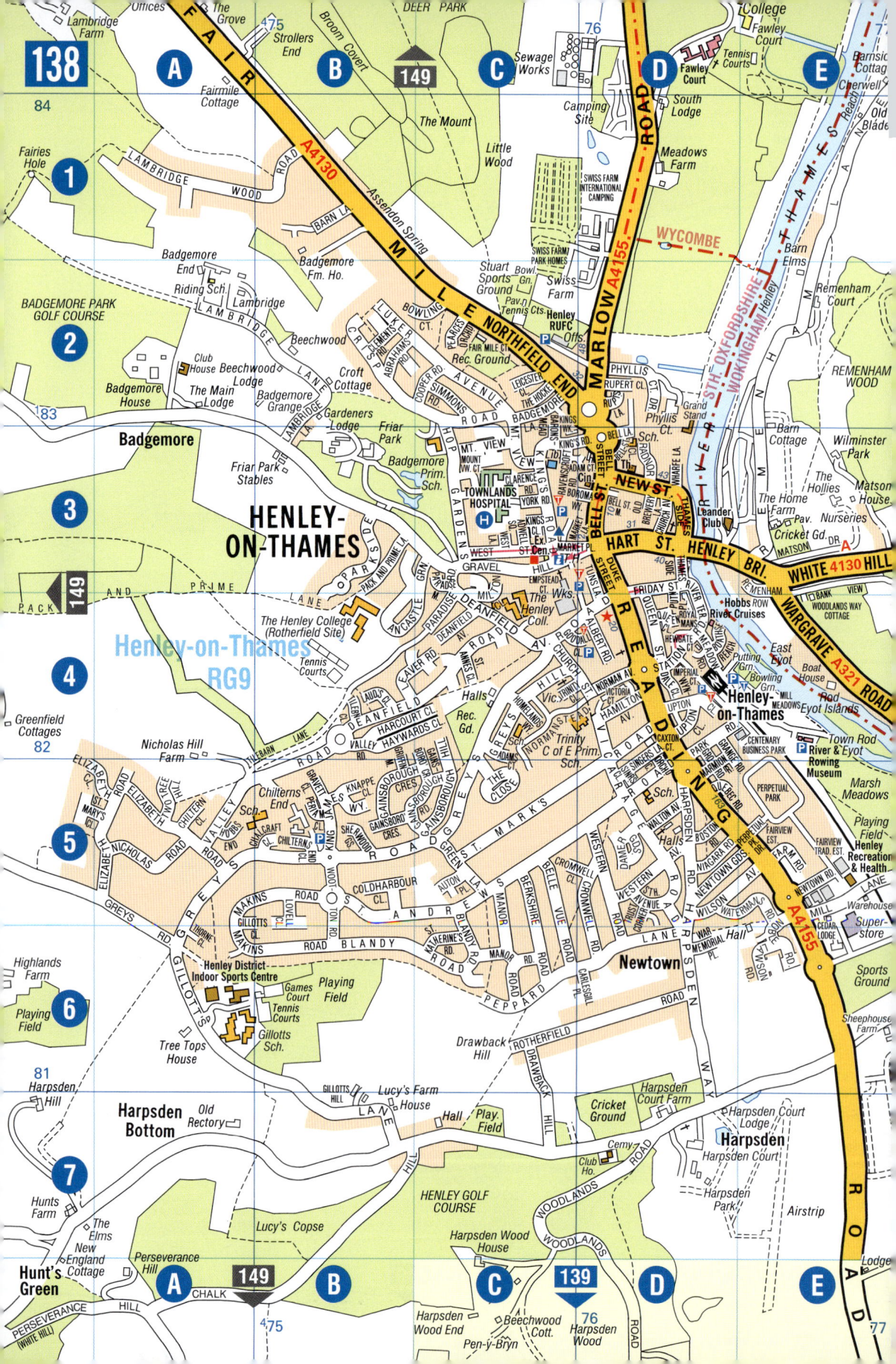

84

A **B** 149 **C** **D** **E**

76

1

Fairies Hole
Offices The Grove
Fairmile Cottage
Lambridge Farm
Strollers End
475
DEER PARK
Broom Covert
149
Sewage Works
College
Fawley Court
Tennis Courts
Barnside Cottage
Cherwell
7
Old Blade

2

BADGEMORE PARK GOLF COURSE
183
Badgemore End
Riding Sch.
Lambridge
Beechwood
LAMBRIDGE WOOD
LAMBRIDGE LANE
The Mount
Little Wood
FAIR MILE
A4130
MILE
ASSENDON SPRING
Camping Site
SWISS FARM INTERNATIONAL CAMPING
Swiss Farm Park Homes
Stuart Sports Ground
Bowl. Gn.
Tennis Cts.
Henley RUFC
South Lodge
Meadows Farm
WYCOMBE
MARLOW A4155
A4155 OXFORDSHIRE
WOKINGHAM
THAMES
Barn Elms
Remenham Court
REMENHAM WOOD

Badgemore Fm. Ho.

3

HENLEY-ON-THAMES
Badgemore
Club House
Beechwood Lodge
The Main Lodge
Badgemore House
Badgemore Grange
Gardeners Lodge
Friar Park
Friar Park Stables
Badgemore Prim. Sch.
Beechwood
Croft Cottage
LUKER AV.
CLEMENTS RD.
ABRAHAMS RD.
COOPER RD.
SIMMONS RD.
BADGEMORE
BOWLING
PARKS RD.
Fair Mile Ct.
Rec. Ground
LEICESTER CL.
THE HOCKEY
AVENUE
KING'S RD.
MT. VIEW
MOUNT VW. CT.
CLARENCE RD.
YORK RD.
KINGS RD.
WEST ST.
MARKET PL.
BELL ST.
NEW ST.
Cin.
LEANDER CLUB
Grand Stand
RUPERT CL.
PHYLLIS CT.
RADNOR
WHARF LA.
HENLEY BRI.
WHITE HILL A4130
Phyllis Ct.
Barn Cottage
Wilminster Park
The Hollies
Matson House
The Home Farm
Nurseries
Cricket Gd.
MATSON DR.
WARGRAVE A321 ROAD
BANK
WOODLANDS WAY
VIEW COTTAGE

TOWNLANDS HOSPITAL
PARK SIDE
HOP GARDENS

4

Henley-on-Thames RG9
Greenfield Cottages
82
Nicholas Hill Farm
The Henley College (Rotherfield Site)
Tennis Courts
PARK AND PRIME LANE
PRIME
149
PACK
DEANFIELD
NEWCASTLE
PARADISE RD.
DEANFIELD AV.
DEANFIELD ROAD
WEAVER RD.
ANNES CT.
MILL
The Henley Coll.
GRAVEL HILL
WEST ST.
EMPSTEAD ST.
The Ct. Wks.
HART ST.
READING
FRIDAY ST.
DUKE STREET
QUEEN ST.
ALBERT RD.
CHURCH
STATION RD.
Hobbs Row
River Cruises
East Eyot
Putting Grn.
Bowling Grn.
Boat House
Rod Eyot
Henley-on-Thames
Town Hall
River & Eyot Rowing Museum
Eyot Islands
MILL MEADOWS
Marsh Meadows

5

Greys
MARY'S CL.
ELIZABETH RD.
ELIZABETH CL.
LIME TREE RD.
THRIFT
NICHOLAS RD.
GREY ROAD
VALLEY RD.
CHILTERN RD.
CHILTERNS END
GRAVEL HILL
CROFT
PERPICK
CHILTERNS
WOOD LANE
Sch.
KNAPPE CL.
JAMES WY.
GAINSBORO CRES.
SHERWOOD
GAINSBOROUGH CRES.
GAINSBOROUGH ROAD
GREAT MARKS
THE CLOSE
ADAMS
GREYS
HOMELANDS
NORMANSTEAD
Sch.
Trinity C of E Prim. Sch.
VICTORIA RD.
HAMILTON AV.
NORMAN AV.
HILL
UPTON CL.
CAXTON CT.
IMPERIAL
Sch.
PARK
BERKSHIRE RD.
WESTERN
NEWTOWN GDNS.
FAIRVIEW
PERPETUAL PARK
CENTENARY BUSINESS PARK
PERPETUAL PARK
Playing Field
Henley Recreation & Health
FAIRVIEW TRAD. EST.

Halls
Rec. Gd.
VALLEY RD.
TILE BARN LANE
HAYWARDS CL.
HARCOURT CL.

6

Highlands Farm
Playing Field
81
Harpsden Hill
Henley District Indoor Sports Centre
Games Court
Tennis Courts
Gillotts Sch.
Tree Tops House
GILLOTTS LANE
MAKINS CL.
THORNE CL.
LOVELL CL.
GILLOTTS RD.
MAKINS ROAD
BLANDY
COLDHARBOUR CL.
ST. ANDREW
KATHERINE'S RD.
CARLESSGL. PL.
ST. MARKS ROAD
CROMWELL CL.
BELLE VUE RD.
MANOR ROAD
DAMER AV.
WESTERN ROAD
HARPSDEN ROAD
WILSON AV.
WATERMAN RD.
NIAGARA RD.
Newtown
WAR MEMORIAL Hall
MILL LANE
CEDAR LODGE
Warehouse
Super-store
Sports Ground
Sheephouse Farm

7

Hunts Farm
The Elms
New England Cottage
Perseverance Hill
Old Rectory
Harpsden Bottom
GILLOTTS HILL
Lucy's Farm House
Hall
Play Field
Drawback Hill
DRAWBACK
ROTHERFIELD WAY
HILL LANE
Cricket Ground
Harpsden Court Farm
Harpsden Court Lodge
Harpsden
Harpsden Court
Harpsden Park
Airstrip
Cerny.
Club Ho.
Lodge

Hunt's Green
PERSEVERANCE HILL (WHITE HILL)
CHALK
149
475
HENLEY GOLF COURSE
Lucy's Copse
Harpsden Wood House
WOODLANDS
139
76
Harpsden Wood End
Pen-y-Bryn
Beechwood Cott.
Harpsden Wood
ROAD

77

F
G
138
H
Sheephouse Farm
J
149
K
78 Lodge
WARGRAVE ROAD
A321

Drawback Hill
PEPPA
ROTHERFIELD
76
ROAD
HARPSDEN
DRAWBACK
WAY
77
RIVER
Hennerton Backwater
81

Hall
Play. Field
Cricket Ground
Harpsden Court Farm
Harpsden Court Lodge
Harpsden Court
Fairacres
Ferry Eyot
1
Reading RG10

HILL
Cemy.
Club Ho.
Harpsden
ROAD
Harpsden Court
Thames Side Court
The Garden House
Bolney Court
Popla Eyot

HENLEY GOLF COURSE
WOODLANDS
Harpsden Park
Airstrip
Bolney Court Farm
Bolney Lodge
Dower House
The White House
Mallards
2
Wargrave Marsh
180 Lower Rivermead Farm

Harpsden Wood House
ROAD
Harpsden Wood Lodge
Lodge
WOODLANDS
Kilnpits
Handbuck Eyot
Lashbrook Eyot
Owl End
3

Harpsden Wood End
Pen-y-Bryn
Beechwood Cott.
Harpsden Wood
Cray Clearing Cott.
Nursery
WOODS
NORTHFIELD
MANOR WOOD GATE
NURSERY CL.
BRAMPTON
BOLNEY TREVOR DR.
AVENUE
NORTHFIELD
MILL
BASMOR
ROAD
LASHBROOK RD
STATION
Lower Shiplake
Willow La.
Henley Sailing Club

Red Hatch
Red Hatch Lodge
Cray Clearing
Cray House
Cray Copse
The Coach House
WHARPSDEN
Thames Poultry Farm House
OAKS
CROWSLEY WAY
ROAD
LOWES CL.
THE LASHBR.
MEAD
LASHBR. CRES.
Lashbrook
Boat Houses
LOWER SHIPLAKE

Upper Bolney House
Ash Farm
BOLNEY
Woodlands
ROAD
Henley-on-Thames RG9
Haileywood
THE CHESTNUTS
BROOKS
BADGERS WLK.
SIDNEY HARRISON HO.
Lashbrook
Lashbrook Farm
4
79

Upper Hailey Wood
Shiplake Wood
ROAD
Haileywood Farm
BASKERVILLE LA.
ROAD
ROAD
Brook
Lash
Andrew Duncan House

Shiplake Woods
137
Lower Hailey Wood
A4155
New Cross
AVENUE
NEW
MILL
Kingsley Gate House
Roman Remains
Lock End
LANE
MILL
LANE
5
Shiplake Lock
Viaduct
Boat House

KILN
LANE
KILN LA.
Shiplake House Farm
Weir
Weir
Sluice
WATERMAN'S WAY
HERONS CT.
Works

Kiln Cottages
SHIPLAKE
ROW
PLOUGH
MEMORIAL
SCHOOLFIELDS
Mem. Hall
ORCHARD CL.
Tennis Cts.
Spts. Gnd.
Shiplake
Playing Field
Playing Field
Pav.
Shiplake House
SOUTH OXFORDSHIRE
WOKINGHAM
Phillimore's Island
LODDON
LODDON
DRIVE
Wargrave
STATION RD.
6
78

LANE
Shiplake C of E Sch.
Bowling Green
PLOWDEN LANE
Shiplake Cross
CHURCH LA.
Shiplake College
The Old Vicarage
Shiplake Hole
Borough Lake
Bridgeman's Bridge
RIVER
Reading RG10

HAMPSTEAD
ROAD
READING
A4155
Shiplakecourt Farm
Warren Hill
The Warren
The Lynch
Borough Marsh
Borough Bridge
St. Patrick's Stream
LODDON
DRIVE
7

HENLEY
BOTTOM
76
Berry
Brook
149
77
Hallsmead Ait
LODDON
Sewage Works
78

F
G
H
149
J
K

WARWICK

Warwickshire Exhibition Centre

Bascote
Stockton
Lower Shuckburgh

15
Longbridge
Whitnash
A426
A425
Southam
A423
A425

B4463
A452
A4087
Tachbrook Mallory
B4455
Ufton
Ufton Fields
B4452
Farm
Napton on the Hill

A46
60
14
13
140
Bishop's Tachbrook
A
Harbury
Bishop's Bowl
B4451
Chapel Green

Sherbourne
Barford
M40
Chesterton
Ladbroke
B
Marston Doles

A429
Chesterton Green
Bishop's Itchington
6
Priors Hardwick
Pri Mar

Wasperton
Ashorne Hall
S
WARWICK
Oxford Canal

Hampton Lucy
Newbold Pacey
Ashorne
5
14
Upper Boddington
Boddi Mea

Charlecote Park NT
Charlecote
Moreton Morrell
B4100
Wormleighton
Byfield Po
Boddi Re

Wartime
Wellesbourne
LIGHTHORNE
18
12
Knightcote
Wormleighton Resr.
Lower Boddington

Wellesbourne Mountford
Watermill
1
Heritage Motor Centre
GAYDON
Northend
Beacon Tower
Fenny Compton
Avon
Aston le Walls

Loxley
A422
250
Walton
B4086
B4455
Compton Verney
Chadshunt
B4100
Burton Dassett Hills
Dassett
Farnborough
Bygones
Claydon
Appletree

Combrook
Butlers Marston
KINETON
Little Kineton
Stone
B4086
Arlescote
Farnborough Hall NT
A423

Ettington
1642 Edgehill
Radway
Warmington
10
Mollington
Cropredy Bridge
Cropredy

Pillerton Hersey
Pillerton Priors
A422
Edge Hill
Ratley
National Herb Centre
Shotteswell
M40
1644
Wardington
Williamscot
W

Newbold on Stour
A3400
B4455
Oxhill
Lower Tysoe
NT
Upton House
Hornton
Horley
Great Bourton
Little Bourton
A361
Cha

Halford
2
Whatcote
Middle Tysoe
Edgehill
Alkerton
A422
Wroxton
Hanwell
Grimsbury
11

Idlicote
Upper Tysoe
Shenington Kart Circuit
Shenington
BANBURY
2

Tredington
Honington Hall
Compton Wynyates
Balscote
Abbey Gardens
Drayton
Neithrop
Overtho

Honington
Winderton
Shutford
Epwell
North Newington
Wa

A429
Shipston-on-Stour
Lower Brailes
Soar Brook
Broughton Castle
Easington

B4035
Upper Brailes
B4035
Sibford Gower
Swalcliffe Barn
Swalcliffe
Broughton
B4035
Bodicote

Barcheston
Willington
Sutton-under-Brailes
18
Burdrop
Tadmarton
A361

Tidmington
Burmington
Sibford Ferris
Adderbury
Milton

Cherington
Stourton
River Stour
Bloxham
Milcombe
Village
B4100
18

Little Wolford
13
3
Whichford
Scotland End
18
Wigginton
12
South Newington
Barford St. John
Barford St. Michael
Clifton
R. Swere
A2260

Barton-on-the-Heath
Long Compton
A3400
Pottery
Hook Norton
Hook Norton Railway Cutting
Swerford
Nether Worton
B4031
Hempton
Deddington

A44
Rollright Stones King Stone
Great Rollright
Swerford
Swalcliffe
North Aston

Little Compton
Whispering Knights
Kings Men
Little Rollright
A361
A
143
Grea ew
Little Tew
Over Worton
B
North Aston

hastleton
NT
Over Norton
Salford
Heythrop
B4022
Ledwell
Duns Tew
Middle Aston
Oxford Canal

ton
Cornwell
Chipping Norton
B4026
A44
Sandford St. Martin
Middle Barton
Steeple

A45
A5
DAVENTRY
Drayton
Staverton
C
A361
B4037
Newnham
Weedon Bec
Badby
Upper Catesby
Lower Catesby
idon
734
Arbury Hill
Packhorse Bri.
Charwelton
16
Byfield
hrp
Hinton
West Farndon
on
Woodford Halse
Eydon
NORTHAMPTONSHIRE
Chipping Warden
pper dington
Culworth
Thorpe Mandeville
mbe
Middleton Cheney
Thenford
Marston St. Lawrence
Greatworth
Halse
Farthinghoe
orth Railway
8
Farthinghoe
A422
Newbottle
Newbottle Spinney
Hinton-in-the-Hedges
Charlton
g's Sutton
Rainsborough Camp
Aynho
Croughton
Aynhoe Park
B4031
A43
Souldern
M40
Fritwell
10
omerton
Fewcott
Ardley
S
CHERWELL VALLEY
B4100
Upper Heyford
Bucknell

Flecknoe
Norton
Fort
60
9
Borough Hill
Dodford
Muscott
Brockhall
Little Brington
Nobottle
New Duston
70
Harlestone Heath
Kingsthorpe
Harpole
A4500
16
Flore
D
Road Weedon
Upper Weedon
Upper Heyford
3
Nether Heyford
Duston
St. James End
Far Cotton
Upton
Eleanor Cross
Kislingbury
Hunsbury Hill
NORTHAMPTON
15a
3
Ironstone Railway
S
A45
A5
Bugbrooke
Rothersthorpe
Collingtree
Milton Malsor
15
A43
1
Little Everdon
Everdon
Everdon Stubbs
Church Stowe
Old Dairy Farm Centre
Upper Stowe
Pattishall
8
Dalscote
Eastcote
Astcote
Cold Higham
Tiffield
Ash Farm Sheep Dairy
Caldecote
Duncote
6
Blisworth
Blisworth Canal Tunnel
Roade
Canal
50
Brick Pits
Stoke, Bruerne
Shutlanger
Hulcote
Nene
Preston Capes
Preston Capes Castle
High Wood & Meadow
Farthingstone
Litchborough
Grimscote
Little Preston
Maidford
Adstone
Foxley
Greens Norton
Towcester
Stoke Park Pavilions
Towcester
Heathencote
Grafton Regis
A508
Canons Ashby House NT
Canons Ashby
NT
Priory Church
Blakesley
Woodend
Bradden
Wood Burcote
Alderton
Moreton Pinkney
Plumpton
Milthorpe
Weston
Weedon Lois
Slapton
Abthorpe
Pury End
Paulerspury
2
A43
Sulgrave Manor
Sulgrave
R. Tove
Wappenham
Bucknell Wood Walks & Pastures
Silverstone
Hazelborough Wood
Whittlebury
A413
Potterspury
A5
Whittlewood Forest
Helmdon
B4525
Syresham
11
Brackley Hatch
Silverstone
18
Lillingstone Lovell
Lillingstone Dayrell
Wicken
Crowfield
Radstone
Biddlesden
Whitfield
18
10
40
Brackley
Turweston
Turweston
Dadford
Stowe
9
NT
Stowe
Akeley
Leckhampstead
A422
Hinton-in-the-Hedges
St. James Lake
i
Shalstone
7
Chackmore
Foxcote Res.
Maids Moreton
River Great Ouse
Thornton
Thornb
Westbury
Evenley
Water Stratford
Buffler's Holt
Radclive
18
Old Gaol
i
3
Mount Pleasant
Buckingham
A421
Mixbury
Finmere
Tingewick
Gawcott
Thornborough Bridge
Singleborou
A421
A421
BUCKINGHAMSHIRE
Cottisford
Hardwick
Newton Purcell
Heth
144
Chetwode
Barton Hartshorn
D
eston Bissett
Padbury
Norbury
Adstock
7
30
A4421
Stoke Lyne
Fringfo
13
Hillesden Church
Addington
A413
Bainton
60
Stratton Audley
Twyford
Steeple Claydon
70
Middle Claydon
Claydon
Wins

142

Gloucestershire

OXF

Places and features (north to south, west to east)

Snowshill

Stanway House & Fountain
Stanway
Didbrook
Hailes
Cotswold
NT Gillets
Hailes Abbey
Wood Stanway
Farmcote
Hyde
Temple Guiting
Kineton
Hawling
Aylworth
Naunton
Barton
Chalk Hill
Hinchwick

A44
Bourton-on-the-Hill
Sezincote
Longborough
Ganborough
Condicote
Donnington Fish Farm
Donnington
Broadwell
Upper Swell
Stow-on-the-Wold
Lower Swell
Maugersbury
Lower Oddington
Upper Oddington
Daylesford

Moreton-in-Marsh
The Four Shire Stone
Barton-on-the-Heath
Cotswold Falconry Centre
Wellington Aviation
Chastleton
Chastleton House NT
Evenlode
Adlestrop
Cornwell

Lon
Com
A3

Rollright Stones King Stone
Kings Men
Little Rollrig
Salf
A44
A436
Church
Sarsde

B4077

Cotswold

982

Upper Slaughter
Lower Slaughter
Old Mill
Model Railway Exhibition
Village Life Exhibition
Model Village
Bourton-on-the-Water
Perfumery
Cotswolds Motoring
Nethercote
Birdland Park & Gardens
Little Rissington
Clapton-on-the-Hill
Great Rissington

Wyck Hill
Wyck Rissington
Icomb
Bledington
Foscot
Church Westcote
Nether Westcote
Idbury
Little Rissington
Fifield

Kingham
Foxholes
Bruern Abbey
Milton-under-Wychwood
Shipton-under-Wychwood

Lyneham
As D'

Ascott Wych

A436
Long Barrow
Salperton
Notgrove
Cold Aston
Hazleton
Hampen
Turkdean

A40
A429

GLOUCESTERSHIRE

Compton Abdale
Hampnett
Farmington
Sherborne
Chedworth
Yanworth
Northleach
Mill End
Mechanical Music
Eastington
NT
Windrush
Great Barrington
Little Barrington

Taynton
Great Barrington

Chedworth Roman Villa NT
Chedworth
Pancakehill
Denfurlong Farm
Fossebridge
Coln St. Dennis
Calcot
Long Barrow
Coln Rogers
Winson
Ablington
Arlington
Arlington Row NT
Bibury
Bibury Trout Farm

Lodge Park NT
Aldsworth
B4425
Westwell
Holwell
Signet
Shilton
Cotswold
Carterton

Calmsden
Barnsley
Ampney Crucis
B4425
A417

Coln St. Aldwyns
Hatherop
Eastleach Turville
Quenington

Eastleach Martin
Cotswold Woollen Weavers
Filkins
Fyfield
Southrop

Swinford
Cross Tree Gallery
Kencot
Broadwell
Alvescot
Blac
Bour

BRIZE NORTON

Tolsey
Burford
Fulbrook
Swinbroc
Asthall
A40

A361
A4020

COTSWOLD HILLS

A429
B4425

Preston
Harnhill
Ampney St. Peter
Ampney St. Mary
Poulton
Driffield
Meysey Hampton
Marsh Hill
Whelford

Milton End
Fairford
Horcott
Fairford

Edward Richardson & Phyllis Amey
Little Faringdon
Langford
Little Clanfield
Grafton

Broughton Poggs
Clanfi
12 12

South Cerney
Butts Farm
Down Ampne
Marston Meysey
Kempsford
Latton

Lechlade on Thames
Father Thames Mon.
Upper Inglesham

Kelmscott
Old Parsonage NT
Buscot
Buscot Park NT

Kelmscott Manor
Eaton Hastings
Littl
A4095

A419
A417

Scotland End
Wigginton
Barford St. John
Barford St. Michael
R. Swere
Aynho
Croughto
A4260
18
10
B4031
Aynhoe Park
M40
A43
Pottery
Hook Norton
A361
South Newington
B4031
Hempton
Clifton
Deddington
Souldern
B41
143
Hook Norton Railway Cutting
Swerford
140
Nether Worton
D
30
S
CHE VA
Swerford
C
Over Worton
North Aston
Fritwell
Somerton
Fewcott
Bayn Gre
10
Great Rollright
Great Tew
Middle Aston
Upper Heyford
Ardley
ghts
A361
Little Tew
Ledwell
Duns Tew
18
Steeple Aston
Lower Heyford
Over orton
Heythrop
Sandford St. Martin
Middle Barton
Roush am Park
Caulcott
Middleton Stoney
Buc
i
Chipping Norton
Church Enstone
B4030
Westcott Barton
Rousham
M40
18
Lidstone
Enstone
Gagingwell
Steeple Barton
Northbrook
B4030
B4026
A44
Cleveley
20
Nethercott
A4095
12
Weston-on-the-green
9
Chadlington
Taston
Kiddington
18
Glympton
Tackley
Kirtlington
Weston-on-the-Green
Spelsbury
B4022
Over Kiddington
B4027
R. Dorn
Middleton Stoney
Shorthampton
Ditchley Park
A4260
B4027
144
Bletchingdon
ly
Chilson
B4437
Charlbury
B4437
Wootton
Shipton-on-Cherwell
Hampton Poyle
Charlton-o Otmoor
inder ood
R. Evenlode
Fawler
Stonesfield
Old Woodstock
Thrupp
O
Finstock
Oxfordshire
Woodstock
H
I
R
E
Mount Skippett
North Leigh Roman Villa
Combe
Blenheim Palace
Oxford
Islip
Leafield
Ramsden
East End
Bladon
19
Kidlington
Noke
Field Assarts
Whiteoak Green
Delly End
New Yatt
North Leigh
Combe Mill
Oxford Bus
Begbroke
Gosford
Woodeaton
B4027
ells
B4022
Asthall Leigh
Minster Lovell Hall & Dovecote
Poffley End
Long Hanborough
Freeland
Church Hanborough
A44
Yarnton
Elsfield
Minster Lovell
Hailey
Crawley
A4095
Barnard Gate
Cassington
OXFORD PEAR TREE
Sunnymead
A40
047
WITNEY
Woodgreen Allotments
Manor Farm
A40
10
Eynsham
S
Wolvercote
Marston
Barton
Curbridge
Cogges
High Cogges
South Leigh
B4449
TOLL Swinford
Godstow Nunnery
Wytham
A34
Park Town
Headington
Botanic
BRIZE Norton
A4095
Ducklington
Farmoor
OXFORD
Light Infantry
A4477
7
A415
Hardwick
Sutton
B4044
North Hinksey Village
Grandpont
Botley
A420
Chawley
Conduit House
South Hinksey
Iffley
Lew
Yelford
Blackditch
Stanton Harcourt Manor
Farmoor Reservoir
Cumnor
18
3
Aston
Brighthampton
Cote
Rack End
Stanton Harcourt
Northmoor
Eaton
Boars Hill
Kennington
Littlemore
Bampton
B4449
Standlake
Bessels Leigh
Appleton
B4017
Foxcombe Hill
Bayworth
Sandford-on-Thames
A4074
Chimney
Duxford
R. Thames or Isis
A420
8
Wootton
Dry Sunningwell
A34
Radley
Nuneham Courtenay
C
147
Longw
Fyfield
Sandford
Cothill
NT
Abingdon
Northcourt
Harcourt
Buckland
Hinton Waldrist
Southmoor
Tubney Frilford
A338
Shippon
ABINGDON
B4015
worth
A420
Pusey
B4508
Kingston Bagpuize
Kingston Bagpuize House
Garford
A415
Marcham
6
Abingdon County Hall Abingdon
Clifton Hampden
Caldec

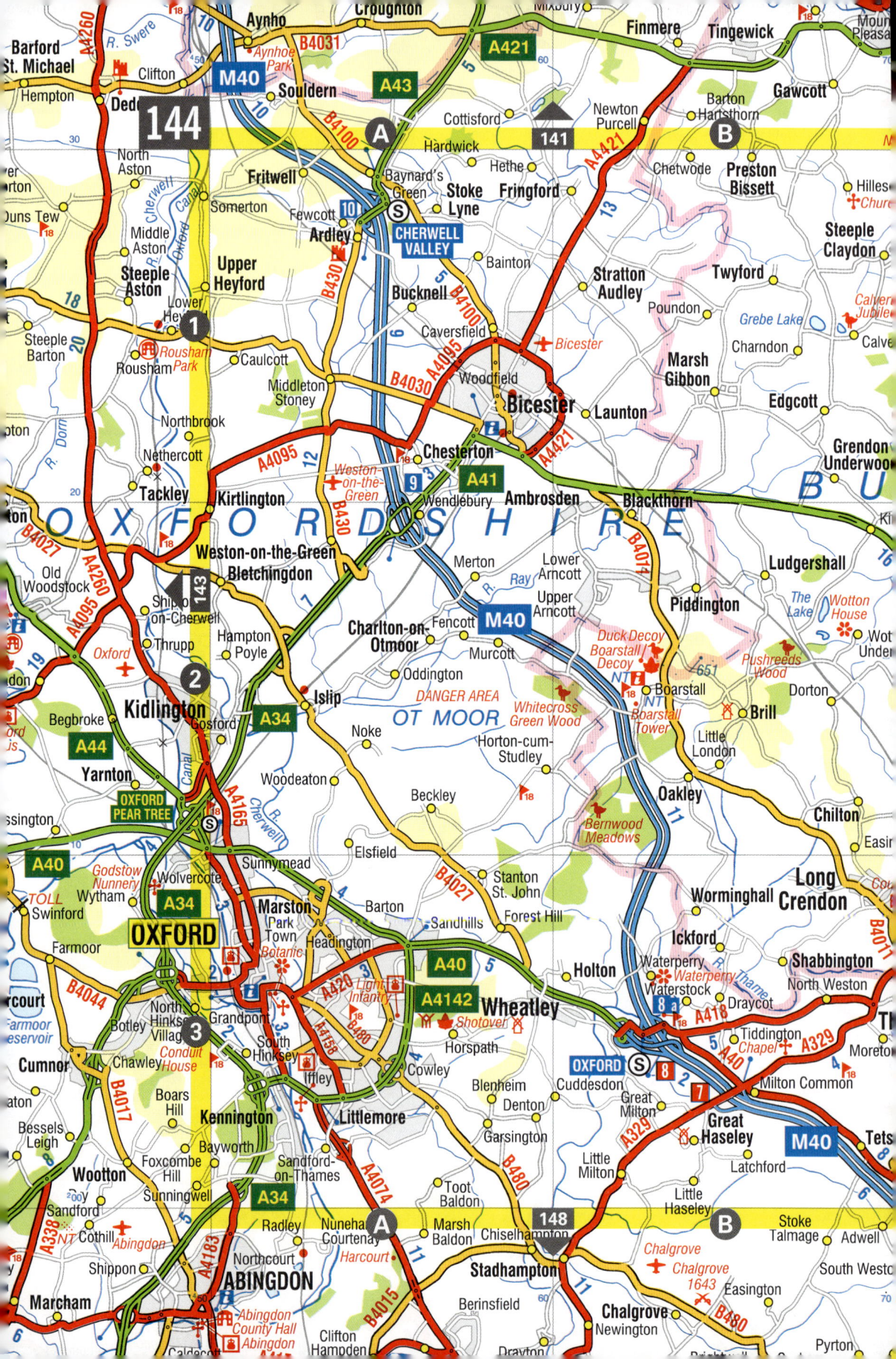

Barford St. Michael
Hempton
Ded...
Clifton
North Aston
Middle Aston
Duns Tew
Steeple Barton
...ton
R. Swere
R. Dorn
M40
A4260
Aynho
Aynhoe Park
B4031
Souldern
Croughton
Finmere
Tingewick
A421
A43
Cottisford
Hardwick
Newton Purcell
Barton Hartshorn
Gawcott
141
A4421
Chetwode
Preston Bissett
Hilles
Chure
Steeple Claydon
Fritwell
Somerton
Fewcott
Ardley
Baynard's Green
Stoke Lyne
Fringford
Hethe
Bainton
Stratton Audley
Twyford
Poundon
Charndon
Calve
Calver Jubilee
Grebe Lake

Upper Heyford
Lower Hey...
Rousham Park
Rousham
Northbrook
Nethercott
Tackley
Middleton Stoney
Bucknell
Caversfield
Bicester
Woodfield
Bicester
Launton
Marsh Gibbon
Edgcott
Grendon Underwoo...
B4100
B430
B4030
A4095
A4421
A41

Steeple Aston
Kirtlington
Weston-on-the-Green
Chesterton
Wendlebury
Ambrosden
Blackthorn
Ludgershall
A4095
B430
Caulcott

OXFORDSHIRE
BU...

Old Woodstock
A4260
A4095
Ship...on-Cherwell
Thrupp
Hampton Poyle
Weston-on-the-Green
Bletchingdon
143
Charlton-on-Otmoor
Fencott
Merton
Murcott
R. Ray
Lower Arncott
Upper Arncott
Piddington
The Lake
Wotton House
Wot...Under
Dorton
Duck Decoy
Boarstall Decoy
Boarstall
Boarstall Tower
Brill
Little London
Pushreeds Wood
651
NT
M40
B4011

Kidlington
2
Gosford
Islip
Noke
Woodeaton
Oddington
DANGER AREA
OT MOOR
Whitecross Green Wood
Horton-cum-Studley
Oakley
Chilton
Easir
Begbroke
A44
Yarnton
OXFORD PEAR TREE
Elsfield
Beckley
Bernwood Meadows
Stanton St. John
Long Crendon
A40
Godstow Nunnery
Wytham
A34
Wolvercote
Sunnymead
B4027
Forest Hill
Worminghall
B4011
Cou...
Swinford
TOLL
Farmoor
OXFORD
Marston
Park Town
Botanic
Barton
Sandhills
A40
Holton
Ickford
Waterperry
Waterperry
Waterstock
Shabbington
North Weston
Draycot
B4044
North Hinksey Village
Botley
Grandpont
Headington
A420
Light Infantry
A4142
Wheatley
Shotover
Horspath
8 a
A418
Tiddington
Chapel
A329
Moreto...
Farmoor Reservoir
Conduit House
South Hinksey
Iffley
Cowley
Blenheim
Denton
Garsington
OXFORD
S
8
7
Cuddesdon
Great Milton
Milton Common
Th...
Cumnor
Chawley
Boars Hill
Kennington
Bayworth
Littlemore
Sandford-on-Thames
Toot Baldon
Little Milton
Great Haseley
Latchford
M40
Tets
Bessels Leigh
Wootton
Foxcombe Hill
Sunningwell
Little Haseley
A34
A4074
Marsh Baldon
Chiselhampton
148
Stoke Talmage
Adwell
South Westo...
Sandford
Cothill
NT
Abingdon
Northcourt
Nuneham Courtenay
Harcourt
Stadhampton
Chalgrove
Chalgrove 1643
Easington
B480
Shippon
ABINGDON
Abingdon County Hall
Abingdon
Berinsfield
Chalgrove
Newington
Marcham
B4015
Clifton Hampden
Drayton
Pyrton
A338
A4183
A4074

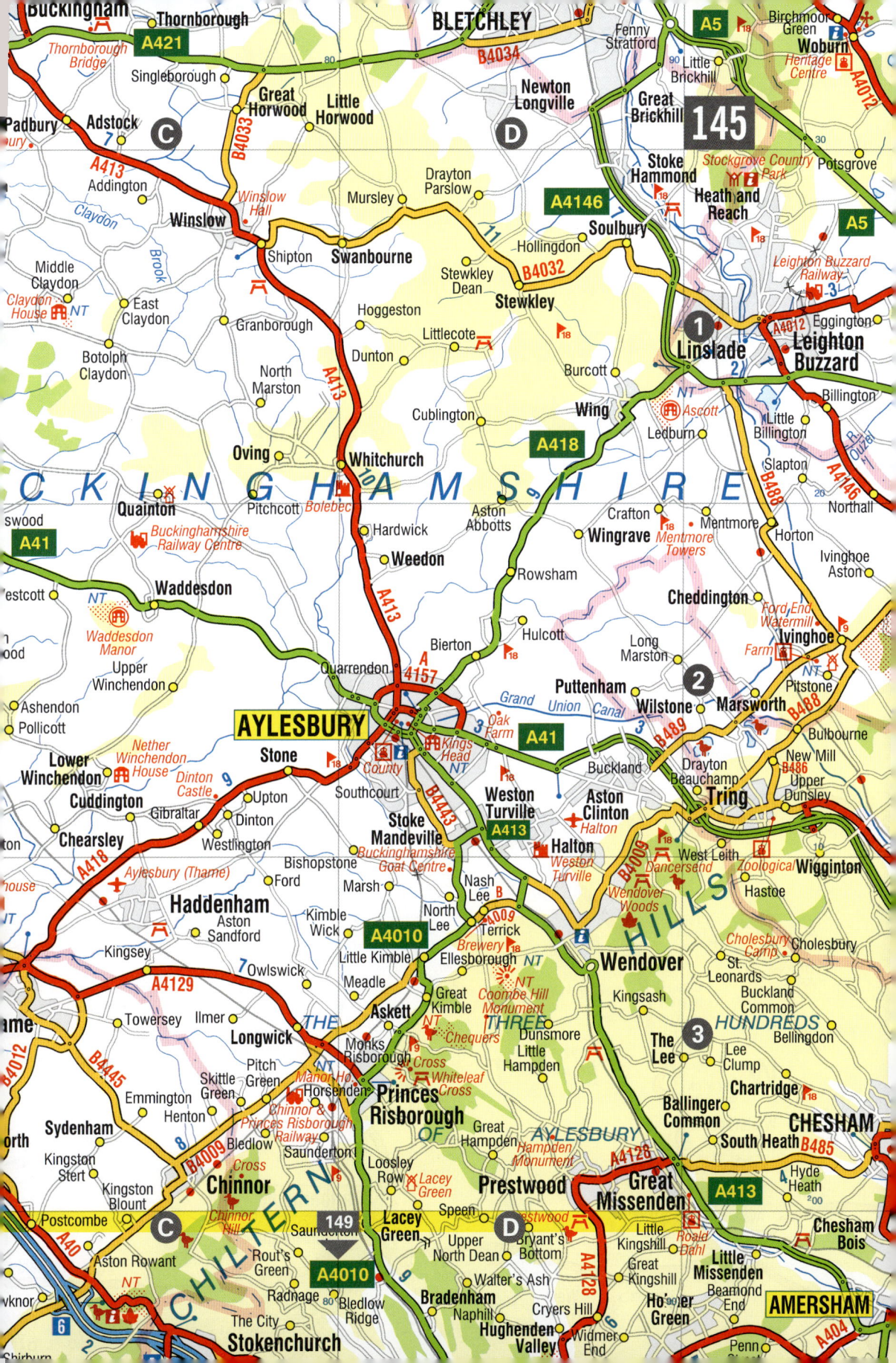

Buckingham
Thornborough
BLETCHLEY
A5
Birchmoor Green
Woburn
Heritage Centre
A421
Thornborough Bridge
B4034
Fenny Stratford
Little Brickhill
A4012
Padbury
Singleborough
B4033
Great Horwood
Little Horwood
Newton Longville
Great Brickhill
Stoke Hammond
Stockgrove Country Park
Potsgrove
Adstock
Addington
A413
A4146
Heath and Reach
A5
Winslow Hall
Mursley
Drayton Parslow
Soulbury
Leighton Buzzard Railway
Winslow
Shipton
Swanbourne
Hollingdon
B4032
Stewkley Dean
Stewkley
Middle Claydon
Claydon House NT
East Claydon
Granborough
Hoggeston
Littlecote
Burcott
Linslade
A4012
Eggington
Leighton Buzzard
Botolph Claydon
North Marston
A413
Dunton
Cublington
Wing
Ledburn
Ascott NT
Little Billington
Slapton
Billington
A41
Oving
Whitchurch
A418
Crafton
Wingrave
Mentmore
Mentmore Towers
Horton
Northall
BUCKINGHAMSHIRE
Quainton
Pitchcott
Bolebec
Hardwick
Aston Abbotts
Ivinghoe Aston
Buckinghamshire Railway Centre
Weedon
Rowsham
Cheddington
Ford End Watermill
Ivinghoe
Waddesdon
Waddesdon Manor
Upper Winchendon
Bierton
Hulcott
Long Marston
Puttenham
Wilstone
Marsworth
Pitstone
Bulbourne
Ashendon
Pollicott
Quarrendon
A4157
Grand Union Canal
B489
Drayton Beauchamp
New Mill
B486
Upper Dunsley
AYLESBURY
A41
Buckland
Tring
Lower Winchendon
Nether Winchendon House
Stone
Kings Head NT
A418
Dinton Castle
Upton
Dinton
Southcourt
County
Weston Turville
Aston Clinton
Halton
West Leith
Zoological
Wigginton
Cuddington
Gibraltar
Westlington
B4443
Stoke Mandeville
A413
Halton
Weston Turville
Dancersend
Hastoe
Chearsley
Bishopstone
Ford
Marsh
Buckinghamshire Goat Centre
Nash Lee
Wendover Woods
HILLS
Cholesbury Camp
Cholesbury
Haddenham
Aston Sandford
Kimble Wick
North Lee
B4009
Terrick
Brewery
Ellesborough
Wendover
St. Leonards
Buckland Common
Bellingdon
Kingsey
Owlswick
Meadle
A4010
Great Kimble
Coombe Hill Monument NT
Kingsash
THREE
Chequers
HUNDREDS
Lee Clump
A4129
Towersey
Ilmer
Askett
Whiteleaf Cross
Dunsmore
Little Hampden
The Lee
Chartridge
Longwick
Monks Risborough
Cross
CHESHAM
Pitch Green
Skittle Green
Manor Ho
Horsenden
Princes Risborough
Great Hampden
AYLESBURY
Ballinger Common
South Heath
B485
Emmington
Henton
Chinnor & Princes Risborough Railway
Saunderton
Hampden Monument
A4128
Great Missenden
A413
Hyde Heath
Chesham Bois
Sydenham
Bledlow
Cross
Loosley Row
Lacey Green
Speen
Prestwood
Little Kingshill
Roald Dahl
Little Missenden
Kingston Stert
B4009
Chinnor Hill
Lacey Green
Upper North Dean
Bryant's Bottom
Great Kingshill
Beamond End
Kingston Blount
Saunderton
Walter's Ash
Hughenden
Cryers Hill
Hodge
AMERSHAM
Postcombe
A40
Rout's Green
A4010
Bradenham
Naphill
Widmer End
Penn
Aston Rowant
Radnage
Bledlow Ridge
Hughenden Valley
The City
Stokenchurch
A404
A4010
149
A40
CHILTERN
Upper Winchendon
THE
OF
Three Hundreds

GLOUCESTERSHIRE

146

WILTSHIRE

A B

142

Queninton
Fyfield
Broughton Poggs
Broadwell
Langford
B4020

Ampney Crucis
A417
Ampney St. Mary
Southrop
A361
Little Faringdon
Little Clanfield
Clanf

Preston
Harnhill
Poulton
Milton End
Fairford
Horcott
A417
Edward Richardson & Phy. Amey
Grafton

Driffield
Meysey Hampton
Marston Hill
Whelford
Lechlade on Thames
Kelmscott Old Parsonage NT
Kelmscott Manor
Eaton Hastings

South Cerney
Butts Farm
A419
Down Ampney
Fairford
Marston Meysey
Kempsford
Upper Inglesham
Father Thames Mon.
Buscot
Buscot Park NT

North End
Ashton Keynes
Latton
Cerney Wick
Castle Eaton
Hannington Wick
R. Cole
Faringdon
Badbury Hill NT 530
Great Coxwell Barn NT
A417
A4095

Chelworth Upper Green
Leigh
Cricklade
R. Thames or Isis
Hannington
Hampton
Highworth
Coleshill
Great Coxwell
B4019
Little Cox
Li

Chelworth Lower Green
A419
Swindon & Cricklade Railway
Broad Blunsdon
B4019
A361
Watchfield
B4508
Longcot
B4508

Purton Stoke
Blunsdon St. Andrew
Stanton Fitzwarren
Sevenhampton
B4000
Shrivenham
VALE

Purton
Widham
Haydon Wick
Penhill
A4311
B4006
Kingsdown
South Marston
A420
Bourton
Woolstone
Compton Beauchamp

B4696
Restrop
Common Platt
Nine Elms
Lydiard Ho.
B4587
B4534
Stratton St. Margaret
A4312
Covingham
Walcot
A419
Ashbury
Waylan Smith
B4507

Lydiard Millicent
Hook
Lydiard Ho.
Even Swindon
Steam
SWINDON
Horpit
Uffington Castle

M4 16
Okus Swindon
A3102
A4259
Coate
Hinton Parva
Bishopstone
Ashdown House NT
Idstone

Woodshaw
North Wroughton
B4006
Jefferies
Wanborough
Liddington

A3102
Wootton Bassett
B4005
Wroughton
Hodson
Badbury
15
Baydon

Elcombe
A4361
Science Museum Wroughton
Clouts Wood Wroughton
Overtown
B4005
Chiseldon
A346
Upper Upham
Woodsend

Bushton
Broad Town
Uffcott
Draycot Foliat
Aldbourne
MEM

Clyffe Pypard
Broad Hinton
Winterbourne Bassett
White Horse 892 Hackpen Hill
Barbury Castle (Fort)
Barbury Castle
Marlborough Downs
Ogbourne St. George
Preston

Clevancy
Berwick Bassett
Ogbourne St. Andrew
Rockley
Ramsbury
Knighton

Yatesbury
Winterbourne Monkton
Great Barn
A4361
Ogbourne Maizey
Whi

Windmill Hill
Alexander Keiller Avebury Manor
Avebury Stone Circle
Avebury
B4003
Marlborough
Axford
A4

Avebury Trusloe
Mon. NT
West Kennett
NT Fyfield
A4
Manton
White Horse
Preshute
Mildenhall
Stitchcombe
A4 Froxfield

White Horse
Beckhampton
Silbury Hill
East Kennett
West Overton
Lockeridge
St. Margaret's
A345
Savernake Forest
Chisbury

A361
West Kennett Long Barrow
The Sanctuary NT
Cadley
Savernake Forest
A346
Litt

Aston Brighthampton B4449 Rack End Cumnor Chawley House B4017 A34 Iffley
Bampton Cote Standlake Northmoor Eaton Boars Hill 450 ennington Littlemore
Chimney R. Thames or Isis 143 A420 Wootton Bessels Leigh Appleton Foxcombe Hill Bayworth Sandford-on-Thames A4074 147
Duxford C Longworth Fyfield Dry Sandford Sunningwell 200
Buckland Hinton Waldrist Southmoor Tubney Frilford A338 NT Cothill Abingdon A4183 Radley Nuneham Courtenay Harcourt
A420 Pusey 8 Kingston Bagpuize Marcham A415 Shippon Northcourt ABINGDON B4015
B4508 Kingston Bagpuize House Garford 6 A4017 Abingdon County Hall Abingdon Clifton Hampden Burc
Charney Bassett Venn Mill Caldecott A415
F O R D S H I R E Hatford R. Ock Charney Mill Lyford A34 Drayton Milton Manor Sutton Courtenay Long Wittenham Pendon Appleford Dor-on- Little Wittenh
Stanford in the Vale Denchworth East Hanney West Hanney Steventon Milton B4016
worth A417 OF WHITEHORSE Baulking Goosey 9 Grove A338 Priory Cottages NT A4130 Milton Hill Harwell Didcot Northbourne East Hagbourne 1
ham Tom Brown's School West Challow Wantage A417 5 Rowstock A4130 Coscote South Moreton
Uffington B4001 East Challow Charlton Ardington West Hendred East Hendred A4185 13 West Hagbourne Aston Upthorne
White Horse Kingston Lisle Park Sparsholt Childrey Vale & Downland East Lockinge Ardington House 148 Upton B4016
Whitehorse Hill Westcot B4507 A338 B4494 East Ginge 11 Chilton A34 Blewbury A417 10
kingston Lisle Letcombe Regis West Ginge 2
Letcombe Bassett 781 Ridge Way West Ilsley
W E S T Lambourn Downs Fawley 11 Farnborough East Ilsley Compton 80
Upper Lambourn B4000 South Fawley Brightwalton Catmore A34
Lambourn Trainers Lambourn Eastbury East Garston Brightwalton Green Chaddleworth Stanmore Beedon Hampstead Norreys Wyld Court Rainforest A
B E R K S H Lambourn Woodlands R. Lambourn Leckhampstead Street Hillgreen Peasemore World's End Bothampstead B4009
S Woodlands St. Mary Great Shefford Leckhampstead Downend A34 3 Eling M4 Yatte
RY M4 14 A338 East Shefford Weston Chieveley 13 Oare Frilsham 1
Crooked Soley Shefford Woodlands Welford Winterbourne CHIEVELEY Hermitage Wellhouse Sta
ditch Straight Soley B4001 Welford Park Welford Ownham B4494 Curridge Longlane B4009 Bu
192 A338 3 Hungerford Newtown Wickham Boxford Snelsmore Common 8 Ashmore Green Cold Ash The Slade Farm Park
ton Foliat Leverton Elcot B4000 Wickham Heath Stockcross 9 Donnington 1644 18 Shaw Upper Bucklebury
gerford C Eddington A4 8 Halfway D Speen 18 Midgham A4 Thatcham
Kennet & Avon 40 Marsh Benham NEWBURY 150 Newbury Thatcham
edwyn The Priory Templeton Kintbury Layland's Green The Folly

A420 · B4017 · A34 · OXFORD · 8 · 2

Cumnor · Chawley House · Iffley · Cowley · Blenheim · Denton · Cuddesdon · Great Milton · Milton Common · A40

Boars Hill · Littlemore · Garsington · Great Haseley · Latchford · M40

Bessels Leigh · Bennington · B480 · Little Milton · Little Haseley · Stoke Talmage · Adwell · South West

Wootton · 148 · Sandford-on-Thames · Toot Baldon · A · 144 · B · Chalgrove 1643 · Easington · Pyrton · Cuxham

Sandford · Cothill · Abingdon · Radley · Nuneham Courtenay · Marsh Baldon · Chiselhampton · B480 · Chalgrove · Newington · Brightwell Baldwin · 10

A338 · Northcourt · Harcourt · Stadhampton

Marcham · ABINGDON · Abingdon County Hall · Clifton Hampden · Burcot · Berinsfield · Drayton St-Leonard · Chalgrove · B4009 · Britwell Salome

Shippon · A415 · Culham · Long Wittenham · Dorchester on Thames · Abbey · Warborough · Berrick Salome · Roke · B480

Caldecott · 1 · Appleford · Little Wittenham · Shillingford · Rokemarsh · Cookley Green

Steventon · Drayton · Milton Manor · Sutton Courtenay · B4016 · R. Thames · A4074 · Benson · Ewelme · B481

Priory Cottages · Milton · A4130 · Brightwell-cum-Sotwell · Slade End · Wallingford · Benson · Nuffield Place

A4130 · Didcot · B4493 · 18 · Wallingford · Crowmarsh Gifford · A4130 · 10

Milton Hill · Harwell · East Hagbourne · North Moreton · Winterbrook · Nuffield

A417 · Northbourne · Coscote · West Hagbourne · South Moreton · Cholsey & Wallingford Railway · Old K

Rowstock · West Hendred · East Hendred · A4185 · Upton · Aston Upthorpe · Cholsey · North Stoke · B4009 · Ipsden · Maharajah's Well · Witheridge Hill

East Ginge · Aston Tirrold · Checkendon · Stoke Row · Sat

West Ilsley · Chilton · 2 · Blewbury · 10 · Moulsford · North Grove · Exlade Street · Wyfold Grange

East Ilsley · A34 · A417 · South Stoke · Woodcote · Cray's Pond · Gallowstree Common · Th

Compton · A329 · Cleeve · B4526 · 13 · CHILTERNS

Aldworth · B4009 · Streatley · NT · Goring · Whitchurch Hill · Cane End · Goring Heath · A4074

Peasemore · World's End · Hampstead Norreys · Wyld Court Rainforest · Ashampstead · Quick's Green · Lower Basildon · Beale Park · Whitchurch-on-Thames · Goring Vineyard · Mapledurham

Hillgreen · Downend · Bothampstead · B4009 · Upper Basildon · Basildon Park NT · TOLL · Pangbourne · Mapledurham House · Caversham Height

A34 · 3 · Eling · Yattendon · Burnt Hill · Tidmarsh · Purley on Thames · River Thames · A329

Chieveley · M4 · 11 · Sulham · A340 · Tilehurst

13 · Oare · Frilsham · Rotten Row · Bradfield · Englefield · North Street · 12 · Calcot Row · READ

CHIEVELEY · Hermitage · Wellhouse · Stanford Dingley · Englefield Ho · Theale · M4 · READING

Curridge · Longlane · Bucklebury · Tutts Clump · South End · Sulhamstead · Trash Green

Snelsmore Common · Ashmore Green · The Slade · Farm Park · A · Chapel Row · Beenham · Burghfield · Burghfield Hill

Donnington · Cold Ash · Upper Bucklebury · A4 · Woolhampton · Padworth · Ufton Nervet · Burghfield Common

Speen · Thatcham · Midgham · Sulhamstead

NEWBURY · Newbury · Thatcham · The Folly

OXFORDSHIRE · BERKSHIRE · WEST · A4

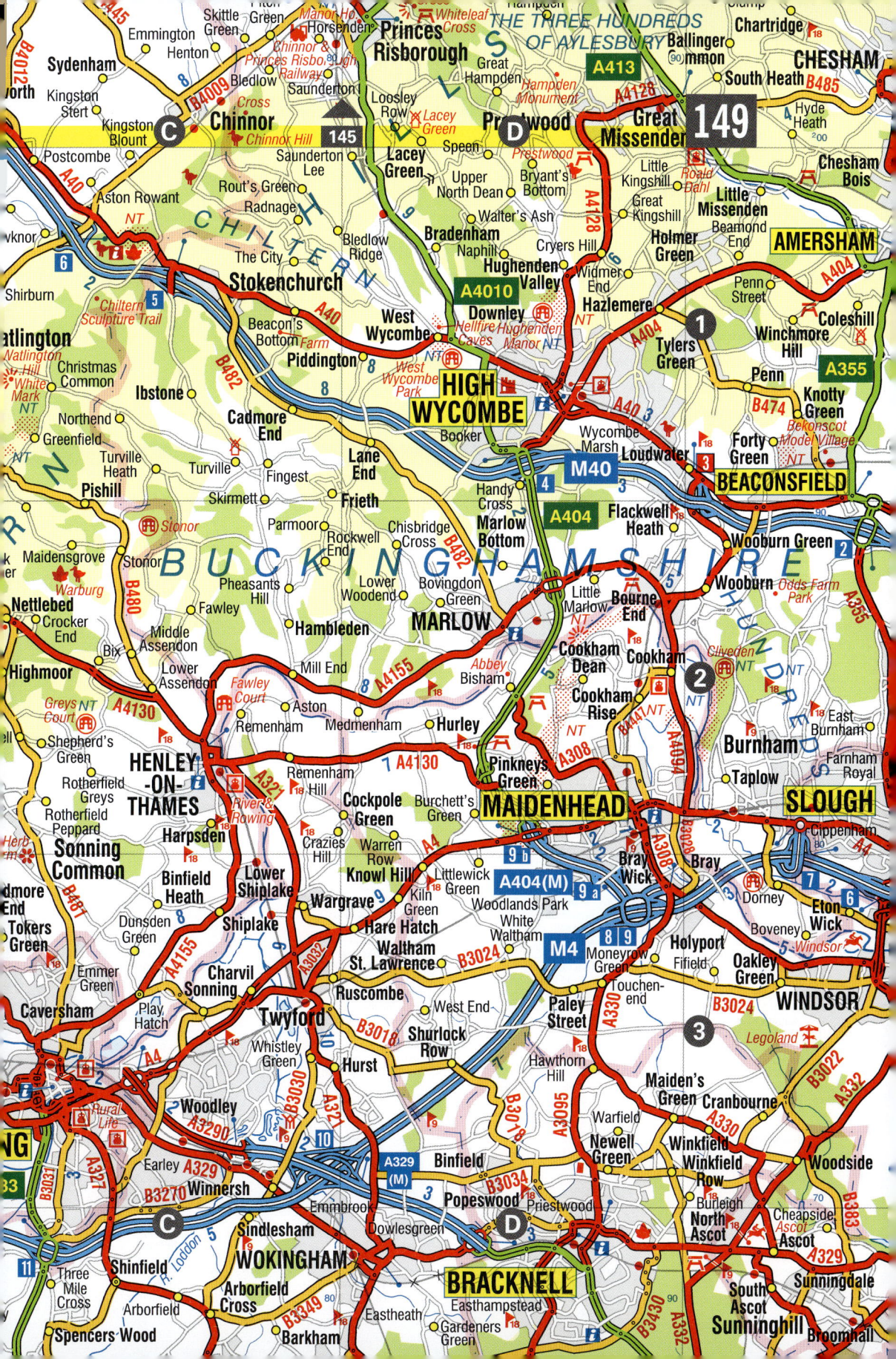

A45 · Skittle Green · Manor Ho · Horsenden · Whiteleaf Cross · Chartridge · Clump · B4012 · Emmington · Henton · Chinnor & Princes Risbo Light Railway · Princes Risborough · Great Hampden · Ballinger Common · Chesham · B485 · Sydenham · Bledlow Cross · Saunderton · Loosley Row · Hampden Monument · Prestwood · South Heath · Hyde Heath · Hawridge

Kingston Stert · Chinnor · 145 · Lacey Green · Prestwood · Great Missenden · 149 · Chinnor Hill · Speen · Little Kingshill · Roald Dahl · Chesham Bois · Postcombe · Saunderton Lee · Upper North Dean · Bryant's Bottom · Great Kingshill · Beamond End · Little Missenden · A40 · Rout's Green · Radnage · Walter's Ash · Cryers Hill · Holmer Green · AMERSHAM · Aston Rowant · NT · Bledlow Ridge · Bradenham · Naphill · Hughenden Valley · Widmer End · Penn Street · A4010 · Coleshill · The City · Downley · Hazlemere · A404 · Winchmore Hill · Stokenchurch · Beacon's Bottom · West Wycombe · Hellfire Caves · Hughenden Manor · Tylers Green · Penn · A355 · Christmas Common · Piddington · West Wycombe Park · HIGH WYCOMBE · Knotty Green · B474 · Ibstone · Cadmore End · Booker · Wycombe Marsh · Loudwater · Forty Green · Bekonscot Model Village · Northend · Greenfield · Turville Heath · Turville · Fingest · Lane End · Frieth · Handy Cross · M40 · BEACONSFIELD · Pishill · Skirmett · Parmoor · Rockwell End · Chisbridge Cross · Marlow Bottom · A404 · Flackwell Heath · Wooburn Green · Maidensgrove · Warburg · Stonor · Pheasants Hill · Lower Woodend · Bovingdon Green · Little Marlow · Bourne End · Wooburn · Odds Farm Park · BUCKINGHAMSHIRE · Nettlebed · Crocker End · Fawley · Hambleden · MARLOW · Cookham Dean · Cookham · Cliveden · Bix · Middle Assendon · Mill End · Abbey · Bisham · Cookham Rise · East Burnham · Highmoor · Lower Assendon · Aston · Medmenham · Hurley · A4155 · A4094 · Burnham · Greys Court · A4130 · Fawley Court · Remenham · Pinkneys Green · A308 · Taplow · Farnham Royal · Shepherd's Green · Rotherfield Greys · HENLEY-ON-THAMES · Remenham Hill · Cockpole Green · Burchett's Green · MAIDENHEAD · SLOUGH · Rotherfield Peppard · River & Rowing · Crazies Hill · Warren Row · A4 · Bray Wick · Bray · Cippenham · A4 · Sonning Common · Harpsden · Lower Shiplake · Knowl Hill · Littlewick Green · 9b · Dorney · Eton Wick · Binfield Heath · Woodlands Park · A404(M) · 9a · Boveney · Dunsden Green · Shiplake · Wargrave · Kiln Green · White Waltham · 8 · 9 · Windsor · Tokers Green · Emmer Green · Charvil · Hare Hatch · Waltham St. Lawrence · B3024 · M4 · Moneyrow Green · Holyport · Oakley Green · Caversham · Sonning · Ruscombe · Fifield · Touchen-end · A330 · WINDSOR · Play Hatch · Twyford · West End · Paley Street · B3024 · Legoland · Rural Life · Whistley Green · Hurst · Shurlock Row · Hawthorn Hill · Maiden's Green · Cranbourne · B3022 · A332 · Woodley · A3290 · Warfield · Newell Green · Winkfield · Woodside · Earley · A329 · Binfield · Popeswood · Priestwood · Winkfield Row · A330 · Winnersh · B3270 · A329(M) · B3034 · North Ascot · Cheapside · Ascot · B3031 · Sindlesham · Dowlesgreen · Burleigh · A329 · Sunningdale · Three Mile Cross · WOKINGHAM · BRACKNELL · Easthampstead · South Ascot · Sunninghill · Shinfield · Arborfield Cross · Eastheath · Gardeners Green · A332 · Broomhall · Spencers Wood · Arborfield · Barkham · B3349

INDEX

Including Streets, Places & Areas, Industrial Estates,
Selected Flats & Walkways, Stations and Selected Places of Interest.

HOW TO USE THIS INDEX

1. Each street name is followed by its Postcode District and then by its Locality abbreviation(s) and then by its map reference; e.g. **Abberbury Rd.** OX4: Oxf . . . .2C **84** is in the OX4 Postcode District and the Oxford Locality and is to be found in square 2C on page **84**. The page number is shown in bold type.

2. A strict alphabetical order is followed in which Av., Rd., St., etc. (though abbreviated) are read in full and as part of the street name; e.g. **Bank Side** appears after **Banks Furlong** but before **Bankside**

3. Streets and a selection of flats and walkways too small to be shown on street map pages **4-121**, appear in the index with the thoroughfare to which it is connected shown in brackets; e.g. **Acacia Cl.** *OX18: Cart* . . . .6E **46** (off Black Bourton Rd.)

4. Addresses that are in more than one part are referred to as not continuous.

5. Places and areas are shown in the index in BLUE TYPE and the map reference is to the actual map square in which the town centre or area is located and not to the place name shown on the map. Map references for entries that appear on street map pages **6-139** are shown first, with references to road map pages **140-149** shown in brackets; e.g. ABINGDON . . . .1G **91 (1D 147)**

6. An example of a selected place of interest is Banbury Mus. 7F **11**

7. An example of a station is **Appleford Station (Rail)** . . . .1C **98**. Included are Rail **(Rail)** and Park & Ride **(Park & Ride)**

8. Service Areas are shown in **BOLD CAPITAL TYPE**; e.g. **CHERWELL VALLEY SERVICE AREA** 5E **28**

9. Map references for entries that appear on large scale pages **4** & **5** are shown first, with small scale map references shown in brackets; e.g. **Abbey Pl.** OX1: Oxf 6D **4** (5J **77**)

GENERAL ABBREVIATIONS

All. : Alley	**Ct.** : Court	**Intl.** : International	**Ri.** : Rise
App. : Approach	**Cres.** : Crescent	**La.** : Lane	**Rd.** : Road
Arc. : Arcade	**Cft.** : Croft	**Lit.** : Little	**Rdbt.** : Roundabout
Av. : Avenue	**Dr.** : Drive	**Lwr.** : Lower	**Shop.** : Shopping
Bk. : Back	**E.** : East	**Mnr.** : Manor	**Sth.** : South
Blvd. : Boulevard	**Est.** : Estate	**Mans.** : Mansions	**Sq.** : Square
Bri. : Bridge	**Fld.** : Field	**Mkt.** : Market	**St.** : Street
Bldgs. : Buildings	**Flds.** : Fields	**Mdw.** : Meadow	**Ter.** : Terrace
Bus. : Business	**Gdn.** : Garden	**Mdws.** : Meadows	**Twr.** : Tower
Cvn. : Caravan	**Gdns.** : Gardens	**M.** : Mews	**Trad.** : Trading
Cen. : Centre	**Gth.** : Garth	**Mt.** : Mount	**Up.** : Upper
Circ. : Circle	**Ga.** : Gate	**Mus.** : Museum	**Va.** : Vale
Cir. : Circus	**Gt.** : Great	**Nth.** : North	**Vw.** : View
Cl. : Close	**Grn.** : Green	**No.** : Number	**Vs.** : Villas
Coll. : College	**Gro.** : Grove	**Pde.** : Parade	**Vis.** : Visitors
Comn. : Common	**Hgts.** : Heights	**Pk.** : Park	**Wlk.** : Walk
Cnr. : Corner	**Ho.** : House	**Pas.** : Passage	**W.** : West
Cott. : Cottage	**Ind.** : Industrial	**Pl.** : Place	**Yd.** : Yard
Cotts. : Cottages	**Info.** : Information		

LOCALITY ABBREVIATIONS

Abin : **Abingdon**	Blox : **Bloxham**	C Ham : **Clifton Hampden**	Fawl : **Fawler**
Add : **Adderbury**	Boar H : **Boars Hill**	Combe : **Combe**	Fenc : **Fencott**
Alk : **Alkerton**	Bod : **Bodicote**	Cos : **Coscote**	Fern : **Fernham**
Alv : **Alvescot**	Bot : **Botley**	Cote : **Cote**	Few : **Fewcott**
Amb : **Ambrosden**	B'ton : **Bourton**	Cot : **Cothill**	Fil : **Filkins**
A'frd : **Appleford**	Bright : **Brighthampton**	Cow : **Cowley**	Fin : **Finmere**
A'ton : **Appleton**	B Bal : **Brightwell Baldwin**	Craw : **Crawley**	Fins : **Finstock**
Ard : **Ardington**	B Sot : **Brightwell-cum-Sotwell**	Cray P : **Cray's Pond**	For H : **Forest Hill**
Ardl : **Ardley**	Bri S : **Britwell Salome**	Crop : **Cropredy**	Free : **Freeland**
Asc W : **Ascott-under-Wychwood**	Briz N : **Brize Norton**	Crow : **Crowell**	Fril : **Frilford**
Ashb : **Ashbury**	Broad : **Broadwell**	Crow G : **Crowmarsh Gifford**	F Hea : **Frilford Heath**
Ast : **Aston**	Brou : **Broughton**	Cudd : **Cuddesdon**	Fring : **Fringford**
A Row : **Aston Rowant**	Buck : **Bucknell**	Cul : **Culham**	Frit : **Fritwell**
A Tir : **Aston Tirrold**	Burc : **Burcot**	C'nor : **Cumnor**	Ful : **Fulbrook**
A Upt : **Aston Upthorpe**	Burd : **Burdrop**	Curb : **Curbridge**	Gall C : **Gallowstree Common**
Badg : **Badgemore**	Burf : **Burford**	Dedd : **Deddington**	Gars : **Garsington**
Bals : **Balscote**	Cane E : **Cane End**	Den : **Denchworth**	Glym : **Glympton**
Bamp : **Bampton**	Cart : **Carterton**	Dent : **Denton**	Goo : **Goosey**
Ban : **Banbury**	Cass : **Cassington**	Did : **Didcot**	Gor : **Goring**
Bar J : **Barford St John**	Caul : **Caulcott**	Dorc T : **Dorchester-on-Thames**	Gor H : **Goring Heath**
Bar M : **Barford St Michael**	Cave : **Caversfield**	Drayc : **Draycot**	Gosf : **Gosford**
Barn G : **Barnard Gate**	Chac : **Chacombe**	Drayt : **Drayton**	G For : **Gozzard's Ford**
Bay : **Bayworth**	Chad : **Chadlington**	Dray L : **Drayton St Leonard**	G Bou : **Great Bourton**
Beck : **Beckley**	Chal : **Chalgrove**	Dry S : **Dry Sandford**	G Cox : **Great Coxwell**
Beg : **Begbroke**	Chalk G : **Chalkhouse Green**	Duck : **Ducklington**	G Has : **Great Haseley**
Ben : **Benson**	Charlb : **Charlbury**	Duns G : **Dunsden Green**	G Mil : **Great Milton**
Ber : **Berinsfield**	Char O : **Charlton-on-Otmoor**	E Cha : **East Challow**	G Roll : **Great Rollright**
Ber S : **Berrick Salome**	Char B : **Charney Bassett**	E End : **East End**	G Tew : **Great Tew**
Bes : **Besslesleigh**	Charv : **Charvil**	E Hag : **East Hagbourne**	Gro : **Grove**
Bic : **Bicester**	Check : **Checkendon**	E Han : **East Hanney**	Hadd : **Haddenham**
Bin H : **Binfield Heath**	Ches : **Chesterton**	E Hen : **East Hendred**	Hail : **Hailey**
Bin : **Binsey**	Child : **Childrey**	E Lock : **East Lockinge**	Hamp : **Hampton Poyle**
Bish : **Bishopstone**	Chilt : **Chilton**	Eaton : **Eaton**	Han : **Hanwell**
Blac L : **Blackbird Leys**	Chin : **Chinnor**	Emm G : **Emmer Green**	Harp : **Harpsden**
Blac B : **Black Bourton**	Chip N : **Chipping Norton**	Ensl : **Enslow**	Har : **Harwell**
B'thorn : **Blackthorn**	Chol : **Cholsey**	Enst : **Enstone**	Head : **Headington**
Blad : **Bladon**	Chu E : **Church Enstone**	Epwell : **Epwell**	Hemp : **Hempton**
B'ton : **Bledington**	Chu H : **Church Hanborough**	Ewel : **Ewelme**	Hen T : **Henley-on-Thames**
Bled : **Bledlow**	C'hill : **Churchill**	Eyn : **Eynsham**	Hethe : **Hethe**
Blet : **Bletchingdon**	Clan : **Clanfield**	F'don : **Faringdon**	H Cog : **High Cogges**
Blew : **Blewbury**	Clay : **Claydon**	Farm : **Farmoor**	Highm : **Highmoor**

Abberbury Av.—Ancastle Grn.

Highw : **Highworth**
Holt : **Holton**
Hook N : **Hook Norton**
Horl : **Horley**
Horn : **Hornton**
Hors : **Horspath**
Hort : **Horton-cum-Studley**
Ids : **Idstone**
Ips : **Ipsden**
Isl : **Islip**
Kenc : **Kencot**
Kenn : **Kennington**
Kidl : **Kidlington**
Ked E : **Kidmore End**
Kingh : **Kingham**
K Bag : **Kingston Bagpuize**
K Blou : **Kingston Blount**
Kingw : **Kingwood**
Kirt : **Kirtlington**
Lang : **Langford**
Laun : **Launton**
Lea : **Leafield**
Letc B : **Letcombe Bassett**
Letc R : **Letcombe Regis**
Lew : **Lew**
Lewk : **Lewknor**
Lit B : **Little Bourton**
Lit Clan : **Little Clanfield**
Lit Cox : **Little Coxwell**
Lit M : **Little Milton**
Litt : **Littlemore**
Lit T : **Little Tew**
Lit W : **Little Wittenham**
Longc : **Longcot**
L Cren : **Long Crendon**
L Han : **Long Hanborough**
L Wit : **Long Wittenham**
Longw : **Longworth**
Lwr A : **Lower Arncott**
Lwr B : **Lower Basildon**
Lwr H : **Lower Heyford**
Lwr S : **Lower Shiplake**
Lwr T : **Lower Tadmarton**
Lyd : **Lyford**
Map : **Mapledurham**
Marc : **Marcham**
Mar B : **Marsh Baldon**
Mars : **Marston**
Mer : **Merton**
Mid A : **Middle Aston**
Mid B : **Middle Barton**
M'ton S : **Middleton Stoney**
Milc : **Milcombe**
Milt : **Milton**
Milt C : **Milton Common**
Milt H : **Milton Hill**
Milt W : **Milton under Wychwood**
Min L : **Minster Lovell**
Moll : **Mollington**
Mon : **Mongewell**
Moul : **Moulsford**
Neth : **Nethercote**
Nett : **Nettlebed**
N'ton : **Newington**
New H : **Newnham Hill**
New Y : **New Yatt**
Nth A : **North Aston**
N Hink : **North Hinksey**
N Leigh : **North Leigh**
N Mor : **North Moreton**
N Sto : **North Stoke**
Nuff : **Nuffield**
Nune C : **Nuneham Courtenay**
Odd : **Oddington**
Over N : **Over Norton**
Overt : **Overthorpe**
Oxf : **Oxford**
Pang : **Pangbourne**
Pep C : **Peppard Common**
Post : **Postcombe**
Pur T : **Purley on Thames**
Rad : **Radley**
Rams : **Ramsden**
Rem : **Remenham**
Rok : **Roke**
Roth G : **Rotherfield Greys**
Roth P : **Rotherfield Peppard**
Row : **Rowstock**
Salf : **Salford**
Sand T : **Sandford-on-Thames**
Sand M : **Sandford St Martin**
Shel : **Shellingford**
Shen : **Shenington**
Shil : **Shillingford**
S Hil : **Shillingford Hill**
Shilt : **Shilton**
Shipl : **Shiplake**
Shipp : **Shippon**
Ship W : **Shipton under Wychwood**
Shott : **Shotteswell**
Shriv : **Shrivenham**
Shut : **Shutford**
Sib F : **Sibford Ferris**
Sib G : **Sibford Gower**
Some : **Somerton**
Sonn C : **Sonning Common**
Soul : **Souldern**
S Hink : **South Hinksey**
Sthm : **Southmoor**
S Mor : **South Moreton**
S New : **South Newington**
S Sto : **South Stoke**
Spar : **Sparsholt**
Spri : **Springwell**
Stad : **Stadhampton**
Stand : **Standlake**
Stan V : **Stanford in the Vale**
Stan H : **Stanton Harcourt**
Stan J : **Stanton St John**
Stee A : **Steeple Aston**
Stev : **Steventon**
Stoke R : **Stoke Row**
Stone : **Stonesfield**
Stra A : **Stratton Audley**
Stre : **Streatley**
Sut : **Sutton**
S Cou : **Sutton Courtenay**
Swal : **Swalcliffe**
Swer : **Swerford**
Syd : **Sydenham**
Tac : **Tackley**
Tad : **Tadmarton**
Tet : **Tetsworth**
Tha : **Thame**
Tid : **Tiddington**
Tin : **Tingewick**
Tok : **Tokers Green**
Toot B : **Toot Baldon**
Tow : **Towersey**
Twy : **Twyford**
Uff : **Uffington**
Up A : **Upper Arncott**
Up H : **Upper Heyford**
Upt : **Upton**
Wal : **Wallingford**
Wan : **Wantage**
Warb : **Warborough**
Warg : **Wargrave**
Watch : **Watchfield**
Water : **Waterstock**
Watl : **Watlington**
Wea : **Weald**
Wend : **Wendlebury**
W Chal : **West Challow**
W Hag : **West Hagbourne**
W Han : **West Hanney**
W Hen : **West Hendred**
W Loc : **West Lockinge**
Westc : **Westcot**
Westc B : **Westcott Barton**
West G : **Weston-on-the-Green**
Wheat : **Wheatley**
Whit H : **Whitchurch Hill**
Whit T : **Whitchurch-on-Thames**
Wilc : **Wilcote**
Wit : **Witney**
Wolv : **Wolvercote**
Wood : **Woodcote**
Woods : **Woodstock**
Wools : **Woolstone**
Woot : **Wootton**
Wort : **Worton**
Wrox : **Wroxton**
Wyf : **Wyfold**
Wyth : **Wytham**
Yarn : **Yarnton**

A

Abberbury Av. OX4: Oxf 2D **84**
Abberbury Rd. OX4: Oxf 2C **84**
Abbey Brook OX11: Did 6B **98**
Abbey Cl. OX14: Abin 1G **91**
Abbey Meadows 1H **91**
Abbey Pl. OX1: Oxf 6D **4** (5J **77**)
OX29: Eyn 5D **70**
Abbey Rd. OX2: Oxf 3B **4** (4H **77**)
OX16: Ban 7C **10**
OX28: Wit 5C **50**
SN6: Watch 2F **65**
Abbey Sailing Club 3G **91**
Abbey Sports Cen.
Berinsfield 3B **94**
Abbey St. OX29: Eyn 5D **70**
Abbey Woods Cl. OX10: Ber 3B **94**
Abbots Cl. RG8: Wood 2C **134**
Abbots Mead OX10: Chol 3F **117**
Abbotswood E. OX3: Head 5H **79**
Abbotswood W. OX3: Head 5H **79**
Abbott Rd. OX11: Did 3B **110**
OX14: Abin 7G **87**
Abelwood Rd. OX29: L Han 2G **53**
ABINGDON 1G **91** (1D **147**)
Abingdon Abbey (remains of)
. . . .*1G 91*
(off Bridge St.)
Abingdon Bus. Pk.
OX14: Abin 7D **86**
Abingdon By-Pass OX1: Kenn . . .3K **83**
OX14: Abin, Rad 2H **87**
Abingdon Cl. OX9: Tha 3H **123**
Abingdon La. OX18: Briz N 2K **47**
Abingdon Mus. *1G 91*
(off Market Pl.)
Abingdon Rd. OX1: Oxf . . .7F **5** (6K **77**)
OX2: C'nor 5J **59**
OX10: Dorc T 4A **94**
OX11: Did 1E **110**
OX13: Stev 4B **96**
OX14: Burc, Cul, C Ham 2H **91**
OX14: Drayt 7C **90**
OX14: S Cou 6J **91**
OX18: Cart 4E **46**
OX29: Bright, Stand 5B **58**
Abingdon Rowing Club 3G **91**
Abingdon Ter. OX11: Did 2K **109**
Abingford By-Pass
OX14: Drayt, Abin 7B **90**
OX14: Drayt, Milt 1B **96**
Ablett Cl. OX4: Oxf 5D **78**
ABLINGTON 3A **142**
Abott Cl. OX11: Did 3B **110**
Abrahams Rd. RG9: Hen T 2B **138**
ABTHORPE 2D **141**
Acacia Av. OX4: Blac L 5H **85**
Acacia Cl. *OX18: Cart* *6E 46*
(off Black Bourton Rd.)
Acacia Gdns. OX13: Sthm 4D **60**
Acacia Wlk. OX16: Ban 4D **10**
OX26: Bic 5E **30**
Acer Wlk. OX2: Oxf 1K **77**
Ackerman Rd. OX7: Chip N 5J **23**
Acland Cl. OX3: Head 4F **79**
Acorn Cl. OX26: Bic 5E **30**
Acorn Way OX16: Ban 4H **11**
Acre Cl. OX3: Head 6H **79**
Acre Ditch OX15: Burd, Sib G . . .5C **14**
Acre End St. OX29: Eyn 5C **70**
Acremead OX33: Wheat 5D **80**
Adam Ct. RG9: Hen T 3D **138**
Adams Ct. RG9: Hen T 4C **138**
ADDERBURY 3H **19** (3B **140**)
Adderbury Ct. OX17: Add 3H **19**
Adderbury Pk. OX17: Add 4G **19**
ADDINGTON 1C **145**
Addison Cres. OX4: Oxf 7C **78**
Addison Dr. OX4: Litt 3F **85**
Addison Rd. OX16: Ban 3E **12**
Addison's Wlk.
OX3: Oxf 4K **5** (4B **78**)
Adeane Rd. OX44: Chal 1B **128**
Adelaide St. OX2: Oxf 1C **4** (2J **77**)
Adkin Way OX12: Wan 5G **105**
ADLESTROP 1B **142**
ADSTOCK 3D **141**
ADSTONE 1C **141**
ADWELL 1B **148**
Adwell Sq. RG9: Hen T 3C **138**
Agnes Ct. OX4: Cow 7F **79**
AKELEY 3D **141**
Akeman Av. OX25: Amb 1G **45**
Akeman Cl. OX5: Kirt 1C **42**
Akeman St. OX5: Kirt 1C **42**
OX7: Rams 4F **39**
OX29: Combe 2D **40**
Alan Bullock Cl.
OX4: Oxf 5K **5** (4B **78**)
Albermarle Dr. OX12: Gro 2G **105**
Albert Rd. RG9: Hen T 4D **138**
Albert St. OX2: Oxf 2C **4** (3J **77**)
OX16: Ban 1F **13**
Albion Pl. OX1: Oxf 6E **4** (5K **77**)
OX7: Chip N *5J 23*
(off Albion St.)
Albion St. OX7: Chip N 6H **23**
ALBURY 1D **122**
Albury Vw. OX9: Tid 1B **122**
Alchester Rd. OX26: Ches 3A **32**
Alchester Ter. OX26: Bic 2F **33**
Aldbarton Dr. OX3: Head 1H **79**
ALDBOURNE 3B **146**
Aldbourne Cl. OX26: Bic 1D **32**
Alden Cres. OX3: Head 1J **79**
Alder Dr. OX25: Amb 1F **45**
Aldergate Rd. OX26: Bic 1C **32**
Alderley Cl. OX18: Cart 6D **46**
ALDERMASTON WHARF 3B **148**
ALDERTON 2D **141**
Aldrich Rd. OX2: Oxf 4J **73**
Aldridge Cl. OX10: Ben 5B **102**
OX14: Abin 5G **87**
ALDSWORTH 2A **142**
Aldsworth Ct. OX28: Wit 4C **50**
ALDWORTH 3A **148**
Aldworth Av. OX12: Wan 5J **105**
Alec Issigonis Way OX4: Cow . . .1G **85**
Alesworth Gro. OX3: Head 7E **74**
Alexander Cl. OX11: Upt 7K **109**
OX14: Abin 4H **87**
Alexandra Rd.
OX2: Oxf 5A **4** (4G **77**)
Alexandra Sq. OX7: Chip N 6G **23**
Alfreds Pl. OX12: E Han 2K **63**
Alfredston Pl. OX12: Wan 6H **105**
Alfred St. OX1: Oxf 5F **5** (4K **77**)
OX12: Wan 6G **105**
Alfred Ter. *OX7: Chip N* *6H 23*
(off Leys App.)
Alfriston Pl. OX16: Ban 4C **10**
Alhambra La. OX4: Oxf . . .6K **5** (5B **78**)
Alice Smith Sq. OX4: Litt 4F **85**
Alison Clay Ho. *OX3: Head* *3F 79*
(off New High St.)
Alister Taylor Av. OX10: Ben . . .7D **102**
ALKERTON 6E **8** (2A **140**)
Allam St. OX2: Oxf 1C **4** (2J **77**)
Allder Cl. OX14: Abin 5G **87**
Allectus Av. OX25: Amb 1G **45**
Allens La. OX25: Up H 3E **26**
Allin Cl. OX4: Blac L 3G **85**
Allin's La. OX12: E Hen 3J **107**
Allnatt Av. OX10: Wal 2H **113**
Allnut Cl. OX49: Watl 6D **128**
All Saints Cl. OX13: Marc 6H **61**
All Saints Ct. OX11: Did 7B **98**
All Saints La. OX14: S Cou 7H **91**
All Saints Rd. OX3: Head 3F **79**
Alma Grn. RG9: Stoke R 6J **131**
Alma Pl. OX4: Oxf 6K **5** (5C **78**)
Alma Rd. OX16: Ban 7G **11**
Almond Av. OX5: Kidl 4F **69**
Almond Rd. OX26: Bic 7E **30**
Alpha Av. OX44: Gars 6B **126**
Alphin Brook OX11: Did 6B **98**
Altus St. OX25: Up H 4G **27**
ALVESCOT 3G **55** (3B **142**)
Alvescot Rd.
OX18: Cart, Alv, Blac B 7B **46**
Alvis Ga. OX16: Ban 5B **10**
Ambassador Av. OX4: Cow 3H **85**
Ambassador Ct. *OX26: Bic* *2F 33*
(off Priory Rd.)
Amberley Ct. OX16: Ban 4C **10**
Ambleside Dr. OX3: Head 1E **78**
AMBROSDEN 2F **45** (2B **144**)
Ambrose Ri. OX33: Wheat 5H **81**
Amey Cres. OX13: Woot 1C **86**
Amory Cl. OX4: Cow 3G **85**
Amos Ct. OX16: Ban 1F **13**
AMPNEY CRUCIS 3A **142**
Ampney Orchard
OX18: Bamp 2H **57**
AMPNEY ST MARY 3A **142**
AMPNEY ST PETER 3A **142**
Amwell Pl. OX10: Chol 2E **116**
Amyce Cl. *OX14: Abin* *5J 87*
(off Yeld Hall Rd.)
Ancastle Grn. RG9: Hen T 4B **138**

Ancholme Cl.—Barford St John

Ancholme Cl. OX11: Did 7C 98
Anchor La. OX11: S Mor 6K 111
Ancil Av. OX26: Laun 1K 33
Andersey Way OX14: Abin 4F 91
Anderson's Cl. OX5: Kidl 3D 68
Andover Cl. OX26: Bic 6G 31
Andover Ct. OX5: Kidl 3G 69
Andover La. OX18: Briz N 5F 47
Andover Rd. OX10: Ben 6E 102
Andrew Rd. OX10: Wal 1G 113
Andromeda Cl. OX4: Blac L 5J 85
Anemone Cl. OX4: Blac L 6H 85
Angelica Cl. OX4: Blac L 5J 85
OX16: Ban 3C 10
Angus Cl. OX16: Ban 5C 10
Anna Pavlova Cl. OX14: Abin 1E 90
Anne Greenwood Cl.
OX4: Oxf 1D 84
Annesley Cl. OX5: Blet 6C 42
Annesley Rd. OX4: Oxf 2D 84
Ansell Way OX7: Milt W 5F 35
Anson Av. OX18: Cart 6E 46
Anson Cl. OX13: Marc 6J 61
OX33: Wheat 5H 81
Anson Rd. OX10: Ben 6E 102
Anson Way OX26: Bic 7G 31
Anthony Hill Rd. OX10: Ben 7C 102
Anvil Cl. SN7: Stan V 6C 62
Anvil La. OX12: Letc R 2G 119
Apley Way OX28: Wit 3C 50
Appleby Cl. OX16: Ban 6A 10
APPLEFORD 1C 98 (1A 148)
Appleford Dr. OX14: Abin 5H 87
Appleford Rd. OX14: S Cou 7J 91
Appleford Station (Rail) 1C 98
APPLETON 1H 61 (3D 143)
Appleton Rd. OX2: C'nor 6H 59
OX13: Longw, Sthm 3B 60
APPLETREE 2B 140
Appletree Cl. OX4: Blac L 6H 85
RG4: Sonn C 4H 135
Approach, The OX26: Bic 7D 30
Apsley Rd. OX2: Oxf 4H 73
ARBORFIELD 3C 149
ARBORFIELD CROSS 3C 149
Arbury Cl. OX16: Ban 4G 13
Arch Hill RG9: Bin H 6H 137
Arden Cl. OX15: Drayt 6K 9
ARDINGTON 5D 106 (2D 147)
Ardington La. OX12: Ard 2D 106
ARDINGTON WICK 2E 106
ARDLEY 6C 28 (1A 144)
Ardley Rd. OX25: M'ton S 5G 29
OX25: Some 1K 25
OX27: Ardl, Buck, Few
6C 28 & 2A 30
Argentan Cl. OX14: Abin 4E 90
Argosy Cl. OX44: Chal 2D 128
Argosy Rd. OX10: Ben 6E 102
OX18: Briz N 5F 47
Argyle St. OX4: Oxf 7C 78
Aristotle La. OX2: Oxf 1H 77
Arkel Cl. OX18: Ful 2E 38
Arkell Av. OX18: Cart 5D 46
Arkwright Rd. OX26: Bic 7G 31
ARLESCOTE 2A 140
ARLINGTON 3A 142
Arlington Cl. OX18: Cart 5E 46
Arlington Dr. OX3: Mars 1B 78
Armstrong Rd. OX4: Litt 5D 84
Arncott Wood Rd.
OX25: Up A 7G 45
Arndale Beck OX11: Did 7D 98
Arnold Rd. OX4: Oxf 7C 78
Arnolds Way OX2: Bot 6C 76
Arnold Way OX9: Tha 5G 123
Arran Gro. OX16: Ban 7E 10
Arthray Rd. OX2: Bot 5D 76
Arthur Evans Cl. OX13: Woot 1B 86
Arthur Garrard Cl.
OX2: Oxf 1D 4 (2J 77)
Arthur St. OX2: Oxf 5B 4 (4H 77)
Arundel Cl. OX18: Cart 5C 46
Arundel Pl. OX16: Ban 1B 12
Arun M. OX11: Did 1E 110
ASCOT 3D 149
ASCOTT 6K 127
ASCOTT D'OYLEY 2J 35
Ascott Rd. OX7: Ship W 6J 35
ASCOTT-UNDER-WYCHWOOD
2J 35 (2C 143)
Ascott-under-Wychwood (Rail)
2J 35
ASHAMPSTEAD 3A 148
Ash Av. OX18: Cart 2E 46
Ashburn Pl. OX11: Did 6C 98
Ashburton La. OX15: Hook N 3C 16
ASHBURY 5C 66 (2B 146)
Ashbury Hill SN6: Ashb 6D 66
Ashby Ct. OX16: Ban 1F 13
Ashby Rd. OX26: Bic 1C 32
Ash Cl. OX5: Kidl 4F 69
OX49: Watl 5C 128
SN7: F'don 3B 56
Ashcombe Cl. OX28: Wit 4E 50
Ashcroft Cl. OX2: Bot 4C 76
OX7: Chad 1C 36
(off Chipping Norton Rd.)
Ashcroft Rd. OX16: Ban 4F 13
Ashdale Av. OX28: Wit 1H 51
Ashdene Rd. OX26: Bic 1C 32
Ashdown House 2B 146
Ashdown Way OX12: Gro 2G 105
Ashenden Cl. OX14: Abin 6G 87
ASHENDON 2C 145
Ashfield Est. OX18: Cart 6D 46
Ashfield Rd. OX18: Cart 6D 46
Ashfields Cl. OX12: E Han 2K 63
Ashfields La. OX12: E Han 2K 63
Ashford Av. RG4: Sonn C 5G 135
Ashgate *OX14: Abin 4F 91*
(off Kensington Cl.)
Ash Gro. OX3: Head 1G 79
OX26: Ches 4A 32
Ash La. OX25: Amb 1G 45
Ashlee Wlk. RG8: Wood 2C 134
Ashlong Rd. OX3: Head 7D 74
Ashmead Rd. OX16: Ban 4B 10
Ashmolean Mus. 3E 4 (3K 77)
Ashmole Pl. OX4: Blac L 3J 85
Ashmole Rd. OX14: Abin 4F 91
ASHMORE GREEN 3A 148
ASHORNE 1A 140
Ashridge OX39: Chin 2F 125
Ashridge Cl. OX16: Ban 4G 13
ASHTON KEYNES 1A 146
Ashurst Ct. OX33: Wheat 6K 81
Ashurst Way OX4: Oxf 3D 84
Ashville Way OX4: Cow 3J 85
ASKETT 3D 145
Aspen Cl. OX26: Bic 5E 30
Aspen Ct. SN7: F'don 2B 56
Aspen Sq. OX4: Blac L 5H 85
Asquith Rd. OX4: Oxf 3D 84
ASTCOTE 1D 141
ASTHALL 2B 142
ASTHALL LEIGH 1B 48 (2C 143)
Astley Av. OX5: Kidl 5G 69
Astley Rd. OX9: Tha 3K 123
ASTON
Bampton 6H 57 (3C 143)
Henley-on-Thames 2C 149
ASTON ABBOTTS 1D 145
ASTON CLINTON 2D 145
Aston Cl. OX10: Wal 3H 113
OX14: Abin 1G 91
OX16: Ban 4G 13
Aston Gdns. OX49: A Row 6F 125
Aston Hill OX49: Lewk 5K 129
ASTON LE WALLS 1B 140
Aston Pk. OX49: A Row 7F 125
Aston Rd. OX18: Bamp 2H 57
OX29: Bright 6A 58
OX29: Duck 7F 49
ASTON ROWANT 6F 125 (1C 149)
Aston Rowant Nature Reserve
Vis. Cen. 1C 149
ASTON SANDFORD 3C 145
Aston St. OX4: Oxf 6C 78
OX11: A Tir 3J 115
ASTON TIRROLD 3J 115 (2A 148)
ASTON UPTHORPE
2H 115 (2A 148)
ASTROP 3C 141
Atkinson Cl. OX3: Head 7H 75
Atkyns Rd. OX3: Head 5H 79
Attwell Row OX18: Cart 4E 46
Atwell Cl. OX10: Wal 2H 113
Atwell Pl. OX3: Head 4G 79
Aubrey Ct. OX4: Oxf 2D 84
Audlett Dr. OX14: Abin 1H 91
Austen Wlk. OX26: Bic 1C 32
Austin Dr. OX16: Ban 5B 10
Austin Pl. OX14: Abin 5F 87
Austin Rd. OX15: Bod 1F 19
Austin's Way OX15: Hook N 1D 16
Auton Pl. RG9: Hen T 5C 138
AVEBURY 3A 146
AVEBURY TRUSLOE 3A 146
Avens Way OX4: Blac L 5H 85
Avenue, The OX1: Kenn 5B 84
OX7: G Tew 1E 24
OX10: S Hil 5G 101
OX15: Blox 3B 18
OX33: Wheat 6H 81
OX39: Chin 2H 125
Avenue One OX28: Wit 6E 50
Avenue Two OX28: Wit 6F 51
Avenue Three OX28: Wit 6F 51
Avenue Four OX28: Wit 5F 51
Avenue La. OX4: Oxf 5C 78
Avenue Rd. OX16: Ban 7H 11
SN6: B'ton 2C 66
Avery Ct. OX2: Oxf 4J 73
Aves Ditch OX25: Caul 7J 27
Avocet Way OX16: Ban 3G 13
OX26: Bic 3H 33
Avonbury Bus. Pk. OX26: Bic 6B 30
Avon Cres. OX26: Bic 7B 30
AVON DASSETT 1B 140
Avon Rd. OX11: Chilt 6H 119
OX13: Shipp 4D 86
Avon Way OX11: Did 6C 98
Awgar Stone Rd. OX3: Head 6H 79
AXFORD 3B 146
Axis Rd. SN6: Watch 3E 64
Axtell Cl. OX5: Kidl 2E 68
AYLESBURY 2D 145
Aylesbury Rd. OX9: Hadd, Tha
3H 123
AYLWORTH 1A 142
AYNHO 3C 141
Aynho Rd. OX17: Add 3J 19
Ayrshire Cl. OX16: Ban 4C 10
Aysgarth Rd. OX5: Yarn 5C 68
Azalea Av. OX5: Kidl 5G 69
Azalea Wlk. OX16: Ban 4D 10
Azor's Ct. OX4: Oxf 2D 84

B

Bablock Hythe Rd.
OX13: Eaton 7F 59
Bk. Bourton Rd. OX18: Clan 4H 55
Back Dr. OX29: Barn G 7D 52
Back La. OX3: Mars 6C 74
OX15: Sib F 6D 14
OX18: Ast 5G 57
OX29: Duck 5G 49
OX29: Eyn 5D 70
Backside La. OX15: Sib G 4C 14
Back St. OX9: Tet 6C 122
Back Way OX44: G Has 7H 121
BADBURY 2A 146
Badbury Cl. SN7: F'don 4B 56
BADBY 1C 141
Baden Powell Way
OX11: Did 2B 110
Bader Dr. OX25: Up H 5H 27
BADGEMORE 3A 138
Badgemore La. RG9: Hen T 2C 138
Badger Cl. OX33: For H 1D 80
Badger La. OX1: S Hink 3J 83
Badgers Copse OX14: Rad 5B 88
Badgers Wlk. RG9: Shipl 4J 139
Badger Way OX16: Ban 4G 13
Badswell La. OX13: A'ton 1H 61
Bagley Cl. OX1: Kenn 4A 84
BAGLEY WOOD 7K 83
Bagley Wood Rd. OX1: Kenn 7K 83
Bailey Cl. OX12: Wan 4G 105
Bailey Rd. OX4: Cow 2F 85
Bailie Cl. OX14: Abin 2F 91
BAINTON 1A 144
Bainton Cl. OX26: Bic 1H 33
Bainton Rd. OX2: Oxf 7H 73
OX27: Buck 2A 30
OX27: Hethe 4F 29
Baker Cl. OX3: Head 3J 79
OX10: Ben 7E 102
OX27: Cave 4F 31
Baker La. OX10: Ben 7E 102
Baker Rd. OX14: Abin 4F 91
Baker's Ct. OX29: L Han 2H 53
Bakers La. OX4: Oxf 2C 84
OX10: B Sot 7E 100
OX11: E Hag 5C 110
OX15: S New 5H 17
Bakers La. OX15: Swal 6F 15
OX15: Tad 6J 15
Bakers Piece OX28: Wit 2F 51
OX39: K Blou 5H 125
Baker's Piece Ho.
OX39: Crow 5J 125
Bakers Sq. SN7: Fern 2H 67
Baker St. OX11: A Tir 2H 115
Bakery La. OX12: Letc R 2G 119
OX18: Clan 6J 55
Baldon La. OX44: Mar B 5J 89
BALDON ROW 2K 89
Baldon's Cl. RG8: Wood 2C 134
Balfour Cotts. OX14: Burc 3K 93
Balfour Rd. OX4: Blac L 4H 85
Balfour's Fld. RG8: Check 7F 131
Ballard Chase OX14: Abin 4G 87
Ballard Cl. OX7: Mid B 6J 25
Ballards Cl. OX7: Ship W 6H 35
BALLINGER COMMON 3D 145
Balliol Cl. OX5: Tac 2K 37
Balliol Ct. OX2: Oxf 1H 77
Balliol Dr. OX11: Did 2E 110
Balliol Ho. OX17: Add 4K 19
Balliol Rd. OX26: Bic 7F 31
Ball La. OX5: Tac 2J 37
Balmoral Av. OX16: Ban 1B 12
(not continuous)
Balmoral Rd. OX11: Did 2D 110
BALSCOTE 2A 140
Baltic Wharf OX1: Oxf 7E 4 (5K 77)
BAMPTON 2H 57 (3C 143)
Bampton Cl. OX4: Litt 3G 85
Bampton Rd. OX18: Ast 6G 57
OX18: Blac B 4J 55
OX18: Clan, Wea 5J 55
OX29: Curb 7A 50
BANBURY 1E 12 (2B 140)
Banbury Bus. Pk. OX17: Add 4K 19
Banbury Ct. *OX14: Abin 1G 91*
(off Vineyard)
Banbury Crematorium
OX16: Ban 2E 10
Banbury Cross 1E 12
Banbury Cross Retail Pk.
OX16: Ban 4E 10
Banbury Hill OX7: Charlb 5C 36
Banbury La. OX17: Ban 5K 11
OX17: Neth 5K 11
Banbury Mus. 7F 11
Banbury Rd. OX2: Oxf 1E 4 (2H 73)
OX5: Kidl 1D 68
OX5: Tac 4F 37
OX7: Chip N 5J 23
OX7: Swer 7A 16
OX15: Blox 2C 18
OX15: Dedd 6C 20
OX15: Shut 2H 15
OX17: Chac 2J 11
OX17: Twy 7J 13
OX20: Woods 2J 41
OX26: Bic 5E 30
Banbury Rd. Crossing
OX7: Chip N 5J 23
(off Banbury Rd.)
Banbury Rd. Rdbt. OX2: Oxf 3H 73
Banbury Station (Rail) 1G 13
Banbury United FC 2G 13
Bandet Way OX9: Tha 6K 123
Banesberie Cl. OX16: Ban 4C 10
Banjo Rd. OX4: Cow 1F 85
Banks Furlong OX26: Ches 3A 32
Bank Side OX29: L Han 7F 41
Bankside OX3: Head 2H 79
OX5: Kidl 1D 68
OX12: W Hen 4G 107
OX16: Ban 2G 13
Bank Vw. RG9: Hen T 3E 138
Bannister Cl. OX4: Oxf 7K 5 (6B 78)
Bannister Rd. OX9: Tha 1A 124
Barberry Pl. OX26: Bic 6E 30
Barbury Dr. OX12: Gro 2G 105
BARCHESTON 2A 140
Barcombe Cl. OX16: Ban 4B 10
Bardolph's Cl. RG4: Tok 2B 136
Bardwell Ct. OX2: Oxf 7K 73
Bardwell Rd. OX2: Oxf 1K 77
Bardwell Ter. OX26: Bic 1E 32
Barfleur Cl. OX14: Abin 4J 87
BARFORD 1A 140
Barford Rd. OX15: Bar J, Blox 4B 18
OX15: Bar M, S New 5H 17
BARFORD ST JOHN 1C 20 (3B 140)

152 A-Z Oxfordshire Atlas

Bishop's Wood—Broad Hinton

Bishop's Wood OX44: Cudd 2C 126
Bisley Cl. OX26: Bic 7G 31
Bitham Rd. OX12: E Lock 7C 106
Bitterell OX29: Eyn 5E 70
BIX 2C 149
Blackberry La. OX4: Blac L 3K 85
OX7: Fins 1G 39
OX44: Toot B 5K 85
BLACKBIRD LEYS 4H 85
Blackbird Leys Leisure Cen. 4H 85
Blackbird Leys Rd.
OX4: Blac L 3G 85
(not continuous)
Blackbird Leys Swimming Pool 4H 85
BLACK BOURTON 3K 55 (3B 142)
Black Bourton Rd. OX18: Cart 5E 46
Blackbull La. OX5: Fenc 5E 44
Blackburn Wlk. OX26: Bic 6G 31
Black Cft. OX12: Wan 4G 105
BLACKDITCH 3A 58 (3D 143)
Blackditch OX29: Stan H 3A 58
Blackfriars Rd.
OX1: Oxf 7E 4 (5K 77)
Blackhall Rd.
OX1: Oxf 2E 4 (3K 77)
Blackhorse La.
OX13: Cot, G For 4A 86
Blacklands OX12: Spar 6A 118
Blacklands Rd. OX10: Ben 4B 102
Blacklands Way OX14: Abin 1D 90
Blackman Cl. OX1: Kenn 4B 84
Blackmore Cl. OX9: Tha 5J 123
Blackmore La. RG4: Sonn C 5J 135
Blacknall Rd. OX14: Abin 3F 91
Blacksmiths Cl.
OX25: West G 2G 43
Blacksmiths La. OX5: Char O 6C 44
OX17: Moll 6C 6
Blacksmiths Mdw.
OX4: Blac L 5J 85
Blackstock Cl. OX3: Head 6H 79
Blackstone Rd. OX10: Wal 1H 113
BLACKTHORN 1K 45 (2B 144)
Blackthorn Cl. OX3: Head 1G 79
OX25: B'thorn 2J 45
Blackthorne Av. OX18: Cart 2E 46
Blackthorn Rd. OX26: Laun 2K 33
Blackwater Way OX11: Did 6D 98
Blackwood Pl. OX15: Bod 6H 13
BLADON 7H 41 (2D 143)
Bladon Cl. OX2: Oxf 4G 73
Bladon Rd. OX20: Woods 5K 41
Blagrave Cl. OX11: Did 1B 110
Blakehope Burn OX11: Did 6C 98
Blake Rd. OX26: Bic 6E 30
Blakes Av. OX28: Wit 4H 51
Blakes Fld. OX11: Did 1A 110
BLAKESLEY 1D 141
Blake Way OX9: Tha 3J 123
Blandford Av. OX2: Oxf 4G 73
Blandford Rd. OX5: Kidl 1E 68
Blandy Av. OX13: Sthm 4D 60
Blandy Rd. RG9: Hen T 6C 138
Blankstone Cl. OX29: Eyn 5C 70
Blay Cl. OX4: Blac L 3H 85
Bleache Pl. OX4: Cow 1G 85
Blecher Ct. OX10: Dorc T 6C 94
BLEDINGTON 7A 34 (1B 142)
BLEDLOW 3C 145
BLEDLOW RIDGE 1C 149
Blencowe Cl. OX27: Cave 4F 31
BLENHEIM 4D 126 (3A 144)
Blenheim Cl. OX11: Did 1B 110
Blenheim Ct. OX5: Kidl 3G 69
Blenheim Dr. OX2: Oxf 4G 73
OX26: Bic 7C 30
OX26: Laun 1K 33
Blenheim Gdns. OX12: Gro 1F 105
Blenheim Hill OX11: Har 3G 109
Blenheim La. OX29: Free 5G 53
Blenheim Orchard
OX12: E Han 3K 63
Blenheim Palace 5G 41
Blenheim Pl. OX10: Ben 6E 102
OX13: Sthm 4C 60
Blenheim Rd. OX5: Kidl 4G 69
OX16: Ban 4G 13
OX33: Hors 6B 80
OX44: Lit M 2H 127
Blenheim Ter. OX7: Chip N 6H 23
Blenheim Way OX33: Hors 6B 80
Blenhiem Ct. OX18: Cart 4D 46
Blenhiem Dr. OX28: Wit 5C 50
Blenhiem La. OX33: Wheat 5F 81
BLETCHINGDON 6C 42 (2A 144)
Bletchingdon Rd. OX5: Isl 4G 43
OX5: Kirt 3B 42
BLETCHLEY 1D 145
BLEWBURY 3D 114 (2A 148)
Blewbury Rd. OX11: E Hag 5D 110
Blewitt Ct. OX4: Litt 4E 84
BLISWORTH 1D 141
Blomfield Pl. OX2: Oxf 1C 4
Blossoms Glade OX14: Rad 1B 88
Blounts Ct. Rd.
RG4: Sonn C 4H 135
RG9: Pep C 4H 135
Blowings, The OX29: Free 4G 53
BLOXHAM 2C 18 (3B 140)
Bloxham Gro. Rd.
OX15: Blox 1D 18
Bloxham Rd.
OX15: Bar J, Bar M 2C 20
OX15: Milc 2J 17
OX16: Ban 7B 12
Bloxham Village Mus. 3C 18
Bluebell Cl. OX26: Bic 7E 30
Bluebell Ct. OX4: Blac L 5J 85
Bluebell Ride OX14: Rad 7B 84
Bluebell Way OX18: Cart 2E 46
Blue Boar St. OX1: Oxf 5F 5 (4K 77)
Blue Row OX7: Over N 3H 23
BLUNSDON ST ANDREW 2A 146
Blythe Pl. OX26: Bic 7B 30
BOARS HILL 6F 83 (3D 143)
BOARSTALL 2B 144
Boathouse Reach
RG9: Hen T 4D 138
Bobby Fryer Cl. OX4: Cow 2H 85
Boddington Rd. OX17: Clay 2C 6
OX29: N Leigh 3C 52
BODICOTE 6G 13 (3B 140)
Bodley Pl. OX2: Oxf 4J 73
Bodley Rd. OX4: Litt 3F 85
Boham's Rd. OX11: Blew 6A 114
Bolney Rd. RG9: Lwr S 2K 139
Bolney Trevor Dr.
RG9: Lwr S 3J 139
Bolsover Cl. OX29: L Han 2G 53
Bolton Rd. OX16: Ban 7E 10
Bonar Rd. OX3: Head 4H 79
Bonds End La. OX15: Sib G 5C 14
Bones La. RG9: Bin H 5H 137
Bonham Pl. OX18: Cart 3D 46
Bonn Sq. OX1: Oxf 5E 4
Bookbinders Ct. OX1: Oxf 5D 4
Book End OX29: Wit 3A 50
BOOKER 1D 149
Booth Rd. OX16: Ban 3E 10
Boot St. OX29: Stone 3A 40
Boreford Rd. OX14: Abin 5J 87
Boroma Way RG9: Hen T 3D 138
Borough Av. OX10: Wal 3H 113
Borough Wlk. OX14: Abin 6F 87
Borrowmead Rd. OX3: Head 7E 74
Bosley Cres. OX10: Wal 3J 113
Bosley's Orchard OX11: Did 1B 110
OX12: Gro 1H 105
Bosley Way OX10: Wal 1F 113
Bostock Rd. OX14: Abin 1F 91
Boston Rd. OX26: Bic 7G 31
RG9: Hen T 5D 138
Boswell Rd. OX4: Cow 2F 85
Botany Gdns. OX10: Crow G 3C 130
BOTHAMPSTEAD 3A 148
BOTLEY 4E 76 (3D 143)
Botley Interchange OX2: Bot 3D 76
Botley Rd. OX2: Oxf 5A 4 (4F 77)
BOTOLPH CLAYDON 1C 145
Bottom Ho. RG4: Sonn C 6H 135
Bottom Yd. OX29: Eyn 6D 70
Boucher Cl. OX12: Gro 2G 105
Boulevard, The OX5: Kidl 1C 68
Boulter Dr. OX14: Abin 4H 87
Boulter St. OX4: Oxf 5K 5 (4B 78)
Boults Cl. OX3: Mars 6C 74
Boults La. OX3: Mars 7C 74
Boundary Brook Rd.
OX4: Oxf 7D 78
Boundary Cl. OX20: Woods 3J 41
Bourlon Wood OX14: Abin 6E 86
Bourne, The OX15: Hook N 2B 16
Bourne Cl. OX2: Oxf 3J 73
OX26: Bic 2D 32
BOURNE END 2D 149
Bourne La. OX15: Hook N 1B 16
Bourne Rd. RG8: Pang 7H 133
Bourne St. OX11: Did 2C 110
BOURTON 2C 66 (2B 146)
Bourton Cl. OX18: Clan 5J 55
OX28: Wit 4C 50
BOURTON-ON-THE-HILL 1A 142
BOURTON-ON-THE-WATER 1A 142
BOVENEY 3D 149
Bovewell OX27: Soul 3H 21
BOVINGDON GREEN 2D 149
Bovingdon Rd. OX18: Cart 4E 46
Bovington's Yd. OX18: Ast 5G 57
BOW 4C 62
Bowbank OX13: Longw 2B 60
Bowbank Cl. OX13: Longw 2B 60
Bower End OX44: Chal 1B 128
Bower Grn. SN6: Watch 2F 65
(not continuous)
Bowerman Cl. OX5: Kidl 3E 68
Bowermans OX7: Ship W 6J 35
Bowgrave Copse OX14: Abin 6K 87
Bowley Ho. OX20: Woods 3H 41
Bowling Ct. RG9: Hen T 2C 138
Bowling Grn. Cl.
OX18: Bamp 1H 57
Bowmont Sq. OX26: Bic 1B 32
Bowmont Water OX11: Did 7B 98
Bowness Av. OX3: Head 1D 78
OX11: Did 3A 110
Bow Rd. SN7: Stan V 5C 62
Bowyer Rd. OX14: Abin 7G 87
BOXFORD 3D 147
Boxhedge Rd. OX16: Ban 7D 10
Boxhedge Rd. W. OX16: Ban 7D 10
Boxhedge Sq. OX16: Ban 7D 10
Boxhill Rd. OX14: Abin 7G 87
Boxhill Wlk. OX14: Abin 7F 87
Box Tree La. OX9: Post 1F 129
Boxwell Cl. OX14: Abin 5J 87
Bozedown Dr. RG8: Whit H 3H 133
Bracegirdle Rd. OX3: Head 4H 79
Bracken Cl. OX18: Cart 3D 46
BRACKLEY 3C 141
BRACKLEY HATCH 2D 141
BRACKNELL 3D 149
Bradburys, The
OX27: Stra A 2K 31
BRADDEN 2D 141
BRADENHAM 1D 149
BRADFIELD 3B 148
Bradford Ct. OX15: Blox 3B 18
Brading Way RG8: Pur T 7A 136
Bradley Arc. OX16: Ban 7B 10
Bradmore Rd. OX2: Oxf 2K 77
Bradshaw Cl. OX25: Stee A 4A 26
Bradstock's Way
OX14: S Cou 3G 97
Braemar Cl. OX18: Cart 2D 46
Braithwaite Cl. OX16: Ban 1C 12
Brake Hill OX4: Blac L 5K 85
Bramber Cl. OX16: Ban 6A 10
Bramble Bank OX28: Wit 2H 51
Bramble La. OX18: Cart 2F 47
Brambles, The OX3: Head 3F 79
Bramblings, The OX26: Bic 2G 33
Brambling Way OX4: Blac L 4G 85
Bramley Cl. OX12: E Han 3K 63
Bramley Cres. RG4: Sonn C 5G 135
Bramley Hgts. OX28: Wit 4D 50
Brampton Chase RG9: Lwr S 3J 139
Brampton Cl. OX14: Abin 6F 87
Brampton Dr. OX18: Cart 5F 47
Brampton Rd. OX3: Head 1J 79
Bramwell Pl. OX4: Oxf 5C 78
Brandon Cl. OX5: Kidl 3E 68
Brantwood Ri. OX16: Ban 2C 12
Brasenose Driftway
OX4: Cow 7H 79
Brasenose Dr. OX5: Kidl 2G 69
Brasenose La.
OX1: Oxf 4F 5 (4K 77)
Brasenose Rd. OX11: Did 1K 109
Brasenose Vs. *OX7: Chip N 6H 23*
(off The Green)
Brashfield Rd. OX26: Bic 6E 30
Brassey Cl. OX7: Chip N 5J 23
BRAY 3D 149
Braybrooke Cl. OX7: Enst 7C 24
BRAY WICK 3D 149
Braze La. OX10: Ben 4C 102
Breach Farm Cotts.
OX10: Chol 6C 116
Breach La. OX29: Hail 1J 49
Brenda Cl. OX16: Ban 2D 12
Brendon Cl. OX11: Did 7K 97
Brent Av. OX11: Did 5C 98
Brentford Cl. OX10: Chol 2D 116
Brereton Dr. OX12: Gro 2G 105
Bretch Hill OX16: Ban 6A 10
Brett Cl. OX9: Tha 4K 123
Brewer Cl. OX13: Stev 5B 96
Brewers Ct. OX14: Abin 2G 91
Brewer St. OX1: Oxf 6F 5 (5K 77)
Brewery La. OX15: Hook N 2A 16
Briar Cl. OX5: Kidl 1D 68
OX16: Ban 4F 13
Briar End OX5: Kidl 1E 68
Briars Cl. RG8: Pang 7J 133
Briar Thicket OX20: Woods 3J 41
Briar Way OX4: Blac L 3J 85
Brice Rd. OX25: Up H 4J 27
Brick Hill OX15: Hook N 3C 16
Brick Kiln La. OX4: Sand T 6E 84
Brickle La. OX15: Blox 2C 18
Brick Row OX15: Swal 6F 15
Bridewell Cl. OX29: N Leigh 4B 52
Bridge Cl. OX11: Did 2D 110
BRIDGE END 1C 100
Bridge End OX10: Dorc T 7C 94
Bridge Farm Cl. OX12: Gro 3H 105
Bridge Hill OX15: Hook N 2C 16
Bridge Ho. Cvn. Pk.
OX14: C Ham 5G 93
Bridge of Sighs 4G 5
Bridges Cl. OX14: Abin 3D 90
Bridge St. OX2: Oxf 5A 4 (4H 77)
OX5: Isl 7H 43
OX14: Abin 1G 91
OX16: Ban 7F 11
OX18: Bamp 2G 57
OX28: Wit 3F 51
Bridge St. Mill Bus. Pk.
OX28: Wit 3F 51
Bridge Ter. OX9: Tha 5K 123
Bridle Cl. OX16: Ban 3G 13
Bridle Path OX12: Char B 2A 62
RG8: Wood 2B 134
Bridle Rd. RG8: Whit H 3J 133
Bridle Way RG8: Gor 4C 132
Bridus Mead OX11: Blew 2E 114
Bridus Way OX11: Blew 2D 114
Briggs Cl. OX16: Ban 2B 12
BRIGHTHAMPTON 5A 58 (3C 143)
BRIGHTWALTON 3D 147
BRIGHTWALTON GREEN 3D 147
BRIGHTWELL BALDWIN 1B 148
BRIGHTWELL-CUM-SOTWELL 6D 100 (1A 148)
Brightwell St. OX10: B Sot 7C 100
BRIGHTWELL UPPERTON 1H 103
BRILL 2B 144
Brill Rd. OX33: Hort 2D 120
Brindley Cl. OX2: Oxf 1H 77
Brinds Cl. RG4: Sonn C 5J 135
Brinkburn Gro. OX16: Ban 5H 11
Brinkinfield Rd. OX44: Chal 1B 128
Bristol Rd. OX26: Bic 7G 31
Britannia Cl. OX18: Cart 3E 46
Britannia Hgts. *OX16: Ban 1F 13*
(off Britannia Rd.)
Britannia Rd. OX16: Ban 1F 13
Britannia Wharf OX16: Ban 1F 13
British Telecom Mus. 7F 5 (5K 77)
Britwell Rd. OX10: Ewel 5G 103
OX11: Did 1B 110
OX49: Watl 6C 128
BRITWELL SALOME 7A 128 (1B 148)
BRIZE NORTON 4J 47 (3C 143)
BRIZE NORTON AIRFIELD 6G 47 (3B 142)
Brize Norton Rd. OX18: Briz N 2J 47
OX18: Cart 5E 46
OX29: Min L 7B 48
Brizewood OX18: Cart 3D 46
BROAD BLUNSDON 1A 146
Broad Cl. OX2: Bot 4C 76
OX5: Kidl 3E 68
OX15: Bar M 3B 20
Broad End OX15: Bod 5G 13
Broad Fld. Rd. OX5: Yarn 5C 68
Broadfields OX4: Litt 4G 85
Broad Gap OX15: Bod 5G 13
Broadhead Pl. OX3: Head 7E 74
BROAD HINTON 3A 146

Broadhurst Gdns.—Carter Cl.

Broadhurst Gdns. OX4: Litt 5D **84**
Broadlands OX3: Mars 5B **74**
Broadmarsh Cl. OX12: Gro 1G **105**
Broad Marsh La. OX29: Free 5G **53**
Broad Oak OX3: Head 5H **79**
Broadoak La. OX12: Spar 5B **118**
Broad Oak Nature Pk. 5J 79
Broadshires Way OX18: Cart 3F **47**
Broad St. OX1: Oxf 4F **5** (4K **77**)
OX14: Abin 1G **91**
OX16: Ban 1F **13**
(not continuous)
OX18: Bamp 2G **57**
SN7: Uff 6G **67**
BROAD TOWN 3A 146
Broad Wlk. OX1: Oxf 6G **5** (5A **78**)
Broadwaters Av. OX9: Tha 5H **123**
Broad Way SN7: Uff 7G **67**
Broadway OX11: Did 2B **110**
OX11: Har 4F **109**
Broadway, The OX5: Char O 6C **44**
OX5: Kidl 5G **69**
Broadway Cl. OX11: Har 4F **109**
OX28: Wit 3B **50**
BROADWELL
Lechlade 3D 54 (3B 142)
Moreton-in-Marsh 1B 142
Broadwell Ct. OX26: Bic 1D **32**
Broadwell La.
GL7: Broad, Kenc, Lang 6C **54**
BROCKHALL 1D 141
Brockholes La. OX49: Bri S 4K **103**
Brocklesby Rd. OX4: Litt 4D **84**
Brocks Way RG9: Shipl 4J **139**
Brode Cl. OX14: Abin 5J **87**
Brogden Cl. OX2: Bot 5F **77**
Brome Pl. OX3: Head 1H **79**
Bromeswell Cl. OX25: Lwr H 6E **26**
Bromsgrove SN7: F'don 3C **56**
BROOKEND 2B 36
Brooke Rd. OX16: Ban 3C **12**
Brookfield Cl. OX7: Milt W 5F **35**
OX10: Wal 5H **113**
Brookfield Cres. OX3: Head 7D **74**
Brookfield Ri. OX15: Tad 7K **15**
BROOKHAMPTON 6H 127
Brookhampton Cl.
OX44: Stad 6H **127**
Brook Hill OX20: Woods 3G **41**
Brook La. OX9: Tha 4G **123**
OX11: Cos, W Hag 5K **109**
OX12: Den 2C **118**
OX28: Wit 1J **51**
OX29: Stone 4A **40**
Brooklime Wlk. OX4: Blac L 5H **85**
Brookmead Dr. OX10: Wal 3H **113**
Brook Rd. OX7: G Tew 2E **24**
OX26: Bic 7C **30**
Brooks Cotts. OX12: Lyd 2D **62**
Brookside OX3: Head 3F **79**
OX7: G Tew 1E **24**
OX9: Tha 3H **123**
OX10: Chol 2E **116**
OX11: Har 3F **109**
OX12: E Han 3J **63**
OX14: Abin 6G **87**
OX15: Hook N 2B **16**
OX44: Dent 3B **126**
OX49: Watl 5D **128**
Brookside Cl. OX9: Tid 1B **122**
Brookside Ct. *OX20: Woods 3G 41*
(off Brook Hill)
OX26: Bic 1E **32**
Brookside Est. OX44: Chal 1B **128**
Brookside Way OX15: Blox 4A **18**
Brooks Row OX29: Lea 5J **39**
Brook St. OX1: Oxf 7F **5** (6K **77**)
OX10: Ben 5B **102**
OX14: S Cou 1G **97**
OX39: K Blou 5H **125**
OX49: Watl 6D **128**
Brook Taylor Ct. OX1: Oxf 6E **4**
Brook Vw. OX4: Blac L 4K **85**
Brook Way OX29: L Han 2G **53**
Broome Way OX16: Ban 6G **11**
BROUGHTON 3B 140
Broughton Castle 3B 140
Broughton Cl. OX3: Mars 7C **74**
BROUGHTON POGGS
............3A 54 (3B 142)
Broughton Rd. OX15: Brou 3A **12**
OX16: Ban 3A **12**
Browning Dr. OX26: Bic 6C **30**
Browning Rd. OX16: Ban 2C **12**
Browns Cl. OX2: Bot 6B **76**
Brown's Hill RG4: Map 7B **134**
Brown's La. OX7: Charlb 5B **36**
OX20: Woods 3G **41**
BRUERN ABBEY 1B 142
Brumcombe La. OX13: Bay 7H **83**
Brunel Cres. OX12: Gro 1G **105**
Brunel Rd. OX11: Did 2K **109**
Brunstock Beck OX11: Did 6C **98**
Brunswick Pl. OX16: Ban 7G **11**
Bryan Ho. OX26: Bic 2E **32**
BRYANT'S BOTTOM 1D 149
Bryan Way OX12: Wan 4J **105**
Bryony Cl. OX4: Blac L 4K **85**
Bryony Gdns. OX18: Cart 2F **47**
Bryony Rd. OX26: Bic 5E **30**
Buchanan Rd. OX25: Up A 7H **45**
Buchan Rd. OX26: Bic 6C **30**
BUCKINGHAM 3D 141
Buckingham Cl. OX11: Did 2D **110**
Buckingham Cres. OX26: Bic 7F **31**
Buckingham Rd. OX26: Bic 7E **30**
OX27: Bic 5G **31**
Buckingham St.
OX1: Oxf 7F **5** (6K **77**)
BUCKLAND
Aylesbury 2D 145
Faringdon 1C 147
BUCKLAND COMMON 3D 145
Buckland Ct. OX5: Kidl 4G **69**
Buckland M. *OX14: Abin 1E 90*
(off Winterborne Rd.)
Buckland Rd. OX12: Char B 2A **62**
OX18: Bamp 2H **57**
BUCKLEBURY 3A 148
Buckler Pl. OX4: Litt 5D **84**
Buckler Rd. OX2: Oxf 4J **73**
Bucklers Bury Rd. OX14: Abin 4J **87**
Buckles Cl. OX14: Abin 1E **90**
BUCKNELL 2A 30 (1A 144)
Bucknell Av. RG8: Pang 7J **133**
Bucknell Rd. OX26: Bic 6C **30**
Buckner's Cl. OX10: Ben 5A **102**
Buckthorn La. OX10: Chol 2E **116**
Budds Cl. OX20: Woods 2J **41**
BUFFLER'S HOLT 3D 141
BUGBROOKE 1D 141
Bugloss Wlk. OX26: Bic 6D **30**
Bulan Rd. OX3: Head 5G **79**
BULBOURNE 2D 145
Bulldog Cl. OX10: Ben 7C **102**
Bull Hill OX7: Chad 2C **36**
Bullingdon Av. OX10: Ber 3B **94**
Bullingdon Rd.
OX4: Oxf 7K **5** (6C **78**)
Bull La. OX9: Tha 4H **123**
OX18: Ast 6H **57**
Bullmarsh Cl. OX25: M'ton S ...5G **29**
Bull Meadow, The
RG8: Stre 6A **132**
Bullockspit La. OX13: Longw ...5B **60**
Bull Ring OX15: Dedd 6C **20**
Bulls Cl. GL7: Fil 3A **54**
Bullsmead OX13: Spri 2F **87**
Bullstake Cl. OX2: Oxf 4G **77**
Bull St. OX18: Ast 6H **57**
Bulrush Rd. OX4: Blac L 5J **85**
Bulwarks La. OX1: Oxf ...4E **4** (4K **77**)
Bungalow Cl. OX3: Beck 4B **120**
Bungalows, The
OX7: Chip N 7H 23
(off Cotswold Cres.)
Buntings, The OX26: Bic 2G **33**
Bunyan Rd. OX26: Bic 6C **30**
Burbush Rd. OX4: Cow 1H **85**
Burchester Av. OX3: Head 1H **79**
Burchester Pl. OX16: Ban 6H **11**
BURCHETT'S GREEN 2D 149
BURCOT 4K 93 (1A 148)
Burcot La. OX10: Dorc T 4C **94**
Burcot Pk. OX14: Burc 3J **93**
BURCOTT 1D 145
Burdell Av. OX3: Head 1K **79**
Burditch Bank OX20: Woot 6H **37**
Burdock Cl. OX26: Bic 6C **30**
BURDROP 5D 14 (3A 140)
Bure La. OX11: Did 7D **98**
Bure Pl. OX26: Bic 1E **32**
BURFORD 4C 38 (2B 142)
Burford Rd. GL7: Fil 2B **54**
OX7: Chip N 6H **23**
OX18: Blac B 1K **55**
Burford Rd. OX18: Briz N 1E **46**
(not continuous)
OX18: Cart 3D **46**
OX18: Ful 3C **38**
OX28: Wit 3D **50**
OX29: Min L, Wit
................5A **48** & 2A **50**
Burgan Cl. OX4: Cow 2G **85**
Burgess Cl. OX14: Abin 1G **91**
Burgess Mead OX2: Oxf 7H **73**
BURGHFIELD 3B 148
BURGHFIELD COMMON 3B 148
BURGHFIELD HILL 3B 148
BURLEIGH 3D 149
Burleigh Rd.
OX29: Blad, Cass 1J **71**
Burlington Cres. OX3: Head 2K **79**
Burlington Gdns.
OX16: Ban 2D **12**
BURMINGTON 3A 140
BURNHAM 2D 149
Burns Cres. OX26: Bic 7C **30**
Burns Rd. OX16: Ban 2C **12**
BURNT HILL 3A 148
Burra Cl. OX4: Sand T 7D **84**
Burr Cl. OX29: Sut 2C **58**
Burrows Cl. OX3: Head 2G **79**
Burrows Hill OX10: Ewel 6G **103**
Burrows Ho. *OX3: Head 4G 79*
(off Old Rd.)
Burr St. OX11: Har 3F **109**
Bursill Cl. OX3: Head 1K **79**
Burswin Rd. OX18: Cart 2D **46**
Burton Cl. OX14: Abin 2E **90**
Burton Pl. OX4: Cow 7H **79**
Burton Taylor Theatre 4E 4
Burwell Cl. OX28: Wit 5C **50**
Burwell Ct. OX28: Wit 5D **50**
Burwell Dr. OX28: Wit 5C **50**
Burwell Mdw. OX28: Wit 6D **50**
Burycroft, The OX14: Cul 4H **91**
Bury Cft. Rd. OX15: Hook N 3B **16**
Buryknowle Pk. OX3: Head 2G **79**
Bury Mead OX29: Stan H 3B **58**
Bury St. OX14: Abin 1G **91**
Busby Cl. OX29: Free 5G **53**
OX29: Stone 3B **40**
Busby's Cl. OX18: Clan 6H **55**
BUSCOT 1B 146
Buscot Dr. OX14: Abin 5J **87**
Buscot Pk. 1B 146
Busgrove La. RG9: Stoke R 7H **131**
Bushes La. RG9: Nett 1G **131**
Bushey Dr. OX18: Clan 7H **55**
Bushey Ground OX29: Min L 4C **48**
Bushey Leys Cl. OX3: Head 7H **75**
Bushey Row OX18: Bamp 2H **57**
Bush Furlong OX11: Did 7E **98**
Bushnell Cl. OX3: Head 2J **79**
BUSHTON 3A 146
Bushy Cl. OX2: Bot 4C **76**
Butcher's Hill OX7: G Tew 3D **24**
Butcher's Row OX16: Ban 7F **11**
Butler Cl. OX2: Oxf 1J **77**
OX15: Blox 1C **18**
OX33: Hors 7C **80**
Butlers Dr. OX18: Cart 6D **46**
BUTLERS MARSTON 1A 140
Butler's Orchard
RG4: Ked E 7F **135**
Butlers Pond RG8: Whit H 3H **133**
Butlers Yd. RG9: Pep C 4H **135**
Butterbur Gdns. OX26: Bic 5E **30**
Butter Cross OX28: Wit 4F **51**
Buttercup Sq. OX4: Blac L 5J **85**
Butter Mkt. OX9: Tha 4H **123**
Buttermilk La. OX29: Lea 7H **39**
Butterwort Pl. OX4: Blac L 4J **85**
Butterwyke Pl.
OX1: Oxf 7F **5** (5K **77**)
Butts, The OX25: Mer 2C **44**
OX29: Stand 6D **58**
Butts La. OX3: Mars 6C **74**
Butts Rd. OX33: Hors 6B **80**
SN7: F'don 4C **56**
Butts Way OX49: A Row 4J **129**
Buzzards Cl. OX17: Lit B 7G **7**
Byeway, The OX16: Ban 6H **11**
BYFIELD 1C 141
Bygones Mus. 2C 6
Byron Cl. OX14: Abin 3D **90**
Byron Rd. OX16: Ban 3C **12**
Byron Way OX26: Bic 7C **30**

C

Cadel's Row *SN7: F'don 3C 56*
(off Southampton St.)
CADLEY 3B 146
CADMORE END 1C 149
Cadogan Pk. OX20: Woods 3H **41**
Cadwell La. OX49: B Bal 3D **128**
Caernarvon Way OX16: Ban 7B **10**
(not continuous)
Calais Dene OX18: Bamp 1H **57**
Calais Rd. OX29: Bright 4A **58**
CALCOT 2A 142
Calcot Cl. OX3: Head 4H **79**
CALCOT ROW 3B 148
Calcroft La. GL7: Broad 5C **54**
Calcroft Rd. OX18: Clan 4F **55**
CALDECOTT 3F 91 (1D 147)
Caldecott Cl. OX14: Abin 2E **90**
Caldecott Ct. *OX14: Abin 2E 90*
(off Caldecott Cl.)
Caldecott Rd. OX14: Abin 2E **90**
Calder Way OX11: Did 7E **98**
CALDESCOTE 1D 141
Caldicott Cl. OX10: Shil 3G **101**
CALMSDEN 3A 142
CALTHORPE 3G 13
Calthorpe Rd. OX16: Ban 2E **12**
Calthorpe St. OX16: Ban 1E **12**
CALVERT 1B 144
Calves Cl. OX5: Kidl 3E **68**
Cambridge Ter.
OX1: Oxf 6F **5** (5K **77**)
Cam Cl. OX11: Did 1C **110**
Camellias, The OX16: Ban 4D **10**
Cameron Av. OX14: Abin 6K **87**
Cameron Ct. *OX16: Ban 1F 13*
(off Britannia Rd.)
Campbell Cl. OX26: Bic 1E **32**
Campbell Rd. OX4: Oxf 1D **84**
Campbells Cl. OX20: Woods 3J **41**
Campden Cl. OX28: Wit 3C **50**
Campion Cl. OX4: Blac L 5J **85**
OX18: Cart 6E **46**
Campion Hall Dr. OX11: Did ...2E **110**
Campion Pl. OX26: Bic 6D **30**
Campion Rd. OX14: Abin 7J **87**
Campion Way OX28: Wit 2H **51**
Camp Rd. OX25: Up H 4F **27**
CAMPSFIELD 1A 68
Canada Cl. OX16: Ban 6F **11**
Canada La. SN7: F'don 3B **56**
Canada Rd. OX16: Ban 6F **11**
Canal Ct. OX12: Wan 3F **105**
Canal Ho. *OX12: Wan 5G 105*
(off Smiths Wharf)
Canal St. OX2: Oxf 2B **4** (3H **77**)
OX16: Ban 1F **13**
Canal Way OX12: E Cha 5D **104**
Candy Way OX13: Woot 1C **86**
CANE END 7B 134 (3B 148)
Cane La. OX12: Gro 2G **105**
Canning Cres. OX1: Oxf 1B **84**
Cannons Fld. OX3: Mars 6C **74**
Canon Hill's Gdns.
SN6: Shriv 6C **64**
CANONS ASHBY 1C 141
Canterbury Cl. OX16: Ban 6J **11**
Canterbury Rd. OX2: Oxf 1J **77**
Capel Cl. OX2: Oxf 4J **73**
Caps La. OX10: Chol 7F **113**
Cardigan St. OX2: Oxf ...2C **4** (3J **77**)
(not continuous)
Cardinal Cl. OX4: Litt 3E **84**
Cardinal Ho. *OX4: Litt 3E 84*
(off Cardinal Cl.)
Cardwell Cres. OX3: Head 3E **78**
Carey Cl. OX2: Oxf 3G **73**
Carfax Tower 5F 5 (4K 77)
Cariad Ct. RG8: Gor 5B **132**
Carlesgill Pl. RG9: Hen T 6D **138**
Carling Rd. RG4: Sonn C 4G **135**
Carlton Cl. OX12: Gro 1F **105**
Carlton Rd. OX2: Oxf 3J **73**
Caroline Ct. *OX20: Woods 3H 41*
(off Oxford Rd.)
Caroline St. OX4: Oxf 5K **5** (4B **78**)
Carpenter Cl. OX4: Litt 4F **85**
Carr Av. OX18: Cart 5C **46**
Carse Cl. OX14: Abin 4J **87**
Carswell Circ. OX25: Up H 5J **27**
Carter Cl. OX3: Head 3J **79**

A-Z Oxfordshire Atlas 155

Everard Cl. OX3: Head 4G 79
EVERDON 1C 141
Eversley Cl. OX7: Chad ...1C 36
Ewart Cl. OX26: Bic 7D 30
EWELME 6G 103 (1B 148)
Ewert Pl. OX2: Oxf 6J 73
Ewin Cl. OX3: Mars 7C 74
Exborne Rd. OX14: Abin ...1E 90
Exe Cl. OX11: Did 1C 110
Exeter Ct. OX5: Kidl 3G 69
  (off Blenheim Rd.)
OX11: Did 2E 110
Exeter Rd. OX5: Kidl 2F 69
EXLADE STREET ...1E 134 (2B 148)
EYDON 1C 141
EYNSHAM 5D 70 (3D 143)
Eynsham Rd. OX2: Farm, Bot ..3H 59
  (not continuous)
OX29: Cass 3G 71
Eyot Pl. OX4: Oxf 6B 78
Eyres Cl. OX10: Ewel 5E 102
Eyre's La. OX10: Ewel 4E 102
Eyston Way OX14: Abin 1D 90

F

Faber Cl. OX4: Litt 4F 85
Fairacres OX14: Abin 1D 90
Fairacres Rd. OX4: Oxf 7C 78
OX11: Did 2B 110
Fair Cl. OX26: Bic 6F 31
Fairfax Av. OX3: Mars 1B 78
Fairfax Cen. OX5: Kidl 5G 69
Fairfax Cl. OX9: Tha 4J 123
OX16: Ban 1C 12
Fairfax Ga. OX33: Holt 5H 81
Fairfax Rd. OX4: Cow 7H 79
OX5: Kidl 5G 69
OX44: Chal 2C 128
Fairfield OX10: Chol 2D 116
Fairfield Cl. OX12: Gro 2G 105
Fairfield Dr. OX28: Wit 5D 50
Fairfield Pl. OX14: Abin 7G 87
OX18: Cart 2E 46
Fairfield Rd. RG8: Gor 5D 132
FAIRFORD 3A 142
Fairford Way OX26: Bic 6G 31
Fairhaven Rd. OX27: Cave ...3F 31
Fairlawn End OX2: Oxf 3G 73
Fairlie Rd. OX4: Cow 3E 84
Fair Mile RG9: Hen T 1A 138
Fair Mile, The OX11: A Tir ..7J 115
Fair Mile Ct. RG9: Hen T ...2C 138
Fairspear Rd. OX29: Lea 4F 39
Fairthorne Way SN6: Shriv ...6B 64
Fair Vw. OX3: Head 6G 79
Fairview Est. RG9: Hen T 5E 138
Fairview Rd. OX16: Ban 2F 13
Fairview Trad. Est.
  RG9: Hen T 5E 138
Fairway, The OX16: Ban 6B 10
Falcon Cl. OX4: Blac L 4G 85
OX16: Ban 2C 12
OX18: Cart 4C 46
Falcon Mead OX26: Bic 2G 33
Falkner's Cl. OX17: Add 3H 19
Fallowfield Cres.
  OX28: Wit 3J 51
Fallowfields OX26: Bic 1F 33
Fallowfields Ct. OX26: Bic ...1F 33
Fallow Way OX16: Ban 4G 13
Falstaff Cl. OX29: Eyn 4D 70
Fane Cl. OX26: Bic 7D 30
Fane Dr. OX10: Ber 3A 94
Fane Ho. OX26: Bic 1E 32
Fane Rd. OX3: Mars 7B 74
Fanshawe Pl. OX4: Cow 1H 85
Fanshawe Rd. OX9: Tha 4K 123
Faraday Av. OX11: Har 5F 119
  (not continuous)
Faraday Rd. OX12: Wan 2D 104
FAR COTTON 1D 141
FARINGDON 3C 56 (1B 146)
Faringdon Rd.
  OX2: C'nor .....5A 82 & 7J 59
OX13: G For 5B 86
OX13: K Bag, Sthm 4C 60
OX13: Shipp 6C 86
OX14: Abin 7D 86
SN6: Shriv 5C 64
SN6: Watch 4D 64
Farleigh Rd. SN6: Shriv 6A 64

Farley Cl. OX29: Stone 2A 40
Farley La. OX29: Stone 2A 40
Farm Cl. OX4: Blac L 5J 85
OX5: Kidl 1G 69
OX18: Ast 6H 57
OX44: Chal 2D 128
RG4: Sonn C 5G 135
Farm Cl. La. OX33: Wheat 5G 81
Farm Cl. Rd. OX33: Wheat 5G 81
FARMCOTE 1A 142
Farm End OX12: Gro 2G 105
OX20: Woods 2G 41
Farmer Pl. OX3: Mars 1C 78
Farmers Cl. OX28: Wit 2F 51
Farmfield Rd. OX16: Ban 3E 12
Farmhouse Cl.
  OX29: Stan H 3B 58
Farmhouse Mdw. OX28: Wit ..6C 50
Farmhouse M. OX49: Watl ...5D 128
FARMINGTON 2A 142
Farmington Dr. OX28: Wit ...4C 50
Farm La. OX29: Craw 2F 49
Farm Mill La. OX28: Wit 5F 51
  (Church Grn.)
OX28: Wit 5G 51
  (Witan Way)
FARMOOR 3H 59 (3D 143)
Farmoor Ct. OX2: Farm 3H 59
Farmoor Reservoir 2F 59
Farm Piece SN7: Stan V 6B 62
Farm Rd. OX14: Abin 5G 87
RG8: Gor 6C 132
RG9: Hen T 5E 138
Farmstead Cl. OX12: Gro ...1G 105
Farm Way OX16: Ban 3H 13
FARNBOROUGH
  Banbury 2B 140
  Wantage 2D 147
Farndon Rd. OX2: Oxf 1J 77
Farnham Ct. OX5: Kidl 3G 69
FARNHAM ROYAL 2D 149
Farriers Cl. OX27: Fring 3J 29
Farriers Ct. OX28: Wit 3F 51
Farrier's Mead OX25: Wend ...7A 32
Farriers M. OX14: Abin 7H 87
Farriers Rd. OX7: Mid B 7J 25
Farringdon Rd. SN7: Stan V ..5B 62
FARTHINGHOE 3C 141
Farthings, The OX13: Marc ...5H 61
FARTHINGSTONE 1D 141
Father Thames Statue 1B 146
Faulder Av. OX18: Cart 4C 46
Faulkner St. OX1: Oxf ...6E 4 (5K 77)
Fawkner Way SN7: Stan V ...6B 62
FAWLER 2C 143
Fawler Rd. OX7: Charlb 7B 36
OX12: Fawl 6H 67
OX29: Stone 3A 40
SN7: Uff 6H 67
FAWLEY
  Henley-on-Thames 2C 149
  Wantage 2C 147
Fawley Cl. OX12: Wan 4G 105
Fawley Court Historic House & Mus.,
  Conference & Retreat Cen.
    .....1E 138
Featherbed La. OX11: Row ...3K 107
OX13: Stev 3K 107
SN6: Ids 7B 66
Feilden Cl. OX29: Duck 5G 49
Feilden Gro. OX3: Head 2D 78
Feltwell Cl. OX18: Cart 4E 46
FENCOTT 5E 44 (2A 144)
Fencott Rd.
  OX5: Char O, Fenc 6C 44
Fennel Way OX14: Abin 7K 87
FENNES Rd. OX16: Ban 1C 12
FENNY COMPTON 1B 140
Fenny Compton Rd.
  OX17: Clay 1B 6
FENNY STRATFORD 1D 145
Fenway OX25: Stee A 3A 26
Ferendune Ct. SN7: F'don ...3B 56
Ferguson Pl. OX14: Abin 7K 87
Ferguson Rd. OX16: Ban ...6G 11
Fermi Av. OX11: Chilt, Har ...6F 119
Ferndale Ga. SN7: F'don 5B 56
Ferndale Rd. OX16: Ban 6B 10
Ferndale St. SN7: F'don 3C 56
Ferne Cl. RG8: Gor 5C 132
Ferngrove SN7: F'don 3C 56
  (off Portway)
FERNHAM 2H 67 (1B 146)

Fernham Rd.
  SN7: F'don, Lit Cox 4B 56
    (not continuous)
SN7: Fern, Shel 2J 67
SN7: Longc 2J 65
SN7: Uff 5G 67
Fernhill Cl. OX5: Kidl 3E 68
OX9: Tid 1C 122
OX15: Milc 2J 17
Fern Hill Rd. OX4: Cow 1G 85
Fernhill Rd. OX5: Beg 3B 68
Fern La. OX18: Cart 2F 47
Ferny Cl. OX14: Rad 4B 88
Ferriston OX16: Ban 5C 10
Ferry Hinksey Rd.
  OX2: Oxf 6A 4 (5G 77)
Ferry La. OX3: Mars 1K 5 (2B 78)
OX10: Moul 7F 117
RG8: Gor 6B 132
RG8: Pang 7H 133
RG8: S Sto 7F 117
Ferry Pool Rd. OX2: Oxf 6K 73
Ferry Rd. OX3: Mars ...1K 5 (2C 78)
RG8: S Sto 7G 117
Ferry Sports Cen. 6K 73
Ferry Wlk. OX14: Abin 2G 91
Fetti Pl. OX7: Milt W 5G 35
OX12: Wan 4J 105
Fettiplace Rd. OX13: A'ton ...2H 61
Fettiplace Rd. OX3: Head ...7H 75
OX13: Marc 5J 61
OX28: Wit 4C 50
FEWCOTT 5B 28 (1A 144)
Fewcott Rd. OX27: Frit 2D 28
Fiddlers Hill OX7: Ship W ...7J 35
Field, The OX13: Dry S 1A 86
FIELD ASSARTS 2C 143
Field Av. OX4: Blac L 4J 85
Field Cl. OX5: Kidl 3G 69
OX5: Yarn 5C 68
OX13: Longw 4C 60
OX29: Stone 2A 40
Fielden Cl. OX10: Ben 7E 102
Fielden Rd. OX10: Ben 7E 102
Fieldfare Cl. OX26: Bic 2F 33
Fieldfare Rd. OX4: Blac L ...5H 85
Field Gdns. OX12: E Cha 5C 104
OX13: Stev 4B 96
Field Ho. Dr. OX2: Oxf 4H 73
Field La. OX44: Cudd 2C 126
Fieldmere Cl. OX28: Wit 4D 50
Field Rd. OX7: Kingh 7C 34
Fieldside OX11: Upt 7K 109
OX14: Abin 6E 86
OX14: L Wit 1F 99
Field St. OX26: Bic 1E 32
Fiennes Rd. OX4: Oxf 3D 84
FIFIELD
  Chipping Norton 2B 142
  Maidenhead 3D 149
Fifteenth St. OX11: Har 5F 119
FILKINS 3A 54 (3B 142)
Filkins Rd. GL7: Fil, Lang 4A 54
Finch Cl. OX3: Head 4F 79
Finchdale Cl. OX18: Cart 4D 46
Finchley La. OX26: Bic 2D 32
FINGEST 1C 149
Finham Brook OX11: Did 6C 98
FINMERE 6J 21 (3D 141)
Finmore Cl. OX14: Abin 7F 87
Finmore Rd. OX2: Bot 5E 76
Finsbury Pl. OX7: Chip N ...5H 23
FINSTOCK 1J 39 (2C 143)
Fir Cl. OX10: Ips 6D 130
Fircroft OX16: Ban 2F 13
OX26: Bic 5F 31
Firebrass Hill OX10: Ewel ...5G 103
Fir La. OX25: Stee A 3B 26
Firs, The OX2: Oxf 4J 73
OX15: Wrox 6G 9
Firs Mdw. OX4: Blac L 6H 85
First Av. OX3: Head 5J 79
OX11: Did 7A 98
First St. OX11: Har 5H 119
First Turn OX2: Oxf 4G 73
Fir Tree Av. OX10: Wal 3G 113
Fir Tree Cl. OX13: Sthm 4D 60
Firtree Cl. OX16: Ban 4B 10
Fir Trees OX14: Rad 7B 84
Fisher Cl. OX14: Drayt 7B 90
OX16: Ban 5H 11
Fishermans Wharf
  OX14: Abin 4G 91

Fisher Row OX1: Oxf 4J 77
Fishers Cl. OX29: Hail 1J 49
Fisher's La. OX7: Charlb 6B 36
Fish Ponds La. OX9: Tha 3G 123
Fitchett Yd. OX14: Abin 1F 91
Fitzcount Way OX10: Wal ...1J 113
Fitzharris Ind. Est.
  OX14: Abin 6F 87
    (off Thornhill Wlk.)
Fitzharry's Rd. OX14: Abin ...7G 87
Fitzherbert Cl. OX4: Oxf 2C 84
Five Mile Dr. OX2: Oxf 3G 73
FLACKWELL HEATH 2D 149
Flatford Pl. OX5: Kidl 1D 68
Flats, The OX7: Kingh 6C 34
Flaxfield Rd. OX4: Blac L ...4J 85
FLECKNOE 1C 141
Fleet Way OX11: Did 2D 110
Fleetwood Way OX9: Tha ...2H 123
Fleming Cl. OX7: Mid B 7K 25
OX26: Bic 6C 30
Fleming Dr. OX7: Mid B 7K 25
Flemings Rd. OX20: Woods ...3J 41
Flemming Av. OX44: Chal ...1B 128
Fletcher Cl. OX5: Yarn 6C 68
SN7: F'don 3D 56
Fletcher Rd. OX4: Cow 7H 79
Flexney Pl. OX3: Head 4G 79
Flexneys Paddock
  OX29: Stan H 3B 58
Flint Hollow OX39: Chin 2F 125
Floral Cl. OX12: Gore 2H 105
FLORE 1D 141
Florence Cl. OX5: Kidl 3G 69
FLORENCE PARK 1E 84
Florence Pk. Rd. OX4: Oxf ...1E 84
Florey's Cl. OX29: Hail 1J 49
Floyds Row OX1: Oxf ...6F 5 (5K 77)
Fludger Cl. OX10: Wal 3H 113
Fluellen Pl. OX26: Bic 6D 30
Fogwell Rd. OX2: Bot 5B 76
Foliat Cl. OX12: Wan 5H 105
Foliat Dr. OX12: Wan 5H 105
Folly Bri. OX1: Oxf 7F 5 (5K 77)
Folly Bri. Ct. OX1: Oxf 7F 5
Folly Ct. OX15: Sib F 6E 14
Folly Cres. SN6: Watch 3D 64
Folly Grn. RG8: Wood 2B 134
Folly Orchard Rd.
  RG8: Wood 1B 134
FOLLY, THE 3D 147
Folly Tower 2E 56
Folly Vw. Cres. SN7: F'don ...4B 56
Folly Vw. Rd. SN7: F'don 4B 56
FORD
  Aylesbury 3C 145
  Cheltenham 1A 142
Ford La. OX10: Dray L 2G 95
OX13: Fril 5F 61
Fords Cl. OX33: Hors 7B 80
FORDWELLS 2C 143
Fordy La. OX12: E Hen 4J 107
Forest Cl. OX7: Milt W 5G 35
OX26: Laun 1K 33
Foresters OX39: Chin 2F 125
FOREST HILL 1E 80 (3A 144)
Forest Rd. OX3: Head 2J 79
OX7: Charlb 6A 36
Forest Side OX1: Kenn 4A 84
Forge Cl. OX10: Ben 5A 102
OX25: Mer 2C 44
OX33: Hort 2C 120
Forge Pl. OX27: Frit 2D 28
Forget-Me-Not Way
  OX4: Blac L 5H 85
Forgeway OX16: Ban 5C 10
Forrest Cl. SN6: Shriv 6A 64
Forster La. OX2: C'nor 6J 59
Forsythia Cl. OX26: Bic 5E 30
Forsythia Wlk. OX16: Ban ...4D 10
Fortescue Dr. OX26: Ches ...4A 32
Forties, The OX44: G Mil 6F 121
Fortnam Cl. OX3: Head 2E 78
Forty, The OX10: Chol 1E 116
FORTY GREEN 1D 149
FOSCOT 1B 142
Foscote Ri. OX16: Ban 2F 13
FOSSEBRIDGE 2A 142
Fosseway, The OX18: Briz N ...4J 47
Foster Rd. OX14: Abin 4G 87
Fosters La. RG9: Bin H 7J 137
Fothergill Pl. OX9: Tha 4H 123
Foundry Cl. OX11: Did 7D 98

H

Hardwick Rd.—High Vw.

Hardwick Rd. OX27: Hethe ...2F **29**
RG8: Whit T ...6H **133**
Harebell Rd. OX4: Blac L ...4J **85**
Harebell Way OX26: Bic ...6D **30**
Harecourt OX12: Wan ...6J **105**
Harefields OX2: Oxf ...3H **73**
HARE HATCH ...3D **149**
Harewood Rd. OX16: Ban ...4G **13**
Harlech Cl. OX16: Ban ...1B **12**
Harlequin Way OX16: Ban ...4D **10**
Harley Rd. OX2: Oxf ...4G **77**
Harlington Av. OX12: Gro ...1H **105**
Harlow Way OX3: Mars ...5C **74**
Harmon Cl. OX27: Cave ...4G **31**
HARNHILL ...3A **142**
Harolde Cl. OX3: Head ...1G **79**
Harold Hicks Pl. OX4: Oxf ...6C **78**
Harolds Cl. OX29: Lea ...6J **39**
Harold White Cl. OX3: Head ...3J **79**
Harper Cl. OX25: Up A ...6G **45**
Harpes Rd. OX2: Oxf ...4J **73**
HARPOLE ...1D **141**
HARPSDEN ...1G **139** (2C **149**)
HARPSDEN BOTTOM ...7A **138**
Harpsden Rd. RG9: Bin H ...5H **137**
RG9: Hen T ...5D **138**
Harpsden Way RG9: Hen T ...6D **138**
Harpsden Wood RG9: Harp ...3G **139**
Harpsichord Pl. OX4: Oxf ...4C **78**
Harrier Pk. OX11: Did ...5A **98**
Harriers Vw. OX16: Ban ...2E **12**
Harrier Way OX26: Bic ...6G **31**
Harris Ct. *OX2: Oxf ...4J 73*
(off Harpes Rd.)
Harrison Pl. OX9: Tha ...3H **123**
Harrison's La. OX20: Woods ...3G **41**
Harris Rd. OX25: Up H ...5H **27**
Harris's La. OX13: Longw ...3B **60**
Harrisville OX25: Stee A ...4B **26**
Harrowby Rd. OX16: Ban ...4F **13**
Harrow Rd. OX4: Cow ...3J **85**
Hart Av. SN7: F'don ...3C **56**
Hart Cl. OX14: Abin ...7K **87**
OX16: Ban ...4E **10**
Hartley Cl. OX10: Shil ...3G **101**
Hartley Ct. OX2: Oxf ...1J **77**
Hartley Russell Cl. OX4: Oxf ...1C **84**
Hart Pl. OX26: Bic ...6G **31**
Harts Cl. OX5: Kidl ...3E **68**
Hartslock Bridleway
RG8: Whit T ...4F **133**
Hartslock Ct. RG8: Pang ...7F **133**
Hart St. OX2: Oxf ...2C **4** (3J **77**)
OX10: Wal ...3J **113**
RG9: Hen T ...3D **138**
Hart St. Pas. OX2: Oxf ...2C **4**
Hart Synnot Ho. *OX2: Oxf ...2J 77*
(off Leckford Rd.)
Harvest Cres. OX18: Cart ...2F **47**
Harvest Way OX28: Wit ...2H **51**
HARWELL ...3F **109** (2D **147**)
Harwell Cl. OX14: Abin ...6H **87**
Harwell Intl. Bus. Cen.
OX11: Har ...5H **119**
Harwell Rd. OX14: S Cou ...3G **97**
Harwood Rd. OX11: E Hag ...4C **110**
Haseley Rd. OX44: Lit M ...2G **127**
Haslemere Gdns. OX2: Oxf ...2H **73**
Haslemere Tramway Est.
OX16: Ban ...1G 13
(off Haslemere Way)
Haslemere Way OX16: Ban ...1G **13**
Hastings Cl. OX16: Ban ...6B **10**
Hastings Dr. OX18: Briz N ...4F **47**
Hastings Hill OX7: C'hill ...1B **34**
Hastings Rd. OX16: Ban ...6B **10**
HASTOE ...3D **145**
Hastoe Grange OX3: Head ...1D **78**
Hatch Cl. OX5: Kirt ...2B **42**
Hatch End OX5: Kirt ...2B **42**
Hatching La. OX29: Lea ...5J **39**
Hatch Way OX5: Kirt ...2B **42**
Hatfield Pits La. OX29: Hail ...1K **49**
HATFORD ...1C **147**
Hathaways OX33: Wheat ...5G **81**
HATHEROP ...3A **142**
Havelock Rd. OX4: Cow ...1F **85**
Haven Cl. OX10: Dorc T ...1C **100**
Haven Va. OX12: Wan ...5H **105**
Havers Av. OX14: Milt ...7E **96**
Hawke La. OX15: Blox ...3B **18**
Hawkes La.
OX15: Burd, Sib F ...6D **14**
Hawkins St. OX4: Oxf ...6C **78**
Hawkins Way OX13: Woot ...1C **86**
Hawksmead OX26: Bic ...3G **33**
Hawksmoor Rd. OX2: Oxf ...3J **73**
Hawkswell Gdns. OX2: Oxf ...5K **73**
Hawksworth OX11: Did ...5A **98**
Hawksworth Cl. OX12: Gro ...1G **105**
HAWLING ...1A **142**
Hawlings Row OX4: Blac L ...5K **85**
Hawthorn Av. OX3: Head ...2G **79**
OX9: Tha ...4G **123**
Hawthorn Cl. OX2: Bot ...5E **76**
OX10: Wal ...3H **113**
Hawthorn Cres. OX12: Gro ...2H **105**
Hawthorne Av. OX13: Abin ...5C **86**
Hawthorn Gro. OX18: Cart ...6D **46**
HAWTHORN HILL ...3D **149**
Hawthorn Rd. OX29: Eyn ...4D **70**
SN7: F'don ...3B **56**
Hawthorns, The OX16: Ban ...3F **13**
Hawthorn Wlk. OX26: Bic ...5F **31**
Hawthorn Way OX5: Kidl ...4F **69**
Haydon Rd. OX11: Did ...1B **110**
HAYDON WICK ...2A **146**
Hayes Av. OX13: Sthm ...5C **60**
Hayes Cl. OX3: Mars ...2C **78**
Hayfield Rd. OX2: Oxf ...7J **73**
Haynes Rd. OX3: Mars ...7B **74**
Hayward Dr. OX18: Cart ...6D **46**
Hayward Rd. OX2: Oxf ...2H **73**
Haywards Cl. OX12: Wan ...5H **105**
RG9: Hen T ...4B **138**
Haywards Rd. OX14: Drayt ...1C **96**
Hayway La. OX15: Hook N ...1A **16**
Hazel Av. OX9: Tha ...4G **123**
Hazel Cl. OX28: Wit ...2J **51**
Hazel Ct. OX4: Oxf ...6E **78**
Hazel Cres. OX5: Kidl ...5F **69**
Hazeldene Cl. OX29: N Leigh ...5B **52**
Hazeldene Gdns. OX16: Ban ...3F **13**
Hazel End OX44: Gars ...5C **126**
Hazel Gdns. RG4: Sonn C ...5H **135**
Hazel Gro. OX10: Wal ...3H **113**
OX26: Bic ...6F **31**
Hazells La. GL7: Fil ...3A **54**
SN6: Shriv ...6C **64**
Hazelmoor La. RG4: Gall C ...5E **134**
Hazelnut Path OX14: Rad ...7B **84**
Hazelrig Dr. OX9: Tha ...4J **123**
Hazel Rd. OX2: Bot ...4D **76**
Hazel Wlk. OX5: Kidl ...5G **69**
HAZLEMERE ...1D **149**
HAZLETON ...2A **142**
Hazleton Cl. OX9: Tha ...4G **123**
HEADINGTON ...2E **78** (3A **144**)
HEADINGTON HILL ...4D **78**
Headington Hill OX3: Head ...3D **78**
HEADINGTON QUARRY ...2H **79**
Headington Rd. OX3: Head ...4C **78**
Headington Rdbt. OX3: Head ...2J **79**
Headley Way OX3: Head ...1D **78**
Healey Cl. OX14: Abin ...2F **91**
Hean Cl. OX14: Abin ...5J **87**
Hearns La. RG4: Gall C ...5E **134**
Hearthway OX16: Ban ...5D **10**
HEATH AND REACH ...1D **145**
Heath Cl. OX3: Head ...5G **79**
OX15: Milc ...2H **17**
Heathcote Av. OX16: Ban ...4G **13**
Heathcote Pl. OX14: Abin ...6K **87**
Heath Dr. RG9: Bin H ...7H **137**
HEATHENCOTE ...2D **141**
Heather Cl. OX18: Cart ...2D **46**
RG4: Sonn C ...5H **135**
Heather Pl. OX3: Mars ...1C **78**
Heather Rd. OX14: Milt ...3E **96**
OX26: Bic ...5E **30**
Heathfield Av. RG9: Bin H ...6J **137**
Heathfield Cl. RG9: Bin H ...6J **137**
Heath La. OX20: Blad ...7H **41**
Heatley Rd. OX4: Litt ...5E **84**
Hedge End OX20: Woods ...4J **41**
Hedge Hill Rd. OX12: E Cha ...5C **104**
Hedgemead Av. OX14: Abin ...6K **87**
Hedgerley OX39: Chin ...2F **125**
Hedges Cl. OX3: Head ...2H **79**
Heigham Ct. SN7: Stan V ...6B **62**
Helen Rd. OX2: Oxf ...4A **4** (4G **77**)
Helen's Way OX10: Ben ...6A **102**
Helleborine Cl. OX4: Blac L ...5J **85**
HELLIDON ...1C **141**
HELMDON ...2C **141**
Helwys Pl. OX5: Kidl ...1E **68**
Hemmingway Dr. OX26: Bic ...1C **32**
HEMPTON ...4E **20** (3B **140**)
Hempton Rd. OX15: Dedd ...6B **20**
HEMTON WAINHILL ...1K **125**
Hendon Pl. OX26: Bic ...6G **31**
Hendred St. OX4: Cow ...7E **78**
Hendred Way OX14: Abin ...6J **87**
Henfield Vw. OX10: Warb ...1G **101**
Hengest Ga. OX11: Har ...3F **109**
Hengrove Cl. OX3: Head ...1G **79**
Henley Av. OX4: Oxf ...1D **84**
Henley Bri. RG9: Hen T ...3D **138**
Henley District Indoor Sports Cen. ...6A **138**
Henley Exhibition Cen. ...3C **138**
HENLEY-ON-THAMES ...3C **138** (2C **149**)
Henley-on-Thames Station (Rail) ...4D **138**
Henley Recreation & Health Cen. ...5E **138**
Henley Rd. OX4: Sand T ...6D **84**
OX10: Dorc T, Shil ...7C **94**
RG9: Shipl ...7K **137**
Henley RUFC ...2C **138**
Henley Sailing Club ...3K **139**
Henleys La. OX14: Drayt ...7C **90**
Henley St. OX4: Oxf ...6C **78**
Henley Way OX10: Ewel ...7G **103**
Hennef Way OX16: Ban ...5F **11**
Henor Mill Cl. OX14: Abin ...5J **87**
Henrietta Rd. OX9: Tha ...3J **123**
Henry Box Cl. OX28: Wit ...5E **50**
Henry Rd. OX2: Oxf ...4A **4** (4G **77**)
Henry Taunt Cl. OX3: Head ...7H **75**
HENSINGTON ...2J **41**
Hensington Cl. OX20: Woods ...3J **41**
Hensington Rd.
OX20: Woods ...3H **41**
Hensington Wlk.
OX20: Woods ...3J 41
(off Flemings Rd.)
HENTON ...3C **145**
HENWOOD ...5B **82**
Henwood Dr. OX1: Woot ...5B **82**
Herald Way OX26: Bic ...6G **31**
Herbert Cl. OX4: Oxf ...6E **78**
Herb Farm, The ...6J **135**
Hereford Way OX16: Ban ...4C **10**
Heritage La. OX7: Asc W ...2H **35**
Herman Cl. OX14: Abin ...7J **87**
HERMITAGE ...3A **148**
Hermitage Rd. OX14: Abin ...2E **90**
Hernes Cl. OX2: Oxf ...4J **73**
Hernes Cres. OX2: Oxf ...4J **73**
Hernes Rd. OX2: Oxf ...4J **73**
Heron Cl. OX18: Cart ...4C **46**
OX26: Bic ...2H **33**
Heron Ct. OX14: Abin ...4G **91**
Heron Dr. OX26: Bic ...2H **33**
Heron Pl. OX2: Oxf ...4J **73**
Heron Rd. OX10: Ben ...6E **102**
Herons Ct. RG10: Warg ...5K **139**
Heron Shaw RG8: Gor ...5C **132**
Heron's Wlk. OX14: Abin ...6G **87**
Heron Way OX16: Ban ...2C **12**
Herringcote OX10: Dorc T ...6C **94**
Herschel Cres. OX4: Litt ...3F **85**
Hertford Cl. OX26: Bic ...7F **31**
Hertford Ct. OX5: Kidl ...3G **69**
Hertford St. OX4: Oxf ...6D **78**
HETHE ...2G **29** (1A **144**)
Hewgate Ct. RG9: Hen T ...4D **138**
Hewitts Cl. OX29: Lea ...6J **39**
Hey Cft. OX29: Eyn ...5D **70**
Heyford Cl. OX29: Stand ...4C **58**
Heyford Hill La. OX4: Litt ...4C **84**
Heyford Hill Rdbt. OX4: Litt ...4C **84**
Heyford Mead OX5: Kidl ...2E **68**
Heyford Rd. OX5: Kirt ...2B **42**
OX25: M'ton S ...5G **29**
OX25: Some ...2K **25**
OX25: Stee A ...4B **26**
Heyford Station (Rail) ...6C **26**
HEYTHROP ...1C **143**
Hibiscus Way OX18: Cart ...2E **46**
Hicks Cl. OX29: Hail ...1J **49**
Hid's Copse Rd. OX2: Bot ...6B **76**
Higgs Cl. OX11: E Hag ...4D **110**
High Acres OX16: Ban ...2G **13**
Highclere Gdns. OX12: Wan ...4G **105**
OX16: Ban ...7A **10**
HIGH COGGES ...5K **51** (3C **143**)
High Cross Way OX3: Head ...7H **75**
Highdown Av. RG4: Emm G ...4E **136**
Highdown Hill Rd.
RG4: Emm G ...3E **136**
HIGHFIELD ...7C **30**
Highfield Av. OX3: Head ...3F **79**
High Furlong OX16: Ban ...5D **10**
(not continuous)
High Ho. Cl. OX18: Clan ...6H **55**
Highland OX16: Ban ...4B **10**
Highlands OX16: Ban ...4C **10**
High Mdw. OX15: Sib G ...4C **14**
HIGHMOOR ...2C **149**
High Rd. OX10: B Sot ...6D **100**
High St. OX1: Oxf ...5F **5** (4K **77**)
OX2: C'nor ...5H **59**
OX3: Beck ...1K **75**
OX5: Char O ...6B **44**
OX5: Isl ...6H **43**
OX5: Kidl ...2F **69**
OX7: Asc W ...2J **35**
OX7: Chip N ...5H **23**
OX7: Fins ...1G **39**
OX7: G Roll ...2B **22**
OX7: Milt W ...6F **35**
OX7: Rams ...2F **39**
OX7: Ship W ...6J **35**
OX9: Tet ...4A **122**
OX9: Tha ...3G **123**
OX10: Ben ...5A **102**
OX10: Dorc T ...6C **94**
OX10: Dray L ...3G **95**
OX10: Ewel ...5E **102**
OX10: Wal ...3H **113**
OX11: Did ...2C **110**
OX11: Har ...3F **109**
OX11: N Mor ...3K **111**
OX11: S Mor ...5J **111**
OX11: Upt ...7K **109** & 1A **114**
OX12: Ard ...5D **106**
OX12: Child ...5E **118**
OX12: E Hen ...4J **107**
OX13: Stev ...5B **96**
OX14: Abin ...1G **91**
OX14: C Ham ...5F **93**
OX14: Cul ...5H **91**
OX14: Drayt ...7C **90**
OX14: L Wit ...1F **99**
OX14: Milt ...5D **96**
OX14: S Cou ...2H **97**
OX15: Bar M ...3C **20**
OX15: Blox ...3C **18**
OX15: Bod ...6G **13**
OX15: Dedd ...6C **20**
OX15: Hook N ...2B **16**
OX15: S New ...5H **17**
OX15: Shut ...2G **15**
OX16: Ban ...1E **12**
(not continuous)
OX17: Add ...3H **19**
OX17: Crop ...2J **7**
OX18: Ast ...5G **57**
OX18: Bamp ...2H **57**
OX18: Burf ...4C **38**
OX20: Woods ...3G **41**
OX25: Up H ...4F **27**
OX27: Soul ...2H **21**
OX28: Wit ...4F **51**
OX29: Eyn ...5D **70**
OX29: Stand ...7C **58**
OX29: Stone ...3A **40**
OX33: Wheat ...5F **81**
OX39: Chin ...1H **125**
OX39: K Blou ...6H **125**
OX44: Chal ...1B **128**
OX44: Cudd ...3C **126**
OX44: Lit M ...2G **127**
OX49: Lewk ...5H **129**
OX49: Watl ...5D **128**
RG8: Pang ...7H **133**
RG8: Stre, Gor ...6A **132**
RG8: Whit T ...6G **133**
RG9: Nett ...2H **131**
SN6: Ashb ...5C **66**
SN6: Shriv ...6B **64**
SN6: Watch ...2C **64**
SN7: Fern ...2H **67**
SN7: Stan V ...6C **62**
SN7: Uff ...7G **67**
Hightown Gdns. OX16: Ban ...3F **13**
Hightown Leys OX16: Ban ...3F **13**
Hightown Rd. OX16: Ban ...2F **13**
High Vw. OX12: E Cha ...6D **104**

Parkside—Primrose La.

Parkside OX20: Woods .3J 41
OX28: Wit .6F 51
OX29: N Leigh .5C 52
OX44: Cudd .2C 126
RG9: Hen T .3B 138
Park Sports Cen., The .4G 81
Parks Rd. OX1: Oxf .1E 4 (2K 77)
Park St. OX7: Charlb .6B 36
OX9: Tha .4H 123
OX20: Blad .7H 41
OX20: Woods .3G 41
Park Ter. OX9: Tha .5J 123
OX12: E Cha .5C 104
PARK TOWN .1K 77 (3A 144)
Park Town OX2: Oxf .1K 77
Park Vw. OX10: Crow G .3C 130
OX12: Wan .5H 105
OX39: Syd .5D 124
Park Wlk. RG8: Pur T .7A 136
Park Way OX3: Mars .5C 74
Parkway Ct. OX4: Cow .2G 85
Parliament Rd. OX9: Tha .3H 123
PARMOOR .2C 149
Parmoor Ct. OX2: Oxf .5J 73
Parry Cl. OX3: Mars .2C 78
Parsley Pl. OX16: Ban .3B 10
Parsonage Cl. OX12: Wan .4K 105
Parson's La. OX10: Ewel .5F 103
Parsons Mead OX14: Abin .6F 87
Parsons Pl. OX4: Oxf .5D 78
Parsons St. OX16: Ban .7E 10
OX17: Add .3H 19
Partridge Chase OX26: Bic .3G 33
Partridge Cl. OX12: Wan .6H 105
Partridge Pl. OX5: Kidl .2D 68
Partridge Wlk. OX4: Blac L .5K 85
Pascal Pl. OX16: Ban .4C 10
Passey Cres. OX10: Ben .5B 102
Paternoster La. OX10: Chol .2E 116
PATH HILL .4K 133
Patrick Haugh Rd.
OX25: Up A .6H 45
Patricks Orchard SN7: Uff .6H 67
PATTISHALL .1D 141
Pattison Pl. OX4: Oxf .3D 84
PAULERSPURY .2D 141
Pauling Rd. OX3: Head .4H 79
Pauls Way OX49: Watl .5D 128
Paxmans Pl. OX16: Ban .2E 12
Paynes End OX27: Cave .4F 31
Peachcroft Cen. OX14: Abin .5J 87
Peachcroft Rd. OX14: Abin .5J 87
Peacock Ho. OX12: Wan .6G 105
(off Post Office La.)
Peacock Rd. OX3: Head .2C 78
Peaks La. OX29: Stone .3A 40
Pearce Ct. OX9: Tha .4H 123
Pearce Dr. OX7: Chip N .6H 23
Pearces Mdw. RG9: Nett .1H 131
Pearces Orchard
RG9: Hen T .2C 138
Pearce Way OX9: Tha .5K 123
Pear Tree Cl. OX7: Milt W .5G 35
Peartree Cl. OX4: Blac L .5J 85
Pear Tree Hill Rdbt.
OX2: Wolv .2F 73
PEASEMORE .3D 147
Peat Moor La. OX13: Marc .1A 90
Peat Moors OX3: Head .5G 79
Pebble Hill Mobile Home Pk.
OX14: Rad .1B 88
Peeble Dr. OX11: Did .3D 110
Peel Cl. OX29: Duck .5G 49
Peel Pl. OX1: Oxf .1A 84
OX18: Cart .5D 46
Peep-O-Day La.
OX14: Abin, S Cou .6F 91
Peers Sports Cen. .3F 85
Pegasus Ct. OX4: Blac L .4J 85
Pegasus Grange OX1: Oxf .6K 77
Pegasus Rd. OX4: Blac L .4H 85
Pegasus Theatre .6C 78
Pelham Rd. OX9: Tha .3K 123
Pelican Pl. OX29: Eyn .4D 70
Pembroke Ct. OX4: Oxf .5C 78
Pembroke Ho. OX17: Add .4K 19
Pembroke La. OX14: Milt .4D 96
Pembroke Pl. OX18: Bamp .1H 57
Pembroke Sq.
OX1: Oxf .6F 5 (5K 77)
Pembroke St. OX1: Oxf .5F 5 (4K 77)
Pembroke Way OX26: Bic .7F 31
Pemscott Cl. OX18: Alv .3G 55
Pendle Ct. OX29: Stone .3A 40
Pendon Mus. .1F 99
Penfield OX7: Over N .3J 23
Penfold Ct. OX3: Head .7E 74
(off Sutton Rd.)
PENHILL .2A 146
Pen La. OX13: Spri .1G 87
OX14: Abin .3G 87
Penley Cl. OX39: Chin .2F 125
PENN .1D 149
Penn Cl. OX14: Abin .5K 87
Pennington Dr. OX9: Tha .3K 123
PENN STREET .1D 149
Pennycress Rd. OX4: Blac L .4K 85
Pennyfarthing Pl. OX1: Oxf .5E 4
Pennygreen La. OX10: B Sot .7D 100
Pennyhooks La. SN6: Shriv .3A 64
Pennypiece RG8: Gor .5C 132
PENNYROYAL .1K 133
Pennywell Dr. OX2: Oxf .3J 73
Penpont Water OX11: Did .7D 98
Penrhyn Cl. OX16: Ban .6A 10
Penrose Cl. OX16: Ban .7C 10
Penrose Dr. OX16: Ban .7C 10
Pensclose OX28: Wit .3G 51
Pensfield OX10: Ben .5K 101
Penshurst Ct. OX4: Oxf .6C 78
Penson's Gdns.
OX4: Oxf .5K 5 (4B 78)
Penstones Ct. SN7: Stan V .6C 62
Pentagon, The OX14: Abin .1J 91
Pen Way OX16: Ban .4D 10
PEPPARD COMMON .2G 135
Peppard Hill
RG9: Pep C, Roth P .2H 135
Peppard La. RG9: Hen T .6C 138
Peppard Rd.
RG4: Emm G, Sonn C .4H 135
Pepper All. OX16: Ban .7F 11
Peppercorn Av. OX3: Head .5H 79
Percy St. OX4: Oxf .7C 78
Peregrine Rd. OX4: Blac L .4G 85
Peregrine Way OX12: Gro .1G 105
OX26: Bic .3G 33
Periam Cl. RG9: Hen T .5B 138
Perimeter Rd. OX11: Chilt .5H 119
Periwinkle Pl. OX4: Blac L .4J 85
Perkins OX1: Kenn .4A 84
Perkins Cl. OX15: Horn .2C 8
Perpetual Pk. RG9: Hen T .5E 138
Perpetual Pk. Dr.
RG9: Hen T .5E 138
Perrin St. OX3: Head .3F 79
Perrot Cl. OX29: N Leigh .4A 52
Perry's Rd. SN7: Stan V .5B 62
Perseverance Hill
RG9: Harp .7A 138
Peterley Rd. OX4: Cow .7J 79
Peters Way OX4: Litt .3F 85
Pether Rd. OX3: Head .4H 79
Pethers Piece OX18: Burf .4B 38
Petre Pl. OX5: Kidl .2G 69
Pettiwell OX44: Gars .7C 126
PHEASANTS HILL .2C 149
Pheasant Wlk. OX4: Litt .5D 84
Phelps, The OX5: Kidl .3E 68
Phelps Pl. OX4: Oxf .4C 78
Philcote St. OX15: Dedd .6C 20
Phipps Rd. OX4: Cow .2G 85
Phoebe Ct. OX2: Oxf .7H 73
Phoenix Picture House
.1C 4 (2J 77)
Phyllis Chiltern Mus. .3J 113
(off St Peter's Pl.)
Phyllis Ct. Dr. RG9: Hen T .2D 138
Pickenfield OX9: Tha .5K 123
Pickett Av. OX3: Head .6H 79
Picklers Hill OX14: Abin .5H 87
PIDDINGTON
Bicester .2B 144
High Wycombe .1D 149
Pieces, The OX18: Bamp .2H 57
Piers Row OX15: Dedd .6B 20
Pigeon Ho. La.
OX29: Chu H, Free .5H 53
Piggy La. OX26: Bic .2E 32
Pike Ter. OX1: Oxf .6E 4 (5K 77)
Pilcher Ct. OX4: Oxf .4C 78
(off St Clements St.)
Pilgrims Cl. SN6: Watch .2F 65
PILLERTON HERSEY .2A 140
PILLERTON PRIORS .2A 140
Pimpernel Cl. OX4: Blac L .4K 85
Pine Cl. OX4: Blac L .3J 85
OX26: Bic .5F 31
OX44: Gars .5B 126
Pinecroft OX18: Cart .5D 46
Pine Ri. OX28: Wit .2H 51
Pines, The SN7: F'don .3B 56
Pine Woods La.
OX13: Longw .3A 60
Pingle Dr. OX26: Bic .2D 32
Pinhill Rd. OX16: Ban .6D 10
Pinkhill La. OX29: Eyn .6D 70
Pinkhill Meadow Nature Reserve
.2F 59
PINKNEYS GREEN .2D 149
Pinnocks Way OX2: Bot .5B 76
Pinsley Rd. OX29: L Han .3J 53
Pioneer Rd. OX26: Bic .5G 33
SN7: F'don .4C 56
Pipe Line OX16: Ban .5F 11
Pipers Cft. OX16: Ban .2C 12
Piper St. OX3: Head .3G 79
Pipit Cl. OX4: Blac L .5H 85
Pipits Cft. OX26: Bic .3G 33
Pipkin Way OX4: Oxf .7D 78
Pipley Furlong OX4: Litt .4E 84
PISHILL .2C 149
PITCHCOTT .1C 145
PITCH GREEN .3C 145
Pitmaston Cl. OX16: Ban .4B 10
Pitreavie Av. OX18: Cart .3E 46
PITSTONE .2D 145
Pitt Rivers Mus.
Banbury Rd. .1K 77
South Parks Rd. .2F 5 (3K 77)
Pitts Rd. OX3: Head .2H 79
Pixey Pl. OX2: Oxf .4G 73
Pixton Cl. OX11: Did .2A 110
Plain, The OX4: Oxf .5K 5 (4B 78)
Plain Rd., The
OX15: Bals, Shut .1H 15
Plane Tree Way OX20: Woods .3J 41
Plantation, The OX17: Crop .2J 7
Plantation Rd.
OX2: Oxf .1C 4 (2J 77)
Plater Dr. OX2: Oxf .1H 77
Players Theatre, The .4H 123
Playfield Rd. OX1: Kenn .7B 84
Playford Ct. OX9: Tha .4H 123
PLAY HATCH .3C 149
Playhouse Theatre
Oxford .3E 4
Playing Cl., The OX7: Charlb .5B 36
Pleck La. OX39: K Blou .4H 125
Plot Rd. OX15: Shut .1H 15
Plough Cl. OX2: Oxf .4G 73
OX10: Shil .3G 101
Plough Cnr. OX39: Syd .5D 124
Plough La. RG9: Shipl .5F 139
Ploughley Cl. OX5: Kidl .3E 68
OX27: Ardl .6C 28
Ploughley Rd.
OX25: Amb, Lwr A .1F 45
Plover Dr. OX4: Blac L .5H 85
Plowden Pk. OX49: A Row .6F 125
Plowden Way RG9: Shipl .6G 139
Plumbe Ct. OX12: Wan .4G 105
Plum La. OX7: Ship W .7J 35
PLUMPTON .2C 141
Plym Dr. OX11: Did .7D 98
Pochard Pl. OX4: Blac L .5J 85
Pocock's Cl. OX18: Bamp .2H 57
POFFLEY END .1K 49 (2C 143)
Poffley End La. OX29: Hail .2K 49
Polecat End La. OX33: For H .1E 80
POLLICOTT .2C 145
Pollocks La. OX10: N Sto .2K 117
Polstead Rd. OX2: Oxf .1J 77
Pond Cl. OX3: Head .2K 79
Pond End Rd. RG4: Sonn C .4J 135
Pond Hill OX29: Stone .3A 40
Pond La. RG4: Map .6C 136
Ponds La. OX3: Mars .6C 74
Pony Rd. OX4: Cow .7J 79
Pooles La. OX7: Charlb .5B 36
Poolside Cl. OX16: Ban .1D 12
Pope's Piece OX28: Wit .3D 50
POPESWOOD .3D 149
Poplar Cl. OX5: Kidl .4G 69
OX16: Ban .4G 13
OX44: Gars .5B 126
Poplar Farm Cl. OX7: Milt W .5F 35
Poplar Farm Rd. OX44: Chal .1C 128
Poplar Gro. OX1: Kenn .5B 84
Poplar Rd. OX2: Bot .4D 76
Poplars, The OX26: Laun .1K 33
Poppylands OX26: Bic .6D 30
Portal Dr. OX25: Up H .4J 27
Portal Dr. Nth. OX25: Up H .4H 27
Portal Dr. Sth. OX25: Up H .5J 27
Port Hill RG9: Nett .1F 131
Port Hill Rd. OX10: Ben .4A 102
Portland Pl. OX7: Chip N .5J 23
Portland Rd. OX2: Oxf .5J 73
OX15: Milc .2J 17
Port Way
OX10: Crow G .6K 113 & 4B 130
OX10: Ips .4A 130
OX12: Wan, W Loc .5K 105
OX25: Caul, Lwr H, Up H .7F 27
Portway OX5: Kirt .1C 42
OX11: Did .3K 109
OX12: Wan .6G 105
OX16: Ban .5C 10
SN7: F'don .3C 56
Portway M. OX12: Wan .6G 105
POSTCOMBE .1F 129 (1C 149)
Post Office La.
OX12: Letc R .2G 119
OX12: Wan .6G 105
Potenger Way OX14: Abin .2E 90
Potkiln La. RG8: Gor H .4B 134
POTSGROVE .1D 145
Potters Ct. OX4: Blac L .5H 85
(off Robin Pl.)
Potters La. OX10: Ewel .7G 103
POTTERSPURY .2D 141
Pottery Flds. RG9: Nett .2J 131
Pottery Piece OX4: Blac L .5H 85
Pottle Cl. OX2: Bot .4C 76
Pott's Cl. OX44: G Mil .4F 121
Poultney Pl. OX18: Cart .4D 46
POULTON .3A 142
Poulton Pl. OX4: Blac L .3J 85
Pound, The OX10: Chol .1E 116
OX12: Wan .5K 105
OX15: Blox .2B 18
Pound Bank OX7: Sand M .4G 25
Pound Cl. OX5: Kirt .2B 42
OX5: Yarn .6C 68
OX29: Duck .5G 49
Pound Ct. OX15: Dedd .6C 20
Pound Cft. OX12: Gro .2G 105
Pound Fld. Cl. OX3: Head .7H 75
Pound Hill OX7: Charlb .5A 36
Pound La. OX10: Chol .1E 116
OX11: Upt .7K 109
OX15: Sib G .5C 14
OX18: Clan .6H 55
OX29: Cass .2H 71
OX33: Stan J .7B 120
POUNDON .1B 144
Pound Piece SN6: Ashb .5C 66
Pound Way OX4: Cow .2F 85
Powell Cl. OX33: For H .1E 80
Powell Ho. OX3: Head .4G 79
(off Old Rd.)
Powys Gro. OX16: Ban .5B 10
Preachers La.
OX1: Oxf .7E 4 (5K 77)
Prebendal Ct. OX7: Ship W .5K 35
Prescott Cl. OX16: Ban .7C 10
Prescott Way OX16: Ban .7B 10
PRESHUTE .3A 146
Prestidge Pl. OX5: Kidl .3G 69
PRESTON
Cirencester .3A 142
Marlborough .3B 146
PRESTON BISSETT .1B 144
PRESTON CAPES .1C 141
PRESTON CROWMARSH .6A 102
Preston Rd. OX14: Abin .3E 90
Prestwich Pl. OX2: Oxf .4G 77
Prestwick Burn OX11: Did .6C 98
PRESTWOOD .3D 145
Prew Cotts. OX7: G Roll .2B 22
Price Cl. OX26: Bic .7F 31
Prichard Rd. OX3: Head .2D 78
Priest Cl. RG9: Nett .1H 131
Priest End OX9: Tha .3G 123
Priest Hill La. OX29: Hail .2H 49
Priest's Moor La.
OX10: Warb .7E 94
PRIESTWOOD .3D 149
Primrose Cl. OX28: Wit .3J 51
Primrose Dr. OX26: Bic .6E 30
Primrose La. OX18: Wea .3G 57

Primrose Pl.—Road Two

Primrose Pl. OX4: Blac L 5J **85**
Primsdown Ind. Est.
OX7: Chip N 5F **23**
Prince Gro. OX14: Abin 4G **87**
Princes Ride OX20: Woods 3J **41**
PRINCES RISBOROUGH 3D 145
Princess Gdns. OX12: Gro 2F **105**
Princes St. OX4: Oxf 5C **78**
Princethorpe Dr.
OX16: Ban 6H **11**
Priors Forge OX2: Oxf 3J **73**
PRIORS HARDWICK 1B 140
PRIORS MARSTON 1B 140
Priory Cl. OX26: Bic 2F **33**
OX33: Hort 2C **120**
Priory Copse RG9: Pep C 4H **135**
Priory Ct. OX2: Oxf 3J **73**
OX26: Bic 2E **32**
Priory La. OX13: Marc 6J **61**
OX18: Burf 4B **38**
OX26: Bic 2E **32**
Priory Mead SN7: Longc 2J **65**
Priory Orchard OX12: Wan 5F **105**
Priory Rd. OX4: Litt 4F **85**
OX12: Wan 6G **105**
OX26: Bic 2F **33**
PRIORY, THE 3C 147
Priory Va. Rd. OX16: Ban 6H **11**
Pritchard Cl. OX10: Ber 2B **94**
Prospect OX29: Stone 3A **40**
Prospect Pk. OX33: Hors 6B **80**
Prospect Pl. OX49: Watl 5D **128**
Prospect Rd. OX11: Upt 7K **109**
OX16: Ban 1F **13**
Prunus Cl. OX4: Blac L 3J **85**
Puck La. OX28: Wit 3E **50**
Pudsey Cl. OX14: Abin 4F **91**
Pugg La. OX29: Eyn 5D **70**
Pugsden La. OX13: Stev 5B **96**
Pulker Cl. OX4: Cow 2F **85**
Pullens Fld. OX3: Head 3D **78**
Pullens La. OX3: Head 3D **78**
Pulling Cl. SN7: F'don 3C **56**
Puma Cl. OX10: Ben 7E **102**
Pumbro OX29: Stone 3A **40**
Pump La. OX9: Tha 4H **123**
Purcell Rd. OX3: Mars . . .1K **5** (2C **78**)
Purland Cl. OX4: Cow 7F **79**
PURLEY ON THAMES
. . . . .7A 136 (3B 148)
Purley Ri. RG8: Pur T 7J **133**
Purley Village RG8: Pur T 7A **136**
Purley Way RG8: Pang 7J **133**
Purslane OX14: Abin 7J **87**
Purslane Dr. OX26: Bic 5D **30**
PURTON 2A 146
PURTON STOKE 1A 146
PURY END 2D 141
PUSEY 1C 147
Pusey La. OX1: Oxf 3E **4** (3K **77**)
Pusey Pl. OX1: Oxf 3E **4** (3K **77**)
Pusey St. OX1: Oxf 3E **4** (3K **77**)
Putman Cl. OX9: Tha 4K **123**
Putman Pl. RG9: Hen T 4D **138**
PUTTENHAM 2D 145
Pye St. SN7: F'don 3D **56**
Pykes Cl. OX14: Abin 5J **87**
Pym Wlk. OX9: Tha 3H **123**
PYRTON 1B 148
Pyrton La. OX49: Watl 5C **128**
Pytenry Cl. OX14: Abin 4J **87**
Pytts La. OX18: Burf 4C **38**

Q

Quadrangle, The
OX20: Woods 2J **41**
OX26: Bic 2E **32**
Quadrangle Ho. OX2: Oxf 4G **73**
Quadrant, The OX14: Abin 1J **91**
QUAINTON 1C 145
Quaker La. OX10: Warb 1G **101**
Quantock Vw. OX11: Did 7K **97**
Quarhill Cl. OX7: Over N 3H **23**
QUARRENDON 2D 145
Quarry Cl. OX7: Enst 7D **24**
OX15: Blox 3A **18**
Quarry End OX5: Beg 3C **68**
Quarry High St.
OX3: Head 3H **79**
Quarry Hollow OX3: Head 3H **79**
Quarry La. OX7: Charlb 5C **36**
Quarry Rd. OX3: Head 3H **79**
OX7: Chad 1C **36**
OX13: Bay 7G **83**
OX28: Wit 1E **50**
Quarry School Pl. OX3: Head . . .3H **79**
Quartermain Cl. OX4: Oxf 7D **78**
Quartermain Rd. OX44: Chal . . .1B **128**
Quebec Rd. RG9: Hen T 5D **138**
Queen Cl. RG9: Hen T 4D **138**
Queen Elizabeth Cl.
OX11: Did 2D **110**
Queen Elizabeth Ct.
*OX29: L Han 3H **53***
(off Glyme Way)
Queen Emmas Dyke
OX28: Wit 4D **50**
Queens Av. OX5: Kidl 3H **69**
OX10: Wal 1G **113**
OX26: Bic 1E **32**
Queens Cl. OX2: Bot 5C **76**
OX9: Tha 2H **123**
OX10: Dorc T 7C **94**
OX29: Eyn 5D **70**
Queen's Cnr. OX18: Clan 6H **55**
Queens Ct. OX26: Bic 1E **32**
RG8: Gor 6C **132**
Queen's Cres. OX15: Drayt 6K **9**
Queen's Ga. OX2: Oxf 3G **73**
Queens La. OX1: Oxf 4G **5** (4A **78**)
OX29: Eyn 5D **70**
Queens Rd. OX9: Tha 5J **123**
OX10: Chol 2E **116**
OX16: Ban 1D **12**
OX18: Cart 5E **46**
Queens St. OX15: Blox 3B **18**
Queen St. OX1: Oxf 5E **4** (4K **77**)
OX10: Dorc T 7C **94**
OX14: Abin 1G **91**
OX15: Hook N 2C **16**
OX18: Bamp 2H **57**
OX29: Eyn 5D **70**
RG9: Hen T 4D **138**
Queens Way OX10: Ben 6E **102**
OX11: N Mor 2J **111**
Queensway OX11: Did 3A **110**
OX16: Ban 2D **12**
QUENINGTON 3A 142
QUICK'S GREEN 3A 148
Quintan Av. OX25: Amb 1G **45**

R

Race Farm La. OX13: K Bag 6E **60**
RACK END 6E 58 (3D 143)
Rack End OX29: Stand 6D **58**
Racquets Fitness Cen. 3H 123
Radbone Hill OX7: Over N 2J **23**
Radcliffe Camera 4G 5
Radcliffe Pl. OX3: Mars 6C **74**
Radcliffe Rd. OX4: Oxf 1C **84**
Radcliffe Sq. OX1: Oxf 4G **5** (4A **78**)
RADCLIVE 3D 141
Radcot Rd. SN7: F'don 1C **56**
Radford Cl. OX4: Oxf 3C **84**
RADLEY 4B 88 (1A 148)
Radley Rd. OX14: Abin 7H **87**
Radley Rd. Ind. Est.
OX14: Abin 6J **87**
Radley Station (Rail) 5C 88
RADNAGE 1C 149
Radnor Cl. RG9: Hen T 3D **138**
Radnor Rd. OX10: Wal 2G **113**
RADSTONE 2C 141
RADWAY 2A 140
Raghouse La.
OX27: Ardl, Frit 3D **28**
Ragnall's La. OX33: Hort 1A **120**
Rahere Rd. OX4: Cow 2F **85**
Railway Cotts. RG8: Gor 6C **132**
Railway La. OX4: Litt 4D **84**
Rainbow Way OX14: Abin 4J **87**
Ralegh Cres. OX28: Wit 5B **50**
Raleigh Pk. Rd. OX2: Bot 6F **77**
Rampion Cl. OX4: Blac L 4K **85**
Ramsay Rd. OX3: Head 2H **79**
RAMSBURY 3B 146
RAMSDEN 3G 39 (2C 143)
Ramsons Way OX14: Abin 7K **87**
Randolph St. OX4: Oxf 6C **78**
Range Rd. OX29: Wit 3A **50**
Rannal Dr. OX39: Chin 2G **125**
RATLEY 2A 140
Rattlecombe Rd. OX15: Shen 7B **8**
Rau Ct. OX27: Cave 3G **31**
Ravencroft OX26: Bic 4G **33**
Ravenscroft Rd.
RG9: Hen T 3C **138**
Ravensmead OX16: Ban 2C **12**
OX39: Chin 2H **125**
Rawdon Cl. SN7: F'don 4D **56**
Rawlins Cl. OX17: Twy 2H **19**
Rawlins Gro. OX14: Abin 7E **86**
Rawlinson Cl. OX7: Chad 1C **36**
Rawlinson Rd. OX2: Oxf 7J **73**
Rawson Cl. OX2: Oxf 3G **73**
Rawthey Av. OX11: Did 5C **98**
Ray Cl. OX11: Did 7D **98**
Raymond Rd. OX26: Bic 6C **30**
Raymund Rd. OX3: Mars 7C **74**
Raynham Cl. OX18: Cart 3E **46**
Ray Vw. OX5: Char O 6B **44**
Reade Av. OX14: Abin 7J **87**
Reade Cl. OX7: Milt W 5G **35**
Reade's La.
RG4: Gall C, Sonn C 5E **134**
READING 3C 149
Reading Rd.
OX10: Chol, Moul, Wal 5F **117**
OX10: Wal 4J **113**
OX11: Har 3D **108**
RG4: Cane E 6B **134**
RG8: Gor 6C **132**
RG8: Lwr B, Stre 6A **132**
RG8: Pang, Pur T 7H **133**
(not continuous)
RG8: Wood 1C **134**
RG9: Hen T, Shipl 4D **138**
Recreation Rd. OX20: Woods . . .3J **41**
SN6: Shriv 5B **64**
Rectory Cl. OX25: Wend 7A **32**
Rectory Cres. OX7: Mid B 7J **25**
Rectory Farm Cl.
OX12: W Han 2H **63**
Rectory La. OX11: A Tir 2J **115**
OX13: K Bag 6E **60**
OX13: Longw 2A **60**
OX20: Woods 3G **41**
OX27: Fring 3J **29**
Rectory Mdw. OX39: Chin 1H **125**
Rectory Rd. OX4: Oxf 5C **78**
OX15: Hook N 1C **16**
RG8: Stre 4A **132**
Red Bri. Hollow
OX1: Oxf, S Hink 2K **83**
Red Bri. Hollow Cvn. Site
OX1: S Hink 2K **83**
Red Copse La. OX1: Boar H 4G **83**
Red Cross Rd. RG8: Gor 6C **132**
Rede Cl. OX3: Head 4H **79**
Red Gallery, The 4H 123
Red Ho. Dr. RG4: Sonn C 5J **135**
Red Ho. Rd. OX15: Bod 6G **13**
Redland Rd. OX3: Head 7E **74**
Red La. OX10: Ips 7B **130**
RG8: Wood 1B **134**
Red Lion Sq. OX1: Oxf . . .4E **4** (4K **77**)
Red Lion St. OX17: Crop 2J **7**
Redmoor Cl. OX4: Litt 4F **85**
Redmoor Ct. OX26: Bic 7D **30**
Red Poll Cl. OX16: Ban 5C **10**
Redwing Cl. OX26: Bic 2G **33**
Redwood Cl. OX4: Blac L 4K **85**
OX13: Sthm 4D **60**
Reed Cl. OX28: Wit 2J **51**
Reedmace Cl. OX4: Blac L 4K **85**
Reedmace Rd. OX26: Bic 6E **30**
Reeds Cl. OX12: Wan 5G **105**
Regal Ct. OX26: Bic 2F **33**
Regal Henley Cinema, The . . .3D 138
Regal Way SN7: F'don 3C **56**
Regent Cinema
Wantage 6G 105
(within The Regent Shop. Mall)
Regent Gdns. OX11: Did 2E **110**
Regent M. SN7: F'don 2C **56**
Regent Shop. Mall, The
*OX12: Wan 6G **105***
(off Newbury St.)
Regent St. OX4: Oxf 7K **5** (6C **78**)
Regis Pl. OX12: Letc R 1G **119**
Reid Cl. OX16: Ban 7D **10**
Reid Pl. OX25: Up H 5H **27**
Reliance Way OX4: Oxf 6E **78**
REMENHAM 2C 149
REMENHAM HILL 2C 149
Remenham La.
RG9: Ast, Rem 3E **138**
Remenham Row RG9: Hen T . . .3E **138**
Remy Pl. OX4: Oxf 1C **84**
Renaissance Pk. OX3: Head 1H **79**
Renault Ho. OX4: Oxf 7C **78**
Rest Harrow OX4: Blac L 4J **85**
Restharrow Mead OX26: Bic 6C **30**
RESTROP 2A 146
Retreat Gdns.
OX10: Crow G 2A **130**
Rewley Abbey Ct.
OX1: Oxf 4C **4** (4J **77**)
Rewley Rd. OX1: Oxf 3B **4** (3H **77**)
Reynard Ct. *OX26: Bic 1E **32***
(off St John's St.)
Reynolds Cl. OX7: Ship W 5J **35**
Reynolds Way OX12: E Cha . . .5C **104**
OX14: Abin 3F **91**
Rhodes House 2G 5 (3K 77)
Richard Gray Ct.
OX1: Oxf 5C **4** (4J **77**)
Richards La. OX2: Oxf 5H **73**
Richardson Ct. *OX4: Oxf 4C **78***
(off Bath St.)
Richards Way OX3: Head 3J **79**
Richens Dr. OX18: Cart 5C **46**
Richman Gdns. OX16: Ban 5B **10**
Richmere Rd. OX11: Did 3C **110**
Richmond Rd.
OX1: Oxf 3D **4** (3J **77**)
Rickyard, The OX12: Ard 5C **106**
OX15: Shut 2G **15**
OX18: Ful 3D **38**
OX44: Chal 2B **128**
Rickyard Cl. OX1: Oxf 3C **4** (3J **77**)
Riddell Pl. OX2: Oxf 3H **73**
Ride, The OX13: F Hea 4J **61**
OX44: Nune C 5H **89**
Riders Way OX39: Chin 2G **125**
Ridge, The OX5: Tac 1K **37**
Ridge Cl. OX16: Ban 2F **13**
Ridgefield Rd. OX4: Oxf 6D **78**
Ridgemont Cl. OX2: Oxf 5H **73**
Ridge Way OX12: Wan 2D **104**
Ridgeway OX1: Boar H 4D **82**
Ridgeway, The OX15: Blox 2C **18**
RG9: Nett 2H **131**
SN6: Ashb 7D **66**
Ridgeway Rd. OX3: Head 2J **79**
OX11: Did 3C **110**
Ridings, The OX3: Head 4J **79**
OX5: Kidl 2E **68**
OX16: Ban 6H **11**
OX29: Lea 7G **39**
OX29: Stone 3A **40**
Ridley Rd. OX4: Cow 7H **79**
Riely Cl. OX29: L Han 2J **53**
Riley Cl. OX14: Abin 2E **90**
Riley Dr. OX16: Ban 5B **10**
Rimes Cl. OX13: K Bag 4E **60**
Rimmer Cl. OX3: Mars 7C **74**
Ringwood Rd. OX3: Head 2K **79**
Ripley Av. OX29: Min L 4C **48**
Rippington Dr. OX3: Mars 1C **78**
Rise, The OX5: Isl 6H **43**
OX17: Twy 3H **19**
OX39: K Blou 5H **125**
RISINGHURST 2K 79
Rissington Dr. OX28: Wit 4C **50**
Ritchie Ct. OX2: Oxf 4J **73**
Rivacres RG8: Whit H 2J **133**
River & Rowing Mus. 4E 138
River Cl. OX14: Abin 3F **91**
River Gdns. RG8: Pur T 7A **136**
River La. RG8: Gor 7B **132**
Rivermead Pk. OX1: Oxf 1A **84**
Rivermead Rd. OX4: Oxf 3C **84**
Riverside OX16: Ban 1G **13**
Riverside Ct. OX1: Oxf . . .7E **4** (5K **77**)
Riverside Gdns. OX28: Wit 3F **51**
Riverside Pk. & Pools 1A 130
Riverside Rd. OX2: Oxf 4G **77**
River Ter. RG9: Hen T 3D **138**
River Vw. OX1: Kenn 5B **84**
OX10: S Hil 5G **101**
Riverview OX4: Sand T 7D **84**
Riverview Rd. RG8: Pang 7G **133**
River Vw. Ter. OX14: Abin 2F **91**
Rivy Cl. OX14: Abin 7K **87**
ROADE 1D 141
Road One OX11: Chilt 6F **119**
Road Two OX11: Chilt 6F **119**

Salisbury Cres.—Skirmett

Salisbury Cres. OX2: Oxf 4J 73
Sallow Cl. OX26: Bic 5F 31
Salmon Cl. OX15: Blox 1D 18
Salop Cl. SN6: Shriv 6B 64
SALPERTON 1A 142
Salter Cl. OX1: Oxf 6K 77
Salt La. OX9: Post 2F 129
Salt Way OX15: Brou 3A 12
OX16: Ban 3D 12
Salvia Cl. OX16: Ban 4C 10
Samian Way OX10: Dorc T 1C 100
Samor Way OX11: Did 2A 110
Samphire Rd. OX4: Blac L 4J 85
Samuelson Ct. OX16: Ban 1F 13
Sandell Cl. OX16: Ban 1D 12
Sanderling Cl. OX26: Bic 3F 33
Sanderling Wlk. OX16: Ban 3G 13
Sanders Rd. OX4: Litt 5F 85
Sandfield Rd. OX3: Head 2E 78
Sandford Cl. OX14: Abin 5J 87
RG8: Wood 2C 134
Sandford Grn. OX16: Ban 6B 10
Sandford La. OX1: Kenn 7B 84
Sandford La. Ind. Est.
OX1: Kenn 7C 84
Sandford Link Rd.
OX4: Litt, Sand T 4D 84
OX44: Nune C 4D 84
SANDFORD-ON-THAMES 6D 84 (3A 144)
Sandford Pk. OX7: Charlb 6C 36
Sandford Ri. OX7: Charlb 6C 36
Sandford Rd. OX4: Litt 5D 84
SANDFORD ST MARTIN 5G 25 (1D 143)
Sandford St. OX7: Westc B 6G 25
Sand Hill SN6: Shriv 5A 64
Sandhill Rd. OX5: Beg 3B 68
SANDHILLS 1K 79 (3A 144)
Sand La. OX3: Beck 2K 75
Sandleigh Rd. OX13: Woot 1B 86
Sandpiper Cl. OX26: Bic 3G 33
Sandpit Hill MK18: Tin 6K 21
Sandpit La. RG4: Duns G 7G 137
Sandringham Rd. OX11: Did 2D 110
Sands, The OX7: Milt W 5G 35
OX10: Ben, Rok 4B 102
Sands Cl. OX2: C'nor 5J 59
OX5: Blet 6C 42
Sands Hill SN7: F'don 5C 56
Sands La. OX15: S New 5H 17
Sands Rd. OX11: S Mor 4J 111
Sands Way OX10: Ben 4A 102
Sand Vw. SN7: F'don 4C 56
Sandy La. OX1: Boar H 5C 82
OX4: Blac L 3H 85
OX5: Yarn 4C 68
OX9: Milt C, Tid 4B 122
OX10: Chol 2D 116
OX13: Sthm 4D 60
OX33: Hors 6C 80
SN6: Shriv 6B 64
Sandy La. W. OX4: Litt 3F 85
Sarajac Av. OX12: E Cha 6C 104
SARSDEN 4D 34 (1B 142)
Sarsden Cl. OX7: Chad 1C 36
SARSDEN HALT 1A 34
Sarsden Rd. OX7: C'hill 3C 34
Sarum Cl. OX18: Briz N 4F 47
SATWELL 1F 137 (2C 149)
Satwell Cl. RG9: Roth G 1G 137
Saunders Cl. OX49: Watl 5D 128
Saunders Rd. OX4: Oxf 7E 78
SAUNDERTON 3C 145
SAUNDERTON LEE 1D 149
Savile Rd. OX1: Oxf 3G 5 (3A 78)
Savile Way OX12: Gro 1F 105
Saw Cl. OX44: Chal 1B 128
Sawpit Rd. OX4: Blac L 3H 85
Saxel Cl. OX18: Ast 6H 57
Saxifrage Sq. OX4: Blac L 5H 85
Saxon Cl. OX10: Wal 3H 113
Saxon Ct. OX3: Head 2F 79
OX10: Ben 5A 102
OX26: Bic 2F 33
Saxon Orchard SN6: Watch 2D 64
Saxon Pl. OX12: Wan 5E 104
RG8: Pang 7H 133
Saxons Cl. GL7: Fil 3A 54
Saxons Heath OX14: L Wit 2G 99
Saxons Way OX11: Did 3D 110
Saxon Way OX3: Head 7E 74
OX28: Wit 5E 50
Saxton Rd. OX14: Abin 3E 90
Sayers Orchard OX11: Did 1A 110
Scampton Cl. OX26: Bic 7H 31
Schilling St. OX25: Up H 4G 27
Schofield Av. OX28: Wit 1E 49
Schofield Gdns. OX28: Wit 1E 50
Schofields Way OX15: Blox 2C 18
Scholar Cl. SN6: Watch 2F 65
Scholar Pl. OX2: Bot 6D 76
Scholars Acre OX18: Cart 3D 46
Scholars M. OX2: Oxf 6J 73
Schongau Cl. OX14: Abin 4E 90
School Cl. OX13: Longw 2B 60
OX13: Stev 5A 96
School Ct. OX2: Oxf 2C 4 (3J 77)
Schoolfields RG9: Shipl 5G 139
School Hill OX17: Moll 6B 6
OX29: Min L 3D 48
School La. OX11: Har 3F 109
OX12: Gro 1G 105
OX13: K Bag 4D 60
OX14: A'frd 1C 98
OX14: Milt 6D 96
(not continuous)
OX16: Ban 7E 10
OX17: G Bou 5G 7
OX18: Blac B 3K 55
OX25: M'ton S 5G 29
OX25: Up H 4F 27
OX29: Min L 3C 48
OX44: Stad 5H 127
OX49: A Row 6G 125
RG9: Stoke R 6H 131
School Paddock OX27: Buck 2A 30
School Pl. OX1: Oxf 7K 77
School Rd. OX5: Kidl 2F 69
OX7: Fins 1J 39
OX12: Ard 5C 106
OX12: W Han 3H 63
School Vw. OX16: Ban 7H 11
School Yd. OX44: Stad 5H 127
Science Pk. OX14: Abin 1J 91
SCOTLAND END 2B 16 (3A 140)
Scotland End OX15: Hook N 2B 16
Scotsgrove Cotts. OX9: Tha 1J 123
Scotsgrove Hill OX9: Tha 1J 123
Scott Cl. OX5: Kidl 3E 68
OX26: Bic 7C 30
Scott Rd. OX2: Oxf 4J 73
Scrutton Cl. OX3: Head 2H 79
Seacourt Rd. OX2: Bot 4D 76
Seacourt Twr. OX2: Bot 4E 76
Sealham Rd. OX29: Duck 5G 49
Second Av. OX11: Did 7A 98
Second St. OX11: Har 7D 108
Sedgefield Cl. RG4: Sonn C 4H 135
Sedgemoor Dr. OX9: Tha 3J 123
Sedgewell Rd.
RG4: Sonn C 4H 135
Seelscheid Way OX26: Bic 4G 33
Seesen Way OX12: Wan 5H 105
Sefton Pl. OX15: Bod 7G 13
Sefton Rd. OX3: Head 2H 79
Segsbury Ct. OX12: Wan 5E 104
Segsbury Rd. OX12: Wan 5E 104
Sellwood Dr. OX18: Cart 4E 46
Sellwood Rd. OX14: Abin 5G 87
Selwyn Cres. OX14: Rad 5B 88
Sermon Cl. OX3: Head 3J 79
Seven Acres OX9: Tha 4J 123
SEVENHAMPTON 1B 146
Seventeenth St. OX11: Har 5F 119
Seventh Av. OX3: Head 5J 79
Severalls Cl. OX10: Wal 1J 113
Severn Cl. OX26: Bic 7B 30
Severn Cres. OX11: Did 2D 110
Severn Rd. OX11: Chilt 6G 119
OX13: Shipp 5E 86
Sewell Cl. OX14: Abin 6K 87
Sewell's La. OX39: Syd 6C 124
SHABBINGTON 3B 144
Shackleton Cl. OX26: Bic 6G 31
Shades, The OX16: Ban 1E 12
(not continuous)
Shadwell Rd. OX10: Ber 3A 94
Shaftesbury Rd. OX3: Head 7H 75
Shakenoak OX29: N Leigh 5C 52
Shakespeare OX29: Eyn 4C 70
Shakespeare Dr. OX26: Bic 6C 30
SHALSTONE 3D 141
Shambles, The *OX9: Tha 4H 123*
(off Butter Mkt.)
Shannon Cl. OX12: Gro 1J 105
Shannon Rd. OX11: Did 2D 110
OX26: Bic 1B 32
Sharland Cl. OX12: Gro 2G 105
Sharman Beer Ct.
OX9: Tha 4G 123
SHAW 3D 147
Shaw Cl. OX26: Bic 1C 32
Shaw's Copse OX14: Rad 5C 88
Sheards La. SN7: Stan V 6C 62
Shearings, The
OX15: Hook N 2B 16
Shearwater Dr. OX26: Bic 3H 33
Sheen Cl. OX27: Cave 4F 31
Sheepstead Rd. OX13: Marc 4H 61
Sheep St. OX7: Charlb 6B 36
OX18: Burf 4A 38
OX26: Bic 1E 32
(not continuous)
Sheepwash La. OX13: Stev 4B 96
Sheepway Ct. OX4: Oxf 2D 84
Sheepways La. RG4: Map 5E 136
SHEFFORD WOODLANDS 3C 147
Sheldonian Theatre 3G 5 (4A 78)
Sheldons Piece
OX49: Watl 5C 128
Sheldon Way OX4: Litt 3F 85
Shelford Pl. OX3: Head 4G 79
Shelley Cl. OX3: Head 3J 79
OX14: Abin 6H 87
OX16: Ban 3C 12
OX26: Bic 7C 30
Shelley Rd. OX4: Oxf 7E 78
SHELLINGFORD 1C 147
SHENINGTON 6D 8 (2A 140)
Shepard Way OX7: Chip N 5J 23
Shepherd Gdns. OX14: Abin 2D 90
Shepherds Cl. OX12: Gro 7F 63
OX25: West G 2G 43
SHEPHERD'S GREEN 1G 137 (2C 149)
Shepherds Hill OX4: Blac L 5J 85
OX25: Stee A 3A 26
Shepstow Gdns. OX16: Ban 1B 12
Sherard Bldg., The OX4: Litt 6E 84
SHERBORNE 2A 142
SHERBOURNE 1A 140
Sherbourne Rd. OX28: Wit 4B 50
Sheriff's Dr. OX2: Oxf 4G 73
Sherwood Av. OX14: Abin 1H 91
Sherwood Cl. OX26: Laun 1K 33
Sherwood Gdns.
RG9: Hen T 5B 138
Sherwood Pl. OX3: Head 1H 79
Sherwood Rd. OX11: Did 1A 110
Shifford La. OX29: Stand 7C 58
Shifford Rd. OX29: Stand 7B 58
Shildeane Dr. OX18: Cart 3D 46
Shillbrook Av. OX18: Cart 2C 46
SHILLINGFORD 3G 101 (1A 148)
Shillingford Ct. OX10: Shil 4F 101
SHILLINGFORD HILL 5G 101
Shilson La. OX7: Charlb 6B 36
SHILTON 1B 46 (3B 142)
Shilton Rd. OX18: Burf 6C 38
OX18: Cart 1B 46
OX18: Shilt 1B 46
SHINFIELD 3C 149
Shinmoor Cl. OX11: Did 7E 98
SHIPLAKE 5G 139 (3C 149)
Shiplake Bottom
RG9: Pep C 3G 135
SHIPLAKE ROW 7K 137
Shiplake Row RG9: Bin H 7K 137
SHIPPON 6D 86 (1D 147)
SHIPSTON-ON-STOUR 2A 140
Ship St. OX1: Oxf 4F 5 (4K 77)
SHIPTON 1C 145
Shipton Ct. OX7: Ship W 6J 35
SHIPTON-ON-CHERWELL 2D 143
Shipton Rd.
OX7: Asc W, Ship W 7K 35 & 4F 35
OX7: Milt W 5G 35
OX20: Woods 3J 41
Shipton Station (Rail) 4K 35
SHIPTON-UNDER-WYCHWOOD 6J 35 (2B 142)
SHIRBURN 1B 148
Shireburn Rd. OX49: Watl 5E 128
Shireburn St. OX49: Watl 5E 128
Shirelake Cl. OX1: Oxf 7F 5
Shirley Pl. OX2: Oxf 1C 4 (2J 77)
Shirvell's Hill RG8: Gor H 3A 134
Shoe La. OX1: Oxf 5E 4 (4K 77)
OX11: E Hag 5C 110
(off Up. Cross La.)
Shooter's Hill RG8: Pang 6F 133
Short, The RG8: Pur T 7A 136
Shorte Cl. OX3: Head 6H 79
Short Furlong OX11: Did 7E 98
SHORTHAMPTON 1C 143
Shortlands Hill OX10: Moul 7B 116
Short St. RG8: Pang 7H 133
SN6: Watch 3D 64
Shotover OX3: Head 3K 79
Shotover Country Pk. 6J 79
Shotover Kilns OX3: Head 4J 79
Shotover Trad. Est.
OX3: Head 4J 79
SHOTTESWELL 2B 140
Shrewsbury Pl. OX18: Bamp 2G 57
Shrieves Cl. *OX14: Abin 4J 87*
(off Bucklers Bury Rd.)
SHRIVENHAM 6B 64 (2B 146)
Shrivenham Hundred Bus. Pk.
SN6: Watch 2C 64
Shrivenham Rd. SN7: Longc 3J 65
SHURLOCK ROW 3D 149
Shute Av. SN6: Watch 4D 64
SHUTFORD 2H 15 (2A 140)
Shutford Rd.
OX15: Lwr T, Shut 2J 15 & 4K 15
SHUTLANGER 2D 141
SIBFORD FERRIS 6D 14 (3A 140)
SIBFORD GOWER 5C 14 (3A 140)
Sibford Rd. OX15: Hook N 1C 16
OX15: Shut 4F 15
Sibthorp Rd. OX1: Oxf 1G 5 (2A 78)
Sideleigh Rd. OX15: Bod 6G 13
Sidings, The OX10: Wal 3G 113
Sidings Rd. OX7: C'hill 2B 34
Sidney Harrison Ho.
RG9: Shipl 4K 139
Sidney St. OX4: Oxf 6C 78
SIGNET 7B 38 (2B 142)
Signet End OX18: Burf 6C 38
SIGNET HILL 6A 38
Silkdale Cl. OX4: Cow 1G 85
Silver Birches OX33: Stan J 7D 120
Silver La. OX12: W Chal 5A 104
OX15: Wrox 6H 9
Silver Rd. OX4: Oxf 6D 78
SILVERSTONE 2D 141
Silver St. OX9: Tet 6C 122
SN6: B'ton 3C 66
SN7: Fern 2H 67
Simmonds Wlk. *OX12: Wan 4G 105*
(off Witan Way)
Simmons Rd. RG9: Hen T 2C 138
Simmons Way OX9: Tha 3H 123
Simon Ho. OX3: Head 2G 79
Simon's Cl. OX33: Wheat 5F 81
Simons La. OX7: Ship W 7J 35
Simpsons Way OX1: Kenn 6B 84
Sinclair Av. OX16: Ban 6B 10
Sinclair Dr. OX16: Ban 6C 10
SINDLESHAM 3C 149
Singers Cl. RG9: Hen T 5D 138
Singers La. RG9: Hen T 5D 138
SINGLEBOROUGH 1C 145
Singletree OX4: Oxf 2E 84
Sinnels Fld. OX7: Ship W 6K 35
Sinnet Ct. OX4: Oxf 5D 78
Sinodun Cl. OX14: L Wit 2G 99
Sinodun Dr. OX10: Wal 1G 113
Sinodun Rd. OX11: Did 3C 110
Sinodun Vw. OX10: Warb 1G 101
Sint Niklaas Cl. OX14: Abin 4E 90
Sires Hill OX10: B Sot 4J 99
OX11: N Mor 4J 99
OX14: L Wit 4F 99
Sir Georges La. OX17: Add 4H 19
Sir Henry Cl. OX16: Ban 3D 10
Siskin Rd. OX26: Bic 2G 33
Sixpenny La. OX44: Chal 2D 128
Sixteenth St. OX11: Har 7C 108
Sixth St. OX11: Har 7C 108
Skarries Vw. RG4: Tok 2B 136
Skene Cl. OX3: Head 4F 79
Skimmingdish La. OX27: Bic 5G 31
OX27: Cave 4F 31
Skinner Rd. OX26: Laun 1K 33
Skippett La. OX7: Rams 2G 39
Skippon Way OX9: Tha 2H 123
SKIRMETT 1C 149

176 A-Z Oxfordshire Atlas

Thames St.—Upthorpe Dr.

Thames St. OX1: Oxf 6D 4 (5J 77)
OX7: Charlb 5B 36
OX10: Wal 3J 113
OX14: Abin 2G 91
OX29: Eyn 5D 70
Thames Vw. OX14: Abin 1H 91
Thames Vw. Ind. Pk.
OX14: Abin 1H 91
Thames Vw. Rd. OX4: Oxf 4C 84
Thame Tennis Club 4K 123
Thanksgiving La.
RG9: Bin H 6G 137
THATCHAM 3A 148
Thatchers Cl. OX15: Epwell 2B 14
The . . . .
Names prefixed with 'The' for example 'The Approach' are indexed under the main name such as 'Approach, The'
THEALE 3B 148
Theatre, The 5H 23
Thelwall Ho. OX4: Oxf 6E 78
THENFORD 2C 141
Thesiger Rd. OX14: Abin 7G 87
Third Acre Ri. OX2: Bot 5C 76
Third St. OX11: Har 5G 119
Thirteenth St. OX11: Har 5F 119
Thistlecroft Cl. OX14: Abin 5J 87
Thistledown Cl. OX4: Blac L 6H 85
Thistle Dr. OX4: Blac L 4K 85
Thompson Av. OX11: Har 7C 108
Thompson Dr. OX27: Cave 3F 31
Thomson Ter. OX4: Litt 4D 84
THORNBOROUGH 1C 145
Thornbury Ri. OX16: Ban 1B 12
Thornbury Rd. OX29: Eyn 5C 70
Thorncliffe Rd. OX2: Oxf 6J 73
Thorne Cl. OX5: Kidl 2D 68
RG9: Hen T 6A 138
Thorney La. OX28: Wit 5B 50
Thorney Leys OX28: Wit 5C 50
Thorney Leys Ind. Pk.
OX28: Wit 6D 50
Thornhill Cl. OX12: Wan 5G 105
Thornhill Wlk. OX14: Abin 6F 87
Thorningdown OX11: Chilt 7J 119
THORNTON 3D 141
Thorpe Cl. OX16: Ban 7H 11
Thorpe Dr. OX16: Ban 7H 11
Thorpe La. OX16: Ban 7H 11
THORPE MANDEVILLE 2C 141
Thorpe Mead OX16: Ban 1H 13
Thorpe Pl. OX16: Ban 7H 11
Thorpes Fld. OX18: Alv 3G 55
Thorpe St. OX11: A Upt 2H 115
Thorpe Way OX16: Ban 7H 11
Three Corners Rd.
OX4: Blac L 4K 85
Three Flds. OX3: Head 5H 79
Three Gables La. RG8: Stre 5A 132
THREE MILE CROSS 3C 149
Three Pigeons Cl.
OX12: Wan 6H 105
Three Poplar Mobile Home Pk.
OX14: L Wit 1F 99
Threshers Ct. *OX18: Cart 2F 47*
(off Beech La.)
Threshers Yd. OX7: Kingh 5C 34
Thrift Pl. OX4: Blac L 4J 85
THRUPP 2D 143
Thrupp La. OX14: Rad 5A 88
Thurne Vw. OX11: Did 1D 110
Thurston Cl. OX14: Abin 2F 91
Tiburn Glen OX11: Did 7C 98
Tichborne OX9: Tha 4J 123
Ticknell Piece Rd.
OX7: Charlb 5C 36
TIDDINGTON 1B 122 (3B 144)
TIDMARSH 3B 148
Tidmarsh La. OX1: Oxf . . .5D 4 (4J 77)
Tidmarsh Rd. RG8: Pang 7G 133
TIDMINGTON 3A 140
Tidmore La. RG8: Wood 1C 134
TIFFIELD 1D 141
Tilbury La. OX2: Bot 3C 76
Tilebarn Cl. RG9: Hen T 4B 138
Tilebarn La. RG9: Hen T 4B 138
Tilehouse Cl. OX3: Head 2H 79
TILEHURST 3B 148
Tilgarsley Rd. OX29: Eyn 4C 70
Tilsley Pk. (Sports Pk.) 4F 87
Tilsley Rd. OX7: Chip N 7G 23
Timber Way OX39: Chin 2G 125
Timms Rd. OX16: Ban 4F 13
Timothy Way OX4: Blac L 4J 85
TINGEWICK 3D 141
Tinkerbush La. OX12: Wan 4G 105
TINKER'S GREEN 4E 136
Tinker's La. OX17: Moll 6C 6
Tirrold Way OX12: Wan 5J 105
Titchener Cl. OX26: Bic 6D 30
Tite La. OX15: Hook N 2C 16
Tithe Ct. OX16: Ban 1C 12
Tithe La. OX17: Add 7K 19
Tithings, The OX15: Swal 6F 15
Titup Hall Dr. OX3: Head 4H 79
TOKERS GREEN 2B 136 (3C 149)
Tokers Grn. La.
RG4: Ked E . . . . .7F 135 & 1B 136
Tollbrook Cnr. OX5: Blet 6D 42
Tollgate Ho. *OX26: Bic 1E 32*
(off North St.)
Tollgate Rd. OX14: Cul 6J 91
Tollington Ct. SN7: F'don 5B 56
Tolsey Mus. 4C 38
Tom Brown's School Mus. 6G 67
TOOT BALDON 1K 89 (3A 144)
Toot Hill Butts OX3: Head 2H 79
Topples La. OX7: Fins 1K 39
Torridge Dr. OX11: Did 7D 98
Tothill OX7: Ship W 5J 35
TOUCHEN-END 3D 149
Tourist Info. Cen.
Abingdon 2G 91
Banbury 7F 11
Bicester 3E 32
Burford 4C 38
Cherwell Valley Service Area
. . . . .5E 28
Didcot 1C 110
Faringdon 2C 56
Henley-on-Thames 3C 138
Kidlington 3F 69
Oxford 4F 5 (4K 77)
Thame 4H 123
Wallingford 3J 113
(within Town Hall)
Witney 4F 51
(off High St.)
Woodstock 3G 41
TOWCESTER 2D 141
Tower Cen., The OX18: Cart 5E 46
Tower Cl. OX13: Marc 6J 61
OX14: Abin 2E 90
Tower Ct. *OX18: Cart 5D 46*
(off Alvescot Rd.)
OX28: Wit 3D 50
Tower Gdns. OX11: Did 7K 97
Tower Hill OX28: Wit 3D 50
Tower Rd. OX10: Ber 2C 94
TOWERSEY 2D 124 (3C 145)
Towersey Dr. OX9: Tha 5K 123
Towersey Rd. OX9: Tha 4K 123
Tower Vw. SN7: F'don 4C 56
Town Cl. OX14: S Cou 2H 97
Town End OX29: Hail 1J 49
Town End Rd. SN7: F'don 4D 56
Town Farm Cl. OX9: Tha 4F 123
Townfarm Cl. OX49: Lewk 6H 129
Town Furlong OX13: A'ton 1H 61
OX15: Bod 6F 13
Town Furze OX3: Head 6G 79
Town Grn., The OX5: Kidl 2G 69
Town Hall & Oxford Mus.
. . . . .5F 5 (4K 77)
Town Pond La. OX13: Sthm 5C 60
TOWNSEND 6E 104
Townsend OX11: Chilt 6J 119
OX11: Har 2F 109
OX14: Abin 3G 91
OX15: Bar M 3C 20
OX16: Ban 7D 10
Townsend Rd. RG8: Stre 5A 132
SN6: Shriv 7A 64
Townsend Sq. OX4: Oxf 7C 78
Town Well End OX27: Frit 2C 28
Toy La. OX7: Chip N 6F 23
Toynbee Cl. OX2: Bot 5E 76
Trafford Rd. OX3: Head 2H 79
Trajan Ho. OX2: Oxf 6B 4 (5H 77)
Tramway Ind. Est., The
OX16: Ban 1G 13
Tramway Rd. OX16: Ban 1G 13
Transport Way OX4: Cow 3J 85
TRASH GREEN 3B 148
Treadwells SN7: Stan V 6C 62
TREDINGTON 2A 140
Treeground Pl. OX5: Kidl 3F 69
Tree La. OX4: Oxf 2C 84
Trefoil Dr. OX26: Bic 6C 30
Trefoil Pl. OX4: Blac L 4K 85
Trefoil Way OX18: Cart 2F 47
Trenchard Av. OX14: Milt 6D 96
Trenchard Circ.
OX25: Up H 3K 27
Trenchard Cl. OX10: Wal 3H 113
TRENCH GREEN 5E 136
Trent Cres. OX26: Bic 7B 30
Trent Rd. OX11: Did 7D 98
Trevor Pl. OX4: Cow 1E 84
Triangle, The OX15: Hook N 2C 16
OX33: Wheat 5H 81
Trill Mill Ct. OX1: Oxf 7F 5 (5K 77)
Trinder Rd. OX12: Wan 6H 105
TRING 2D 145
Trinity Cl. OX14: Abin 5J 87
OX16: Ban 6A 10
OX26: Bic 7F 31
RG9: Hen T 4C 138
Trinity Rd. OX3: Head 3J 79
Trinity St. OX1: Oxf 7D 4 (5J 77)
Trinity Way OX17: Add 4K 19
Tristram Rd. OX29: Duck 5G 49
Troika Cl. OX16: Ban 4C 10
Trot's La. OX7: Ship W 7J 35
Troy Cl. OX3: Head 6H 79
Troy La. OX5: Kirt 3B 42
Truelocks Way OX12: Wan 4J 105
Truemper Gro. OX27: Cave 3F 31
Trust Cnr. RG9: Hen T 5D 138
Tubb Cl. OX26: Bic 1C 32
Tubbs Cl. OX12: Gro 2G 105
Tubbs La. OX26: Ches 4A 32
TUBNEY 1D 147
Tucker Rd. OX4: Blac L 3H 85
Tuckers Rd. SN7: F'don 3D 56
Tuck's La. OX13: Longw 1B 60
Tudor Cl. OX4: Oxf 2C 84
OX10: Wal 3H 113
OX16: Ban 4F 13
Tudor Ct. OX2: Bot 5B 76
Tudor Ct. Pk. OX2: Bot 5B 76
Tuer, The *OX29: Eyn 5D 70*
(off High St.)
Tullis Cl. OX14: S Cou 2G 97
Tulwick La. OX12: Gro 7H 63
Tumbledown Hill OX2: C'nor 4H 59
Tumbling Bay Ct. OX2: Oxf 4A 4
Tuns La. RG9: Hen T 3D 138
Turberville Cl. OX14: Abin 2F 91
TURKDEAN 2A 142
Turl St. OX1: Oxf 4F 5 (4K 77)
Turn Again La.
OX1: Oxf 6E 4 (5K 77)
Turnagain La. OX14: Abin 2G 91
Turnberry Cl. OX26: Bic 6G 31
Turner Cl. OX4: Cow 7G 79
Turner Rd. OX14: Abin 3E 90
Turners Cl. OX14: Rad 5C 88
Turner's Grn. OX49: Bri S 7A 128
Turner's Grn. La.
OX49: Bri S . . . . .1K 103 & 7A 128
Turnpike Rd. OX2: Bot 7C 76
OX27: Cave 4G 31
Turnstone Grn. OX26: Bic 3G 33
TURVILLE 1C 149
TURVILLE HEATH 1C 149
TURWESTON 3D 141
TUTTS CLUMP 3A 148
Tweed Cres. OX26: Bic 7B 30
Tweed Dr. OX11: Did 5C 98
Twelfth St. OX11: Har 7C 108
Twelve Acre Dr. OX14: Abin 4J 87
Twentieth St. OX11: Har 7A 108
Twitchers All. *OX26: Bic 1E 32*
(off Field St.)
Two Rivers Ind. Est.
OX28: Wit 6F 51
Two Tree Hill RG9: Hen T 5A 138
TWYFORD
Banbury 1H 19
Buckingham 1B 144
Reading 3C 149
Twyford Av. OX17: Twy 1H 19
Twyford Gdns. OX17: Twy 1H 19
Twyford Gro. OX17: Twy 1H 19
Twyford Rd. OX17: Twy 1H 19
Twynhams Rd. OX5: Tac 2K 37
Ty-Craig OX26: Bic 2F 33
TYLERS GREEN 1D 149
Tyndale Rd. OX4: Oxf 6K 5 (5B 78)
Tyne Av. OX11: Did 7C 98
Tynedale Pl. OX33: Wheat 5H 81
Tyne Rd. OX13: Shipp 5D 86
Tyne St. OX11: Did 2D 110
Tyrell Cl. SN7: Stan V 6B 62
Tyrrells Cl. OX11: Har 4E 108
Tyrrell's Way OX14: S Cou 3F 97
Tyte End OX7: G Roll 2C 22

U

UFFCOTT 3A 146
UFFINGTON 6G 67 (2C 147)
Uffington Castle 2B 146
Uffington White Horse 2C 147
UFTON 1A 140
UFTON NERVET 3B 148
Ulfgar Rd. OX2: Oxf 4G 73
Ultimate Picture Palace, The
. . . . .6K 5 (5C 78)
Underhill OX10: Moul 7E 116
Underhill Cir. OX3: Head 1J 79
Unicorn St. OX15: Blox 3B 18
Unicorn Theatre 1H 91
Union Sq. OX20: Woot 7H 37
Union St. OX4: Oxf 5C 78
OX16: Ban 7D 10
OX20: Woods 3H 41
Union Way OX28: Wit 4D 50
University Mus. 2F 5 (3K 77)
University of Oxford
(University Field Station)
. . . . .4B 72
Untons Pl. SN7: F'don 3D 56
Upavon Way OX18: Cart 6C 46
Upland Ct. OX2: Oxf 4H 73
Upland Pk. Rd. OX2: Oxf 4H 73
Uplands Ri. OX17: Lit B 7G 7
UPPER ARNCOTT 6H 45 (2B 144)
UPPER ASTROP 3C 141
Upper Barr OX4: Cow 2F 85
UPPER BASILDON 3A 148
UPPER BODDINGTON 1B 140
Up. Bolney Rd. RG9: Harp 3F 139
UPPER BRAILES 3A 140
Up. Brook Hill
OX20: Woods 3H 41
UPPER BUCKLEBURY 3A 148
Up. Campsfield Rd.
OX20: Woods 5K 41
UPPER CATESBY 1C 141
Upper Comn. La. SN7: Uff 6H 67
Upper Crale SN7: Stan V 5B 62
Upper Cres. OX29: Min L 4C 48
Up. Cross La. OX11: E Hag 5C 110
UPPER DUNSLEY 2D 145
Upper End OX7: Ship W 7J 35
OX18: Ful 2D 38
Up. Fisher Row
OX1: Oxf 4C 4 (4J 77)
Upper Grn. SN7: Stan V 5C 62
UPPER HEYFORD
Bicester 4F 27 (1D 143)
Northampton 1D 141
Up. High St. OX9: Tha 4H 123
Up. Icknield Way
HP27: Bled 1K 125
OX39: Chin 4H 125
UPPER INGLESHAM 1B 146
UPPER LAMBOURN 2C 147
Upper Mdw. OX3: Head 4H 79
UPPER NORTH DEAN 1D 149
UPPER ODDINGTON 1B 142
Up. Red Cross Rd.
RG8: Gor 6C 132
Upper Rd. OX1: Kenn 3A 84
UPPER SLAUGHTER 1A 142
UPPER STOWE 1D 141
UPPER SWELL 1A 142
UPPER TYSOE 2A 140
UPPER UPHAM 3B 146
Upper Wlk. OX44: Nune C 6H 89
UPPER WARDINGTON 2B 140
Upperway Furlong
OX11: Did 7E 98
UPPER WEEDON 1D 141
UPPER WINCHENDON 2C 145
Up. Windsor St. OX16: Ban 2E 12
UPPER WOLVERCOTE 4G 73
Upthorpe Dr. OX12: Wan 4H 105

Upton—Wentworth Rd.

UPTON
Aylesbury 2C 145
Burford 4A 38
Didcot 7K 109 (2A 148)
Northampton 1D 141
Upton Cl. OX4: Litt 4F 85
OX14: Abin 6H 87
RG9: Hen T 4D 138
Upton Ct. OX16: Ban 1E 12
Upway Rd. OX3: Head 7E 74
Upwood Dr. OX18: Cart 3E 46
Usher Dr. OX16: Ban 4B 10
Usk Way OX11: Did 6D 98
Uxmore Rd. RG8: Check 7F 131

V

Vale & Downland Mus. & Vis Cen. 6G 105
Vale Av. OX12: Gro 1H 105
Valence Cres. OX28: Wit 3B 50
Valentia Cl. OX5: Blet 6B 42
Valentia Rd. OX3: Head 3E 78
Vale Rd. OX11: Har 7C 108
OX28: Wit 4C 50
Valetta Way OX10: Ben 6E 102
Valley Cl. RG8: Gor 6C 132
Valley Rd. MK18: Fin 6J 21
OX16: Ban 2F 13
OX33: Hors 7D 80
RG9: Hen T 5A 138
Valley Vw. OX17: G Bou 4G 7
OX25: Lwr H 6E 26
Vanalloys Bus. Pk.
RG9: Stoke R 6J 131
Vanbrugh Cl. OX20: Woods 2G 41
Van Dieman's SN7: Stan V 5B 62
Van-Diemans La. OX4: Cow 3F 85
Van Dieman's Rd. OX9: Tha 5H 123
Van Diemens Cl.
OX39: Chin 1G 125
Vane Rd. OX9: Tha 4K 123
Vanner Rd. OX28: Wit 2G 51
Varsity Pl. OX1: Oxf 1A 84
Vauxhall Way OX11: Did 7A 98
Venables Cl. OX2: Oxf 1C 4 (2J 77)
Venneit Cl. OX2: Oxf 2B 4 (3H 77)
Venners Water OX11: Did 6D 98
Venn Mill 1D 147
Ventfield Cl. OX33: Hort 2B 120
Venvell Cl. OX7: Enst 7C 24
Verbena Way OX4: Blac L 5H 85
Verinia Ct. OX20: Woods 3J 41
Verlam Gro. OX11: Did 7E 98
Vermont Dr. OX20: Woods 2G 41
Vernon Av. OX2: N Hink 7F 77
Vernon Ho. OX7: Chip N 6H 23
Vervian Cl. OX26: Bic 5E 30
Vestry Cl. OX12: Gro 7F 63
Vetch Pl. OX4: Blac L 4J 85
Vicarage Cl. OX4: Litt 4E 84
OX12: Gro 1H 105
OX18: Ast 6G 57
OX44: Chal 1C 128
Vicarage Ct. OX1: Oxf 7A 78
OX16: Ban 1F 13
(off Calthorpe Rd.)
Vicarage Flats OX17: Crop 2J 7
Vicarage Gdns. OX17: Crop 2J 7
Vicarage Hill OX12: E Cha 6D 104
Vicarage La. OX1: Oxf 7K 77
SN6: Shriv 6C 64
Vicarage Rd. OX1: Oxf 7K 77
OX5: Kidl 2G 69
OX11: Did 2C 110
OX13: Stev 5A 96
RG9: Hen T 4D 138
Victoria Ct. OX1: Oxf 4E 4 (4K 77)
OX3: Head 3E 78
OX26: Bic 2F 33
RG9: Hen T 4D 138
Victoria Mead OX9: Tha 5J 123
Victoria Pl. *OX7: Chip N 5H 23*
(off Market St.)
OX16: Ban 7G 11
Victoria Rd. OX2: Oxf 4J 73
OX14: Abin 1E 90
OX26: Bic 1F 33
Victoria Ter. OX15: Dedd 6C 20
Victor St. OX2: Oxf 2C 4 (3J 77)
Viking Dr. OX11: Did 3D 110
Viking Ter. OX10: Ben 6E 102
Village Farm Ct.
OX25: West G 2G 43
Villas, The OX2: Oxf 2H 77
Villeboys Cl. OX14: Abin 7K 87
Villiers Ct. OX4: Oxf 2E 84
Villiers La. OX4: Oxf 2E 84
Villiers Rd. OX26: Bic 1D 32
Viner Cl. OX28: Wit 2G 51
Vineyard OX14: Abin 1G 91
Vineyard Cl. OX16: Ban 6E 10
Violet Way OX4: Blac L 6H 85
Virginia Way OX14: Abin 4E 90
Viscount Ind. Est.
OX18: Briz N 6J 47
Volunteer Way SN7: F'don 4D 56

W

Wadard's Mdw. OX28: Wit 4G 51
WADDESDON 2C 145
Wadham Cl. OX26: Bic 7F 31
Waine Rush Vw. OX28: Wit 4F 51
Waites Cl. OX18: Ast 6H 57
WALCOT
Chipping Norton 5A 36
Swindon 2A 146
Walford Rd. OX15: Sib F 6D 14
Walk, The OX5: Isl 6H 43
Walker Cl. RG8: Wood 1B 134
Walker Dr. OX9: Tha 5K 123
Walkers Cl. OX29: Free 5G 53
Walker's Height OX7: Fins 1J 39
Wallace Cl. OX14: Abin 3F 91
Wallbrook Ct. OX2: Bot 4E 76
Walled Gdns. OX14: Rad 4B 88
Waller Dr. OX16: Ban 3C 12
WALLINGFORD 3J 113 (2B 148)
Wallingford Mus. 2H 113
Wallingford Rd.
OX10: Chol, Wal 1E 116
OX10: Mon, N Sto 6H 117
OX10: Shil 4G 101
OX11: N Mor 2K 111
RG8: Gor, S Sto 6H 117
RG8: Stre 6A 132
Wallingford Station
Cholsey and Wallingford Railway 3G 113
Wallingford St. OX12: Wan 6G 105
Walls, The SN7: Stan V 6C 62
Walnut Cl. OX20: Woot 7H 37
OX26: Bic 6F 31
OX28: Wit 4D 50
RG4: Sonn C 5G 135
Walnut Ct. SN7: F'don 3C 56
Walnut Gdns. OX17: Clay 2C 6
Walnut Ri. OX25: Some 1K 25
Walnut Tree Ct. RG8: Gor 6C 132
Walnut Trees Hill SN6: Ashb 5D 66
Walpole Cl. OX26: Bic 6C 30
Walsingham Cl. OX15: Blox 3A 18
Walter Bigg Way OX10: Wal 2H 113
Walterbush Rd. OX7: Chip N 7G 23
WALTER'S ASH 1D 149
Waltham Ct. RG8: Gor 4C 132
Waltham Gdns. OX16: Ban 7J 11
WALTHAM ST LAWRENCE 3D 149
WALTON 1A 140
Walton Av. OX17: Twy 2J 19
RG9: Hen T 5D 138
Walton Cl. OX15: Bod 6G 13
Walton Cres. OX1: Oxf 2D 4 (3J 77)
Walton La. OX1: Oxf 2D 4 (3J 77)
WALTON MANOR 2J 77
Walton Mnr. Ct.
OX2: Oxf 1C 4 (2J 77)
Walton St. OX1: Oxf 3J 77
OX2: Oxf 1C 4 (2J 77)
Walton Well Rd.
OX2: Oxf 1A 4 (2H 77)
WANBOROUGH 2B 146
Wanbourne La. RG9: Nett 2H 131
Wandle Beck OX11: Did 6C 98
Wansbeck Dr. OX26: Bic 7B 30
Wansbeck Wood OX11: Did 6D 98
WANTAGE 6G 105 (2D 147)
Wantage Leisure Cen. 6G 105
Wantage Rd. OX10: Moul 7C 116
OX10: Wal 1F 113
OX11: Did 2K 109
OX11: Har 4E 108
RG8: Stre 4A 132
WAPPENHAM 2D 141
Warbler Wlk. OX4: Blac L 5H 85
WARBOROUGH 1G 101 (1A 148)
Warborough Rd. OX10: Shil 3G 101
OX12: Letc R 2G 119
Warburg Cres. OX4: Blac L 3J 85
WARDINGTON 2B 140
Wards Cres. OX15: Bod 7G 13
Ward's La. OX7: Fins 1J 39
Wards Mobile Home Pk.
OX3: Mars 5C 74
Wards Rd. OX7: Chip N 5J 23
OX7: Ship W 7J 35
Ware Rd. SN7: Stan V 6A 62
WARFIELD 3D 149
WARGRAVE 3C 149
Wargrave Rd.
RG9: Hen T 4E 138 & 1K 139
RG10: Warg 1K 139
Wargrave Station (Rail) 6K 139
WARKWORTH 2B 140
Warkworth Cl. OX16: Ban 5B 10
Warmans Cl. OX12: Wan 5E 104
War Memorial Pl.
RG9: Hen T 6D 138
WARMINGTON 2B 140
Warnborough Rd. OX2: Oxf 1J 77
Warneford Hall OX3: Head 4E 78
Warneford La. OX3: Head 4E 78
Warneford Rd. OX4: Oxf 5D 78
Warner Cres. OX11: Did 3A 110
Warren Cres. OX3: Head 4G 79
Warren Hill OX44: Stad 6H 127
WARREN ROW 2D 149
Warren Vw. OX44: Lit M 1G 127
WARWICK 1A 140
Warwick Cl. OX14: Abin 7H 87
OX18: Cart 4C 46
SN7: Stan V 6C 62
Warwick Ct. OX26: Bic 6G 31
Warwick Rd. OX16: Ban 5B 10
OX17: Ban, Han 1K 9
Warwick St. OX4: Oxf 6C 78
Wasbrough Av. OX12: Wan 5F 105
Washford Glen OX11: Did 7D 98
Washington Ter. OX7: Mid B 7K 25
WASPERTON 1A 140
Wastie La. OX29: Eyn 5D 70
Wastie's Orchard
OX29: L Han 2H 53
WATCHFIELD 3D 64 (1B 146)
Watcombe Rd. OX49: Watl 6D 128
Watercress Cl. OX15: Bod 6G 13
WATER EATON 7K 69
Water Eaton La. OX5: Gosf 4H 69
Water Eaton Rd. OX2: Oxf 4K 73
Waterford Rd. OX28: Wit 3H 51
Water La. OX7: Charlb 4A 36
OX7: Lit T 3B 24
OX10: Dray L 3G 95
OX15: Blox 2C 18
OX17: Add 4H 19
OX25: Stee A 4A 26
OX27: Few 6B 28
OX28: Wit 2J 51
OX29: Craw, Wit 1B 50
OX29: Hail 2K 49
Waterloo Dr. OX16: Ban 7G 11
Waterloo Wlk. *OX28: Wit 4F 51*
(off Waine Rush Vw.)
Waterman Rd. RG9: Hen T 5D 138
Waterman's La.
OX10: B Sot 6C 100
Watermans Reach OX1: Oxf 7F 5
Waterman's Way
RG10: Warg 6K 139
Watermead OX5: Kidl 2H 69
WATERPERRY 1H 121 (3B 144)
Waterperry House (Horticultural Cen.) 1H 121
Water Rd. OX9: Tow 2D 124
Waterside Ct. OX28: Wit 3F 51
WATERSTOCK 2K 121 (3B 144)
WATER STRATFORD 3D 141
Water St. OX25: Some 1K 25
Watery La. OX12: Spar 5B 118
OX14: C Ham 4G 93
OX15: Hook N 2B 16
Watery La. Path
OX10: Crow G 2A 130
Wates Way OX16: Ban 4G 11
Watling La. OX10: Dorc T 7C 94
WATLINGTON 5D 128 (1B 148)
Watlington Ind. Est.
OX49: Watl 5C 128
Watlington Rd.
OX4: Cow, Blac L 3J 85
OX10: Ben 5A 102
OX44: Gars 3J 85
OX49: Lewk 7F 129
Watlington St. RG9: Nett 1H 131
Watlington White Mark 1C 149
Watson Cres. OX13: Woot 7B 82
Watson's Cl. OX18: Cart 6E 46
Watts La. OX11: Blew 3D 114
Watts Way OX5: Kidl 2F 69
Waveney Cl. OX11: Did 1D 110
OX26: Bic 1B 32
Waverley Av. OX5: Kidl 3G 69
Waxes Cl. OX14: Abin 5K 87
Wayfaring Cl. OX4: Blac L 6H 85
Wayfarings OX26: Bic 5E 30
Wayland Av. OX12: Wan 2D 104
Wayland Cres. OX11: Chilt 6H 119
Wayland Rd. OX12: Gro 1G 105
Wayland's Smithy 2B 146
Waynflete Rd. OX3: Head 1J 79
Wayside Grn. RG8: Wood 1B 134
WEALD 4F 57
Weald St. OX18: Wea 4F 57
Wear Rd. OX26: Bic 1B 32
Weaver Cft. OX11: Did 6D 98
Weavers Cl. OX28: Wit 5E 50
Weavers Ct. *OX18: Cart 2F 47*
(off Trefoil Way)
Weavers Ground OX18: Briz N 4F 47
Webb Cl. OX16: Ban 6G 11
Webb Cres. OX7: Chip N 6G 23
Webbs Cl. OX2: Wolv 4E 72
OX7: Chad 1C 36
Webb's Way OX5: Kidl 2G 69
Webster Cl. OX9: Tha 3H 123
Wedgwood Rd. OX26: Bic 7G 31
WEEDON 2D 145
WEEDON BEC 1D 141
Weedon Cl. OX10: Chol 3F 117
Weedon Ct. OX10: Wal 2H 113
WEEDON LOIS 2D 141
Weeping Cross OX15: Bod 6G 13
Weir La. OX25: B'thorn 1K 45
Weirs La. OX1: Oxf 1A 84
Welch Way OX28: Wit 4D 50
Weldon Rd. OX3: Mars 1C 78
Weldon Way OX9: Tha 4J 123
WELFORD 3D 147
Welford Gdns. OX14: Abin 6H 87
Welland Av. OX11: Did 7E 98
Welland Cl. OX13: Shipp 5D 86
Welland Cft. OX26: Bic 7B 30
Well Bank OX15: Hook N 2C 16
Weller Cl. OX10: Ber S 1B 102
WELLESBOURNE 1A 140
Wellesbourne Cl.
OX14: Abin 7J 87
Wellesley Cl. OX16: Ban 7G 11
Wellesley Wlk. OX28: Wit 4F 51
Well Hill OX7: Fins 1J 39
WELLHOUSE 3A 148
Wellington Av. OX16: Ban 6G 11
Wellington Cl. OX26: Bic 6G 31
Wellington Cotts.
OX7: Charlb 7B 36
Wellington Pl.
OX1: Oxf 2E 4 (3K 77)
Wellington Sq.
OX1: Oxf 2D 4 (3J 77)
SN6: Watch 3D 64
Wellington St.
OX2: Oxf 2C 4 (3J 77)
OX9: Tha 4H 123
Well La. OX15: Alk 6E 8
OX29: Stone 3A 40
Wellshead OX11: Har 4F 109
Wellsprings OX10: B Sot 7D 100
Well St. OX12: Ard 5D 106
Well Vw. RG9: Stoke R 6H 131
WENDLEBURY 7A 32 (2A 144)
WENDOVER 3D 145
Wenlock Cl. OX11: Did 7K 97
Wenman Rd. OX9: Tha 6J 123
OX28: Wit 4C 50
Wenrisc Dr. OX29: Min L 4C 48
Wensium Cres. OX26: Bic 7B 30
Wensum Dr. OX11: Did 7D 98
Wentworth Rd. OX2: Oxf 4J 73
OX9: Tha 4J 123

Wesley Cl.—Windrush Sports Cen.

Wesley Cl. OX4: Blac L 4H 85
OX26: Bic 6C 30
Wesley Dr. OX16: Ban 2D 12
Wesley La. OX26: Bic 1E 32
Wessex Cl. SN7: F'don 3D 56
Wessex Ind. Est. OX28: Wit 6F 51
Wessex Rd. OX10: Ben 6E 102
OX11: Did 2B 110
Wessex Way OX12: Gro 2G 105
OX26: Bic 2F 33
Westacott Rd. OX26: Bic 5G 33
WEST ADDERBURY 4G 19
West Av. OX14: Abin 5H 87
West Bar OX16: Ban 1E 12
Westbeech Ct. OX16: Ban 1E 12
Westbourne Ct. OX15: Blox 4C 18
West Brook OX12: Gro 7G 63
Westbrook SN7: F'don 3C 56
Westbrook Grn. OX11: Blew 3C 114
Westbrook St. OX11: Blew 3C 114
WESTBURY 3D 141
Westbury Cres. OX4: Cow 2E 84
WEST CHALLOW 5A 104 (2C 147)
West Chiltern RG8: Wood 2B 134
(not continuous)
WESTCOT 6A 118 (2C 147)
Westcote Cl. OX28: Wit 5B 50
Westcot La.
OX12: Spar, Westc 4A 118
WESTCOTT 2C 145
WESTCOTT BARTON
. . . . .7H 25 (1D 143)
West Ct. OX16: Ban 7G 11
West Cft. OX10: Ber 2B 94
W. Down La. OX13: Marc 4H 61
West Dr. OX11: Har 7B 108
WEST END 3D 149
WESTEND 1C 36
West End OX7: Kingh 5C 34
OX10: B Sot 7C 100
OX10: Chol 2D 116
OX15: Horn 3C 8
OX18: Shilt 2A 46
OX20: Woot 7H 37
OX26: Laun 2K 33
OX28: Wit 2F 51
OX29: Combe 6E 40
West End Cl. OX26: Laun 2K 33
West End Ind. Est. OX28: Wit . . .3F 51
West End La. OX25: Mer 2C 44
Western Av. OX11: Did 2D 110
RG9: Hen T 5D 138
Western By-Pass Rd.
OX2: Wolv, Wyth, Bot 5D 72
Western Cres. OX16: Ban 2G 13
Western Rd. OX1: Oxf . . .7F 5 (6K 77)
RG9: Hen T 5D 138
WEST FARNDON 1C 141
Westfield OX11: Har 3E 108
(not continuous)
Westfield Cl. OX4: Oxf 7E 78
OX10: Ben 5B 102
OX12: Gro 2G 105
Westfield Cres. RG9: Shipl 4K 139
Westfield Rd. OX10: Ben 4A 102
OX10: Chol 7B 116
OX14: L Wit 2F 99
OX28: Wit 2E 50
OX33: Wheat 4F 81
Westfields OX14: Abin 7E 86
Westfield Way OX12: Wan 5J 105
Westgate Shop Cen.
OX1: Oxf 5E 4 (4K 77)
WEST GINGE 7F 107 (2D 147)
West Grn. SN7: Lit Cox 7A 56
West Gro. OX2: Oxf 4J 73
WEST HAGBOURNE
. . . . .6K 109 (2A 148)
WESTHALL HILL 3B 38
Westhall Hill OX18: Ful 3B 38
WEST HANNEY 3H 63 (1D 147)
W. Hawthorn Rd. OX25: Amb . . .1G 45
WEST HENDRED 4G 107 (2D 147)
West Hill OX12: Wan 6F 105
Westholme Ct. OX26: Bic 2F 33
WESTHORP 1C 141
WEST ILSLEY 2D 147
WEST KENNETT 3A 146
Westland Rd. SN7: F'don 4B 56
Westlands Av. OX25: West G . . .2G 43
Westlands Dr. OX3: Head 7E 74
West La. OX29: Craw 3F 49
RG9: Hen T 3C 138
Westleigh Dr.
RG4: Sonn C 6H 135
WEST LEITH 2D 145
WESTLINGTON 2C 145
WEST LOCKINGE 6B 106
Westminster Way OX2: Bot 4E 76
OX16: Ban 6H 11
Westmoor La. OX18: Ast 6G 57
WESTON
Newbury 3C 147
Towcester 2C 141
WESTON-ON-THE-GREEN
. . . . .2G 43 (2A 144)
Weston Rd. OX5: Blet 6C 42
OX49: Lewk 5F 129
WESTON TURVILLE 2D 145
WEST OVERTON 3A 146
West Oxfordshire Mus. Cen. . . .3F 51
(within Witney and District Mus.)
W. Oxon Ind. Pk.
OX18: Briz N 4F 47
West Quay OX14: Abin 4G 91
Westrup Cl. OX3: Mars 2C 78
West St Helen St.
OX14: Abin 2G 91
West St. OX2: Oxf 5A 4 (4H 77)
OX7: Chip N 6H 23
OX7: Kingh 5C 34
OX12: Child 6D 118
OX12: Spar 5B 118
OX15: Shut 2G 15
OX16: Ban 6G 11
OX26: Bic 7D 30
RG9: Hen T 3C 138
West Vw. OX4: Oxf 2D 84
Westwater Way OX11: Did 7E 98
West Way OX2: Bot 4D 76
Westway RG8: Gor 4C 132
WESTWELL 3B 142
Westwood Rd. OX29: Wit 3A 50
WEST WYCOMBE 1D 149
Weycroft OX11: Did 6D 98
Weyland Rd. OX3: Head 3H 79
Weymann Ter. *OX4: Oxf* *6E 78*
(off Saunders Rd.)
Wey Rd. OX10: Ber 3C 94
Wharf, The OX12: Wan 5G 105
RG8: Pang 7G 133
Wharf Cl. OX14: Abin 2G 91
Wharfe La. RG9: Hen T 3D 138
Wharf La. OX25: Some 1K 25
OX27: Soul 3F 21
Wharf Rd. OX10: Shil 3F 101
Wharton Rd. OX3: Head 2G 79
WHATCOTE 2A 140
Wheatcroft Cl. OX14: Abin 5H 87
Wheatfields OX11: Did 3K 109
WHEATLEY 5G 81 (3A 144)
Wheatley Bus. Cen.
OX33: Wheat 5H 81
Wheatley Cl. OX16: Ban 4G 13
Wheatley Rd. OX5: Isl 7H 43
OX33: For H 1E 80
OX44: Gars 2A 126
Wheatsheaf Yd.
OX1: Oxf 5F 5 (4K 77)
Wheelers End OX39: Chin 2G 125
WHELFORD 1A 146
WHICHFORD 3A 140
Whimbrel Cl. OX26: Bic 2G 33
Whimbrel Way OX16: Ban 3G 13
Whirlwind Way OX10: Ben 6E 102
WHISTLEY GREEN 3C 149
Whitamore Row
RG9: Hen T 5D 138
(off Trust Cnr.)
WHITCHURCH 1D 145
WHITCHURCH HILL
. . . . .2J 133 (3B 148)
WHITCHURCH-ON-THAMES
. . . . .6G 133 (3B 148)
Whitchurch Rd. RG8: Pang 7H 133
Whitebarn OX1: Boar H 3C 82
Whitecross OX13: Abin 2D 86
Whitehall Cl. OX29: Min L 4B 48
Whitehall La. RG8: Check 7F 131
White Hart OX3: Mars 6C 74
White Hart Cl. OX10: Ben 5A 102
White Hart Wlk. SN7: F'don 3C 56
White Hill RG9: Harp 7A 138
RG9: Rem 3E 138
White Hill La. OX1: Woot 5B 82
Whitehills Grn. RG8: Gor 6C 132
Whitehorns Farm Rd.
OX12: Wan 5K 105
Whitehorns Way OX14: Drayt . . .7B 90
White Horse SN7: Uff 6H 67
White Horse Bus. Pk.
SN7: Stan V 6A 62
White Horse Cres.
OX12: Gro 2F 105
White Horse Leisure & Tennis Cen.
. . . . .7K 87
White Horse M. OX18: Burf 5C 38
Whitehouse Cl. OX13: Shipp 6D 86
Whitehouse La. OX7: Chip N . . .5H 23
White Ho. Rd.
OX10: N Sto . . . .2K 117 & 5A 130
Whitehouse Rd.
OX1: Oxf 7E 4 (6K 77)
RG8: Wood 2B 134
Whiteleys Cl. OX11: Did 1C 110
White Lion Wlk. OX16: Ban 7F 11
Whitelock Rd. OX14: Abin 6G 87
WHITEOAK GREEN 2C 143
White Post Rd. OX15: Bod 5G 13
White Rd. OX4: Cow 1H 85
OX12: E Hen 3K 107
Whites Forge OX13: A'ton 2H 61
White Shoot OX11: Blew 6D 114
White's La. OX14: Rad 4A 88
Whitethorn Way OX4: Blac L 4H 85
WHITE WALTHAM 3D 149
White Way OX5: Kidl 3F 69
Whiteway OX17: Moll 5B 6
WHITFIELD 3D 141
Whitley Cres. OX26: Bic 7G 31
Whitley Dr. OX25: Up H 4H 27
Whitley Rd. OX10: Wal 4G 113
WHITNASH 1A 140
Whitson Pl. OX4: Oxf 6D 78
Whittington Pl. OX18: Cart 6D 46
WHITTLEBURY 2D 141
Whittle Rd. OX9: Tha 4K 123
WHITTONDITCH 3B 146
Whittons Cl. OX15: Hook N 1C 16
Whitworth Pl.
OX2: Oxf 2B 4 (3H 77)
Wick Cl. OX3: Head 1H 79
OX14: Abin 5K 87
WICKEN 3D 141
Wick Farm Pk. Cvn. Pk.
OX3: Head 7H 75
Wick Grn. OX12: Gro 7F 63
WICKHAM 3C 147
WICKHAM HEATH 3D 147
Wicks Cl. OX18: Clan 6H 55
WIDHAM 2A 146
WIDMER END 1D 149
Widmore La. RG4: Sonn C 4J 135
WIGGINTON
Banbury 3A 140
Tring 2D 145
Wigginton Rd. OX15: S New 5F 17
Wigod Way OX10: Wal 1H 113
Wilberforce St. OX3: Head 3G 79
Wilcher Cl. OX11: E Hag 4C 110
WILCOTE 3K 39
Wilcote La. OX7: Rams 3H 39
Wilcote Riding
OX7: Fins, Wilc 1J 39
Wilcote Rd. OX3: Head 1J 79
OX29: E End 1A 52
Wilcote Vw. OX29: N Leigh 4C 52
Wilcox Rd. OX7: Chip N 4H 23
Wilder Av. RG8: Pang 7J 133
Wilding Rd. OX10: Wal 1G 113
Wildmere Cl. OX16: Ban 4G 11
Wildmere Ind. Est.
OX16: Ban 4G 11
Wildmere Rd. OX16: Ban 4G 11
WILDMOOR 6F 87
Wildmoor Ga. OX14: Abin 6F 87
Wilkins Rd. OX4: Cow 1G 85
Willes Cl. SN7: F'don 3C 56
William Bliss Av.
OX7: Chip N 6H 23
William Cl. OX16: Ban 6B 10
William Kimber Cres.
OX3: Head 2H 79
William Lucy Way
OX2: Oxf 1B 4 (2H 77)
William Morris Ct. *OX3: Head 1J 79*
(off Stowfort Rd.)
William Orchard Cl.
OX3: Head 1F 79
WILLIAMSCOT 2B 140
Williamscot Hill OX17: Chac 1J 11
WILLIAMS HILL 7H 37
William Smith Cl. OX7: C'hill . . .3C 34
Williamson Way OX4: Oxf 4D 84
William St. OX3: Mars 2C 78
WILLINGTON 3A 140
Willis Ct. OX7: Ship W 5J 35
Willoughby Rd. OX16: Ban 4F 13
Willow Brook OX14: Abin 1E 90
Willowbrook OX29: Stan H 3A 58
Willowbrook Leisure Cen. 7C 98
Willow Cl. OX5: Yarn 5C 68
OX44: Gars 5C 126
OX49: Watl 5C 128
Willow Ct. La. OX10: Moul 6E 116
Willow Dr. OX18: Cart 3F 47
OX26: Bic 5E 30
Willow La. OX12: Wan 7G 105
OX14: Milt 4E 96
RG10: Warg 3K 139
Willow Mead OX44: Chal 2C 128
Willow Rd. OX9: Tha 3H 123
OX16: Ban 5F 13
OX25: Amb 1F 45
OX39: Chin 2G 125
Willows, The OX1: Woot 7B 82
OX12: Gro 3G 105
OX28: Wit 3G 51
Willows Ct. RG8: Pang 7G 133
Willows Edge OX29: Eyn 4C 70
Willows Ga. OX27: Stra A 1K 31
Willow Tree Cl. OX13: Shipp 6D 86
Willow Wlk. OX2: Oxf 1A 4 (2G 77)
(not continuous)
Willow Way OX4: Blac L 4H 85
OX5: Beg 3B 68
OX14: Rad 7B 84
Wills Rd. OX11: Did 1K 109
Wilmot Cl. OX28: Wit 6D 50
Wilmots OX44: Toot B 1K 89
Wilmot Way OX12: Wan 4J 105
Wilsdon Way OX5: Kidl 2E 68
Wilsham Rd. OX14: Abin 2G 91
Wilson Av. RG9: Hen T 5D 138
Wilson Pl. *OX4: Oxf* *4C 78*
(off Cave St.)
Wilsons Cl. OX14: L Wit 1F 99
Wilson Way OX27: Cave 3F 31
WILSTONE 2D 145
Wimblestraw Rd. OX10: Ber 3B 94
Wimborn Cl. OX15: Dedd 6B 20
Wimborne Av. OX16: Ban 7D 10
Winaway OX11: Har 4E 108
Winchelsea Cl. OX16: Ban 4B 10
Winchester Cl. OX16: Ban 6H 11
Winchester Rd. OX2: Oxf 1J 77
Winchester Way OX12: Wan . . .5F 105
WINCHMORE HILL 1D 149
Windale Av. OX4: Blac L 4H 85
Windale Ho. OX4: Blac L 4H 85
WINDERTON 2A 140
Windle Gdns. OX26: Bic 1C 32
Windmill Av. OX26: Bic 6E 30
Windmill Cl. OX9: Tow 2C 124
OX15: Dedd 6B 20
OX16: Ban 2F 13
OX29: N Leigh 5B 52
Windmill Hgts.
OX29: N Leigh 5B 52
Windmill La. OX33: Wheat 6E 80
Windmill Pl. OX12: E Cha 6C 104
Windmill Rd. OX3: Head 2G 79
OX9: Tha 5H 123
OX9: Tow 2C 124
OX29: N Leigh 5B 52
Windmill St. OX15: Dedd 6B 20
Windows Ct. OX33: Wheat 6H 81
WINDRUSH 2A 142
Windrush OX16: Ban 5D 10
(not continuous)
Windrush Cl. OX12: Gro 1G 105
OX18: Burf 4C 38
OX28: Wit 3C 50
(not continuous)
Windrush Ct. OX14: Abin 1D 90
OX18: Burf 5C 38
OX28: Wit 5F 51
Windrush Ind. Pk. OX29: Wit . . .2A 50
Windrush M. OX11: Did 6E 98
Windrush Pk. Rd. OX29: Wit 3A 50
Windrush Rd. OX10: Ber 4B 94
Windrush Sports Cen. 4F 51

A-Z Oxfordshire Atlas 181

N.B. Where Hospitals and Hospices are not named on the map, the reference given is for the road in which they are situated.

ABINGDON HOSPITAL 1D **90**
Marcham Road
ABINGDON
OX14 1AG
Tel: 01235 205700

BICESTER COMMUNITY HOSPITAL 2E **32**
King's End
BICESTER
OX26 6DU
Tel: 01869 604000

CHIPPING NORTON WAR MEMORIAL HOSPITAL
. . . . .5H **23**
Horsefair
CHIPPING NORTON
OX7 5AJ
Tel: 01608 641682

CHURCHILL HOSPITAL 5F **79**
Old Road
Headington
OXFORD
OX3 7LJ
Tel: 01865 741841

DIDCOT COMMUNITY HOSPITAL 2K **109**
Wantage Road
DIDCOT
OX11 0AG
Tel: 01235 205860

DOUGLAS HOUSE HOSPICE 6D **78**
Magdalen Road
OXFORD
OX4 1RZ
Tel: 01865 794749

FIENNES CENTRE 2F **13**
Hightown Road
BANBURY
OX16 9BF
Tel: 01295 229301

FOSCOTE BMI HOSPITAL, THE 2F **13**
2 Foscote Rise
BANBURY
OX16 9XP
Tel: 01295 252281

HELEN HOUSE CHILDREN'S HOSPICE 6D **78**
37 Leopold Street
OXFORD
OX4 1QT
Tel: 01865 728251

HORTON HOSPITAL .2F **13**
Oxford Road
BANBURY
OX16 9AL
Tel: 01295 275500

JOHN RADCLIFFE HOSPITAL 1F **79**
Headley Way
Headington
OXFORD
OX3 9DU
Tel: 01865 741166

KATHARINE HOUSE HOSPICE 3K **19**
Anyho Road
Adderbury
BANBURY
OX17 3NL
Tel: 01295 811866

LITTLEMORE MENTAL HEALTH CENTRE 5E **84**
Sandford Road
Littlemore
OXFORD
OX4 4XN
Tel: 01865 778911

MANOR HOSPITAL 2F **79**
Beech Road
OXFORD
OX3 7RP
Tel: 01865 307777

NUFFIELD ORTHOPAEDIC CENTRE 4G **79**
Old Road
Headington
OXFORD
OX3 7LD
Tel: 01865 741155

OXFORD CHILDREN'S HOSPITAL 1E **78**
Headley Way
Headington
OXFORD
OX3 9DU
Tel: 01865 741166

PARK HOSPITAL 4F **79**
Old Road
Headington
OXFORD
OX3 7LQ
Tel: 01865 226213

RADCLIFFE INFIRMARY 1D **4** (2J **77**)
Woodstock Road
OXFORD
OX2 6HE
Tel: 01865 311188

ST LUKE'S HOSPITAL 3F **79**
Latimer Road
OXFORD
OX3 7PF
Tel: 01865 228800

SIR MICHAEL SOBELL HOUSE HOSPICE 5F **79**
Churchill Hospital
Old Road
OXFORD
OX3 7LJ
Tel: 01865 225860

SUE RYDER CARE - NETTLEBED HOSPICE
. . . . .2J **131**
Joyce Grove
Nettlebed
HENLEY-ON-THAMES
RG9 5DF
Tel: 01491 641384

THAME COMMUNITY HOSPITAL 4J **123**
East Street
THAME
OX9 3JT
Tel: 01844 212727

TOWNLANDS HOSPITAL 3C **138**
York Road
HENLEY-ON-THAMES
RG9 2EB
Tel: 01491 637400

WALLINGFORD COMMUNITY HOSPITAL 4H **113**
Reading Road
WALLINGFORD
OX10 9DU
Tel: 01491 208500

WANTAGE HOSPITAL 5H **105**
Garston Lane
WANTAGE
OX12 7AS
Tel: 01235 205801

WARNEFORD HOSPITAL 4E **78**
Roosevelt Drive
Old Road
Headington
OXFORD
OX3 7JX
Tel: 01865 741717

WITNEY COMMUNITY HOSPITAL 4E **50**
Welch Way
WITNEY
OX28 6JJ
Tel: 01993 209400

OXFORD UNIVERSITY COLLEGES & HALLS

covered by this atlas

with their map square reference

All Souls College 4G **5**

Balliol College 3F **5** (3K **77**)
Blackfriars 3E **4**
Brasenose College 4G **5**

Campion Hall 6F **5**
Christ Church College 5F **5** (4K **77**)
Corpus Christi College 5G **5** (4A **78**)

Exeter College 4F **5**

Green College 1D **4** (2J **77**)
Greyfriars 6C **78**

Harris Manchester College & Chapel 3G **5**
Hertford College 4G **5**

Jesus College 4F **5**

Keble College 2F **5** (3K **77**)
Kellogg College 2E **4**

Lady Margaret Hall 1A **78**
Linacre College 2H **5** (3A **78**)
Lincoln College 4F **5**

Magdalen College 4J **5** (4B **78**)
Mansfield College 2G **5** (3A **78**)
Merton College 5H **5** (4A **78**)

New College 4G **5** (4A **78**)
Nuffield College 4D **4**

Oriel College 5G **5**

Pembroke College 6F **5**

Queen's College 4H **5**

Regents Pk. College 3E **4**

St Anne's College 1E **4** (2K **77**)
St Antony's College 2J **77**
St Benet's Hall 2E **4** (3K **77**)
St Catherine's College 3J **5** (3B **78**)
St Cross College
　　Pusey St. 3E **4**
　　St Cross Rd. 3J **5** (3B **78**)
St Edmund Hall 4H **5** (4A **78**)
St Hilda's College 6J **5** (5B **78**)
St Hugh's College 1J **77**
St John's College 3F **5** (3K **77**)
St Peter's College 4E **4**
St Stephen's House .5C **78**
Somerville College 2D **4** (3J **77**)

Templeton College 3A **84**
Trinity College 3F **5** (3K **77**)

University College .5G **5**
University College (annexe) 7J **73**

Wadham College 3G **5** (3A **78**)
Wolfson College 7A **74**
Worcester College 4D **4** (3J **77**)
Wycliffe Hall 2K **77**